BEHIND THE SCENES IN

American Government

Peter Woll   BRANDEIS UNIVERSITY

BEHIND THE SCENES IN

American Government

Personalities and Politics

Ninth Edition

HarperCollins*CollegePublishers*

Acquisitions Editor: Maria Hartwell
Project Coordination and Cover Design: York Production Services
Cover Illustration: David Omar White
Production: Sunaina Sehwani/Linda Greenberg
Compositor: ATLIS Graphics & Design, Inc.
Printer and Binder: R.R. Donnelley & Sons Company
Cover Printer: New England Book Components, Inc.

Behind the Scenes in American Government, Ninth Edition

Library of Congress Cataloging-in-Publication Data
Behind the scenes in American government : personalities and politics
  / [compiled by] Peter Woll.
      p.   cm.
   ISBN 0-673-52325-X
   1. United States—Politics and government—20th century.
I. Woll, Peter, 1933–
JK271.B533   1993
320.973—dc20   93-2596
                                                          CIP

  94 95 96 9 8 7 6 5 4 3

For Jon and Cindy

CONTENTS

PREFACE

This book is designed to be an exciting supplementary text for introductory American government courses. It presents politics through the eyes of participants, focusing on the personalities of those who shape the way the political game is played and who place their individual imprints on public policies. The text also can be used to complement the wide range of courses that analyze parties and political campaigning, interest groups and lobbyists, the media and political consultants, the presidency, Congress, the courts, and the bureaucracy.

Politics is, by any measure, fascinating. But its fascinating qualities are not often conveyed to students because many books and courses concentrate on structures and processes at the expense of the individuals who constitute the lifeblood of politics. And it is, after all, the people in politics who shape its character, just as they themselves are shaped by it. This book illustrates both how character and personality influence politics and the ways in which political institutions and processes, such as the presidency and political campaigning, affect the personalities and actions of those who are directly, and sometimes indirectly, involved. Vignettes of famous politicians, pressure group leaders, journalists and political consultants, members of Congress, White House staffers and presidential advisers, Supreme Court justices, and top-level bureaucrats are collected in the book. By introducing students to the colorful and powerful personalities who are to be found in politics, I hope to make American government the lively subject that it should be.

WHAT'S OLD, WHAT'S NEW

This exciting new ninth edition of *Behind the Scenes in American Government* focuses on the politics of the 1990s and the Clintonization of Washington. The first baby-boomer president and first lady have wrought political changes that in many ways are as great as the upheavals of the 1960s, which they participated in and witnessed. The text looks at politics through eyewitness accounts of participants, written by the participants themselves or political reporters and journalists closely attuned to political personalities and the political process.

As in earlier editions, the rationale for the changes in the ninth edition is to keep the text up-to-date by including profiles of the most contemporary leading political personalities and depictions of their roles in the constantly evolving political process.

Chapter One: Playing the Game: Politicians, Power, and People

All of the selections in this chapter are new. The chapter first focuses on Bill and Hillary Clinton, James Carville, George Stephanopoulos, and other youthful members of the Clinton team who embarked on what at first seemed a quixotic quest for the presidency. The first three selections discuss, respectively, how the New Hampshire primary helped to define Clinton as a presidential candidate, the role of Hillary Clinton in the campaign, and the team behind Bill and Hillary.

The chapter next illustrates the poignancy of losing in an excellent piece by *Time* columnist Hugh Sidey, "Going Gently into the Night." And, because no account of the 1992 presidential campaign would be complete without a portrayal of the role of Ross Perot, the chapter includes two portrayals of the Texas billionaire and his political odyssey.

Finally, on a different tack, Chapter 1 concludes with a behind-the-scenes account of the clash between Clarence Thomas and Anita Hill, a defining event that overshadowed the 1992 presidential campaign in many ways, particularly by producing a greater than normal turnout of women voters, the majority of whom voted for Clinton.

Chapter Two: Pressure Groups and Lobbyists

The ninth edition retains the extremely popular pieces by writers Evan Thomas ("Influence Peddling in Washington") and Haynes Johnson ("When Money Talks, Washington Listens"). One new selection, by *Newsweek* writer Eleanor Clift and her reporters, depicts the impact pressure groups will have on the Clinton administration as it seeks changes in public policies. And students will be delighted to read the highly revealing account of the powerful lobbyist Robert Gray, of the Washington firm of Hill and Knowlton, in the other new selection, "Lord of the Lies," by *Washington Monthly* writer Susan B. Trento.

Chapter Three: The Media and Political Consultants

A new reading in this chapter "Loathe the Media," by Ken Auletta gives a provocative glimpse of the role of the media in the 1992 presidential campaign. The chapter retains two highly popular selections. Larry J. Sabato, a household name among political scientists, is the author of "How Political Consultants Choose Candidates." And former Carter Press Secretary Jody Powell contributes the provocative account of how presidents deal with the media in "The Right to Lie."

Chapter Four: The Presidency

With the exception of the classic James David Barber selection, "Presidential Character, Style, and Performance," and George E. Reedy's portrayal of the White House staff, the selections in Chapter 4 are all new.

The ninth edition of *Behind the Scenes* adds lively accounts of the Clinton presidency, including the unprecedented role that Hillary Clinton has assumed as first lady, to this chapter on the presidency. Michael Kelley and Maureen Dowd describe six relationships that could make or break the new president in the selection, "The Company He Keeps." *Wall Street Journal* reporters James M. Perry and Jeffrey H. Birnbaum depict the possibility of a co-presidency in the amusing piece, " 'We' the President." Other new selections discuss the White House perks that President Clinton promised to derail and the role of a little-publicized presidential advisor. *Newsweek* reporter Tom Morganthau's ominous account of the Cuban missile crisis, "At the Brink of Disaster," based upon secret Russian file documents released in 1992, is also new to this edition.

Chapter Five: The Congress

New selections in this chapter deal with the impact of the 1992 congressional and presidential elections on Capitol Hill and with emerging legislative leaders. Adam Clymer's "House Revolutionary" profiles Georgia Republican Newt Gingrich, a colorful member who is in the news on almost a daily basis. He has made the position of House Republican whip into one of national leadership for his party.

In another new selection, Alison Mitchell tells the poignant story of how New York Congressman Thomas J. Downey, who had forged a very successful career in the House, lost touch with his constituency and lost the 1992 election. It is "a cautionary tale of how the power and prerequisites of Washington can seduce [all members of Congress]; of how even the brightest star of the post-Watergate era could eventually seem to the voters as too much like the insiders he once scorned."

Continued in this chapter are the popular selections that focus on how different personal styles affect the attainment of power within the House and the Senate. The portraits of powerful chairmen, Michigan Congressman John Dingell, West Virginia Senators Robert Byrd and John D. Rockefeller IV, and Massachusetts Senator Edward Kennedy, should be highlighted in any introductory American government course, where Congress is one of the most popular topics.

Chapter Six: The Supreme Court

With the important exception of Bob Woodward's and Scott Armstrong's classic piece, "The Brethren and the Abortion Decision," which gives a behind-the-scenes account of *Roe v. Wade* (1973), all of the selections in this chapter are new, up-to-date portrayals of Supreme Court justices. In Ruth Marcus's selection, Justice Harry Blackmun, who for the past twenty years has borne much criticism for his *Roe* decision, is portrayed. Paul M. Barrett, in another new selection, writes about Justice David Souter, who has become an important force on the Court despite his unassuming style. John Lancaster and Sharon Lafraniere portray the controversial justice Clarence Thomas and his role on the Court in two selections. And, finally, Jeffrey Rosen discusses the style of Antonin Scalia in "The Leader of the Opposition."

Acknowledgments

I am especially indebted to Elaine Herrmann, who has assisted me over the years with this and other projects. Her extraordinary skills and especially her good humor in the face of the many pressures that always accompany writing and publishing a book have saved many a day for me. I also would like to thank my editor, Maria Hartwell, for guiding the book through the production process with skill and extraordinary professional competence. It is always a delight to work with her.

Peter Woll

PLAYING THE GAME: POLITICIANS, POWER, AND PEOPLE

Chapter
One

This chapter's selections illustrate the complex political forces that impact candidates, elected officials, and their aides. Politics is both a personal and a team contact sport. Presidential candidates in particular must be willing to walk through the fire of relentless criticism and often embarrassing media scrutiny. Candidates and elected officials also must contend with an increasingly volatile electorate, which the media, including talk show hosts, have stirred to the boiling point in the quest for higher ratings. Highly individualist tele-democracy with "candidate" parties has replaced a classical democratic process that, in theory at least, was defined by aggregative and competitive political parties that gave voters a meaningful electoral choice.

W HEN PRESIDENT BILL CLIN-
TON took his oath of office on
January 20, 1993, he rode a
wave of popular approval and high expectations. He was *Time*'s Man of the
Year for 1992, and he and his increasingly popular wife, Hillary, adorned the
covers of other national magazines,
which generally portrayed them in a fa-
vorable light. Forgotten were the dark days of the early Clinton campaign, when
Time ran a cover depicting Clinton as a
"Slick Willy" and asked the question,
"Can This Man Be Trusted with the Presidency?" How a political campaign reveals character and tests candidates is the
subject of the following lively account of
Clinton's struggle in New Hampshire at
the outset of his successful race for the
presidency.

1 Curtis Wilkie
THIRTY-THREE DAYS THAT DEFINED A CANDIDATE

Bill Clinton's time was expiring in New Hampshire. Worn down by illness,
his voice frayed by fatigue, his jogger's body swollen from the consumption
of junk food, he seemed to be fighting a losing battle. A freezing rain cast a
treacherous glaze on the highway as he was driven to Nashua less than 60
hours before the polls opened. Still, Clinton was encouraged when he
arrived at the event and saw that an overflow crowd had come to hear him
on the Saturday night before the primary. It was a good sign, he told his
wife.

Hillary Clinton was not so sanguine. "How do we know," she said, "that
they're not just coming to see the freak show?"

By that final weekend, the campaign had acquired the characteristics of a
carnival, a frantic crusade, a portable Chautauqua. In little more than a
month, it had taken Clinton on a journey from the cover of *Time* magazine to
the tawdry scandal sheets sold at supermarket checkout stands, keelhauled
him through a controversy that renewed the pain of Vietnam, and plunged
him into a free fall in popularity.

It was one of the most extraordinary passages for a candidate in American
political history, carried out on a Bruegelian landscape peopled with angry
and skeptical voters. And even though Clinton had expected the accusations that bushwhacked him in New Hampshire and had developed plans to
deal with them, no one fully anticipated the intensity of the storm.

Today, the Arkansas governor is on the threshold of the Democratic

"Thirty-three Days that Defined a Candidate," by Curtis Wilkie, *The Boston Globe*, July 12,
1992. Reprinted courtesy of The Boston Globe.

presidential nomination because he withstood the turbulence in New Hampshire, enduring where others had failed. In the last campaign, two of the party's most promising candidates, Gary Hart and Joe Biden, were forced out early, in the face of questions about their character.

Clinton has survived numerous tests en route to the Democratic convention in New York, fighting off formal opponents in a long season of primaries while fending off Washington oracles who whispered that a new Democratic candidate would emerge to save the party. But it was his performance in New Hampshire that gave him his commanding position in New York this week.

In the beginning, Clinton never considered New Hampshire critical to his interests. A credible finish in the Yankee state, he figured, was all he needed to return to the South poised to claim a cluster of primaries in the old Confederate states and march from there to the nomination.

That was before a series of crises converged on Clinton, like a forbidding confluence of planets, that turned the primary into what one of his aides described as a "live-or-die situation." For 33 days this winter, Clinton's political career hung in the balance.

His problems defied the broad strategy he had developed in 1991, as well as the quick-fix gimmicks his advisers conceived in the heat of the moment. The New Hampshire primary became Bill Clinton's personal battle, and by the final days it was clear that his survival depended on his tenacity, his relentless optimism, and his inner reserves.

As early as last summer, as he reached his decision to run for president, Clinton was braced for adversity. In particular, he discussed his reputation as a philanderer, the subject of many rumors in political circles, with his closest friends and advisers. He laid out the dimensions of the problem and asked at one point, "Should this disqualify me?" He was assured that it was not an insurmountable obstacle.

His wife was included in these delicate consultations, and the Clintons finally decided to confront the issue together by publicly admitting to a history of "difficulties" in their marriage, problems that they said had been resolved. In private meetings with potential contributors, Clinton dealt with uncomfortable questions by quietly acknowledging he had been involved in extramarital affairs and emphasizing the present strength of his marriage. In an attempt to put down one persistent rumor, he blurted out at a closed-door meeting with Chicago Democrats: "Listen, I don't have a black baby."

The Clinton strategy was formally embodied in the governor's remarks to a group of Washington reporters last September. With Hillary at his side, Clinton said: "Like nearly everybody who has been together 20 years, our relationship has not been perfect or free of difficulties. But we feel good about where we are, and we believe in our obligation to each other." He indicated that he would not be drawn into specific discussions of alleged romances. The statement, he said, "ought to be enough" to answer the question of his fidelity to his marriage vows.

Several weeks later, his campaign was tested for the first time. A young aide, Steve Cohen, heard a Little Rock radio talk-show host discussing a story in *Penthouse* magazine in which a rock 'n' roll groupie claimed that Clinton had propositioned her. Cohen reported the news to Clinton's deputy campaign manager, George Stephanopoulos, who quickly collected affidavits from several of Clinton's associates who had witnessed the encounter. They swore that the woman had approached Clinton and been rebuffed.

The story enjoyed the mini-life of celebrity that Andy Warhol forecast for mankind—one metion on CNN Headline News the next day. Stephano-poulos immediately pounced on CNN, offered documentation to refute the woman's claim, and rebuked the producers for airing the story. The item was dropped.

That night, in Little Rock, a few members of Clinton's staff celebrated with pizzas, and Cohen was given the nickname Scoop. The Clinton campaign felt confident that the sex issue had been settled.

Another cloud still hovered in the background. It involved Clinton's draft record, a topic that had come up sporadically since he entered politics. But it had been dealt with as recently as his reelection campaign for governor in 1990, and there was no reason to believe that the issue would explode in the presidential campaign.

By the new year, Clinton's future looked prosperous. Gov. Mario Cuomo of New York had decided not to enter the race, and Gov. Douglas Wilder of Virginia, who threatened to strip Clinton of vital black support, dropped out eight days into January.

Then, on January 16, a blemish appeared like the first, faint signs of a malignancy. It was a Thursday, the day of the week that became known as "garbage day" in the Clinton campaign, for it was on Thursdays that advance copies of *Star*, a national tabloid, were released.

Star's first broadside was a regurgitation of allegations that Clinton had used public funds to carry on affairs with five different women. The charges grew out of a lawsuit filed during the last gubernatorial race by a former state employee sacked for using his office phone to promote the Nicaraguan contras.

News agencies had investigated the allegations and failed to find any corroboration. The Clinton campaign was equipped with denials from the women named as Clinton's mistresses, including a night-club singer named Gennifer Flowers. Nevertheless, the *Star* story seeped into daily tabloids the next day and precipitated the first mob scene of the political season. As soon as Clinton arrived in New Hampshire to attend a health-care conference at

the Sheraton-Tara Hotel, a mock-Tudor fortress in Nashua, he was surrounded by reporters, photographers, and camera crews.

Maintaining a smile and an air of bemusement, Clinton followed a
preordained plan. He described the story as old and false and ridiculed the
source, dismissing *Star* as a newspaper "that says Martians walk on earth
and cows have human heads." Although more than a score of reporters
were on hand for the exchange with Clinton, editors at television networks
and most newspapers made judgments not to use the story.

By mid-January, Clinton was leading his closest challenger, former
Massachusetts Sen. Paul E. Tsongas, by 12 percentage points in *Boston Globe*
polls in New Hampshire, and he was featured on the cover of *Time* magazine
as "the Democrats' rising star."

Then Stephanopoulos got a tip that *Star* planned a new expose involving
Flowers. A few hours later, flying from Little Rock to Manchester on the next
"garbage day," Clinton's small charter plane made a stop in Washington to
pick up a consultant the governor had recently hired—James Carville,
a shrewd and bombastic strategist who specializes in the tactics of confrontation.

Although the members of Clinton's entourage were apprehensive over
the new development, Clinton was in a bluff mood when he arrived at a
Manchester hotel, not recognizing the enormity of his problem until he
reached his private suite. His staff had located a copy of *Star*, and a
telephone facsimile of the article was waiting for him. He quickly read
through the lurid account, with the headline "They Made Love All Over Her
Apartment. . . ."

Clinton had suspected for weeks that Flowers might become the source of
allegations—she had called him once and told him she had been offered
$50,000 to make public charges—but the story was stunning.

Emotions in the room ran from sinking sensations to a determination to
fight back. Clinton's aides wondered, with false hope, if the mainstream
press might again ignore the allegations. They knew that any counteroffensive would have be undertaken in tandem with Hillary Clinton. She was
reached in Atlanta, where she was campaigning. After learning details of
the allegations, she said she was ready to fly wherever necessary to make a
joint appearance with her husband.

Meanwhile, Stephanopoulos obtained from Little Rock a copy of a
year-old letter from Flowers' lawyer. It contained a threat to sue a radio
station because a talk-show host "wrongfully and untruthfully alleged an
affair between my client, Gennifer Flowers, and Bill Clinton. . . ." Stephanopoulos had copies of the letter reproduced for distribution to reporters.

Without knowing whether a frenzy awaited them, Clinton and his aides
set off, an hour late, for a campaign appearance in Claremont. New

Hampshire was enveloped in ice and fog and gloom. They wanted to fly but were forced to drive.

Clinton was burdened further by the knowledge that he had to return to Arkansas that night to handle last-minute appeals in connection with the execution of Rickey Ray Rector, condemned for killing a policeman. With events closing in around him, Clinton tried to keep his serenity. As the van carried him slowly over the icy roads, he read *Lincoln on Leadership*.

It was midafternoon by the time Clinton reached the American Brush Co. in Claremont, and news of Flowers' allegations had spread to a group of waiting reporters. He was cornered by questions as soon as he stepped into the foyer of the building. "It isn't true," he said, shaking his head sadly. "She's obviously taking money to change her story." Peppered by questions, he said flatly, "The affair did not happen."

Clinton worked his way past the pack of reporters and went on to deliver a speech inside the small factory without a sign that he was troubled. But he knew, instinctively, that he had erred by departing from his decision not to discuss specific rumors.

Clinton and his aides retreated to an upstairs office and spent the rest of the darkening afternoon on the telephone. Clinton talked with his wife, his aides, and others he trusted.

Stephanopoulos phoned Carville, who was in Manchester, to tell him that Clinton had been hit hard with questions on the Flowers case. "We can't be eaten up by this thing," Carville said, urging that Clinton "get in front of the story."

As they considered a forum to address the issue, they were contacted by Ted Koppel, who planned to use the sex allegations as his topic that evening on ABC's "Nightline." Stephanopoulos also talked to an ABC executive about a Clinton appearance on "Prime Time Live" that same night. There was a timing problem. Clinton was more than 50 miles from his chartered plane. A mixture of freezing rain and snow was falling. And the situation was complicted by the fact that arrangements had to be made for his wife to join him at ABC's studios in Washington in a few hours.

For a moment, decision-making was frozen. The network news shows carried no mention of the allegations other than a reference in a profile of Clinton on NBC. Downstairs, restive reporters, standing in line for one pay telephone, were having difficulty convincing their editors that the story was worthy of publication. Clinton felt that he might get another reprieve.

But WMUR-TV in Manchester, New Hampshire's major television station, carried a report from Claremont, showing Clinton pelted with questions, and the Associated Press soon moved a story. The furies were finally set in motion.

Sometime after 7:30 P.M., the van carrying Clinton began a meandering, erratic drive. He was hopelessly late for an event in Plymouth, at least two hours away in deteriorating conditions, but he headed in that direction anyway. Meanwhile, Clinton's aides kept up conversations with ABC. They explored the possibility of appearing the next day on "Good Morning America" and were discouraged to learn that the Clintons could get no more than six minutes on the air. A network executive tried to sell them on "20/20," a Friday-night ABC program, but Clinton ruled out an appearance on the same night as the Rector execution in Arkansas. Reluctantly, Clinton gave up the attempt to go to Plymouth and abandoned plans to appear immediately on TV. He returned, instead, to Manchester and flew back to Little Rock, traveling much of the night to keep the grim duty of presiding over the execution of Rickey Ray Rector.

He also needed to regroup politically, because the next morning the Flowers story would be in every newspaper in the nation.

Clinton spent the day in seclusion, a practice he had followed on other execution days. It was a time for brooding. Paul Begala, one of his advisers, attempted to encourage him by sending a message: "Life breaks us all, but some of us emerge stronger in the broken places." The aphorism, Begala noted with some irony, was popularized by Max Cleland, the secretary of state of Georgia who had lost three limbs in Vietnam and was supporting Sen. Bob Kerrey for president.

Meanwhile, Clinton's campaign staff committed the governor to weekend appearances on CNN's "Newsmaker Saturday" as well as "This Week with David Brinkley," on ABC. Then Steve Kroft, a "60 Minutes" correspondent, called to offer a spot on the most popular news show on television, boasting an audience of millions that would be expanded because it would appear immediately after the Super Bowl. Stephanopoulos asked for a guarantee that the show would be promoted with unsensational language. In exchange, the Clintons agreed to give CBS an exclusive interview, and other appearances were canceled.

Clinton and his wife returned to New England for a rally in Manchester, New Hampshire, Saturday night, where a youthful crowd packed a downtown gymnasium, cheering the couple. After the event, in the comfort of the Ritz-Carlton hotel in Boston, the Clintons gathered with a few friends and advisers. Although the conversation drifted away from the political crisis, everyone in the room was preoccupied by the Clintons' date the next morning. "60 Minutes" would begin taping before noon.

James Carville, his nerves taut, woke the next morning weeping. Other Clinton aides were tense but tried to hide their emotions. The group assembled in the Clintons' suite for final preparations before the interview, which would take place in one of the hotel's stately rooms with a fireplace.

Mandy Grunwald, a media consultant, advised the Clintons that this would not be a normal political interview. Kroft, she said, had an entertainment orientation and was likely to ask questions that seemed disjointed. She predicted he would be persistent on the subject of adultery.

Hillary Clinton, who would later display the toughness of a courtroom lawyer during the interview, began to cry. She was distressed, she said, over the impact the show might have on their daughter, Chelsea, who was 11 at the time.

The candidate was outwardly dispassioniate. He was prepared to acknowledge, implicitly, that he had been involved in affairs. But he was determined to do it his own way.

Once they were on the set, Don Hewitt, the producer of "60 Minutes," urged Clinton to deal with the adultery question openly and to follow with an arching exposition of his political dreams. It could become a historic moment in American politics, Hewitt said. It could also be one hell of a TV show.

The taping went on for more than an hour. Kroft made about a dozen passes at the adultery question. Clinton stuck to his formula. He repeated his denial that he had been involved with Flowers. He admitted he had caused "pain in my marriage." And, near the end, he observed: "I think most Americans who are watching this tonight, they'll know what we're saying. They get it."

Watching the monitors in a control room, most of Clinton's aides were quietly weeping and thinking that he had survived the crucible. Before he left the Ritz-Carlton, Clinton had lunch with a journalist and defended his vagueness on the show. "If I say 'no,' you all will just go out and try to prove me wrong. And if I say 'yes,' that will mean there is no end to it. I'm not complaining, though; I signed on for the whole ride. If I made any mistake, it was talking about all this at all."

Less than 15 minutes of the Clintons' interview aired that night. The campaign had no major quarrel with the editing, but one line was omitted that Clinton's aides wished had been used: In a philosophical moment, Clinton had said, "No one wants to be judged on the worst moment of his life."

For many of Clinton's supporters, the worst moment of the campaign occurred the next day. Gennifer Flowers' sponsors convened a press conference in Manhattan, and most of it was televised live by CNN. She said she had loved Bill Clinton and insisted that he was "absolutely lying."

The spectacle led every network news show that evening, enjoying priority over a significant turn of events in Russia, the Middle East peace talks, and a Supreme Court decision. Clinton was campaigning in Louisiana and did not see Flowers' performance, but his aides watched in horror. Begala could not believe what he had seen. He thought: The networks just led with a failed lounge singer with a bad dye job holding a press conference at the Waldorf-Astoria to lie about us. He quickly came up with the "cash for trash" expression that Clinton would subsequently use to describe his accusers.

That night, Clinton's support fell dramatically, for the first time, in a poll conducted for the *Globe* in New Hampshire.

After an absence of several days, Clinton returned to New Hampshire on

Wednesday, February 5, ill and feverish. During a speech at a Concord school, he constantly wiped perspiration from his face and drank two quarts of water. He had to cancel the rest of his schedule and went to bed at Day's Hotel, a modest lodging place in Manchester, which he had made his unofficial headquarters.

Clinton, however, was unable to rest. He learned that *The Wall Street Journal* was preparing to publish a story suggesting that in 1969 he had maneuvered his way out of the draft.

The key source was Col. Eugene Holmes, an ROTC officer at the University of Arkansas when Clinton enrolled in the program to get a deferment from his draft board. After Clinton broke the agreement, he was reclassified 1-A on October 30, 1969. For 33 days—exactly the same period he would dangle in New Hampshire more than two decades later—Clinton was exposed to the draft, but there was no call-up. On December 1, 1969, a draft lottery was held. Clinton's birthday drew a high number that spared him. *The Wall Street Journal* quoted Holmes: "Bill Clinton was able to manipulate things so that he didn't have to go in."

Clinton was staggered. He had always called Holmes his "first line of defense" when his draft record was raised in Arkansas campaigns, and he had often referred reporters to Holmes, who was retired. First, Gennifer Flowers had changed her story, and now Holmes, Clinton's erstwhile defender, was accusing Clinton of manipulation.

Clinton's staff realized it was an explosive situation. They retrieved by fax from Little Rock papers from Clinton's draft file and simulated a press conference in his hotel room, interrogating him on details of the case.

But nothing prepared him for the scene Thursday morning. There was a sense of déjà vu in Nashua when he was again engulfed by a wave of reporters and photographers in the same lobby of the Sheraton-Tara Hotel where he had been besieged by questions about extramarital affairs. Cameras and lights were poked toward his face. Reporters encircled him. Questions struck like hail. He admitted being "bitterly opposed" to the war but denied that he had evaded it. He nearly lost his equilibrium in the violence of the exercise. In the midst of the turmoil, he lamented, "This is an unbelievable rewriting of history."

Stephanopoulos, who was becoming a specialist in damage-control, produced copies of a story from the *Arkansas Democrat-Gazette* last October that dealt with the dispute over Clinton's lack of military service. In the article, Holmes, the former ROTC commander, said he had treated Clinton "just like I would have treated any other kid."

Although the draft story was front-page news on Friday, Clinton was not asked about the subject during questions from an audience at New Hampshire Technical College, in Stratham. Again, members of the campaign staff thought they had weathered the difficulty, heartened by a report from a private focus group conducted by their pollster, Stan Greenberg, that showed little hostility toward Clinton over the draft issue.

"I don't have anything more to say about it," Clinton told reporters as he left New Hampshire to spend a weekend at home. His departure from the state turned out to be one of the greatest tactical errors of the campaign. While Clinton took a break, the political environment in New Hampshire was roiling, and his local organizers implored the Little Rock headquarters to bring Clinton back for the time remaining. They feared he was losing command of the situation.

On Sunday night, February 9, Clinton met with key members of his staff at the governor's mansion in Little Rock to go over a battle plan. They were troubled by a new *Globe* poll that showed that Clinton and Tsongas were effectively tied.

There were suggestions that the campaign buy time for a television show in which Clinton would take spontaneous questions from viewers. There was talk of a fighting speech that would blame the Republicans for the perfidy that had hit the Clinton campaign. There were surrogates to deploy. And there were new television spots to consider, in which Clinton's chief TV consultant, Frank Greer, wanted to portray the governor "talking over the heads of the tabloid press."

Just before midnight, Greenberg telephoned with numbers from his latest survey in New Hampshire. An aide announced to the room: "There's big trouble in River City." Clinton had fallen from a peak of 37 percent support to 17 percent in a matter of days. It seemed that the bottom had dropped out of the campaign.

Begala was put to work on the draft of a short speech for Clinton, who rarely uses prepared texts. Others awakened Hershel Gober, the director of veterans' affairs for Arkansas, to tape a testimonial for Clinton that Greer would get on New Hampshire radio stations within hours.

Clinton went to bed late that night knowing that if he failed ignominiously in New Hampshire, his dream would die. He had eight days to save his campaign.

Clinton, his wife, and a few aides headed back to New Hampshire early Monday. On the way, Clinton marked up Begala's text, which raised the specter of a "Republican attack machine" orchestrating Clinton's misery.

He intended to deliver the speech as soon as he landed at a small airport near Nashua, and to declare that he would "fight like hell" for the last eight days. But his campaign could not get clearance for a political event at the airport.

One of the few journalists to meet the plane was Mark Halperin, an ABC producer who had covered Clinton all year. Halperin had a document to deliver, a copy of a letter, written by Clinton to Col. Holmes more than 22 years ago, describing his aversion to the draft.

Halperin gave the letter to Stephanopoulos, who had been wrestling with his own pessimism for days. The Clinton aide quickly scanned it. As soon as his eyes settled on the second paragraph, in which Clinton offered thanks "for saving me from the draft," Stephanopoulos had one thought: It's over.

The Clinton group squeezed into a tiny room at the airport to weigh the latest crisis. Clinton quickly read the letter and momentarily brightened. "This is mine," he told his wife. "I remember writing this letter." Imbued with a politician's ability to discover silver linings, Clinton said it proved his point that he had made himself "available for the draft." Others were not so sure. Stephanopoulos was despondent. Begala's legs trembled. But Carville, a Louisiana Catholic who had thought hours before that the campaign was *in extremis*, saw the possibility of redemption. He began shouting, which is his fashion. He described the letter in scatological terms, but he told Clinton it was "your friend."

The letter had come into ABC's hands over the weekend through an anonymous fax that the network eventually traced to Lt. Col. Clinton Jones, another former officer at the ROTC unit.

Jim Wooten, one of the network's chief political reporters, was handling the story, and Halperin asked Clinton to meet with him for an interview. After a desultory appearance in Nashua, where Clinton delivered his "fight like hell" message with little gusto, the candidate sat down with Wooten in a room at a Londonderry yogurt factory he had visited and insisted the letter vindicated his assertions.

Clinton assumed the story would break in a few hours on ABC's "World News Tonight." But as night fell and Clinton waited in Manchester for a flight to New York, he heard from Wooten that the story was going to be delayed. The reporter was troubled by discrepancies between what Clinton Jones and Bill Clinton had said, and he wanted more time to sort it out.

For want of an office, Clinton took over the men's room at the airport. The governor perched on a lavatory, and his aides huddled around him, pondering what course to take next. Carville urged Clinton to release the letter immediately. Clinton was reluctant. He felt Wooten had been fair with him, and he did not want to steal "Wooten's scoop."

He flew to New York and claimed at a $1,000-a-plate dinner that "reports of my demise are, as Mark Twain said, premature."

On the flight back to New Hampshire, Clinton and his wife appeared in good spirits. They played pinochle with a couple of reporters. He bantered about garbling the Twain quote, and he and Hillary reminisced about the antiwar movement, even though the reporters did not know about the existence of the letter. Clinton also talked about Southern politics, and he recalled the travails of another governor, Bill Allain of Mississippi, who was accused a few days before an election in 1983 of consorting with a gang of homosexual transvestites. Though Allain was elected, Clinton recalled. "He never recovered from that."

When they landed at Keene, it was after midnight. Clinton was hungry. The group found a Dunkin' Donuts shop that was open. He wolfed down a bowl of soup and two bagels with tuna salad. Then, before leaving, he engaged an astonished customer in a long discussion on health care. There was no sign that the letter was preying on his mind.

The next afternoon, Clinton was hit from another direction. Ted Koppel, whose "Nightline" program is independent from ABC's "World News Tonight" operation, contacted David Wilhelm, Clinton's campaign manager in Little Rock, and told him: "It is important that the governor and I talk."

Koppel also had a copy of the draft letter. Clinton's aides never made a public complaint, but privately they were troubled that leaks seemed to flow naturally toward ABC, a network where several executives had a strong Republican pedigree. It fed the campaign's paranoia over Republican plots.

The document that Koppel had received was at least a fourth-generation copy. A "World News Tonight" producer had obtained the letter from Jones in South Carolina and asked a hotel clerk to make copies. The intrigued clerk made himself a copy and faxed it to an acquaintance, a Washington businessman named James Tully, who travels in military-intelligence circles. Tully sent a copy to Clinton's political office in Washington, a move that mystified Clinton aides there, who knew nothing of the letter. He also sent a copy to former Air Force Maj. Gen. Richard Secord, a figure in the Iran-contra affair. Secord had it sent to "Nightline."

Because of Secord's background, Koppel was concerned that he might be drawn into a "dirty tricks" operation. He told Wilhelm, vaguely, he was "under the impression that my source might have gotten it from someone in the Pentagon."

He was surprised to learn from Wilhelm that ABC had already interviewed Clinton on the subject. "Obviously, the right hand doesn't know what the left hand is doing," Koppel said.

Sensing that the letter represented a dramatic story, Koppel was anxious to get Clinton on "Nightline," regardless of Wooten's prior interest. Koppel and Clinton's aides began discussing details. Stephanopoulos wanted to know where the letter had come from. "It beats the shit out of me," Koppel said. But he repeated his "impression" that it had come from the Pentagon.

Clinton's advisers felt that Koppel's answer reinforced their claim that their campaign was under attack by the Republican administration. It also played into Carville's demand for Clinton to go public with the letter.

On Wednesday, February 12, less than a week before the primary, Clinton triggered a day of high drama by calling Koppel at home. He said he hoped to release the letter and wanted to confirm that it had been leaked by the Pentagon. Koppel said again that it was his "impression." He warned Clinton that he was leaping to a conclusion.

Late that morning, Clinton called a press conference in a hangar of the Manchester airport, where a large American flag was hung as a backdrop. As his aides distributed copies of his letter, Clinton said: "Mr. Koppel confirmed to me that it is his understanding that ABC received a letter from two different sources, both of whom got it from the Pentagon. If this is true, the leak violates the Federal Privacy Act." Clinton said he would appear on "Nightline" that night to "discuss all of this."

The letter, a painful, eloquent, three-page epistle from a troubled time, coupled with Clinton's charge that "George Bush and the Republican Party will do anything it takes to win," burst upon the campaign like a thunderstorm.

Afterward, Clinton asked one of his state coordinators, Patricia McMahon, how she felt the event had gone. "I thought you did a very good job," she assured him. She said the letter was so moving it must have been leaked by a friend.

After hearing of Clinton's charge, Koppel's source contacted him again and described the circuitous route the letter had taken. In a late afternoon conversation with Clinton, Koppel told the candidate the letter had not come from the Pentagon.

Clinton new the letter was creating a political earthquake, and now he realized that his contention that he was the victim of a Republican plot was discredited. A *Globe* poll completed that evening would show he had fallen 11 points behind Tsongas.

As he boarded his 16-seat plane to fly to an event in Claremont, Clinton looked tired and stricken. As he moved to his seat, he greeted one of the passengers, Thomas Edsall of *The Washington Post*. Edsall and his wife had written a book Clinton admired, a book that described how Democratic Party policies, perceived as too soft on blacks, had driven away conservative whites. Another reporter told Clinton he had recently written of him and Edsall in the same paragraph, suggesting that Clinton was better experienced than the other Democratic candidates to deal with the racial problems the Edsalls had written about. "I was," Clinton said with resignation.

"What do you mean, 'I was'?" he was asked.

"Oh, hell, I *am*," he said, putting the verb in the present tense. "It's just that I'm so busy fighting wars that are 23 years old. . . ."

A large audience was waiting in Claremont, and another Arkansan was asked to give a long introduction, to enable Clinton to meet privately with some of his local supporters.

David Matthews was a throwback to the old school of passionate Southern oratory, a former state representative who had responded to the negative reports from New Hampshire by suspending his law practice in the little town of Rogers, Arkansas, and coming to the state to help his friend. This was his first real chance, and his light blue eyes burned like dry ice.

He started with a joke about the Baptist preacher whose description of Jesus Christ as "the only perfect man" was challenged by a man in the back pew:

"Brother Jones, are you saying you're perfect?"

"Oh, no, I'm just standing up for my wife's first husband."

Matthews went on to attack Gennifer Flowers' veracity, and he excoriated another supermarket tabloid for a headline that said "Clinton Likes Four-Way Sex with Black Hookers."

"You probably haven't heard the one about him being buck naked in a tree at the University of Arkansas, protesting the war," Matthews shouted.

Dee Dee Myers, Clinton's press secretary rolled her eyes and wondered: Where is he going?

Actually, Matthews was moving skillfully from low comedy to graceful poignance. He said that Clinton was neither perfect nor a "two-headed monster," and he related the story of how the Arkansas governor had befriended a boy gravely ill with cancer, and how the boy had been inspired.

Clinton was standing in the wings by now, listening. He covered his moist eyes with his oversized hands and bowed his head. He was struggling not to cry openly, but, somehow, he also seemed to be drawing a second wind.

During his Claremont speech Clinton fought off one heckler, then he flew to Dover for an Elks Club apperance that has by now taken on mythic proportions. Garry Trudeau, who was there, later had one of his *Doonesbury* characters describe the talk as "the most extraordinary political speech I've ever heard."

In the Dover address, Clinton described his political career as the "work of my life" and said his dreams represented the "vision thing" that Bush flippantly dismissed. "I hope you never raise a child without the vision thing," he told the crowd. "Life would be bleak and empty without the vision thing."

He reminded the New Hampshire audience that Bush had won a second chance in the state in 1988 after losing the Iowa caucuses and had subsequently spent "three hours here, mostly on his way to and from Kennebunkport, while you tripled your unemployment, welfare, and food-stamp rates."

It was a bravura performance. Surrounded by a few hundred spectators in an underlit and crowded room, the candidate was like a man on trial, making a closing argument for himself.

"They say I'm on the ropes because other people have questioned my life, after years of public service," he bellowed, his hoarse voice rising. "I'll tell you something—I'm going to give you this election back, and if you'll give it to me, I won't be like George Bush. I'll never forget who gave me a second chance, and I'll be there for you till the last dog dies."

The day was still not finished. Clinton had to return to Manchester to appear on "Nightline." Koppel, handling the interview from Washington, seemed oddly deferential, as though he felt responsible for the misunderstanding. Much of the half-hour program was consumed as Koppel read the entire letter, while the screen showed Clinton, listening and nodding. The candidate was not only embracing the letter, he was spreading its word through newspaper advertisements reproducing the text.

It was midnight when the show was over, and there was a glimmer of hope. It was a triumph, Clinton's aides told him, and they exchanged high-fives, like athletes.

For days, an exasperated Clinton had been complaining to his staff about his schedule in New Hampshire and demanding more grass-roots events. "Just turn me loose," he said.

On the Thursday before the primary, he began a breakneck schedule that took him back and forth across the densely populated areas in the southern part of the state. He bought a half-hour of TV time for two consecutive nights to submit to random questions from a statewide audience. He spoke at schools and addressed the Legislature. He prowled suburban shopping malls near Salem and Nashua, and he walked the streets of seacoast towns.

During a visit to a home for the elderly in Nashua on the final Friday, Clinton watched Mary Annie Davis break into tears as she described how she and her husband could no longer afford prescription drugs. To comfort the sobbing woman, Clinton suddenly knelt on the floor and hugged her.

In the next room, Stephanopoulos was trying to discourage an editor of the *Nashua Telegraph* from publishing a story involving new allegations by a former campaign volunteer. The disgruntled source claimed he had overheard Clinton and Arkansas Lt. Gov. Jim Guy Tucker discussing a new job for Gennifer Flowers. Stephanopoulos insisted that the conversation dealt with a Clinton aide named Gloria. The newspaper decided to drop the matter for lack of supporting evidence.

After the Nashua event, a relieved Stephanopoulos was preparing to tell Clinton that the latest problem had been resolved when he realized the candidate was still so overcome with emotion that he could not speak. It was the only time Stephanopoulos saw the governor close to breaking.

But the mood was upbeat as the Clinton team flew from Manchester to Keene that night. He had climbed back to within seven points of Tsongas in the *Globe* poll. On a portable television in the front of the plane, David Matthews was watching the news on WMUR-TV. He could make out, through static and snow, a scene of Clinton hugging the elderly woman earlier in the day. He yelled at the candidate, who was sitting in the rear of the 16-seat plane: "I don't know whether it's a good story or another sex scandal, but you led the news."

On Saturday, Clinton and his wife went to the Mall of New Hampshire, a labyrinth on the outskirts of Manchester that was teeming with weekend shoppers. It was supposed to be a half-hour stop, with the rest of the afternoon devoted to preparation for the primary's final debate the following night.

Clinton refused to leave. Standing in a McDonald's, he greeted knots of people who waited patiently to talk with him. It was not like a receiving line, with a word and a handshake, but an evangelical ceremony. He listened as much as he talked, and sometimes spent five to ten minutes with a couple of voters.

Hillary Clinton was standing a few feet away, detached for the moment from the clutter of cameras. A reporter suggested that while she might not like the comparison, the scene was reminiscent of Lyndon B. Johnson's irrepressible campaign for the presidency in 1964, when it seemed as if LBJ wanted to shake every hand in America.

"I never saw Johnson," she said, "and I don't want to denigrate him. But my impression was that with Johnson it was all take. He took strength from his supporters, but he gave nothing back. If you look at Bill, you'll see that it's reciprocal. He gives as well as he takes."

A few minutes later, an incident took place as if on cue. A young man without a job, holding his small daughter in his arms, began to cry as he told Clinton of his anxiety that he might lose his home. The candidate reached out and held the man's arms until he regained his composure.

After 2½ hours, Clinton's aides finally persuaded the candidate to leave the mall. As he was departing, a reporter asked facetiously if he also liked fund-raising, generally regarded as the most loathsome task for a politician. "Usually, I do," Clinton confessed. "But I like this best of all."

That night in Nashua, the people in the packed house who came to see Clinton seemed to have been drawn more by his magnetism than by the freakish aspects his wife had feared.

The primary was approaching, and it was apparent that even if Clinton failed to win, he would finish, at worst, a respectable second, a result that would enable him to continue his campaign. Before a single vote was cast, he had won a grudging concession from his rivals that he was a candidate who would not quit, and his supporters were attributing his survival to the power of his presence and the strength of his will.

Clinton would have to draw upon these resources again and again as he struggled toward the nomination in the primaries after New Hampshire. From the beginning, the candidate felt he could overcome any adversity if he could somehow reach the voters personally. He said it was important "to stand for something bigger than yourself."

And as he proclaimed himself the "Comeback Kid" at his primary-night rally in Merrimack, he added: "At least I proved one thing—I can take a punch."

ONE OF THE MOST DISCUSSED topics of the 1992 presidential campaign was the "Hillary factor." Hillary Clinton, the candidate's wife and a graduate of both the prestigious Wellesley College and Yale Law School, epitomized the successful career woman who emerged from, but was not necessarily based in, the feminist movement of the 1960s and early 1970s.

Hillary Clinton became a metaphor for the politician's spouse who pursues an independent career but who may use the politician's influence to gain, in the view of critics, an unfair advantage over the competition.[1] The following account of Hillary Clinton's character and style points to the certainty that she will symbolize a new kind of first lady and reshape the character of the office.

2 Margaret Carlson
ALL EYES ON
HILLARY

You might think Hillary Clinton was running for President. Granted, she is a remarkable woman. The first student commencement speaker at Wellesley, part of the first large wave of women to go to law school, a prominent partner in a major law firm, rated one of the top 100 lawyers in the country—there is no doubt that she is her husband's professional and intellectual equal. But is this reason to turn her into "Willary Horton" for the '92 campaign, making her an emblem of all that is wrong with family values, working mothers and modern women in general?

The Republicans clearly think so. Hillary has been such a constant target of G.O.P. campaign barbs that Bill Clinton recently wondered aloud whether "George Bush was running for First Lady." In making her a focus of their attack strategy, the Republicans seems to have calculated that they can shave votes off Governor Clinton's total by portraying his wife as a radical feminist who prefers the boardroom to the kitchen. And they may be right. In the latest *Time*/CNN poll, 74% of the respondents said their votes would not be affected by their views of Hillary; but among the remainder, almost twice as many said they would vote against Clinton (14%) as for him (9%) based on their opinion of his wife. If the Hillary factor can mean the difference of a couple of percentage points, it could provide a critical margin in a close election.

The foundations of the anti-Hillary campaign were carefully poured and were part of a larger effort to solidify Bush's conservative base. Republicans dug up—and seriously distorted—some of her old academic articles on children's rights. Rich Bond, the chairman of the Republican National

[1]See Katherine Boo, "The Hillary Loophole," *Washington Monthly*, May 1992, 26–30.

17

Committee, caricatured Hillary as a lawsuit-mongering feminist who likened marriage to slavery and encouraged children to sue their parents. (She did no such thing.) Richard Nixon warned that her forceful intelligence was likely to make her husband "look like a wimp." Patrick Buchanan blasted "Clinton & Clinton" for what he claimed was their agenda of abortion on demand, homosexual rights and putting women in combat.

Rarely has the spouse of a presidential candidate been so closely scrutinized and criticized by the political opposition. To a large extent, the controversy swirling around Hillary Clinton today reflects a profound ambivalence toward the changing role of women in American society over the past few decades. Hillary, who personifies many of the advances made by a cutting-edge generation of women, finds herself held up against what is probably the most tradition-bound and antiquated model of American womanhood: the institution of the First Lady.

The President's wife, as Eleanor Roosevelt once wrote, was to be seen and not heard, a discreet adornment to her husband's glory. Never mind that Mrs. Roosevelt broke most of her own rules with her high-profile tours and a vocal interest in civil rights. Most of those who followed in her footsteps remained true to the traditional backseat role, and those who ventured too close to the policymaking arena—Rosalynn Carter sitting at the Cabinet table, for instance—were harshly criticized. And there are some sound reasons for concern. The President's spouse is potentially the second most powerful person in government but is beyond accountabilty. Yet for reasons that are both social and generational, Barbara Bush will almost certainly be the last of the traditional First Ladies. Whoever follows her is likely to shatter the mold—particularly if it is a woman with the professional achievements, the career ambitions and the activist bent of Hillary Clinton.

Still, Mrs. Clinton would have done well at the outset to have conformed more to the traditional campaign rules for aspiring First Ladies: gaze like Nancy Reagan, soothe like Barbara Bush and look like Jacqueline Kennedy. By not doing that, to some extent, Hillary played into the hands of her critics. At first she seemed insufficiently aware that she was not the candidate herself. Instead of standing by like a potted palm, she enjoyed talking at length about problems and policies. At one coffee in a living room in Manchester, New Hampshire, people were chatting amiably about the cost of groceries when she abruptly launched into a treatise on infant mortality. She sometimes took longer to introduce her husband than he did to deliver his speech. She, and he, should have known that quips like "People call us two-for-one" would arouse the traditionalists.

Her image as a tough career woman probably peaked in March, when Democratic gadfly Jerry Brown charged that her law firm benefited unfairly from her marriage to the Arkansas Governor. After she shot back, "I suppose I could have stayed home, baked cookies and had teas," many minds snapped shut on the Hillary question faster than you can say sound bite. (Almost no one reported the rest of what she said: "The work that I have done as a professional, a public advocate, has been aimed . . . to assure that women can make the choices . . . whether it's full-time career, full-time motherhood or some combination.")

Ironically, Hillary's natural desire to shield her daughter from the glare of publicity only fed suspicions that she valued the role of high-powered lawyer over that of wife and mother. Instead of using Chelsea in photo ops in New Hampshire, where a sweet family portrait might have helped counter the Gennifer Flowers story, Hillary kept her daughter back in Little Rock with her grandparents. To this day, Chelsea has never been interviewed and is still only rarely photographed.

All this made Hillary a perfect foil for Barbara Bush, the composed matron for whom hard-edged feminism is as foreign as an unmade bed. That she looks and acts as if she is above the political fray only makes her a more potent force within that very arena—although her most conspicuous activities are politically neutral, like hugging sick babies, promoting literacy and ghostwriting best sellers for her dog. Twice as popular as her husband, she can have it both ways when she wants to. No one would think to label America's favorite grandmother cynical when she lets it be known that she is pro-choice, while her husband is doing everything possible to make abortion a crime. Mrs. Bush has also worked hard to conceal her role in the White House, which can be every bit as ferocious as was Nancy Reagan's, especially when she believes the President is not being well served. She can turn on a bulldog disposition when warranted. "You people are just not as important as you think you are," she once growled to a group of journalists she thought were tormenting her husband.

Although Mrs. Bush initially said Hillary bashing should be off limits, she reversed herself later on the grounds that Mrs. Clinton was playing such a prominent role and had spoken out on public policy. The President agreed and got in a few swipes of his own about Hillary's legal writings. Then Marilyn Quayle chimed in, insisting in an interview that as a representative of "the liberal, radical wing of the feminist movement," Mrs. Clinton was absolutely fair game.

Seated on the couch in the living room of the Arkansas Governor's mansion last week, with Bill and Chelsea waiting to have a rare family dinner, Hillary responded to the Republican onslaught more in sadness than in anger. "I really don't know what to make of it," she told *Time*. "What recently has happened has been part of a very sad and cynical political strategy. It's not really about me. I find it hard to take a lot of that personally, since the portrait is a distorted, inaccurate one."

The unprecedented headlining of Barbara and Marilyn at the Republican National Convention last month was above all an attempt to score points on the family-values front by depicting them as paragons of stay-at-home motherhood. The First Lady's approach was typically gentle and low-key, invoking her years of driving carpools, den mothering and going to Little League games. Marilyn, however, took the white gloves off with a strident critique of the choices and values Hillary Clinton represents. "Not everyone [in our generation] believed that the family was so oppressive that women could only thrive apart from it," she said. "Most women do not wish to be liberated from their essential natures as women."

But there are signs that such tactics may backfire on the Republicans. The latest *Time*/CNN poll shows, for example, that only 5% of likely voters consider family values the main campaign issue and that Marilyn Quayle is the least popular of the three women, with a 37% approval rating, compared with 40% for Hillary and 76% for Barbara. Only 14% felt Hillary does not pay enough attention to her family.

Bush campaign strategists, in fact, have sought to tone down the anti-Hillary rhetoric in recent weeks. In their own postconvention surveys, the Republicans found that a hard core of about 10% to 15% of voters strongly dislike the Arkansas Governor's wife. But the internal surveys also indicated this anti-Hillary sentiment is firm and needs no boosting, while the great majority of the public finds the assaults on her insulting, meanspirited and beside the point.

The Clinton camp, meanwhile, came to the same conclusion. A sampling taken by Democratic pollster Stan Greenberg showed that Hillary's favorability ratings shot up 8 or 9 points right after the Republican Convention. All the Hillary bashing in the Astrodome, says Clinton's top campaign strategist, James Carville, "played to a decent advantage for us. The Republican Party in Houston made a collective fool of itself in attacking Hillary. People want to hear other things in an election campaign than a distorted 1974 scholarly article."

The main reason for the backlash is obvious: by taking after Hillary the way they did, the Republicans unnecessarily angered moderates, who saw the attack as one on women in general. By going after women who work, they got at the élite Murphy Browns—a small contingent—but also snagged the middle- and working-class Roseannes, creating solidarity among both groups, who aren't confident enough in their new roles to take a presidential strike force with equanimity. Scratch the surface of any mother and she wonders if she is doing it right, whether she works full time, part time or not at all. A note from the teacher saying Junior is having trouble with long division can make a trial lawyer wonder if she should write briefs from the kitchen table. Ask a stay-at-home mother at a cocktail party what she does, and she looks at you as if you just asked if you could have one of her fingers as an hors d'oeuvre. She is wondering if she will ever be able to get back into the job market again and is worried that if her children don't turn out a lot better than those of the woman doing arbitrage deals down the block, she will have wasted her life.

While the Republicans were busy painting Hillary as an overly ambitious careerist, she seemed to be consciously modifying her style. In the past few months, she has softened her image (much to the dismay of some feminists), grinning and gripping like a mayor's wife and baking cookies to show she is not a harridan. She has even learned to stand at the back of the stage and look at Bill with a convincing imitation of the Nancy Reagan gaze.

In person and off the podium, Hillary Clinton is neither a killer lawyer nor the adoring spouse of the bus tours. Riding in the back seat of a car during a New York campaign swing, she wolfs down popcorn while worrying about whether Chelsea got her booster shots. She jokes about only making the teams for sports like volleyball and softball—and laments that she didn't have the foresight to concentrate on profession-enhancing pastimes like tennis and golf. While Bill can go for long stretches of time on the road, she says she has to head back frequently to Little Rock to "make a cup of tea, hang out with Chelsea, take an afternoon nap. If I don't get back there, I don't feel grounded."

Running parallel to this homing instinct is what friends describe as a growing spirituality over the past few years. Though the fact is not trumpeted—even in the face of Republican family-values attacks—Hillary, a Methodist who claims to have been "religiously committed since child- hood," carries her favorite Scriptures (*Proverbs, Psalms, Corinthians, Beati- tudes*) wherever she goes. She and Bill regularly pray with Chelsea at bedtime. "As I have grown older," says Hillary, "I have tried to synthesize my personal beliefs with the way I act in the world and to try to keep growing. It's a very important part of who I am and what I think my life should mean."

Friends describe Hillary as someone who tends toward the earnest and serious but who nonetheless has a playful side. "She laughs harder than anyone at the jokes, but she is always a little surprised when she herself gets off a good line," says Mark McLarty, who has known the Governor since they attended Miss Mary's Kindergarten together in Hope, Arkansas, and is now chairman of the board of Arkla Inc., a huge natural-gas conglomerate. Prominent Washington lobbyist Liz Robbins, an old friend of both Clintons, marvels at the fact that Hillary manages to stay in touch while less busy people do not. "Hillary is a very inclusive person, which you don't usually find in successful women," says Robbins.

While not the life of a party, Hillary tends to get into the spirit of an evening. She's the one to "try the new meal—hippopotamus stew—or order the blue drink," says television producer Linda Bloodworth-Thomason. Most socializing is done at home, in the kitchen and breakfast room and around the piano. (All three Clintons play the instrument, says Hillary, "but none of us is what you'd call good.") They play Pictionary, Scrabble and a cutthroat card game called Hungarian Rummy.

Before the campaign switched into high gear, the Clintons would eat dinner at least once a week with Bill's mother and stepfather and Hillary's parents, who moved from Chicago to Little Rock a few years ago. On such occasions, says Dorothy Rodham, Hillary's mother, they all subscribe to the theory that it is more important who is around the table than what's on it—which is fortunate for Hillary, who admits she served black beans, chili and leftovers from an official dinner as last year's Christmas meal.

There is no mistaking that Hillary is a strong and determined woman, used to dominating whatever situation she is in by force of mind. Although the campaign plays down her role, she is the talent that test-drives the Governor's ideas, punches holes in his theories, comments on his speeches and often identifies the weak spots in his campaign operation and helps get them corrected. She is one of the people who can convince him it's better to make three points in a speech than six, and the only one who can make sure he gets to bed on time rather than shooting the breeze with staff members into the wee hours, as he likes to do. Hillary herself ensures that Clinton's Arkansas supporters are properly used in his presidential quest. Says campaign aide Betsy Wright: "She has the analytic ability to make certain that the decisions he is leaning toward are ironclad." Mrs. Clinton is certain to be one of the key players in the room when her husband finally sits down to prepare for his crucial—though still unscheduled—debates with President Bush.

The gravest error the Republicans may have made was not resting their case with Barbara Bush. Instead they also spotlighted Marilyn Quayle as the symbol of their baby-boomer professional woman who gave it all up for the man she loves. Those worried about Hillary Clinton being a co-President (although in 11 years as First Lady in Arkansas, no one accused her of being co-Governor) should take a look at Mrs. Quayle's activities. She was her husband's campaign manager and has an office near his in the Old Executive Office Building, where she spends much of her time. In joint interviews, she doesn't hesitate to correct her husband.

An intelligent and capable manager who can rightly claim much of the credit for Dan's success, Marilyn Quayle has a vindictive streak that often undercuts her strengths. While aides go out of their way to point out what a nice guy her husband is, one Republican handler admits that "Marilyn doesn't have a lovable side."

Mrs. Quayle's personality and career choices should no more be a campaign issue than those of Mrs. Clinton. But the Vice President's wife has gone out of her way to criticize Hillary on points where she has labeled criticism of herself as unfair. When stories surfaced in 1988 about her parents' adherence to the teachings of Fundamentalist preacher "Colonel" Robert B. Thieme Jr., known for attacking homosexuals, liberals and the United Nations, she fumed that religion was a private matter. But recently she told a friend she considered it "very significant" that the Governor and his wife attended different churches.

While Mrs. Quayle is urging women who care about their children not to work, she is constantly buzzing around the world and the country helping her husband campaign to keep his job. Having adopted disaster relief as her personal crusade, she has visited numerous disaster sites in the U.S. and abroad during the past four years. Just last week she was off to Florida, as a highly visible member of the board of the Federal Emergency Management Agency. She has also traveled to all 50 states on behalf of the party, raising more than $1 million for the campaign. Almost any paying job, short of flight attendant, would give her more time at home with her kids.

And she has found time to co-author a potboiler novel called *Embrace the Serpent* and to take a nine-state book tour. Some critics point out, however, that she would never have landed a sweetheart book deal—Crown Publishers churned out 75,000 copies instead of the usual 6,000 for a first novel—if she had not been married to the Vice President. Marilyn Quayle's activities demonstrate nothing more than the fact that in the modern age, talented, ambitious women need not hide their skills nor divert their energies. Although politically unthinkable for a Republican at the moment, what would be wrong with a qualified lawyer like Maryiln Quayle—or Hillary Clinton—holding an important government job, if earned by merit? Robert Kennedy was his brother's Attorney General, and both the President and the country were well served.

Last week Hillary Clinton sought to reclaim a bit of her policy role by saying she intended to take a more "comprehensive" role in the White House, meaning she would be an active "voice for children" and an advocate of programs to promote their interests. "I have recollections of extraordinary policy roles taken by Eleanor Roosevelt and very strong positions on the environment by Lady Bird Johnson," she told *Time*.

First Spouses have always had some influence on the President, no matter how much that influence was hidden or downplayed. Woodrow Wilson's wife Edith was the virtual President during her husband's long illness. And it is impossible to imagine Presidents from George Washington to George Bush not listening to the counsel of the one person in the world upon whom they can count to have their joint interests at heart. Bush is a better President for having Barbara Bush at his side. So why shouldn't Dan Quayle get the benefit of Marilyn Quayle's intellect and instincts? And why shouldn't Bill Clinton have the benefit of Hillary Clinton's? And why then shouldn't the country get the same benefit? Perhaps it is time to admit that "two for one" is a good deal.

BEHIND EVERY SUCCESSFUL politician is a dedicated and skilled team that does everything from advancing the candidate's trips to writing his or her speeches. "Experts" in every category advise the candidate; for example, media consultants devise complex strategies that shape the candidate's image on television and in the press. Personal style determines the extent to which a candidate takes a hands-on approach to the campaign. But even candidates who like to hold the reins of power find that their campaigns are always significantly influenced by their staffs. There is no doubt that Bill Clinton exercised unusually close control over his campaign; nevertheless, James Carville, Clinton's top campaign advisor and, in Gary Wills's colorful language, "Clinton's hell-raiser," was perhaps more than any other advisor, responsible for Clinton's victory.[1] In addition to Carville, the Clinton team included a core of talented individuals who, in their own ways, exerted influence on the campaign, as the following selection reveals.

3 Walter Shapiro with Priscilla Painton
THE TEAM BEHIND BILL AND HILLARY

For Bill Clinton and Al Gore, Iowa last week became their own Field of Dreams. A shimmering summer's day was just beginning its slow fade into dusk as the eight-bus caravan pulled into Manchester for a carefully orchestrated "unscheduled" stop. The local Democrats had done their part—a crowd of nearly 1,000 had been waiting for several hours to gambol in the limelight. Gore, fast becoming the Ed McMahon of political warm-up acts, gave his patter-perfect introduction, complete with the mawkish reminder that Clinton's father died three months before Clinton was born. Then Clinton clambered up onto the small outdoor podium for a quick rendition of his stump speech. Knowing all too well how easily this political magic can fade, he tried to inoculate himself by warning, "In the next 88 days, those Republicans will try to scare you to death. Clinton and Gore—those young fellows—will go hog wild, and things will be terrible. For the only way those Republicans can be elected is to scare you to death."

Afterward, Clinton worked his way down the rope line, waving, shaking, touching, posing, always smiling, his blue dress shirt damp with perspiration, the Secret Service agents clinging to his belt when he leaned far into the crowd. The faces of Manchester conveyed the *Music Man* message that

[1]Gary Wills, "Clinton's Hell-raiser," *The New Yorker*, 12 October 1992, 92–101.

"there's nothing halfway about the Iowa way to greet you." The mood was warm and enveloping as Clinton heard each message of encouragement. "We owe it all to you." "You're doing great." "You'll be a great President."

None of this, of course, is conclusive. Friendly crowds and sunny poll numbers can be a fatal August illusion. But for now, the mood of the Clinton campaign is a kind of dazed humility at the wondrous workings of fate. Says campaign manager David Wilhelm, who originally dreamed up the notion of putting the Clinton campaign on wheels: "I'd love to be able to say that we knew it would strike this chord. It just isn't true."

Hard to remember that at the end of the California primary in early June, the Clinton campaign was impelled forward by little more than a grim sense of inevitability. Clinton was physically drained from the gauntlet of primaries; the candidate's message of change had been pre-empted by Ross Perot; and the campaign structure in Little Rock had so many fancy titles and overlapping responsibilities that decisions had to be made by consensus—or not at all.

Against this backdrop of drift and looming defeat, Clinton, prodded by his wife Hillary, belatedly realized that the campaign structure in Little Rock had to be revamped for the general election. It had become too much a mirror of Clinton's own personality, particularly his tendency to skirt conflict, paper over differences and thus tolerate confusion. "He's got good political instincts, but the problem is that he's so facile and adroit that people come away thinking they've heard what they want to hear," says a senior campaign adviser. Hillary does not have this problem. "She's quicker to clarify and make decisions than Bill," says Carolyn Staley, a longtime friend of the candidate's.

While the public relations effort to mold Hillary into a traditional my-heart-belongs-to-hubby First Lady means that campaign insiders are reluctant to publicly acknowledge her substantive role, her imprint on the staff shake-up seems clear. With Hillary as the principal guardian of the candidate's body and mind, it is telling that just before the convention she propelled the couple's longtime friend Susan Thomases—a sometimes confrontational New York City lawyer—into the powerful slot of head scheduler. In that role Thomases serves Hillary's agenda to make sure Clinton's tendency to please everyone—to let discussions drag on, to keep on the campaign trail until he's robotic with fatigue—does not get the better of him.

"One of the reasons she wanted me to do the scheduling is that she knows I understand that her husband needs sleep and needs time to think," says Thomases. Until recently, she was the epicenter for controversy within the campaign, which may explain why she has received scant public credit for shrewd judgments like doggedly promoting the bus-tour idea within the Clinton camp. Top strategist James Carville defends her in these terms: "The most powerful force in the universe is inertia, and Susan is the most anti-inertia person I know."

Clinton himself, as a ranking insider put it, is "the real manager of this campaign." On the morning after the convention, Clinton told his top aides that he was restructuring the operation. The decision stemmed in part from a campaign flare-up in early June, when several senior staffers complained directly to the candidate about Thomases' tendency to meddle in areas like polling that were far outside her formal role as Hillary's staff director. The ultimate resolution was Thomases' new job as the campaign's internal Dr. No—the final authority to resist demands on Bill Clinton's time. In a larger shift, campaign chairman Mickey Kantor was in effect kicked upstairs to handle long-term planning on such contingencies as a Clinton-Gore transition as well as handholding the egos of Democratic powers.

Thus emerged the unlikely trio that now holds day-to-day responsibility for directing the campaign—Carville, George Stephanopoulos and Betsey Wright. Each represents a different facet of the totality that is Clinton. Carville is the grit, the guts and the unyielding determination. Stephanopoulos, like the candidate a Rhodes scholar, mirrors Clinton's thinking and intuits his likely responses. Wright, Clinton's chief of staff during most of his years as Arkansas Governor, is the keeper and the ardent defender of his record.

Carville and Wright are the dominant agenda-setting forces at the 7 A.M. staff meeting in the third-floor war room of the Little Rock headquarters. Even now, the Clinton campaign has an informality that would make a Republican organizational purist wince. Wright, in fact, laughingly calls the campaign structure mystical. To understand the dramatic summer transformation of Clinton's candidacy from junker to juggernaut, take a closer look at the triumphant trio in Little Rock.

The Ragin' Cajun

Carville, 47, is a constant study in coiled tension; he holds his body Marine-style rigid; his brooding brow and his closely cropped, sparse hair all convey the same message as the T-shirts and pressed jeans that he favors: This is not a man to be messed with. As Carville describes himself: "I walk the edge between being colorful and controversial."

Carville was a late bloomer—a Vietnam-era Marine (who was never sent to Vietnam); a Louisiana lawyer reluctant to practice; a political hired gun who moved into the front rank of Democratic consultants only by masterminding last year's upset Pennsylvania Senate victory of Harris Wofford. Carville first met Clinton last summer through another client, Georgia Governor Zell Miller, and joined the campaign in November. Carville's first impression of Clinton: "So this is what major league pitching looks like." But baptism in the big leagues can be brutal, and so it was for Carville, who field-marshaled Clinton's give-no-ground-defense against the fusillade of charges—ranging from adultery to draft dodging—that almost destroyed the candidate before the New Hampshire primary.

Yet by April, Carville was a little lost. As an admirer within the Clinton camp puts it: "When James isn't in charge, he tends to lose interest." It wasn't that Carville loafed, it was more that he craved a new adrenaline high. As even he admits, "After the New York primary, I was working, but I didn't put my helmet back on until after California." Now the first among equals in the campaign, Carville is the Count of the Counterpunch, calling the political ploys and postures, the stratagems and sound bites that make up daily campaign gamesmanship.

If Carville is motivated by one principle, it is "Hit 'em back hard." Nothing better reflects his combative personality than the inspirational slogans he posts in the war room. On the central issue of the campaign: THE ECONOMY, STUPID. And on the need for rapid response: SPEED KILLS—BUSH. Carville's ambitions begin and end with politics, for as he says, "I wouldn't live in a country whose government would have me in it."

The Alter Ego

Stephanopoulos' influence in the campaign is no secret—he is handed over 100 telephone-message slips a day. But still, as a campaign insider puts it: "Everybody underestimates him. He looks like he's 14 years old." With a shock of dark brown hair, a boyish face and an imperturbable, almost brusque manner, Stephanopoulos, 31, is the ultimate quick study. Joining the campaign last summer, after being heavily wooed by Bob Kerrey, Stephanopoulos became Clinton's constant traveling companion throughout the primaries. His mastery of Clinton's ideas and his ability to anticipate the candidate's reactions to any situation is uncanny. Stephanopoulos' explanation: "He's a great teacher."

Stephanopoulos was no slouch as a student either. The son of a dean in the Greek Orthodox Church, he attended Columbia University, where he won his Rhodes. His career in politics was precocious. Starting out as a congressional aide, Stephanopoulos became a deputy communications director for the 1988 Michael Dukakis campaign, where he banged out the political message of the day. After the Dukakis debacle, Stephanopoulos almost left politics for a key job helping run the New York City Public Library before Congressman Richard Gephardt, now House majority leader, offered him a top staff position. Recruited last summer, Stephanopoulos pressed the Clinton campaign hard to get exactly what he wanted—the post of communications director.

A pivotal moment in the campaign came in May, when Stephanopoulos was detached from Clinton's side to manage the nerve center in Little Rock. Suddenly, good ideas that had been kicking around the campaign were carried out. Media adviser Mandy Grunwald had been arguing for months that Clinton should do "The Arsenio Hall Show." In fact, Clinton's come-back may well have begun on Arsenio, when the image of Slick Willie gave way to Saxophone Bill. On a more substantive level, Stephanopoulos directed the drafting of Clinton's new economic plan, now a campaign centerpiece. As Robert Shapiro, a ranking Clinton economic adviser, puts it: "When George says something has to be done, everyone knows he's speaking for Clinton."

The Secretary of Defense

Wright, 48, first met Clinton when both were young liberal idealists working in her native Texas on the 1972 George McGovern campaign. In the mid-1970s she gravitated to Washington, where she ran the Women's National Education Fund, recruiting women candidates for office. After Clinton was defeated for re-election as Governor in 1980, he called upon Wright to run his comeback crusade. She accepted instantly beause, as she recalls, "it was always important to me that strong political feminists have relationships with strong male politicians. And Bill Clinton has no problem with strong women."

Wright's reward from the victorious Clinton: he named her his chief of staff, a post she held until 1990. Wright, whose reputation for political toughness belies a far softer interior, had some lonely years serving as the lightning rod for criticism of the Governor. In the late 1980s, she confided with a laugh. "I've made great progress here. When I came in, they hated me for being a woman. Now they only hate me for being the Governor's chief of staff." After a stint chairing the Arkansas Democratic Party, Wright drifted out of politics—thereby avoiding the early shakedown months of the Clinton campaign. But she returned to Little Rock in the spring to run the campaign's research operation, aggressively defending the Clinton record from Republican attacks and probing press queries.

Her rapid rise in the campaign hierarchy—symbolized by her new title of deputy campaign chairman—was not without political infighting and mo-ments of drama. But her position is secure because of her deep allegiance to both Clinton and Hillary. During much of the 1980s, Wright spent half her life at the Governor's mansion with the Clintons and their daughter Chelsea. But beyond Wright the loyalist, there is also Wright the champion archivist: the computerized database on the Clinton record that she devel-oped allows her to retrieve any crucial document in minutes.

When South Carolina's Republican Governor Carroll Campbell recently criticized Clinton as a typical tax-and-spend liberal. Wright dug into the files and found a 1989 letter from Campbell praising his Arkansas colleague, which was gleefully released to the press. When she hears about a new G.O.P. attack, Wright is apt to give a rich Texas chuckle, and then say with puckish enjoyment, "I think I've got something on that. Let me check." Likely as not, the result is another Clinton gotcha.

A winning campaign inevitably turns everyone associated with it into a political genius on a par with F.D.R. mastermind James Farley, an honor held only as long as the polls stay high. But the real tests for Carville, Stephanopoulos and Wright will come with the bruising fall contest. In the meantime, the campaigners can recline in their bus seats, roar down the highway and enjoy the cheering throngs. As Wright puts it for all of them: "I'm going to remember these days when things get tough."

POLITICS IS ALWAYS ABOUT winners and losers, glorious victories and crushing defeats. Election day in a presidential campaign is the Super Bowl of politics, and the candidates' headquarters are the campaign locker rooms, with exultant victors and stunned losers. How power shifts affect the candidates, their families, and close advisors is the subject of the following glimpse behind the scenes of presidential politics.

4 Hugh Sidey
GOING GENTLY INTO THE NIGHT

A piece of George Bush's soul has been crushed. He will hide it behind his patrician grace in his season of defeat. Rejected by the American people, a life's ambition cut short, a political finale cast in defeat—a heavy burden even for a man of Bush's discipline. Yet this cruel ritual is the heart of democracy.

Like the office itself, the pain of an incumbent's defeat has to be immense. A friend of Jimmy Carter's watched him confront the fact he would not be re-elected in 1980 and said, "a part of him died." Jerry Ford clung to his hope for victory into election night, but as always with good politicians there comes a moment when truth confronts them and they accept it. When Ohio slipped out of Ford's grip on that fateful night in 1976, he got up from his chair in front of his television set and said, "That's it." Tears streamed down his face and that of Joe Garagiola, former baseball player and sports commentator, who had campaigned desperately for Ford in the final hours. The two old friends hugged each other in their silent despondency.

Later Rex Scouten, chief White House usher, remembers walking with Ford to his bedroom on that night, saying something about Ford's long, distinguished public career and how it might be best for him to move on and think of himself. Ford looked at Scouten with a great hurt in his eyes. "I don't believe so," he said. None of them ever do.

There probably is no easy way for the loser to endure the transition of presidential power. He is faced with the exuberance of the winner, impatient to get into the White House. He is surrounded with the political disarray of his expiring Administration. By most measures, the change from Bush to Bill Clinton will be less traumatic than others. The anti-Bush tide was running for weeks. Only blind fanatics—and that does not include Bush—could see a good chance of redemption in the last campaign days.

"Going Gently Into the Night," by Hugh Sidey, *Time* Magazine, November 16, 1992. Copyright © 1992 Time Inc. Reprinted by permission.

The worst hours in presidential power shifts follow the unexpected episodes like the assassination of John Kennedy. On Air Force One bringing both Kennedy's body and Lyndon Johnson, the new President, back to Washington, there played out a scene of anguish and exhilaration, a weird struggle contained in the hurtling fuselage. Devastating sorrow among the Kennedy people turned to a blind hatred against the statutory heirs to power. The Johnson group, though stunned by the death of Kennedy, could scarcely contain their satisfaction at gaining the office that had eluded them in the electoral process.

Back at the White House the most devastating images were those of the physical changes taking place inside the old building, like the pictures of the Kennedy rocking chairs piled on a furniture dolly being rushed out the side door even before Kennedy's funeral was over. There was no choice. The White House staff perpetuated the hearbeat of American authority.

Richard Nixon made the final decision to yield the presidency, and the inevitability of his departure had been writ large for days. Still, the pain was intense. Not long before Nixon made that final wave from the door of his helicopter, Alexander Haig, then the White House chief of staff, met with a friend in the shadowy Map Room in the basement of the Mansion. "He will be dead within a year," said Haig of Nixon, having witnessed an emotional wound beyond anything Haig the soldier had seen before.

Nixon recovered, as did Ford and Carter, though even today their disappointment lingers. Politicians know the risks of their game, but like soldiers in battle they all expect the other person to be laid low. Lyndon Johnson was renowned for a cast-iron political gut, but even he had a soft core. While he secretly decided not to run in 1968 rather than risk defeat, there is strong evidence that he never cleansed himself of despair. Being out of power may have hastened his death down at his ranch four years after leaving the White House.

Even in a programmed transition after eight years in office, there is a sadness and a frantic shifting of the complex internal gears of the White House, which must serve one man up to his departure on Inauguration Day, then welcome the newcomer a few hours later. At the end of that sunny, joyous day in 1981 when Ronald Regan was sworn in, Usher Gary Walters pulled down the U.S. flag that had flown over the White House and tucked it away; eight years later, he and the assembled staff gave it to the departing President. Even the Gipper choked up, and so did Walters and all the others. End of the Reagan home at 1600 Pennsylvania Avenue.

Over in the working West Wing, Reagan had stoically stepped in for a last look around the Oval Office, perhaps the world's most recognized symbol of political authority. Then he fished in his pocket, pulled out the code card for nuclear attack and asked huskily, "What do I do with this?" That Godlike hold over life and death vanished from his fingers and into a military aide's hands and later to Bush's pocket.

When an election decrees a new White House resident, the outgoing President and his governing team must continue to operate for another 10 weeks. That in turn dictates that the home must continue to be familiar, comfortable and functional. Family pictures stay on the walls and tables, favorite desserts are served up at night, fresh flowers placed at every turn. Then, when the First Family departs for the Capitol and the Inaugural, the resident staff and supplemental crews launch a furious assault. By the end of the great Inauguration parade, say around 5 P.M., the new President and his family enter the White House furnished and decorated in the private quarters to fit their style and taste. Inside, the staff must contemplate new habits, accommodate strange kids, house new dogs or cats, position new furniture and pictures and make sure that sadness yields to cheer, tears turn to smiles.

The greater burden in these days of passing the power will fall on Barbara Bush. The change in the business end of the White House is a stodgy ritual. The Clinton people don't want to get entangled in the last days of Bush decision making, and so they will do little more than learn how to operate the machinery and scout the office space, then wait for the moment of truth when they can claim the desks and issue orders. But Barbara, wife and nester, must dismantle a home and shift a family. Walters and his crew by tradition will wait until the immediate pain of defeat subsides and the First Lady signals she is ready to make plans. Then the staff, renowned for its sensitivity, will feel their way into the new routine.

It took a White House servant three tries back when Harry Truman moved in to get the formula that Bess and Harry liked for their nightly old fashioned cocktail. The final solution: double the shot of bourbon. The flower arrangers went from Nancy Reagan's lower, denser bouquets to airy sprays favored by Mrs. Bush. Pastry impresario Roland Mesnier boosted his cookie output when the Bushes arrived trailing various combinations of their eight (now twelve) grandchildren. Walters, who is no cat lover, remembers being sent to Blair House in 1977 to bring Amy Carter's cat, Misty Malarkey Ying Yang, over to its quarters in the White House. Walters got a firm but nervous grip on Misty, tenderly threaded his way through the amused crowds on Pennsylvania Avenue who were waiting for the Inauguration parade. Both Walters and Misty were relieved to get safely inside the White House. The cat loved the new home; Walters even grew to like Misty.

Now and then there is a bump or two in the changing of the presidential family. Legend has it that Lyndon Johnson asked French chef René Verdon, who had been installed by Jackie Kennedy, if he could cook Texan. "I don't cook fried chicken, corn bread or barbecue," said Verdon, who soon left to open a restaurant in San Francisco.

For the most part the bittersweet drama goes along without any lasting rancor. Peaceful change is what democracy is all about, and the people who play the political game despite their frayed feelings know the rules and respect them. On election night when Bush had conceded to Bill Clinton, and the White House in its weary sadness had dimmed and paused for a few hours, one could loiter on Pennsylvania Avenue and marvel anew at the magic in this old system of ours. No tanks guarded the White House gates. No troops cordoned the streets. The greatest political power on the face of the earth had been taken from one man and given to another, and it was done with only the riffle of an autumn breeze around the big house that George Washington built.

SINCE THE 1992 PRESIDENTIAL election, the media spotlight on Texas billionaire Ross Perot, who ran not so much as a third-party candidate but as a self-proclaimed "citizens' choice," continues. Perot has had an important impact on politics by encouraging citizens to send Washington a message. Perot proclaimed that his movement was directed toward active democracy. As the following assessment of Perot indicates, he achieved remarkable success at the polls without the support of an organized political party. His campaign reflected telecommunication democracy in action.

5 Laurence I. Barrett
MUTINY IN
PEROTLAND

For Lloyd Wells, serving as a volunteer in Ross Perot's advocacy group United We Stand America "was one of the most euphoric experiences of my life." Wells, 72, had been an activist for decades, agitating against orthodox politics. It was the fulfillment of his dreams when Perot arrived on the scene and organized a popular rebellion against the major parties. But this month the Maine chapter of Perot's organization ejected Wells and two others for alleged insubordination. Last week Wells was helping to organize a competing group in Maine and began coordinating with disaffected Perotistas elsewhere. "We're going to promote Perot's agenda without Perot," said Tim Beal, one of the Maine rebels. "We need an eloquent spokesperson, but we don't need a dictator."

Nationally, Perot's standing prospers. Though his Dallas headquarters refuses to disclose current numbers, the group has recruited more than 1 million members since January and appears to be growing steadily. In a *Time*/CNN poll last week, Perot's favorable rating, 54%, was virtually the same as Bill Clinton's, at 57%.

Below the waterline, however, Perot's effort to build a national organization of many millions is springing leaks. By the estimate of some dissidents, there are now about 100 small splinter groups of Perot defectors. Loosely organized so far, they keep in touch with one another through a phone-and-fax network. Roger Lindholm, a Phoenix, Arizona, business consultant, now edits one of several newsletters for disgruntled activists.

The prime source of friction is that Perot wants to focus his group's energy on attracting more followers, while the members already on board want to push the Perot agenda by lobbying legislatures and backing local candidates. Now that Perot has built an army, it is itching to fight battles over such issues as taxes and legislative term limits. But Perot won't let them do so, leading disgruntled Perotistas to claim the group has become like a giant pyramid scheme, existing only for the purpose of growing larger. The dispute has produced a sharp discrepancy between Perot's self-image as a mere servant of the volunteers and his need to impose discipline on a movement fueled by independence. "I'm Ross, you're the boss," he tells his followers. When they take that slogan literally, conflict occurs.

The upheaval in Maine is a vivid example. When Wells complained that the national group was developing "military industrial organizational procedures," Perot headquarters ignored him, so he attempted to incorporate the Maine chapter independently of Dallas. He also went public with his criticism. Stephen Bost, the Maine coordinator appointed by Dallas, responded by summoning Wells to appear before an "ad hoc committee on grievances." Wells states that the meeting took the form of a tribunal, accusing him of disrupting the membership drive and damaging Perot's image. "If names had been stones," Wells said, "I'd be black and blue or dead." Though the panel ruled that Wells could remain in the organization, Bost later refunded Wells' $15 membership fee and a $100 contribution he had made. The Perot alumni network depicted Wells as a martyr for the cause.

Meanwhile, a rump group in Idaho may become a model for other rebels. About 200 of Perot's most zealous supporters, operating under the title of United We Stand Idaho, is focusing its efforts on such local issues as county land policy. Because that clashed with Dallas' post-election strategy of concentrating on recruitment, the national headquarters has now sanctioned a second, larger Idaho chapter and is trying to quash the independent group.

The dispute over goals is proving deeply divisive. Some activists want to use United We Stand America as the foundation of a new national political party—an idea Perot has considered but put aside. Other followers hope to endorse candidates for local and federal office, using Perot's preachments as criteria. Dallas is not ready for that tactic yet. The restless centurions also want to act out Perot's reformist script in concrete political ways.

About two dozen state directors have quit or been pushed out since Perot began organizing the present incarnation of United We Stand America in January. Tom Wing, who had led the Perot faction in Illinois as a volunteer since last summer, was dumped in March. His interim successor, Janice Horner, says Wing lost favor because he wanted control. The real problem, Wing charges, was that he was building an activist group intending, among other things, to pressure the Illinois congressional delegation to support Perot's policy proposals. According to Perot's rhetoric, that should have been welcomed by headquarters, but Dallas disapproved. "We were told," Wing says, "that the only appropriate activity after the election was getting members signed up."

Some of the turmoil results from confusion and personal rivalries that are inevitable in a ballooning new organization of amateurs. Perot distances himself from these problems, relying on a handful of emissaries to keep order. These agents often impress the locals as tough but incompetent. Says one defector: "He's got people in command whom he trusts—that's all that counts, not whether they're good or bad."

Similar gripes are heard from the Northeast to the Southwest. Most vocal are veterans who stuck with Perot through his erratic presidential campaign and now think he is abandoning the movement's original goals in favor of gratifying his ego. Quipped Joyce Shepard, a county leader in New York: "I feel as if I've remarried an abusive husband."

In Dallas Perot's senior advisers dismiss the dissenters as a tiny minority. Darcy Anderson, once a real-estate executive for Perot and now executive director of the group, said last week, "We grew so quickly, with no infrastructure in place. Now we're building the foundations." That effort includes hiring a full-time director in each state. All but two of the 21 named so far have come from the cadre of volunteers. Eventually members in each congressional district will elect a local leader. These district coordinators in turn will select state executives from their own ranks. Once those layers are in place, presumably the rank-and-file will not feel irrelevant.

The national headquarters, however, will still exert ultimate control. Each state chapter is to receive a "license," much like a fast-food franchise, from Dallas, and Perot will retain the right to cancel a chapter's accreditation. Explained Clay Mulford, the national group's general counsel: "We don't want to be held responsible for every action they may take."

Yet the huge mechanism Perot is building still lacks a goal more concrete than expanding its patron's political influence. John White, Perot's chief economic consultant a year ago, predicts the instability will continue. The movement, White says, contains "no unifying principle other than the personality of Ross Perot. So it's hard to keep it together." A current Perot adviser concedes that "they have to decide in Dallas what they're really going to be."

Perot seems to be in no hurry to do that, any more than he is bothered by the mutiny of some of his followers. Perot has established himself as a large enough political force to rattle both the White House and Congress. He will buy more television time in which to argue his positions and pitch membership in his national group. Meanwhile, network and local talk shows give him ample free air time, helping to keep his poll ratings lofty.

Gordon Black, the independent pollster now doing surveys for Perot, forecasts that United We Stand America will have close to 10 million dues-paying members by the end of the year. Even half that number would be impressive. At that point, Perot envisions a dramatic unveiling of his organization's numerical strength, along with a new assertion of his issues agenda. He will display that heft just as the congressional election campaign starts, aiming at pressuring candidates. His followers can hardly wait.

6
A BRIDE, A CORPSE . . .

White House officials are under orders to speak no ill of Ross Perot: no point in generating more TV sound bites. But by last week political strategist Paul Begala could no longer contain himself. Perot, said Begala, "will say anything to get attention. He is just one of those folks who, when he goes to a wedding, he wants to be the bride. When he goes to a funeral, he wants to be the corpse."

Which testifies to how deep Perot is getting under the presidential skin. Not just because of the personal nature of his needling either—although that is getting extreme. Sample insults from his latest round of TV interviews: Clinton is "still doing things the Arkansas way, like trying to give the travel business as a political payoff . . . the President [is] . . . trying to flimflam the American people." All this in addition to Perot's now celebrated crack that he would not hire Clinton for any job above middle management.

The White House cannot just shrug off such barbs; it takes Perot seriously as a political threat. In the latest *Time*/CNN poll, 52% of the respondents have a generally favorable opinion of Perot, while only 50% have a similar opinion of Clinton personally (and many fewer approve of the job he is doing as President). On Perot's current major bugbear, the North American Free Trade Agreement, 63% agree with him that it will result in a loss of American jobs, vs. only 25% who believe with Clinton that it will create jobs.

The Administration is beginning to . . . well, not shoot but talk back. Clinton, pressed by reporters for a response to Perot, said, "Well, we know he doesn't like my state . . . but that doesn't have much to do with America." Three senior officials—Trade Representative Mickey Kantor, Labor Secretary Robert Reich and Council of Economic Advisers chairwoman Laura Tyson—appeared at a press briefing to answer in advance the attacks on NAFTA Perot was preparing to make in a TV speech Sunday night.

Administration officials are also trying to set up a special task force charged with further monitoring and answering Perot's assaults on NAFTA, but it is not staffed yet. Even so, the Administration seems stumped. Suffering in silence or making restrained replies when unavoidable plainly is not working. But trading raspberry for raspberry with Perot might only lower Clinton's presidential dignity without being very effective either; it is Perot's natural style but hardly Clinton's. The White House has not yet found a way out of that dilemma.

POLITICAL PUNDITS HER-
alded 1992 as the "year of the
woman," referring to the unusually large number of women elected to
federal, state, and local offices. The event
that ignited women was the Senate Judiciary Committee hearings on the nomination of Clarence Thomas to the Supreme
Court and its investigation of Anita Hill's
graphic charges that Thomas had sexually harassed her while she was an employee and he the chairman of the Equal
Employment Opportunity Commission.
Writing for *The Boston Globe*, editorial
commentator Loretta McLaughlin expressed the widely held view that the
president's continued support of Thomas
after Anita Hill's charges "alienated—
and energized—women voters as nothing else had before. Anita Hill became
the national symbol of unfair treatment of
women—both in her allegations of sex-

ual harassment against Thomas and the
scorn she was subjected to by the all-
male Senate Judiciary Committee. That
shameful scene will never be repeated.
But it spawned the Year of the Women."[1]

Over 2,500 women ran for public
office in 1992, and many were elected,
including Senators Dianne Feinstein and
Barbara Boxer in California, Mosele R.
Braun in Illinois, and Patty Murray in
Washington. In Pennsylvania, political
novice Lynn Yeakel almost unseated incumbent Arlene Specter, a seasoned
campaigner and popular senator who
won by a close vote.

A fascinating behind-the-scenes account of the Hill-Thomas clash that became a major political event and that
helped to bring about the year of the
woman unfolds in the following selection.

7 Gloria Borger and Ted Gest with Jeannye Thornton
THE THOMAS-HILL EPISODE:
THE UNTOLD STORY

The charges of sexual harassment against a Supreme Court nominee had
stunned the nation—and the Senate Judiciary Committee had just begun its
public inquisition. But even before Anita Hill faced Clarence Thomas,
Chairman Joseph Biden took his colleagues behind closed doors in a session
that now seems prophetic: "We're all going to be losers here. We can't do
what we know we should all do as lawyers. We should have an executive
session. But unfortunately, gentlemen, we will never be able to do that. The
public would be outraged."

By the time the incredible hearings ended three days later, the public was

[1] *The Boston Globe*, 4 November 1992, 19.

outraged anyway—over a conundrum it could not solve, over a process that seemed unfair, over the inept performance of a male-dominated Senate. One year later, the questions of the Thomas-Hill affair remain unanswered, yet the political impact could not be more certain: A record number of women are running for Congress, supported by political action committees for women that are now among the largest fund-raisers in the nation. The Equal Employment Opportunity Commission reports a substantial jump in sexual-harassment complaints. And the country is still arguing every day about what happens between men and women.

Moreover, Anita Hill has become a folk hero to a large segment of the public—and is much in demand on the lecture circuit. Just after the confirmation battle ended, polls showed the public overwhelmingly believing Thomas over Hill, by a 60-to-20-percent margin. A new *U.S. News* poll shows a dramatic shift in sentiment to a dead heat—at 38 percent each.[*] The survey also shows a big change in the way the public thinks Hill was treated: Last year, only 8 percent thought the Judiciary Committee had treated her unfairly; that number has now jumped to 39 percent. Yet while the public remains angry with the Senate, a majority still believes it did "the right thing" in confirming Thomas.

A *U.S. News* investigation into the story reveals that the committee's probe was doomed from the start. While neither Hill nor Thomas would comment, dozens of other key players did, revealing a process overpowered by the extreme political tactics and interests of the left and the right. As one key Thomas strategist summed up: "It had all the sleaze and slime of politics. When it was over, all I wanted to do was go home and take a shower."

Part 1: The News

Late on the third day of the often mind-numbing Thomas confirmation hearings—September 12, 1991—Biden was tapped on the shoulder and beckoned to a private room by aide Ronald Klain. There, he learned for the first time what had been whispered around Washington for weeks—that a young law professor who had worked for Thomas at the Equal Employment Opportunity Commission was saying that during the time he was in charge of enforcing laws against sexual harassment he had harassed *her*. "When did this happen? Where did you get it? Have you talked to this person?" Biden sputtered. Anita Hill was no kook, he was told, and had been talking to aides of other committee members. Biden stopped short, then barked: "Let them get back to her and tell her to call. Give our number."

A goddamn bombshell is sitting here, Biden thought, as he returned to the hearing. Later that day, Hill spoke twice to Biden investigator Harriet Grant

[*]*U.S. News* poll by Princeton Survey Research Associates of 1,002 adults, September 11–15. Margin of error is plus or minus 3 percentage points. 1991 poll data from a *New York Times*/CBS News survey.

but refused to allow her name to be revealed to other senators—or to Thomas. Biden was in a box: He couldn't ask for a full investigation by the FBI unless the accuser came forward so Thomas could respond in an FBI interview. He couldn't even notify the nominee. In the end, it took three weeks and a leak to the press to get Hill's charges out.

It was clear from the start that the stakes in the Thomas nomination were too high for an easy confirmation. From the day George Bush anointed Thomas as the successor to retiring Justice Thurgood Marshall, it was war. The White House did not want to lose the fight over this black, conservative federal appeals court judge the way Ronald Reagan lost the 1987 nomination of Robert Bork. For their part, liberal interest groups knew this justice might be the one to doom the right to abortion.

At first, both sides thought the fight would center on Thomas's ideology, not on his character. Still, it would be fought with images aimed at TV audiences, like a political campaign. At the White House, a working group run by former White House Chief of Staff Kenneth Duberstein and including then Bush Chief of Staff John Sununu, congressional liaison Fred McClure, vice presidential Chief of Staff William Kristol and chief White House counsel C. Boyden Gray settled on its "Pin Point" strategy: Depict Thomas as a man from humble beginnings in a small Georgia town, a conservative still sympathetic to minorities' and women's interests. A special target of this appeal was Southern Democrats, whose black constituencies leaned toward Thomas. The other part of the plan was to "soften" Thomas's often hard-edge legal philosophy and to obfuscate his views on abortion. During his practice "murder boards," the team's advice was simple: Eliminate the histrionics.

While the contest for public approval unfolded, a private drama, too, was underway. Within days of Bush's July 1 announcement, Hill, a law professor at the University of Oklahoma, called her old law school friend Gary Phillips, a lawyer at the Federal Communications Commission. After 10 minutes of small talk, Phillips realized that neither had raised the big news about her former boss. What did she think about the Thomas nomination? Hill paused, then said: "I never told you this before, but I was sexually harassed by Clarence Thomas." Stunned, Phillips wondered if she planned to report her story; she seemed inclined to keep it quiet. Over the next few weeks, Phillips told friends he knew a woman who had been harassed by Thomas. The story made the rounds with much speed.

In late July, a partisan passed the rumor about the Oklahoma law professor to the liberal Alliance for Justice. Top staffers Nan Aron and George Kassouf checked a school directory and came upon Anita Hill's name. After mulling over what to do, Aron passed the tip to an aide of liberal Ohio Democrat Howard Metzenbaum's—who, in turn, told other Metzenbaum aides.

The information was hardly treated as a smoking gun. In mid-August,

Metzenbaum staffer Gail Laster mentioned the harassment rumor to fellow Labor Committee staffer Ricki Seidman, who worked for Ted Kennedy. Neither pursued it in the crush of other work. Just five days before the confirmation hearing, Laster called Hill. The professor, startled to find a Senate staffer on the line, did not volunteer anything.

Coincidentally, Seidman phoned Oklahoma the next day. She mentioned harassment to Hill, and got enough vague responses to make the issue seem worth pursuing. She learned that Hill had attended Yale Law School with Metzenbaum aide James Brudney and called her back, suggesting the two classmates speak. They did—on the first day of confirmation hearings—and that was the first time that Hill spelled out her charges. Brudney reported them to Metzenbaum; the senator ordered that Biden's staff be informed.

Publicly, meantime, the hearings grew testy as Thomas stonewalled substantive questions about his legal philosophy. Democrats were furious—and incredulous—at his claim that he had never discussed *Roe v. Wade*; conservatives weren't much happier. That left character questions as the only way to deny Thomas the nomination. Still, Biden was determined that Hill's charges would not surface unless she authorized it.

Misunderstandings blocked progress for a crucial week: Hill figured her charges were being circulated among senators with no name attached. But Biden was keeping a lid on them—in fairness to both Hill *and* Thomas. Even so, the circle of those who knew was widening. Sen. Patrick Leahy of Vermont suggested that the FBI be called in despite Hill's reticence. But the chairman nervously played a waiting game with Hill.

Back in Norman, Okla., Hill agonized about what course to take during long walks with fellow law Prof. Shirley Wiegand. On September 19—eight days before the committee was set to vote—Hill called Washington and was told that panel members would not be informed of her charges unless she allowed her name to be used. After another weekend of soul-searching, Hill finally faxed her charges to the committee on September 23, authorizing an FBI probe so Thomas could be informed of her allegations. But she still insisted on public anonymity.

Now, her complaint could be quietly revealed to White House lobbyists and to Sen. John Danforth, Thomas's political chaperone. It was left to handler McClure to call Thomas at his home in suburban Virginia two days later to tell him the FBI would be visiting that day. After the session with the FBI, the judge was disconsolate. He phoned Pamela Talkin, who had served as his chief of staff at the EEOC, to ask: "What might I have done that could have led to such a misunderstanding?" He denied it all.

The Judiciary Committee was also befuddled. Biden had told committee Democrats of Hill's charges, but ranking GOP member Strom Thurmond had not told most of his Republican colleagues. Some Democrats embarked on feverish fact finding. Paul Simon of Illinois called Hill the day before the vote. She sounded convincing, but Simon reiterated that her statement would not be circulated to all members of the Senate until she attached her name to it. A frustrated Hill decided she could no longer hold back, and a telephone chain began: Friends contacted Harvard Law Prof. Charles Ogletree, who then enlisted colleague Laurence Tribe to reach Biden aide Klain—a former Tribe student—a few hours before the morning voting session. Klain arranged for Hill's statement to be hand-delivered to members minutes before the session. Still, Hill had one more stricture: Senators could not *publicly* discuss her charges. The committee split 7 to 7 on the nomination. Anita Hill remained under wraps.

Biden was privately amazed that the Hill charges had not leaked out, since the group of those in the know had reached critical mass—17 senators in all, countless staffers, Hill friends and administration officials. The circle was so wide that a feminist activist told a top abortion-rights fund-raiser in the Chicago suburbs that the pending Hill charges might be a big money-maker for feminists.

Inevitably, journalists got wind of Hill's bombshell. Legal-affairs reporters Nina Totenberg of National Public Radio and Timothy Phelps of *Newsday* called Hill to ask for comment. Although initially refusing them, Hill gave in after Totenberg read to her from her own statement to the committee.

Hill did not imagine how explosive her charges would be; the White House did. When *Newsday's* Phelps called for comment, White House aides did more than issue a denial. They told him who could vouch for Thomas's character, including Phyllis Berry Myers, who had worked with both Thomas and Hill at the EEOC—and who said the charge was inconceivable. On Sunday morning, both *Newsday* and National Public Radio broke the story. The Senate later hired New York Lawyer Peter Fleming to investigate the leak, but an exhaustive inquiry failed to determine its origin.

Part 2: The Chaos

After the stories broke, the White House damage-control operation could not keep some pro-Thomas Democrats from getting cold feet. Danforth had a hard time controlling his fury—at both the leak and the wavering politicians. In an angry call to Biden at home in Delaware Sunday night, he insisted the Senate vote be held on Tuesday as scheduled, railed about the leak and dressed down the chairman for "losing control of his committee"—a charge that did not sit well. Danforth's decibel level made even his own allies uncomfortable because Biden was still going to be the ultimate arbiter.

Even before Danforth's shot across the bow, though, Biden had already spent much of the weekend on the telephone ("probably $400 in phone bills") trying to figure out the next steps, both for the Senate and for himself. He phoned Senate Majority Leader George Mitchell, aides, outside political advisers, lawyers and fellow senators. The problem was a political Catch-22:

"We can't vote with this thing out there," Biden told his fellow Democrats, but Hill wanted her name kept secret.

By Monday, Biden and his male colleagues were being skewered—by women for not paying enough attention to Hill's charges, by Democrats for not calling off the vote immediately and by Republicans for considering a delay. One persuasive argument in favor of postponement was whispered in the Democratic cloakroom: *If this guy goes on the court, this is impeachable stuff.* But the delay was cinched when Hill held a nationally televised press conference in Oklahoma. The Capital's phone lines were so jammed that senators could not get through to their own offices. Overnight, Anita Hill had become a national symbol, and Joe Biden—the Senate's expert on crimes against women—had become a target of those he had always worked to defend. "This ain't about Anita Hill and this ain't about Clarence Thomas," he told anyone who would listen. "This is about a power struggle going on in this country between men and women. This is the biggest thing you can imagine."

Faced with the public outcry, a number of Democrats who had been leaning toward Thomas adopted a strategy pushed by Leahy: They said they would vote against Thomas unless the vote was delayed. Sens. Dennis DeConcini of Arizona, Joseph Lieberman of Connecticut and Daniel P. Moynihan of New York were game. That news convinced even Danforth—who had tried to hold support by releasing Thomas's phone logs detailing friendly calls from Anita Hill. After frenzied meetings that moved around the Capitol like "a floating crap game," as Biden put it, the vote was delayed for one week. The hearings on Hill's charges would take place in three days.

Once the timing was settled, a key Democratic staffer figured the fight was over before it even started: *This will settle absolutely nothing. The votes will be there for Thomas so long as senators can say there was some sort of investigation, no matter how bad.* And everyone knew how nasty it would get. Republican Sen. Alan Simpson, who still smarts from his experience, sent an early warning: "Anita Hill will be sucked into the very thing she wanted to avoid most. And maybe we can ruin them both." Colorado Republican Hank Brown, a new Judiciary Committee member, wanted to find out about this woman firsthand. He phoned Hill and took notes during the call: "Never wanted this public." "Never initiated calls." "Said 'no comment' when asked about sexual harassment at first." When he hung up, he said nothing. *She's credible*, he thought.

Hill was hardly prepared for what she faced. She first met with her team of legal advisers just 60 hours before the hearings. Two law professor allies, Emma Coleman Jordan and Judith Resnik, assembled a team that included Ogletree and veteran constitutional lawyer John Frank. Hill was grilled on her story, with legal *éminences grises* like Lloyd Cutler looking on. No one doubted they had a good witness.

Moral support.   Among those offering private moral support was Biden. The day the vote was postponed, he walked into the Senate cloakroom about 9 P.M. and called her, even though he wasn't sure he should. "You did great," he said, referring to her Monday press conference. "All you have to do when you come before this committee is just tell your story like you did. You will do just fine."

Among Biden's advisers, there was a debate. His political future arguably hung in the balance, and they pondered the questions Biden asked of himself: *Do I go out and kill him? Or do I try to act as a judge?* The judge won, and Biden now allows he could have "taken on" his GOP colleagues a bit more. Fellow Democrats agree. At the time, they were wary of a direct assault on Thomas. Polls showed him increasingly popular. And some committee liberals like Metzenbaum, Kennedy and Simon were already under suspicion of having leaked the news. At a Wednesday caucus of committee Democrats, a benign strategy was chosen: Become seekers of the truth. The aggressive Leahy and the folksy Howell Heflin were chosen as designated interrogators.

The Republicans at their strategy session Thursday night had a vastly different mission: Defend Thomas. Their goal was to provide enough political cover that the Democrats who had been with Thomas could stay with him. White House strategists and Danforth were there; Duberstein was on the speakerphone. The decision was made to try to get Thomas to testify first. Key GOP players had already designated Arlen Specter of Pennsylvania and Orrin Hatch of Utah as the questioners. Specter—a deft former Philadelphia prosecutor who is also a moderate supporter of abortion rights—would take on Hill, and Hatch would question Thomas. Some friends warned Specter to go easy on Hill. He was eager to display his prosecutorial skills in the limelight, but he could not have been more off base in his political calculations.

By this point, Clarence and Virginia Thomas had reduced their circle to a precious few intimates—the Danforths and Mark Paoletta, a lawyer from the White House who became a friend during the ordeal. The night before the Friday hearings, Clint Bolick, an ex-EEOC co-worker, called the Thomases. "We're going for it," Ginny told him. Bolick and other friends worried that Thomas might withdraw. Allies hoped Ginny had talked him into holding firm, though they winced at times at her other advice. Later, friends would recoil at her decision to have the couple appear in *People* magazine.

Part 3: The Event

Just before heading into the bright lights, Biden prepared to use Hill's original statement to publicly justify the hearings. But aide Cynthia Hogan told him he was still handcuffed: "You're not authorized to use this." Biden erupted, saying he thought it had all been cleared. It had not. The problem was that Hill's attorneys did not want the committee to go over her testimony with Thomas—the first witness—until she had had a chance to speak for herself.

The first few minutes of the open hearing provided a real look at the behind-the-curtain confusion. Republican Hatch insisted he should be able to use Hill's statements in public, and Biden cut him off. The brawl continued until the chairman pounded his gavel—and then went at it with Hatch and others behind closed doors. They all exploded, Biden among the loudest: "There's drive-by shootings. This will be the first time in history you're going to have a drive-by character assassination."

By the time Thomas and Hill had given their opening statements, the nation was locked in a fierce and irreconcilable he-said, she-said battle. And by the time Biden questioned Hill that afternoon, he knew he was going to have to make it even worse. All the experts in sexual harassment had told him he had to establish the elements of the alleged crime—in detail. With Biden leading, Hill described how Thomas "measured his penis size in terms of length," spoke of pornographic films and recalled an incident with pubic hairs on a Coke can. The Republican comeback was not very tough at first, though Specter accused Hill of perjury in her recounting of early discussions with Senate aides. "We couldn't attack her without looking sleazy," says a key committee Republican.

By Friday night, the folks at the White House were depressed. Hill had been a strong witness, and some staffers were saying as much to reporters. When Duberstein heard what was coming from his own allies, he went ballistic, calling White House Chief of Staff John Sununu and letting him have it. "You guys are throwing more arrows at Clarence Thomas than the interest groups," he growled from a phone in Danforth's office. "Tell them to stop, now." The next task was less simple: Get the committee to allow Thomas to testify again Friday night so that his final testimony would dominate the day's news cycle. When Biden suggested the panel reconvene in the morning, Duberstein politely suggested Thomas might hold a press conference in front of the committee's closed doors—and tell how he had been held back from telling his side of the story. Thomas appeared in prime time at 9 P.M., breathing life into his confirmation with his characterization of the hearing as a "high-tech lynching."

For the rest of the weekend, Thomas spent most of his time away from home in Danforth's office. First Lady Barbara Bush wanted to invite the Thomases to a social dinner with a large group, but McClure nixed the idea. Danforth, meantime, was having a difficult time juggling his roles—politician, minister, tactician. His intensity became difficult to deal with, even for his allies. In the sanctity of his office, Danforth became Thomas's chief consoler and confidant. Throughout the weekend, sources say, the Danforths and Thomases prayed together in the office, religious tapes sometimes playing in the background.

Debunking the charges.   Meanwhile, the chaos backstage at the hearing was unimaginable. No charge from Hill—about pubic hairs on Coke cans or porno-movie star Long Dong Silver—was left unanswered. Hatch suggested the pubic reference came from "The Exorcist" and that the X-rated movie detail had been borrowed from a Kansas court case—a citation that had been quickly unearthed by government lawyers. Leahy charged that vast executive-branch resources were deployed to debunk Hill's testimony. And Democrats complained that orchestrated phone banks were bombarding their offices.

Interminable arguments among committee members centered on what was permissible to use in public. During the Saturday session, for example, the committee gathered in Kennedy's conference room across the hall. Each side was outraged at what the other side was doing, especially with confidential and unsubstantiated reports. Biden demanded an "absolute commitment" that no one would read from FBI reports in public. He went around the room: "Strom, do you agree? Ted, do you agree?" Somehow, Hatch slipped into the bathroom while Biden was calling the roll. Biden walked out thinking he had won unanimous agreement. Then Hatch began to read from the FBI report at the hearing. He had never signed in blood like the others and wasn't going to be bound by it. (Before the hearings, the White House announced that the FBI report had cleared Thomas. Biden disputed the account—and received a call from FBI Director William Sessions to thank him for setting the record straight. Later, Biden privately complained to Bush: "You've been head of the CIA. You know better.")

The disagreements over the scope of the hearings extended to other matters. Republicans wanted to subpoena medical and employment records—to check out rumors about Hill's stress-related illness while at the EEOC, whether she had ever been asked to leave a private law firm or whether she had ever charged sexual harassment at any other job. Some Democrats, meantime, threatened to get even by asking more about Thomas's interest in pornography. Biden wanted none of it; the committee followed, with party-line votes.

By Saturday afternoon, decorum was shot: Simpson spoke of the "stuff coming in over the transom"—and one year later he still smarts over being likened to Joseph McCarthy. The staffs of some Republican senators were becoming very aggressive in pursuing tips about Hill. So much material was coming in by fax and by telephone that Biden unilaterally declared a "12-hour rule"—no side could use information unless it had been in hand at least 12 hours. "If we had just worn our lawyer clothes and not our politician clothes," says Simpson, "we would have called this absurd thing to a halt."

But it steamed on. Former Hill students provided the most leads for eager GOP staffers. Plenty were willing to say she had been a lousy teacher with a political point of view, but there was disagreement over what that would prove. Most strange, though, were claims contained in what staffers referred to as the "pube affidavit." It was sent in by Lawrence Shiles, a former Hill law student at Oral Roberts University. He alleged that he and two peers had received back papers with "10 to 12 short black pubic hairs. . . . At that time, I made the statement . . . that either she had a low opinion of our work or she had graded our assignments in the bathroom." The other students refused to confirm the story in public. Still another, who says he saw the papers, told his father the story as they watched the hearings together. His father, a Simpson friend, called the senator. Soon the former student's phone was ringing—mostly calls from GOP staffers, telling the student his testimony had been requested "from the highest levels" at the White House and the Senate. Hill's attorneys called the story "absurd."

Danforth wanted to pursue the claims, while others on the team remained skeptical, particularly since no one could even prove it was pubic hair. So the allegations never became public. By this time, though, some worried that Danforth was in danger of crossing the line: Two psychiatrists sat in his outer offices during the hearing weekend who were experts in an affliction called erotomania, which had been suggested as an explanation for Hill's charges. When the hearings ended Sunday night, Danforth wanted to present them to the press. "We had to hold him back," says a pro-Thomas staffer, and they did.

Perhaps the most controversial backroom debate revolved around Angela Wright, a North Carolina reporter who claimed to have been the target of unwanted sexual advances by Thomas when both worked at the EEOC. In a telephone interview, she told Senate aides before the hearings that Thomas "made comments about women's anatomy quite often" and that he "did consistently pressure me to date him." At one seminar, she added, he "commented on the dress I was wearing" and inquired, "What size are your breasts?" She was rushed to Washington by Friday and waited all weekend to tell her story.

Silent witness. In a political nanosecond, Republicans unearthed unflattering details. Ricky Silberman, a Thomas backer who was EEOC vice chairman, told reporters Wright was a "grossly incompetent" employee. Personnel files revealed that Wright had been fired from a congressional job for being "absent without leave." She had quit another government job and called her supervisor a "fool" who was biased against her because she is black. The GOP plan was to show that Wright would be destroyed if she testified. Duberstein warned Democrats: "You guys better be careful if Angela Wright turns out to be Angela Wrong."

Biden says he pushed for Wright to testify but sent word to her lawyer, Gil Middlebrooks, that the hearing could be rough. The Democrats were split: Some liberals reportedly worried that Wright, if a weak witness, could undermine Hill's case. One year later, committee Democrats are still arguing.

When Biden announced the schedule for Sunday evening, it looked as if Wright would appear at 2 or 3 A.M. Also waiting in the wings to corroborate Wright's account was Rose Jourdain, a fellow EEOC worker who was prepared to come to the hearings by ambulance from a hospital where she was recovering from surgery. None of it happened. Wright now charges that Biden aide Cynthia Hogan pressured her attorney to withdraw his client as a live witness and instead submit her statement for the record. Hogan insists there was no pressure and that Wright's attorney seemed relieved. Wright says Biden's staff "is lying" and adds that she finally succumbed when it became apparent that hardly anyone would be around to hear her story. A footnote: Democrat Simon now says that he was later "startled" to learn of Jourdain's corroboration, adding that had it been known by more senators at the time, it "would have toppled Thomas."

Democrats believed that another appearance by Hill could sway the outcome, in part because instant polls showed that the majority of viewers believed Thomas. Late Sunday evening, when Biden heard that Hill might not return, he had his staff track her down in her hotel. "Wake her," he told them. After a 10-minute phone conversation, Biden lost. "What good would it [have done] to continue sparring with the senators?" asks Hill's friend, Shirley Wiegand. "Sooner or later you have to get the hell out of Dodge." Hill partisans thought they had scored points with her witnesses and by releasing details of a polygraph she had passed. (In fact, that prompted some Thomas allies to urge him to consider a polygraph, too. Thomas did consider it but quickly nixed the idea as "unseemly.") By 11:30 Sunday night, Biden aide Jeff Peck called Duberstein: If Hill won't testify, then will Thomas agree not to return? Duberstein passed on the good news to Danforth. The excited senator called his friend Clarence, dialing a wrong number first.

The theories.   One year after the showdown, a host of educated guesses substitutes for real knowledge about what happened between Clarence Thomas and Anita Hill. Thomas's true believers, like Danforth, see the saga as a Washington morality tale in which the evil special interests out to defeat Thomas were willing to pressure a relative innocent—who might possibly have suffered harassment at the hands of another man—into claiming the man was Thomas. Hill's own motivation, some Republicans speculate, could have been political; revenge against a man she loved or hated, or, some whisper, the result of something even more emotionally complicated.

Hill's partisans say that it is the judge whose lifestyle should have been more closely examined. They note that after her charges became public, roughly half a dozen current or former female government employees made it known that Thomas had made sexual comments. But only one, an ex-EEOC employee named Sukari Hardnett, ever went public with the charge, and she did not testify. Despite repeated inquiries by Senate aides, FBI agents, friends and journalists, the women never would come forward because they were intimidated by Thomas and the process.

Some subscribe to a more benign, mixed approach: that Thomas, given his interest in X-rated movies dating back to law school, may have made what he thought were innocuous comments to Hill that either were crude enough to be offensive or were misinterpreted by her. After a decade she finally decided to speak out. And a whole nation listened.

Pressure Groups and Lobbyists

Chapter Two

Since the publication of David Truman's classic, *The Governmental Process*, in 1951, many political scientists have become enamored of the "group theory" of politics.[1] Although the origins of group theory date back at least as far as John C. Calhoun, who stated its premises and implications in his posthumously published work, *A Disquisition on Government*, in 1853, real acceptance of the group theory did not come until the twentieth century. There are two essential premises of group theory: (1) individuals function in the political process only through groups; (2) the interaction of political interest groups produces the national interest. Today, group theory is not as widely accepted as it once was. Theodore Lowi, in particular, has led an attack on the group theorists' second assumption.[2] But the idea that politics is essentially a group process, rather than an individual process, remains largely unchallenged. The extreme expression of this view treats groups anthropomorphically, that is, as if they were persons. But groups are not mystical entities that can exist apart from the individuals who act as their leaders and members or from the important intermediaries, such as the Washington lawyers, between pressure groups and government.

Individual character, personality, and style affect the ways in which pressure groups interact with government. The selections in this chapter have been chosen to demonstrate the personal dimension of the group process.

[1]David B. Truman, *The Governmental Process* (New York: Alfred A. Knopf, 1951).

[2]Theodore J. Lowi, *The End of Liberalism*, 2nd ed. (New York: W.W. Norton, 1979).

THE PRACTICE OF LOBBYING IS as old as government itself. Lobbying styles and techniques have changed over the years in response to different political environments. The crasser forms of influence peddling in the nineteenth century, which often included outright bribery of state and national legislators, have given way to subtler techniques. A vast lobbying corps continues to roam the capital's corridors of power, seeking to influence legislators and other government officials. But laws as well as social and political customs circumscribe, at least to some degree, their freedom to act. They certainly cannot, for example, do what railroad tycoon Jay Gould did in attempting to influence the Albany legislature in his competition with railroad magnate Cornelius Vanderbilt in the late nineteenth century. Gould arrived in the state's capital with a valise stuffed with $500,000 in greenbacks with the obvious intention of bribing the lawmakers. His behavior, in the words of one of the time's chroniclers, had "the most frenzying and overstimulating effect . . . which it would take many years of disciplined machine leadership to eliminate."[1]

While modern-day lobbying may be less crude than in the past, the Washington lobbying corps has expanded in numbers and power. Many individuals have turned positions of public trust into private gain as former members of Congress, staffers, and administration officials become high-paid lobbyists. The following depiction of lobbying in the 1980s highlights the personalities, styles, and techniques that are involved. Also discussed is the perennial question of what, if any, limits should be placed upon lobbying.

8 Evan Thomas
INFLUENCE PEDDLING IN WASHINGTON

The hallway is known as "Gucci Gulch," after the expensive Italian shoes they wear. At tax-writing time, the Washington lobbyists line up by the hundreds in the corridor outside the House Ways and Means Committee room, ever vigilant against the attempts of lawmakers to close their prized loopholes. Over near the House and Senate chambers, congressmen must run a guantlet of lobbyists who sometimes express their views on legislation by pointing their thumbs up or down. Not long ago, Senator John Danforth, chairman of the Senate Commerce Committee, could be seen on the Capitol steps trying to wrench his hand from the grip of a lobbyist for the textile industry seeking new protectionist legislation. Though Danforth himself

---

[1]Quoted in Edgar Lane, *Lobbying and the Law* (Berkeley and Los Angeles: University of California Press, 1964), p. 24.

wants help for the shoe, auto, and agricultural industries in his native Missouri, the senator—an ordained Episcopal minister—rolled his eyes heavenward and mumbled, "Save me from these people."

There have been lobbyists in Washington for as long as there have been lobbies. But never before have they been so numerous or quite so brazen. What used to be, back in the days of Bobby Baker, a somewhat shady and disreputable trade has burst into the open with a determined show of respectability. Tempted by the staggering fees lobbyists can command, lawmakers and their aides are quitting in droves to cash in on their connections. For many, public service has become a mere internship for a lucrative career as a hired gun for special interests.

With so many lobbyists pulling strings, they may sometimes seem to cancel one another out. But at the very least, they have the power to obstruct, and their overall effect can be corrosive. At times the halls of power are so glutted with special pleaders that government itself seems to be gagging. As Congress and the administration begin working this month to apportion the deepest spending cuts in America's history and to sort out the most far-reaching reform of the tax laws since World War II, the interests of the common citizen seem to stand no chance against the onslaught of lobbyists. Indeed, the tax bill that emerged from the House already bears their distinctive Gucci prints, and the budget is still filled with programs they have been able to protect.

Of course, the common citizen often benefits from various "special interest" breaks (for example, a deduction for home mortgages or state and local taxes). One man's loophole is another man's socially useful allowance, and one man's lobbyist is another man's righteous advocate. Nonetheless, the voices most likely to be heard are often the ones that can afford the best-connected access brokers.

As the legislative year cranks up, the whine of special pleaders resonates throughout the Capitol:

In the Senate Finance Committee, heavy industries like steel and autos, led by veteran Lobbyist Charles Walker, are working to restore tax breaks for investment in new equipment that were whittled down last fall by the House Ways and Means Committee.

In the House and Senate Armed Services Committees, lobbyists for weapons manufacturers are fanning out to make sure that lawmakers do not trim their pet projects from the defense budget.

In the Senate Commerce Committee, business lobbyists are pressing for legislation to limit liability for defective products. They face fierce opposition from consumer groups and personal-injury lawyers.

Throughout the House and Senate, lobbyists for interests ranging from commercial-waterway users to child-nutrition advocates are laboring to spare their favorite federal subsidies from the exigencies of deficit reduction.

A superlobbyist like Robert Gray, a former minor official in the Eisenhower administration who parlayed his promotional genius and friendship with the Reagans into a $20-million-a-year PR and lobbying outfit, is in the papers more than most congressional committee chairmen. He would have his clients believe that he is at least as powerful. "In the old days, lobbyists never got any publicity," says veteran Lobbyist Maurice Rosenblatt, who has prowled the halls of Congress for several decades. "Congressmen didn't want to be seen with notorious bagmen. But now," he shrugs, "the so-called best lobbyists get the most publicity."

Influence peddling, says Jack Valenti, head of the Motion Picture Association and no mean practitioner of the craft, "is the biggest growth industry around." The number of registered domestic lobbyists has more than doubled since 1976, from 3,420 to 8,800. That figure is understated, however, since reporting requirements under a toothless 1946 law are notoriously lax. Most experts put the influence-peddling population at about 20,000—or more than 30 for every member of Congress. Registered lobbyists reported expenditures of $50 million last year, twice as much as a decade ago, but the true figure is estimated at upwards of $1.5 billion, including campaign contributions.

What does the money buy? "Everybody needs a Washington representative to protect their hindsides, even foreign governments," says Senator Paul Laxalt. "So the constituency for these people is the entire free-world economy." Joseph Canzeri, a former Reagan aide who calls himself a Washington "facilitator," notes, "It's a competitive business. There are a lot of wolves out there. But there are a lot of caribou in government too."

In the amoral revolving-door world of Washington, it has become just as respectable to lobby as to be lobbied. Ronald Reagan may have come to Washington to pare down the size of the Federal government, but many of his former top aides have quit to profit off Big Government as influence peddlers. None has been more successful more swiftly than Reagan's former deputy chief of staff Michael Deaver, who may multiply his White House income sixfold in his first year out of government by offering the nebulous blend of access, influence, and advice that has become so valued in Washington. Other Reaganauts now prowling Gucci Gulch include ex-Congressional Liaison Kenneth Duberstein and two former White House political directors, Lyn Nofziger and Ed Rollins. "I spent a lot of years doing things for love. Now I'm going to do things for money," Rollins told the *Washington Post* after he left the White House. By representing clients like the Teamsters Union, Rollins, who never earned more than $75,000 a year in government, boasts that he can earn ten times as much.

Former administration officials are often paid millions of dollars by special interests to oppose policies they once ardently promoted. This is particularly true in the area of foreign trade, as documented by the *Washington Post* a week ago. For example, Reagan has ordered an investigation into the unfair trade practices of South Korea. That country will pay former Reagan aide Deaver $1.2 million over three years to "protect, manage and expand trade and economic interests" of the nation's industry. Deaver refuses to say exactly what he will do to earn his fee, but he has hired Doral Cooper, a former deputy trade representative in the Reagan administration, as a lobbyist for his firm. Japanese semiconductor and machine-tool firms are also charged by the administation with engaging in unfair trade practices. They have hired Stanton Anderson, who had served as director of economic affairs for the administration's 1980 transition team.

Foreign governments are particularly eager to retain savvy Washington insiders to guide them through the bureaucratic and congressional maze and polish their sometimes unsavory images in the U.S. The Marcos government in the Philippines has retained the well-connected lobbying firm of Black, Manafort & Stone for a reported fee of $900,000. Another Black, Manafort client is Angolan rebel Jonas Savimbi. Not to be outdone, the Marxist regime of Angola hired Bob Gray's firm to front for it in Washington. Two years ago, Gray told *Time* that he checks with his "good friend," CIA Director William Casey, before taking on clients who might be inimical to U.S. interests. It is unclear just what Casey could have said this time, since the CIA is currently funneling $15 million in covert aid to Savimbi to help his rebellion against the Angolan regime. Last week outraged Savimbi backers chained themselves to a railing in Gray's posh offices in Georgetown and had to be forcibly removed by local police.

Lobbyists call themselves lawyers, government-affairs specialists, public relations consultants, sometimes even lobbyists. They offer a wide array of increasingly sophisticated services, from drafting legislation to creating slick advertisements and direct-mail campaigns. But what enables the big-time influence peddlers to demand upwards of $400 an hour is their connections. "I'll tell you what we're selling," says Lobbyist Frank Mankiewicz. "The returned phone call."

Old-time fixers such as Tommy "the Cork" Corcoran and Clark Clifford were not merely practiced lawyers but had some genuine legislative expertise to offer. Lately, however, Washington has seen the rise of a new breed of influence peddler, whose real value is measured by his friends in high places—particularly in the White House. Clifford prospered no matter who was in office; after the Reagans go home to California, it is hard to believe that Deaver or Gray will remain quite such hot commodities.

There is, and has long been, a strong whiff of scam about the influence-peddling business. Its practitioners like to imply that they have more clout than they truly do. In the post-Watergate era, power has been fractionated on Capitol Hill. Where a few powerful committee chairmen once held sway, Congress has become a loose federation of 535 little fiefdoms. This has made a lobbyist's job more difficult, but it hardly means that Congress has been liberated from the thrall of special interests. Well-intentioned congressional reform has been subverted over the years by the proliferation of lobbyists and the spiraling cost of election campaigns, two trends that go together like a hand and a pocket. The result has often been institutional paralysis. The very fact that Congress and the White House felt compelled to enact the Gramm-Rudman measure, requiring automatic spending cuts, it a monument to the inability of weak-willed legislators to say no to the lobbyists who buzz around them.

President Reagan has tried to sell his tax-reform bill as the supreme test of the public interest vs. the special interests. In pitching his campaign to the public, he has accused special interests of "swarming like ants through every nook and cranny of Congress," overlooking, perhaps, that many of the most prominent ants are his former aides. Few lobbyists, however, seem especially offended by his rhetoric, and certainly their livelihoods are not threatened. Indeed, many lobbyists candidly admit that true tax reform would actually mean more business for them, since they would have a fresh slate upon which to write new loopholes.

The way lobbyists have feasted on the president's tax-reform bill illustrates why the bill is known in the law firms and lobbying shops of K Street as the "Lobbyists' Full Employment Act." The 408-page proposal first drafted by the Treasury Department 16 months ago, known as Treasury I, was called a model of simplicity and fairness. It would have swept the tax code virtually clean of loopholes for the few in order to cut tax rates sharply for the many. But the 1,363-page tax bill sent by the House to the Senate last December is so riddled with exemptions and exceptions that the goal of fairness was seriously compromised, and simplicity abandoned altogether.

The lobbyists wasted no time biting into Treasury I. Insurance executives calculated that such loophole closings as taxing employer-paid life insurance and other fringe benefits would cost the industry about $100 billion over five years. Led by Richard Schweiker, who was President Reagan's Secretary of Health and Human Services before becoming head of the American Council of Life Insurance, the industry launched a $5 million lobbying campaign that can only be described as state of the art.

Even before the Treasury had finished drafting its original plan, the insurers were showing 30-second spots on TV that depicted a bird nibbling away at a loaf of bread labeled "employee benefits." An actress in the role of frightened housewife exclaimed, "We shouldn't have to pay taxes for protecting our family!" Life insurance agents around the country were revved up by a 12-minute film entitled *The Worst Little Horror Story in Taxes*. In the film, Senate Finance Chairman Robert Packwood, a strong advocate of preserving tax breaks for fringe benefits, was shown urging the public to write their congressmen. The insurers also mounted a direct-mail campaign that inundated Congress last year with 7 million preprinted, postage-paid cards. The campaign was successful: by the time the bill passed the House of Representatives last December, the insurance lobby figured that it had managed to restore about $80 billion of the $100 billion in tax breaks cut out by Treasury I. The insurers hope to win back most of the rest when the bill is reported out by the Senate Finance Committee this spring.

Threats to close a single loophole can bring scores of lobbyists rallying round. The original Treasury proposal sought to eliminate Section 936 of the U.S. Tax Code, which gives tax breaks worth some $600 million to companies that invest in Puerto Rico. Treasury Department officials conceded that the tax break helped create jobs by luring business to the island, but figured that each new job was costing the U.S. Treasury about $22,000. To defend Section 936, a coalition of some 75 U.S. companies with factories on the island formed a million-dollar "Puerto Rico–U.S.A. Foundation" and hired more than a dozen lobbyists, including Deaver. Last fall Section 936 advocates flew some 50 congressmen and staffers to Puerto Rico on fact-finding trips.

Deaver, meanwhile, coordinated a lobbying campaign aimed at National Security staffers and officials in the State, Commerce, and Defense Departments. The strategy was to cast Section 936 as a way to revive the president's moribund Caribbean Basin Initiative and erect a bulwark against Communism in the region. Some two dozen companies with plants in Puerto Rico promised that if Section 936 was retained, they would reinvest their profits in new factories on other Caribbean islands. During a tense moment in the negotiations with the administration, Deaver even managed to place a ground-to-air call to Air Force I as it flew to the Geneva Summit last November. He wanted to alert Secretary of State George Shultz to stand fast against the maneuverings of tax reformers at the Treasury. Not surprisingly, the Treasury gnomes were overwhelmed. Later that month the administration committed itself to preserving Section 936.

The fabled "three-martini lunch," threatened by the Treasury Department's proposal to end tax deductions for business entertainment, was preserved as at least a two-martini lunch after heavy lobbying by the hotel and restaurant industry. In the House-passed bill, 80 percent of the cost of a business lunch can still be deducted. The oil-and-gas lobby managed to restore over half the tax breaks for well drilling removed by the original Treasury bill. Lawyers, doctors, and accountants won an exemption from more stringent new accounting rules. The lobbying by lawyers was a bit crude: congressmen received letters that were supposedly written by partners of different law firms but were all signed by the same hand. No matter. Though congressional etiquette demands that each constituent's letter be answered personally, "We just let our word processors talk to their word processors," shrugged a congressional staffer.

The real deal making was done over so-called transition rules, which postpone or eliminate new taxes for certain individual businesses. The House-passed bill is studded with some 200 transition rules, which have been written to protect pet projects in a congressman's district or large industries with particular clout on the Hill. Drafted behind closed doors, these rules are written in language designed to make it difficult to identify the real beneficiaries. One transition rule, for instance, waives the cutbacks on investment tax credits and depreciation for the fiberoptic networks of telecommunications companies that have committed a certain number of dollars for construction by a certain date. It turns out that just two companies profit from the exception: AT&T and United Telecom.

Not every lobbyist made out in the wheeling and dealing, by any means. Some were a little too greedy. The banking lobby pushed an amendment that would actually *increase* its tax breaks for bad-debt reserves. The lobbyists figured that they were just making an opening bid; their real aim was to protect existing tax breaks. To their surprise, however, the amendment passed in the confusion of an early Ways and Means Committee drafting session. When jubilant banking lobbyists began shouting "We won! We won!" outside the hearing room, some Congressmen became angry. Giving more tax breaks to the already well-sheltered banking industry was no way to sell voters on tax reform. The amendment was repealed.

Despite the predations of lobbyists, a tax-reform bill may be signed into law this year. But it must first survive the Senate, and already the advocates are queuing up to be heard. "I wish there were a secret elevator into the committee room," laments Senator David Pryor of Arkansas, a member of the Finance Committee. "Whenever I go there to vote, I try to walk fast and be reading something."

Some congressmen may try to avoid lobbyists, but many have come to depend on them. "God love 'em," quips Vermont Senator Patrick Leahy. "Without them we would have to decide how to vote on our own." Sarcasm aside, lobbyists do serve a useful purpose by showing busy legislators the virtues and pitfalls of complex legislation. "There's a need here," says Anne Wexler, a former Carter administration aide turned lobbyist. "Government officials are not comfortable making these complicated decisions by themselves." Says Lobbyist Van Boyette, a former aide to Senator Russell Long of Louisiana: "We're a two-way street. Congress often legislates on issues without realizing that the marketplace has changed. We tell Congress what business is up to, and the other way around."

Lobbyists and government officials alike are quick to point out that lobbying is cleaner than in earlier eras, when railroad barons bought senators as if they were so much rolling stock. "It's an open process now," says Jack Albertine, president of the American Business Conference, a trade association of medium-size, high-growth companies. "All sides are represented, the contributions are reported, and the trade-offs are known to everybody. In the old days you never knew who got what until a waterway project suddenly appeared in someone's district."

In some ways the growth of interest groups is healthy. Capitol Hill at times seems like a huge First Amendment jamboree, where Americans of all persuasions clamor to be heard. Movie stars plead on behalf of disease prevention, Catholic clerics inveigh against abortion, farmers in overalls ask for extended credit, and Wall Street financiers extol the virtues of lower capital-gains taxes. No single group dominates. When the steel, auto, and rubber industries saw the Reagan administration as an opening to weaken the Clean Air and Clean Water acts, the "Green Lobby," a coalition of environmental groups, was able to stop them.

But not every voter has a lobby in Washington, "Sometimes I think the only people not represented up here are the middle class," says Democratic Congressman Barney Frank of Massachusetts. "The average folks—that's what bothers me." Of course, that is not entirely true; many ordinary citizens are represented by such lobbies as the National Association of Retired Persons and Common Cause.

Lobbyists cannot afford to rely solely on well-reasoned arguments and sober facts and figures to make their case. In the scramble to win a hearing, they have developed all manner of stratagems designed to ingratiate themselves and collect IOUs.

Helping congressmen get reelected is an increasingly popular device. Veteran Washington Lobbyist Thomas Hale Boggs, Jr., is on no fewer than 50 "steering committees" set up to raise money for congressional election campaigns. By night, "Good Ole Boy" Boggs can be found shmoozing at Capitol Hill fund raisers, where lobbyists drop off envelopes containing checks from political action committees at the door before digging into the hors d'oeuvres. By day, Boggs lobbies congressmen, often the same ones for whom he has raised money the night before. Lately high-power political consulting firms such as Black, Manafort & Stone have taken not only to raising money for candidates but actually to running their campaigns: planning strategy, buying media, and polling. These firms get paid by the candidates for electioneering services, and then paid by private clients to lobby the congressmen they have helped elect. In the trade this cozy arrangement is known as "double dipping."

Special-interest giving to federal candidates has shot up eightfold since 1974, from $12.5 million to more than $100 million by the 1984 election. Nonetheless, PACs can give no more than $5,000 to a single campaign, and all contributions are publicly filed with the Federal Election Commission. "Elections are so expensive that the idea of a PAC's having inordinate influence is ridiculous," says Boggs.

Some congressmen are not so sure. "Somewhere there may be a race of humans who will take $1,000 from perfect strangers and be unaffected by it," dryly notes Congressman Frank. Says Congressman Leon Panetta of

California: "There's a danger that we're putting ourselves on the auction block every election. It's now tough to hear the voices of the citizens in your district. Sometimes the only things you can hear are the loud voices in three-piece suits carrying a PAC check."

Even the most reputable influence peddlers use their political connections to build leverage. As director of the 1984 GOP Convention, Lobbyist William Timmons, a quietly genial man who represents such blue-chippers as Boeing, Chrysler, ABC, and Anheuser-Busch, controlled access to the podium. GOP senators lobbied him for prime-time appearances. A *Wall Street Journal* reporter described Senator Pete Domenici of New Mexico, who was running for reelection in the fall of 1984, thanking Timmons a bit too effusively for allotting time for him to address the convention. "You told me you'd give me a shot," gushed Domenici. "So I appreciate it, Brother."

Family ties help open doors. Tommy Boggs's mother, Lindy, is a congresswoman from Louisiana; his father, the late Hale Boggs, was House majority leader. Other congressional progeny who as lobbyists have traded on their names for various interests: Speaker Tip O'Neill's son Kip (sugar, beer, cruise ships); Senate Majority Leader Robert Dole's daughter Robin (Century 21 real estate); Senator Paul Laxalt's daughter Michelle (oil, Wall Street, Hollywood); and House Appropriations Committee Chairman Jamie Whitten's son Jamie Jr. (steel, barges, cork).

Then there is so-called soft-core (as opposed to hard-core) lobbying. Since the real business of Washington is often conducted by night, a whole cottage industry has grown up around the party-giving business. Michael Deaver's wife, Carolyn, is one of half a dozen Washington hostesses who can be hired to set up power parties, which bring top government officials together with private businessmen. "Facilitator" Canzeri puts on charitable events to burnish corporate images, like a celebrity tennis tournament that drew scores of Washington lobbyists and netted $450,000 for Nancy Reagan's antidrug campaign. Lobbyists, not surprisingly, work hard not just at reelecting congressmen but also at befriending them. Congressman Tony Coelho of California describes the methods of William Cable, a former Carter administration aide who lobbies for Timmons & Co. "Three out of four times," says Coelho, "he talks to you not about lobbying, but about sports, or tennis—I play a lot of tennis with him—or your family. He's a friend, a sincere friend." Congressman Thomas Luken of Ohio is so chummy with lobbyists that he has been known to wave at them from the dais at committee hearings.

Congressmen often find themselves being lobbied by their former colleagues. More than 200 ex-congressmen have stayed on in the capital to represent interest groups, sometimes lobbying on the same legislation they helped draft while serving in office. Former Congressmen are free to go onto the floor of Congress and into the cloakrooms, though they are not supposed to lobby there. "Well, they don't call it lobbying," shrugs Senator Pryor. "They call it visiting. But you know exactly what they're there for."

Congressional staffers also cash in by selling their expertise and connections. Indeed, members of the House Ways and Means Committee were concerned that the president's tax-reform bill would provoke an exodus of staffers into the lobbying ranks. Their fears were not unfounded: the committee's chief counsel, John Salmon, quit to work as a lobbyist for the law firm of Dewey, Ballantine; James Healey, former aide to Committee Chairman Dan Rostenkowski, quit to join Black, Manafort.

As congressmen became more independent of committee chairmen and party chieftans, they have tended to listen more to the folks back home. Predictably, however, lobbyists have skillfully found ways to manipulate so-called grass-roots support. Direct-mail outfits, armed with computer banks that are stocked with targeting groups, can create "instant constituencies" for special-interest bills. To repeal a 1982 provision requiring tax withholding on dividends and interest, the small banks and thrifts hired a mass-mailing firm to launch a letter-writing campaign that flooded congressional offices with some 22 million pieces of mail. The bankers' scare tactics were dubious—they managed to convince their depositors that the withholding provision was a tax hike, when in fact it was set up merely to make people pay taxes that they legally owed. But the onslaught worked. Over the objections of President Reagan and most of the congressional leadership Congress voted overwhelmingly in 1983 to repeal withholding.

Onetime liberal activists who learned grass-roots organizing for such causes as opposition to the Vietnam War now employ these same techniques on behalf of business clients. Robert Beckel, Walter Mondale's campaign manager in 1984, has set up an organization with the grandiose title of the Alliance to Save the Ocean. Its aim is to stop the burning of toxic wastes at sea. Beckel's fee is being paid by Rollins Environmental Services, a waste-disposal company that burns toxic waste on land.

Grass-roots organizations sometimes collide. Lobbyist Jack Albertine recently established the Coalition to Encourage Privatization. Its public policy purpose: to enable private enterprise to run services now performed by the government. Its more immediate goal: to persuade Congress to sell Conrail to the Norfolk Southern Railroad. In the meantime, Anne Wexler has been building the Coalition for a Competitive Conrail, a farm-dominated group pushing for Morgan Guaranty as the prospective purchaser.

Booze, broads, and bribes—what nineteenth-century congressional correspondent Edward Winslow Martin called "the levers of lust"—are no longer the tools of the trade. This is not to say, however, that lobbyists have stopped wining and dining congressmen and their staffs. Public records indicate that Ways and Means Chairman Rostenkowski spends about as much time playing golf as the guest of lobbyists at posh resorts as he does holding hearings in Washington.

Though it has become more difficult to slip a special-interest bill through Congress in the dead of night, it is not impossible. In 1981, when a group of commodity traders began lobbying for a tax loophole worth $300 million, then Senate Finance Chairman Dole poked fun at the commodity traders on the Senate floor. "They are great contributors. They haven't missed a fund-raiser. If you do not pay any taxes, you can afford to go to all the fund-raisers." But then commodity PACs and individual traders increased their contributions to Dole's own political action committee from $11,000 in 1981–1982 to $70,500 in 1983–1984. Dole, engaged in a campaign to become Senate majority leader, badly needed the money (his PAC contributed some $300,000 to 47 of the Senate's 53 Republicans). In a late-night tax-writing session in the summer of 1984, Dole quietly dropped his opposition to the tax break for the commodity traders, and it became law.

Such victories inspire other loophole-seeking businessmen to hire guides through the congressional maze, at any price. There is no shortage of hungry lobbyists ready to relieve them of their money. "You get hustlers in Washington who get hooked up with hustlers outside of Washington, and the money moves very quickly," says Peter Teeley, former press aide to Vice President George Bush and now a Washington PR man. "Some people are getting ripped off." Says Senator Pryor: "Businessmen are very, very naive. It's amazing what they pay these lobbyists. The businessmen panic. They really don't understand Washington."

As one of the most successful lobbyists in town, Bob Gray naturally has his detractors, and they accuse him of overselling businessmen on his ability to solve all their Washington problems with a few phone calls. "Gray is so overrated it's unbelievable," says one U.S. senator. "He makes a big splash at parties, but his clients aren't getting a lot for their money." Gray insists that he never promises more than he can deliver. But his own clients sometimes grumble that, for a fat fee, they get little more than a handshake from a Cabinet member at a cocktail party.

When the big lobbying guns line up on opposite sides of an issue, they tend to cancel each other out. Threatened with a takeover by Mobil Oil in 1981, Marathon Oil hired Tommy Boggs's firm to push a congressional bill that would block the merger. The firm managed to get the bill through the House by using a little-known procedural rule at a late-night session. In the Senate, however, Mobil—represented by former Carter aide Stuart Eizenstat—was able to stop the bill when Senator Howell Heflin of Alabama blocked consideration on the Senate floor. Heflin is a friend of Mobil Chairman Rawleigh Warner.

"We're getting to the point of lobbylock now," says Lobbyist Carl Nordberg. "There are so many lobbyists here pushing and pulling in so many different directions that, at times, nothing seems to go anywhere." The most pernicious effect of the influence-peddling game may simply be that it consumes so much of a congressman's working day. Every time a congressman takes a PAC check, he is obliged at least to grant the contributor an audience. The IOUs mount up. "Time management is a serious problem," says Frank. "I find myself screening out people who just want to bill their clients for talking to a congressman." The lobbyists are not unmindful of congressional impatience. Lobbyist Dan Dutko, for instance, has a "five-second rule"—all background documents must be simple enough to be absorbed by a congressman at the rate of five seconds per page. It is no wonder that Congress rarely takes the time to debate such crucial national security questions as whether the U.S. really needs to build a 600-ship Navy, as the Reagan administration contends; most congressmen are too preoccupied listening to lobbyists for defense contractors telling them how many jobs building new ships will create back in the district.

In theory at least, there is a partial cure to the growing power of the influence-peddling pack: further limits on campaign expenditures and public financing of elections. But Congress is not likely to vote for these reforms any time soon, in large part because as incumbents they can almost always raise more money than challengers can. Certainly, most congressmen have become wearily resigned to living with lobbyists. They are sources of money, political savvy, even friendship. In the jaded culture of Washington, influence peddlers are more envied than disdained. Indeed, to lawmakers on the Hill and policymakers throughout the Executive Branch, the feeling increasingly seems to be: well, if you can't beat 'em, join 'em.

Cashing In on Top Connections

After former White House Deputy Chief of Staff Michael Deaver quit last May to become a "public affairs consultant," he drove about town for a while in a dark blue Dodge, very much like the limousines that transport top Executive Branch officials. The car served to get Deaver where he was going in more ways than one: in status-conscious Washington, it was a not-so-subtle reminder of his White House connections. Now Deaver has given up the status symbol of public power for one of private wealth. These days he rides in a chauffeur-driven Jaguar XJ6 equipped with a car phone that keeps him plugged in to some of the highest offices in the land.

The onetime California PR man who followed Ronald Reagan to Washington five years ago has cashed in. As a White House official, he had to moonlight by writing a diet book, while his wife Carolyn went to work for a PR outfit, throwing parties on behalf of private clients. But now a dozen corporations and foreign countries, including CBS, TWA, South Korea, Singapore, and Canada, pay him annual retainers that are, he says, "in the six figures." This year he should take home around $400,000—at the White House, his top salary was $70,200.

What makes Deaver so valuable? "There's no question I've got as good access as anybody in town," says Deaver, as he reclines on a couch in his tastefully appointed office overlooking the Lincoln Memorial. Alone among departing White House aides, Deaver was permitted to keep his White House pass. He also still chats regularly on the phone with Nancy Reagan. But Deaver insists that he never discusses his clients' problems with the first lady or the president. Actually, Deaver says, he does not do much lobbying.

Nor does he do any public relations work, or legislative drafting, or direct mail, or polling, or any of the sorts of services performed by most high-powered influence shops. So what exactly does he do?

"Strategic planning," he says somewhat airily. His clients tell him "where they want to be vis-à-vis Washington in three to five years, and I help them develop a plan to get there." In fact, although Deaver is a relative newcomer to Washington, it is hard to think of a lobbyist who has a better sense of how the Reagan administration works or who has more clout among the Reaganauts. And in a city where perception is often reality, Deaver is known as a master imagemaker who kept Reagan's profile high and bright. It is not hard to see why the government of South Korea, under fire for unfair trade practices abroad and repression of political dissidents at home, would want to hire him, even at Deaver's asking price of $1.2 million for a three-year contract. "There's a new breed in Washington," says Canadian Ambassador Allan Gotlieb. "Consultants about consultants." Canada hired Deaver—at $105,000 a year—for "his unique knowledge of how this government works from the inside," says Gotlieb.

There are some who think that Canada got more than gossip and advice from Deaver. Though the former deputy chief of staff was rarely involved in policy details at the White House, the *Washington Post* reports that before he left, he showed surprising interest in the debate over acid rain. It was Deaver who is believed to have persuaded Reagen to accede to the request of the Canadian government for a special commission to investigate the problem and make recommendations. The commission's report, issued in January, called for much stronger measures to reduce acid rain than the administration had previously sought.

Canada was one of the first clients signed up by Deaver. Acting on complaints from Democratic Congressman John Dingell of Michigan, the General Accounting Office is now investigating Deaver's role for possible conflict of interest. The public official turned private sage dismisses the charges, noting that while he played a role in creating the acid-rain commission, he had nothing to do with its report. "What I did at the White House was part of my public responsibilities. If I'd gone back there after leaving and tried to influence the acid-rain study, that would be a different story. But I really can't understand what the conflict is."

Under the Ethics in Government Act, Deaver is legally barred from discussing private business matters with anyone in the White House for a period of one year after leaving office. "I can't ask the president or anyone in the White House for anything now," he shrugs. Then, brightening, he adds, "I can, starting in May, though."

The Slickest Shop in Town

A lobbyist can perform no greater favor for a lawmaker than to help get him elected. It is the ultimate political IOU, and it can be cashed in again and again. No other firm holds more of this precious currency than the Washington shop known as Black, Manafort.

Legally, there are two firms, Black, Manafort, Stone & Kelly, a lobbying operation, represents Bethlehem Steel, the Tobacco Institute, Herba-life, Angolan "Freedom Fighter" Jonas Savimbi, and the governments of the Bahamas and the Philippines. Black, Manafort, Stone & Atwater, a political-consulting firm, has helped elect such powerful Republican politicians as Senator Phil Gramm of Texas and Senate Agriculture Committee Chairman Jesse Helms.

The political credentials of the partners are imposing. Charles Black, 38, was a top aide to Senator Robert Dole and the senior strategist for President Reagan's reelection campaign in 1984. Paul Manafort, 36, was the political director of the 1984 GOP national convention. Roger Stone, 33, was the Eastern regional campaign director for Reagan in 1984 and is now one of Congressman Jack Kemp's chief political advisers. Peter Kelly, 48, was finance chairman of the Democratic National Committee from 1981 to 1985. Lee Atwater, 34, was Reagan's deputy campaign manager in 1984 and is now Vice President George Bush's chief political adviser. Alone among the firm's partners, Atwater sticks to advising electoral candidates and does not lobby.

The partners of Black, Manafort say that the lobbying and political-consulting functions are kept separate. "It's like a grocery store and a hardware store," insists Black. "You can't buy eggs at a hardware store and you can't buy tires at the grocery." Yet these are but fine distinctions in Washington, where the firm is considered one of the most ambidextrous in the business, the ultimate supermarket of influence peddling. "You are someone's political adviser, then you sell yourself to a corporation by saying you have a special relationship with Congress," says Democratic Media Consultant Robert Squier, who does no lobbying himself. Is it proper to get a politician elected, then turn around and lobby him? "It's a gray area," sidesteps Squier. Charges Fred Wertheimer, president of the public-interest lobbying group Common Cause: "It's institutionalized conflict of interest."

It certainly is good for business. The partners charge six-figure fees to lobby and six-figure fees to manage election campaigns. As a result, they take home six-figure salaries. (Their stated aim is to make $450,000 apiece each year; they are assumed to have achieved it last year.) They unabashedly peddle their access to the Reagan administration. The firm's proposal soliciting the Bahamas as a client, for instance, touted the "personal relationships between State Department officials and Black, Manafort & Stone" that could be "utilized to upgrade a backchannel relationship in the economic and foreign policy spheres."

When Savimbi came to Washington last month to seek support for his guerrilla organization, UNITA, in its struggle against the Marxist regime in Angola, he hired Black, Manafort. What the firm achieved was quickly dubbed "Savimbi chic." Doors swung open all over town for the guerilla leader, who was dapperly attired in a Nehru suit and ferried about in a stretch limousine. Dole had shown only general interest in Savimbi's cause until Black, the Senate Majority leader's former aide, approached him on his client's behalf. Dole promptly introduced a congressional resolution backing UNITA's insurgency and sent a letter to the State Department urging that the U.S. supply it with heavy arms. The firm's fee for such services was reportedly $600,000.

The Black, Manafort partners have woven such an intricate web of connections that the strands become entangled at times. Lobbyist Kelly served as finance chairman of the National Democratic Institute, a public-interest organization established by Congress to promote democracy in underdeveloped countries. The institute recently sent observers to try to ensure a fair election in the Philippines. Yet Kelly's firm, for a reported $900,000 fee, represents Philippine President Ferdinand Marcos, who stands accused of having stolen the vote. Manafort for one sees no conflict. He points out that the firm urged Marcos to try to make the elections more credible to American observers. "What we've tried to do is make it more of a Chicago-style election and not Mexico's," he explained.

As a political firm, Black, Manafort represents Democrats and Republicans alike—and sometimes candidates running for the same seat. Kelly, for instance, is doing some fund raising for Democratic Senate candidates John Breaux in Louisiana, Bob Graham in Florida, and Patrick Leahy in Vermont. Atwater and Black are consultants for the Republican opponents in these contests. In the race for the 1988 Republican presidential nomination, Atwater advises Bush, while Stone advises Kemp. Stone and Atwater's offices are right across the hall from each other, prompting one congressional aide to ask facetiously, "Why have primaries for the nomination? Why not have the candidates go over to Black, Manafort & Stone and argue it out?"

Stone and Atwater present a contrast in styles. Stone, who practices the hardball politics he first learned as an aide to convicted Watergate co-conspirator Charles Colson, fancies $400 suits and lawn parties. With his heavy-lidded eyes and frosty demeanor, he openly derides Atwater's client, Vice President Bush, as a "weenie." Atwater, an impish "good ole boy" from South Carolina, wears jeans and twangs an electric guitar. Both, however, drive Mercedes.

For all its diverse interests, the firm remains "loyal to the president," says Black. "We would never lobby against Star Wars, for example." The firm has nonetheless attacked the president's tax-reform bill on behalf of corporate clients seeking to preserve their loopholes, and it did not hesitate to lobby for quotas on shoe imports on behalf of the Footwear Industries of America, even though Reagan strongly opposed the bill as protectionist. And at times the firm does show some selectivity. A few years back, it turned down Libya's Muammar Qaddafi as a client.

P RESIDENT CLINTON BEGAN his administration with grand plans to solve the nation's problems. He had promised a new health care system, an invigorated economy, cutbacks in and reallocation of defense appropriations, and a variety of tax reforms. The following selection depicts the entrenched Washington interests that Clinton faced in his quest for change.

9 Eleanor Clift with Pat Wingert, Mary Hager, and Bob Cohn
FACING THE POWERS THAT BE

Lobbyists, entrenched forces in Congress and self-interested friends will try to stymie Clinton's efforts. A look at four key arenas of combat:

The Medical Lobby Lineup

Memo to incoming White House junior staff: volunteers required for taking on an interest group. Immediate, sweeping reform is the goal. The group? Oh, it's more than twice the size of the military-industrial complex. And a lot better dug in.

The target is the health business. When dark horse Harris Wofford won election to the Senate in 1991 promising top-to-bottom reform of health care, other politicians took notice. By 1992 nearly all candidates for office, including Bill Clinton and George Bush, were advocating action regarding what many now call the health-industrial complex. Everybody wants something done. How strongly can the health system resist change?

Very strongly, if dollars are any measure. In the year 1973 an important line was crossed—health care became more expensive than defense. Since then military spending has shown long-term decline, while health-care expenditures continually rise. This year the Pentagon will consume about 6 percent of the GNP, while health costs will gobble up 13 percent. "Defense and medicine have become the same," says Richard Smith, public-policy director of the Washington Business Group on Health. "The people wear uniforms, technology is in the driver's seat, and both cost far too much."

Americans receive good health care by many measures, but judged by cost effectiveness the U.S. system may be the worst in the world. The United States spends more per capita on health than any nation, yet is the sole Western country in which medical expenses don't buy universal coverage for all citizens.

Clinton has said that health reform will be a priority of his administration. But imagine tackling a system with more than double the entrenched lobbying clout of the Pentagon. "Only all-out reform has a chance," asserts Rep. Jim Cooper, a Tennessee Democrat. "Health-care special interests have enough power to block tinkering. We've got to get them falling back on their heels with a broad program that changes everything."

Countries like France and Denmark that offer high-quality universal coverage at lower cost than the United States are able to do so partly because their governments took on the health lobby years ago, when its economic dimensions were smaller. With each year doctors, hospitals and insurers control more dollars, acquiring greater lobbying leverage. This suggests that that delay in "all out" reform will only make the problem worse, as medicine's share of the GNP keeps growing. The medical-lobby lineup:

Doctors.   Physicians are among the wealthiest segments of society, each averaging $164,300 in income in 1990. They spend freely to influence government decisions, with the American Medical Association always one of the top PAC donors.

In recent years an increasing number of doctors have come to favor some program to aid the "medically indigent," the estimated 35 million Americans with no health insurance. Doctors favor the idea for two reasons: one altruistic, because universal care is a moral imperative; one selfish, because this reform could make doctors even richer.

Thirty years ago nearly all physician groups lobbied against Medicare; later, realizing Medicare allowed them to raise prices, doctors embraced it warmly. A similar progression of attitudes now applies to the medically indigent. Increasingly doctors realize that with a new government or employer-financed universal-care program, they could charge for services now rendered on a charity basis.

A working estimate is that universal care would increase U.S. medical costs $50 billion a year, wiping out the peace dividend in a single stroke. Health-care advocates therefore assume that new cost controls must accompany universal care. But most physician lobbies want only new payments, not accompanying controls. In California, the state AMA affiliate is furiously resisting a proposal that combines universal coverage with cost containment.

The docs' lobby has long suffered from sleeplessness and other chronic symptoms, worrying that the public will realize that physician wealth is unique to the United States. In what used to be West Germany, which has top-quality medical care, doctors earn about 25 percent less than here. Reducing U.S. physician incomes to the German level, perhaps by cuts in federal reimbursements, would save about $45 billion a year, enough to finance universal care and still leave doctors very well off. Is this possible? "The political system has shown so little courage on physicians' incomes that the best most of us hope for is stopping future growth," says Rashi Fein, an economist at Harvard Medical School.

Hospitals.   The U.S. hospital industry, at $256 billion in 1990, is nearly the size of the Pentagon. Those who have crossed paths with hospital accounts offices know that when it comes to money, many hospitals are now tougher than Schwarzkopf. Their lobbying can be as aggressive.

Hospitals will support new benefits for the uninsured, both because it's the right thing to do and because it will create payments for care that hospitals now give away. But like most doctors, most hospitals oppose combining new benefits with new controls. Clinton advisers have spoken of "global budgets" for hospitals. Under this plan, hospitals would receive annual lump-sum payments, rather than submit individual bills for each patient treated: the idea is to break the pass-along mentality. Hospital lobbyists are expected to fight to the death against this notion, since health "providers" love to pass costs along.

One political problem that may cut into hospital-lobby clout: avarice at the top. *The New York Times* recently reported that while medical prices ran 114 percent ahead of inflation in the last decade, pay for hospital executives escalated at 142 percent. Paul Marks, CEO of New York's nonprofit Sloan-Kettering Cancer Center, makes well over $1 million a year; H. Richard Nesson, head of nonprofit Brigham & Women's Hospital in Boston, made $872,000 in 1991. Marks and Nesson thus earn much more than the amount that got William Aramony in hot water as head of the United Way. And since the primary source of revenue to hospitals is government, hospital CEOs are annexing their opulence from the taxpayer, whereas Aramony's pay came entirely from donations.

Insurers.   Advocates of government-financed systems like those of Western Europe now say that what they want is a "single payer" plan. This soothing, neutral term plays better than "socialized medicine"—except with insurance companies. If government were the "single payer," medical insurers would be out of business.

No national health-care system could be adapted without shutting down part of the insurance industry. But just as society may be better off with some resources diverted from defense contractors to domestic needs, the health-care system might be better off with fewer workers involved in unproductive paper-shuffling of insurance claims. America spends as much as a breathtaking $130 billion per year on health overload, enough to fund universal care and cut medical costs simultaneously.

Clinton seems likely to propose reforms under the buzzphrase "managed competition." One idea should be government-set basic health-insurance terms, so that buyers can make meaningful comparisons between plans. Another should be a ban on "adverse risk selection," under which insurers bar coverage for pre-existing conditions or drop policyholders who become gravely ill.

Such standards would violate one of the great sacred cows of 20th-century American politics—state regulation of insurers. Insurance lobbyists have beaten back every attempt at nationwide standards, preferring to work the 50 statehouses on a divide-and-conquer strategy. Federal health-insurance rules would open the door to federal scrutiny of auto, life and property insurance: longstanding goals of consumer advocates. Expect many, many millions of dollars of your premiums to be spent resisting this development.

The Wofford factor.   How will Congress respond to health-industry lobbying? One hopeful note is the Wofford Factor. Incumbents left Capitol Hill in huge numbers this fall, replaced by candidates who ran on issues like health-care reform. Last year's old-boy Congress, which retreated in terror before the health lobby many times, might have been too timorous to attempt substantial reform. This year's group may have the combination of courage and foolishness necessary for the task. If so, the greatest change in health care since the 1965 creation of Medicare may be in store.

"Iron Triangle" Veterans

George Bush whittled from the Pentagon budget in each of his four years as president. Bill Clinton, eager to avoid being painted as another soft-on-defense Democrat, stayed quietly on Bush's heels during the fall campaign. What little he had to say about defense policy heavily overlapped Bush's message. His proposed five-year, $1.3 trillion Pentagon budget is only 5 percent smaller than Bush's. While Clinton proposed deeper troop cuts in Europe and a new commitment to retraining laid-off defense workers for the civilian job sector, both men offered essentially the same pared-down vision of the post-cold-war military.

The truth is that both plans merely nibble at the edges of a system in need of fundamental restructuring. To pay for a new domestic agenda and fashion a smaller but highly mobile military for 21st-century threats, Clinton will have to make far deeper cuts. That means fighting the military's "Iron Triangle," the cozy alliance of the Pentagon, its contractors and their friends on Capitol Hill. They're all dug in like battle-hardened infantry:

Congress.   The defense industry may be hurting, but its political-action committees still ponied up $4.4 million for congressional campaigns in 1992. The money is bound to help certain weapons projects survive. Even some of Clinton's closest supporters are committed to programs that should be killed. Sen. Sam Nunn backs the $37 billion Protection Against Limited Strikes system (PALS), a poor-man's Strategic Defense Initiative designed to destroy incoming intercontinental ballistic missiles (ICBMs). But PALS won't be ready in time to deal with the only significant security threat the country faces: the residual arsenal of nuclear weapons in the former Soviet Union. It would be far cheaper to buy the missiles. Ukraine is asking for cash and security guarantees in exchange for the ICBMs it inherited.

The pork barrel will bedevil many proposed reductions. Sen. Strom Thurmond offers a case in point. The ancient South Carolinian has been entitled to the top Republican slot on the Senate Armed Services Committee for years, but yielded it to Sen. John Warner so he could concentrate on other assignments. Thurmond recently said he is now claiming the seat to defend South Carolina from impending cutbacks. The state has 11 military installations, including the complex of air, naval and Marine bases around Charleston, generating $3.6 billion a year in wages and state contracts. And Thurmond certainly won't be the only member of Congress circling the pork wagons. Pressure will come from other levels of government as well. The Bush administration proposes cutting reserves from their 1987 peak of 1.1 million to 925,000 by 1997. Even this modest decrease has stalled in Congress because of pressure from the nation's governors. In many states, reserve pay is a key source of supplemental family income. Clinton is sure to hear from his ex-colleagues if he also pushes for cuts.

The Pat Schroeder factor.   [This is] a rubric for various lobbies close to the heart of the Democratic Party. Their two biggest military objectives: repealing the ban on gays and allowing women into combat. Clinton risks squandering political capital in Congress and the Pentagon if he is pushed to move too hard too soon on these questions. The debates won't go away. A presidential commission recently recommended allowing women on some naval warships, but rejected them for infantry and air combat. Clinton bought himself some time by kicking the gay issue over to a yet-to-be appointed study group. Sooner or later, though, he'll be forced to deliver.

The military mind-set.   Armies invariably learn more from defeat than they do from victory. Desert Storm is no exception. While the gulf war stands as an impressive technical triumph, the performance of individual services and weapons systems tells a far more ambiguous story. In a world where mobility will be the key to future military success, it took the army six months to move two corps to Saudi Arabia. Clinton will face considerable resistance in getting the military to take a clear-eyed look at the changes it must make. To force those reforms, he'll need a defense secretary capable of nothing less than what James Forrestal did when he shaped the military's cold-war missions in the late 1940s. Despite the many milestones since— including the reductions of the Bush-Powell era—Forrestal's architecture, designed for a single, now nonexistent Soviet foe, remains largely in place.

Colin Powell.   It's difficult to overstate his influence. He's the most powerful chairman of the Joint Chiefs since George Marshall—perhaps too powerful for Clinton's long-term political health. The Bush administration's proposal for shrinking uniformed forces from 1.9 million to 1.6 million by 1997 is Powell's brainchild. Earlier this year he insisted that any further reductions would jeopardize national security. But he's softened his stance recently, acknowledging Clinton's proposal for deeper cuts—to 1.4 million by 1997. The truth is that both Clinton and the Joint Chiefs will have to face the prospect of more radical reductions. Cutting troops is the quickest way to free up money for domestic programs.

The big showdown is likely to come over any attempt by the newcomers to radically alter the missions of the individual service branches to reflect new budgetary and strategic realities. Powell is likely to resist. He's working on his own reappraisal of service missions, and sources say it proposes minimal changes. "That's Colin," said a senior colleague. "He's very pro-army and he's very conservative." Powell's term as chairman is up in September. Clinton might want to ease him into a high-level cabinet job. Or the new president may decide that Powell is a power-that-be that he can be without.

Doing Business with Business

The business lobbies in Washington are awaiting Bill Clinton with roses in one hand—and a war club tucked behind the back in the other. Business, like everyone else, wants to start off right with any new president. Hence the roses. And though he's a Democrat, Clinton is admired by most business groups for his fix-the-economy-first campaign and for his record of consultation and compromise with business as governor of Arkansas. "This is not Mr. Dukakis coming in," says William Archey, the No. 2 man at the U.S. Chamber of Commerce. "This is not a Democrat who is knee-jerk adversarial to business."

But there's still the war club. During the campaign, Clinton made dozens of social, legal, tax and labor proposals that industry deplores. These include proposals to cap executive pay, raise taxes on the rich, bar the permanent hiring of strikebreakers in labor disputes, restore the closed shop in union contracts and require every business to provide 12 weeks of unpaid family leave annually for any employee. Business claims that these proposals would erode efficiency or ruinously raise costs. Some lobbies will concede certain issues to Clinton. "Family leave and the rich man's tax are going to pass the new Congress in 20 minutes anyway," says Jack Albertine, a Washington lobbyist, so "why waste your ammo on a lost cause?" But the National Federation of Independent Business, a grass-roots giant with more than 600,000 members, is conceding nothing. "We're going to take it issue by issue," says John Motley, director of federal relations for the NFIB. "We'll support Clinton where we can, but we will fight him when we must."

Yet as Clinton starts out, nearly all business lobbies—even the NFIB—are upbeat. The president-elect indicated that he will focus his first 100-day policies on improving economic growth, in part by pushing a temporary investment tax credit, while simultaneously attacking the long-term deficit in the budget. These are the top priorities of business, too. "He's addressing our agenda," says John Ong, chairman of both B.F. Goodrich and the Business Roundtable, the country's big-business lobby. The manufacturing sector looks to Clinton's presidency with outright hope. The president-elect vowed to use government to rebuild the U.S. manufacturing base, notes

Jerry Jasinowski, president of the National Association of Manufacturers. Jasinowski has been dickering with Clinton aides since early October. "The Clinton administration is going to be quite open to business suggestions. It'll do anything reasonable to boost jobs, productivity and growth," predicts Jasinowski.

The high-tech–electronics industry is even happier. Clinton met last summer with Silicon Valley executives, led by John Young of Hewlett-Packard and Roger Johnson of Western Digital, and crafted a subsidy program. He promised to make the 20 percent research-and-development tax credit permanent (worth $1 billion), to establish a high-tech civilian research-and-development agency ($5 billion to $10 billion) and to build a new telecommunications "interstate highway" hooking up all civilian research and educational library computer databases nationwide ($1 billion to $5 billion). "We're tired of fighting Japan's corporate state all by ourselves," says Johnson. "Bill Clinton has a program to get this country moving."

Some industries are directly in Clinton's line of policy fire—and they're openly grousing. Charles DiBona of the American Petroleum Institute notes that Clinton pledged to prohibit production in all big potential oilfields under U.S. control (the Arctic National Wildlife area, offshore California). Clinton also said that he would cut back U.S. oil consumption by 2 million barrels a day by the year 2000 to curb the greenhouse effect. "The domestic oil industry has lost 450,000 jobs in the last decade—72,000 last year alone," DiBona says. "[Clinton] means more trouble—and worse." And Clinton vowed to boost the corporate average fuel economy (CAFE) standard from 27.5 miles per gallon to 40 miles per gallon by the year 2000. U.S. automakers, struggling through their third year of red ink, claim they lack the know-how and the cash to meet that goal. What to do? Pray. Mike Stanton, lobbyist for the Motor Vehicle Manufacturers Association of the United States, was heartened by Clinton's remarks during a campaign stop in Michigan in early October. When challenged on the new CAFE standard, Clinton "said that he didn't want to do anything that would cost jobs," says Stanton. "We find that encouraging."

If—and when—it comes to a fight with Clinton, the business lobbies are already preparing their strategy: grass roots, grass roots and more grass roots. William Archey of the chamber notes that there will be 110 new lawmakers in the House next year and that domestic policy dominates voter concern, to the total exclusion of foreign policy, more than at any time since 1936. "National security—a president's showcase—isn't even in the top 10 issues," says Archey. "This means power shifts to the Congress, where members will vote the views of the folks back home." The chamber and the NFIB have elaborate newsletter and wire communications with their members. The nets include computerized telecommunications systems that can trigger letters and phone calls from important local business leaders—within hours if necessary—to every member of Congress on Capitol Hill.

This kind of muscle doesn't guarantee business victories: congressional Democrats thwarted business interests in numerous votes last year. But the NFIB's Motley has done his congressional nose count for next year and says that he's encouraged. He figures that he can count on 165 of the 176 Republicans in the House, as well as an additional 30 conservative Democrats. "This leaves me with one to two dozen votes to scramble up elsewhere when we're really sweating a vote," says Motley. "That should be doable on a lot of issues." Motley hopes that it won't come to that too often. Despite Clinton's promises to liberals during the campaign, he's the only current governor ever to have won an NFIB plaque as a "Guardian of Small Business"—one of the NFIB's highest awards.

With Friends Like These

Saying no to your friends is hard. But if Bill Clinton is truly "a different kind of Democrat," he will disappoint his liberal allies. They know that. In a rare moment of mutual understanding, liberal interest groups are lying back, respecting Clinton's difficult balancing act, and not putting the squeeze on him. As least not yet. Sobered by 12 years out of power, these groups have less of a sense of political entitlement. They know how fragile their hold on power is with a president who won because he moved the Democratic Party to the middle. But self-restraint is not a popular virtue among activists of any kind. And the betting is that President Clinton will eventually feel the heat from his progressive friends.

How hard they push for their pet programs and how Clinton handles the onslaught will be a central theme of his presidency. What could save Clinton is the memory of Jimmy Carter being overwhelmed by the demands from his own party. "For those of us who remember, that tempers our sense of expectation," says former Arizona governor Bruce Babbitt, a contender for a top environmental post. A Carter health-care proposal and legislation curbing hospital costs failed mostly because they weren't far-reaching enough to please Sen. Ted Kennedy and an array of interest groups. The chance to draft more politically correct bills ended with the election of Ronald Reagan. Clinton's transition chief, Vernon Jordan, was among Carter's earliest critics. Then head of the Urban League and a longtime Carter friend, Jordan hurt the new president's credibility by charging that he had not fulfilled promises made to the civil-rights community.

This time, interest groups are packaging their demands differently. They are avoiding big price tags and tailoring their wish lists to fit Clinton's trimmed-down agenda. Their strategy in some key areas:

Education.   Teachers are among the Democratic Party's biggest financial backers and voting blocs. They want Clinton to be the "Education President" that Bush never was and fully fund Head Start, rebuild inner-city schools and turn high schools into technology centers. Clinton supports these goals, but not all at once. The 2 million-member National Education Association is a major player in presidential politics. This year the group gave the Clinton campaign more than $1 million. In 1984, the NEA presented Democratic nominee Walter Mondale with a list of programs that added up to $11 billion. Mondale's eager acquiescence tagged him as a tool of the special interests and another tax-and-spend Democrat, labels the party is still trying to shake. This time, the NEA's proposals are more modest. "We don't have a lock on anything," says NEA president Keith Geiger. The union may have downsized its dollar expectations. But it still poses trouble for Clinton on philosophical grounds. The NEA opposes public-school choice across district lines, and national service as a way for college students to repay federal student loans—programs at the heart of Clinton's reform agenda.

Environment.   The Green Group, a coalition of environmental organizations, recently broadened its franchise to include population-control advocates and the Children's Defense Fund, where Hillary Clinton is a board member. "If it is narrowly defined as just birds and bees, nobody is going to play," says Jay Hair, head of the National Wildlife Federation. Environmentalists, who have a strong ally in Al Gore, are biding their time to let Clinton build political capital with Congress and the voters. For now, they are asking for things that don't cost money: elevating the Environmental Protection Agency to cabinet level; lifting anti-abortion controls on international family-planning programs; convening a summit on the spotted owl controversy in the Northwest. "We don't want to ruin what could be a good relationship any sooner than we have to," says Jim Maddy of the League of Conservation Voters. Environmental concerns have never been one of Clinton's priorities. But he sees potential in environmental cleanup as an industry of the future.

Women.   Clinton promised repeatedly in his campaign to include women in equal numbers in his administration. To help him keep that pledge at all levels, women's groups are sending long lists of names to the Little Rock transition office. This week the National Political Congress of Black Women will unveil its list to make sure African-American women are represented. Pro-choice groups would like Clinton to press for Freedom of Choice legislation, but he does not want a contentious battle over abortion rights to divert him from his economic agenda. Instead, Clinton is expected to sign executive orders immediately that lift the ban on abortion counseling in federally funded clinics, allow fetal-tissue testing and ease import restrictions on RU-486, the French abortion pill.

Cities.   In traditional political terms, Clinton "owes" very little to big-city mayors. His campaign was pitched toward white suburban voters, who are now a voting majority. During the campaign, a $35 billion package to revive the cities was treated coolly by Clinton. But the cities should benefit from Clinton's emphasis on job training and public investment in rebuilding the nation's crumbling infrastructure. The Rev. Jesse Jackson, who traveled tirelessly to register new voters for Clinton, wants early White House leadership on statehood for the District of Columbia.

Clinton's best defense is to keep a relentless focus on his economic agenda. And the interest groups understand that: cramming bits and pieces of their agenda into an omnibus economic package will occupy them for the coming weeks and months. But once at the table, will they be able to take no for an answer? Clinton will also face strong opposition from senior citizens' groups to any kind of deficit-reduction package that includes restraints on entitlements. Many organizations have flourished over the last decade because they had a clear enemy in the White House, but pillorying enemies is a lot easier than promoting patience. If Clinton is to prevail, he must reverse the natural order.

T HE FOLLOWING SELECTION picks up the theme suggested in the first selection in this chapter, stressing that a· major way in which money talks in Washington is to hold out the lure to public servants that once they leave government they will be able to profit from their experience by obtaining lucrative jobs. Top government officials obtain valuable experience and contacts that can put them in good stead later in the private sector. But ethics laws constrain what public officials can do for a period of time after they leave office; they cannot, over the short term, profit from their prior government experience. However, the possibility always exists that at least some officials may, while still in office and with a view toward their private sector future, bend what they are supposed to do in the public interest in the direction of special interest demands.

10 Haynes Johnson
WHEN MONEY TALKS, WASHINGTON LISTENS

Joseph A. Califano, Washington insider, examined the invitations he had received in the morning mail: To attend a breakfast honoring a congressman—and contribute $250. To another breakfast for a congressman—and another $250. To a kickoff breakfast for a political campaign committee—and $1,000. To black tie dinners for Democratic candidates—and $1,000 each. To an event honoring a congressional committee chairman too busy with Washington duties to campaign in his home district—and $250. To a dinner honoring the years of public service of a retiring U.S. senator—another $1,000. To separate functions for three other members of Congress—and contributions of $250 to $350 apiece.

"For the last year I've kept all the invitations to fund-raisers I've received," said Califano, a Washington lawyer, former Cabinet officer and presidential adviser. "It's mind-blowing. In just a year I've got well over a couple of thousand invitations to fund-raisers of one kind or another, from both parties."

Other participants in Washington's political circus say they receive the same inundation of requests for money—one of every three pieces of mail he receives, according to one prominent lawyer.

Of course, Califano and others like him are being asked for money partly because they are making so much themselves. Colleagues say Califano earns nearly $1 million a year providing advice and legal counsel based in part on experience gained during his years as a White House aide and as secretary of Health, Education and Welfare.

Money plays a vastly greater role in the political life of the capital than it did a generation ago, according to many involved then and now. There is more of it to be made, they say, and more people seeking to make it more openly, and more blatantly, than ever. That is the first point many of them make about what might be called the "Deaver Syndrome," the rush of former government officials to profit from private dealings with the government they just served.

Not that the relationship between money and politics presents a new phenomenon in Washington. Money continues to be the "mother's milk of politics," the common denominator of the democratic system.

There is nothing new, either, about the city's recurrent seizures of conscience over the state of capital ethics like the one provoked recently by questions growing from the Washington dealings of Michael K. Deaver. This trusted adviser and public relations counselor to Ronald Reagan instantly translated his government contacts and access to high places into a multimillion-dollar business when he left the White House last May.

Since the days of George Washington, former high government officials have offered to sell their valued expertise and access to policymakers and legislators in Washington. Since then, too, tales of capital corruption have repeatedly scandalized or titillated the nation.

But today's capital ethics do seem new. Old-style corruption—venal politicians exchanging votes and favors for cash, vicuna coats and Persian rugs—is for the most part a thing of the past. At least that is the belief of a score of prominent, longtime Washingtonians interviewed about the present ethical climate of the nation's capital, many of whom agreed to speak about what one called "this sensitive subject" only if their names were not used.

In place of the old venality, many of those interviewed say, is a new prevailing attitude, symbolized now by the Deaver case—an attitude of insensitivity to the appearance of conflicts of interest.

"What's different is very clear," says Fred Wertheimer of Common Cause, the self-described citizens' lobby. "As a given, there's always been influence peddling, inside dealing . . . ranging from activities that might fit the definition of acceptable conduct to improprieties to ethical violations to statutory violations to criminal violations. This administration does not recognize this area as an issue. It is a nonissue, a nonreality, and I question whether you could find any presidential statement [from Reagan] explaining why it's important to have honesty and integrity in government, why you need standards of public service. . . .

"There is no message coming out of this administration that anything is wrong about all this. Now that's different. In the past, the key to influence peddling was that it was secret, private, people didn't know about it. Why?

Because it was considered wrong. Not necessarily by the people who did it, but ultimately it was judged wrong in the public arena. When it came out on the table, it lost. Now blatant public influence peddling is fine. . . .

"I have this image that I play around with of an administration that rode in from the West to tame the evil government, and rode in with the fresh air of the West to clean up this polluted air center, and now they're moving in, they're running around town like classic Washington insiders and they are feeding off the government."

That may be an exaggeration, but different attitudes about the lines between public and private life in Washington do seem to be reflected at top levels of the Reagan administration. An incident at the White House underscored this.

The president had invited members of the committee appointed to oversee his presidential library to a dinner. As one person who was there recalled:

"He had a big breakfast the next day in the White House and the head of the Hoover Institution [Dr. W. Glenn Campbell], who's head of the Reagan library committee, got up and said two things which showed how really insensitive some of these people are to this problem. He said, 'You know we have the tremendous advantage of raising money for this library while there's a sitting president.' Two, he says, 'You notice we have Mrs. Weinberger on this committee [Defense Secretary Caspar's wife]. Oh, boy, when Mrs. Weinberger goes to those defense contractors.' He said that. Just totally insensitive. But that's what this is all about. That's the story."

Asked about that incident, Campbell says, "I may or may not have said something close to that. The fact that we have a sitting president is self-evident, isn't it? There's no question about that. Now Mrs. Weinberger is a member of the Board of Governors and I may have said something like that as a joke, and only as a joke. To the best of my knowledge Mrs. Weinberger would never approach defense contractors. She has too much good sense to do so, and I have not and would not ever ask her to do so. This teaches me again that in Washington you cannot even make a joke without someone misinterpreting it as a serious remark."

Reagan met with key backers of his library project in Los Angeles just before leaving on his trip to Asia. Campbell said there that he hopes to raise $80 million to $100 million, but added that the list of donors will not be released.

For much of its history, Washington has attracted ambitious people seeking power and profit as well as opportunities to serve the public. And for much of its history, the making of deals and trading of influence was an accepted staple of Washington life.

It is said, for instance, that when Congress was debating whether to grant federal land to the railroads, the lobbyists literally "camped in brigades around the Capitol building." In the Ulysses S. Grant administration, when lobbyists bought and sold congressmen like sacks of potatoes and influence peddling became enshrined as a political device, Mark Twain captured the corruption in Washington during what he called "The Gilded Age." A decade later, Henry Adams, scion of presidents and social arbiter of Washington manners and morals, also turned to fiction to describe in his *Democracy* the story of a "political society full of corruption, irresponsible ambition, and stupidity."

That kind of climate, perhaps always exaggerated, continued into this century, producing scandals from Teapot Dome to Watergate that reinforced the public impression of Washington as a center of corruption. At the same time, each scandal brought a reaction and, over time, new laws, ethical codes of conduct for government, and greater public awareness and scrutiny, especially in the so-called post-Watergate era.

Public scrutiny, public disclosure, whistle-blowing, and increasing use of leaks from within government about wrongdoing have exerted a powerful check on corruption, longtime Washingtonians agree. The new rules have made it much easier to expose cases of malfeasance, a fact that may contribute to the large numbers of Reagan administration officials caught in embarrassing situations since 1981.

Today's corruption, if such a word applies, stems more from changing attitudes that make "cashing in" more acceptable, from the proliferation of lobbying groups and political action committees and from the greater amounts of money to be made.

More people appear to be drawn to government not as a career, but as a means to cash in on their public service as quickly and profitably as possible, according to lawyers and lobbyists. One observer describes this as the desire "to do two years and then come out and make a big hit. They all think that they're going to be able to be bigger earners, bigger hitters, than they were before they went in. I'm not sure it works, but that's the mythology, that's the legend, and they do come [to town] with that in mind."

At the same time, the number of jobs in which people are paid to try to influence policy in Washington has mushroomed, in private business and in the "public interest" sector. For example, the files of the Foundation for Public Affairs include the names of about 2,500 public interest organizations representing almost every conceivable political viewpoint—and all involved in the legislative or lobbying process.

Add these to the public relations firms such as that founded by Deaver after leaving the White House, the growing number of law firms, consulting groups, corporate and union offices, and firms dealing with foreign governments, and one has an enormously expanding world of people seeking to influence the government.

But according to many Washington insiders, the results these "fixers" achieve often are negligible. Obviously, special interest lobbying can produce tangible results in the form of tens of millions of dollars for clients on such major congressional legislation as the 1981 tax bill. Still, the view is widely held that much "rainmaking" is as fraudulent as . . . well, as attempts to make rain.

"My judgment has been that most of the time the people who are taking the huge fees are guilty of false pretenses," says one person intimately involved with the lobbying process. "Not in the criminal sense that you could prosecute them for it, but they're total charlatans because they can't do anything. In a sense, they're really stealing from a bunch of scoundrels. And the con men out there who are coming in here to create the fix, you know are the biggest patsies in the world. So it's just a bunch of con men working on each other and I don't think they affect the result.

"It's a rarity when you see an important decision in government affected by an old school tie or an attempt to influence the official. I don't really think there is the kind of corruption or venality in government that the existence of all these fixers suggests. The principal corruption is the corruption of the pretenses *they* make as to what they can do when they lift these gargantuan fees off these hicks when they come to Washington. They come in, you know, with shoes and they go out without shoes."

Those involved in the process of representing clients who deal with the government resent being tagged as "influence peddlers," and see much of the news media as naively preoccupied with the occasional scandal while missing the larger picture of the way the process works.

Leonard Garment, who served in the Nixon White House and now practices law in Washington, says, "I don't think this city could work without lobbyists. Nor would the Constitution actually be a live enterprise without lobbies because that's the way one petitions for the redress of grievances.

"This is a country that is so large that the federal notion of representative government saturates our life, and that's very much the case with lobbying. Is it different now than it has been in an earlier time that I'm familiar with? Yes, but everything is bigger. . . .

"And [there are] a lot more of people who had nothing to do with government. They come here not to be part of the public life experience. They come here to be lobbyists. It's like becoming a periodontal surgeon without going to dental school. They're working on the patients without much in the way of real experience. . . .

"And everybody's got a lobbyist. It's like private businesses having jet aircraft. The accoutrements of modern life. . . . The general impression is that unless you have somebody representing you, you're in trouble. It's clumsy but roughly correct that they are like a lot of blind people groping in a closet. They know they should have somebody to explain the jargon, to read the hieroglyphics of this mysterious pre-Mayan culture called Washington. And they're told that there [is] this whole group of special guys that you find at the headwaters of the Potomac and if you say the right words they'll put you in a canoe and take you up there and help you find your way into the mysterious culture."

"I'll tell you what's different about Washington now," says a lobbyist for a major trade association who for years was a key congressional aide. "Money. It's just more pervasive. This proliferation of the PACs [political action committees], these around-the-clock fund-raisers. . . . All for money. Everyone expects it. It has to be done. You have to raise that money— 'hitting the drum,' as they say—and you have to give it.

"Unless you hit the drum, you're not in the game. Unless you give your 'max' [a PAC can contribute a maximum of $5,000 per election to a candidate, and an individual citizen can give up to $1,000 per candidate], unless you lay out your $5,000 at a fund-raiser, you don't have access. Now that only buys a return call. I'll give you a concrete example of what money buys. I can take out of my pocket right now and show you a line in the proposed tax legislation that, if deleted, will cost my industry billions of dollars—billions, that is. Now this afternoon, three lobbyists—big, big contributors—are meeting with Sen. X on the tax bill. Others can't get in the front door. So the question is which one gets to tell his message directly. And if you don't go to those fund-raisers, if you don't hit the drum, if you don't 'max out,' you don't get in the door. They don't even return your phone calls."

To Califano, the new importance of money has had an adverse effect on the political system: "The influence of money has turned Congress into an institution that resembles the state legislatures in the days of Lincoln Steffens."

To others, such as former senator J. William Fulbright, the Arkansas Democrat whose congressional hearings on corruption at the end of the Truman administration led him then to decry "the moral deterioration of democracy," today's climate makes the past seem almost innocent. "We never even had fund-raisers here when I was in the Senate," says Fulbright, now a Washington lawyer. "They were all held in Arkansas."

The new flood of money, coupled with the flow of people from government into private practice in Washington, leads some to fear that the situation is bound to grow worse. One lobbyist speaks darkly about a "return to the Robber Baron era," when the "special interests" were virtually able to dictate legislation.

Most interviewed, however, were far less pessimistic. Many argue that a rigorous application of existing rules and guidelines would head off a new era of venality.

"There happens to be, in my view, a good set of rules about ethical conduct on the books . . ." Common Cause's Wertheimer says. "But ethical conduct is a combination of things. It's rules and guidelines. It's attitudes and atmosphere. It's oversight and enforcement. So we have the rules and the guidelines to a good degree. We have neither the attitudes and atmosphere nor the enforcement. And it all goes back to the tone established by this administration."

11 Susan B. Trento
LORD OF
THE LIES

In the old days, when Robert Gray was a staffer in the Eisenhower White House and had visitors in his office, he'd have his secretary interrupt him from time to time with fake telephone calls from the President. Back then, the occasional deception helped the Nebraska native wire his White House career. Three decades later, the tricks were the same but the stakes a little higher. This time around, deception helped Bob Gray set the American agenda.

"A reporter would walk in, and he would instruct his executive assistant to come in and announce there was a call from the White House," a former Gray and Company executive recalls. "Totally fabricated. They would come in and they would say, 'Mr. Gray, Mr. Meese is on the phone,' and he would pick up a dead line, carry on a conservation of four or five short, rapid sentences as though he was in constant communication and hang up. And then, of course, the reporter, dazzled, would report that a White House phone call came in."

Access: The illusion of it has long been the energy source of Washington's unelected power elite—the lobbyists, PR sorcerers, and counselors who work their quiet magic on the nation's laws in back rooms the general public doesn't even know exist. And no one has nurtured that illusion better or longer than Bob Gray, one of Washington's most powerful and most respected, influence peddlers. For 30 years, at his own firm and at Hill and Knowlton, he's set a standard—not a particularly high one—for what Washington lobbying can get away with.

Of course, Gray would probably relate his story as a Horatio Alger tale: A boy from Hastings, Nebraska, comes to Washington, works hard, and makes it to the top. When he started in the world of public relations in 1961, he had no expertise in either government or substantive policymaking. But he did have a talent for making people believe he was well-connected, and in the power-crazed world of Washington, he found an audience not only eager to believe he was a player, but willing to pay him handsomely to prove it.

In relatively short order, his illusion became reality: Gray did favors for people; he thrived on the party circuit; he was a perfect host and perfect guest. He cultivated Washington society wives, raised money for the

"Lord of the Lies," by Susan B. Trento, The Washington Monthly, September, 1992. Reprinted with permission from The Washington Monthly. Copyright by The Washington Monthly Company, 1611 Connecticut Avenue, NW, Washington, D.C. 20009. (202) 462-0128.

Republican party, and took care of the politically powerful. Soon enough, Gray *did* know almost everyone in town who mattered. And he knew exactly how to profit from that knowledge: Take all comers, regardless of who they are. Whether the client was Haiti's "Baby Doc" Duvalier of the Church of Scientology, the only criterion was that the client paid—and paid well.

Gray's professional life is a study of how, if it's done right, pulling strings for profit can come to look an awful lot like status. But it's not, unfortunately, the story of one man. In part because of Gray's success, the brand of insider politics he fine-tuned has become an entrenched and unhappy part of our legislative process. Any any understanding of how we got here must take into account the career of Robert Keith Gray.

In 1961, the year he parlayed his White House experience into a power position in public relations, Gray went as respectable as Washington could get. As vice president and director of the D.C. office of Hill and Knowlton, Gray had signed on to perhaps the most conservative firm in the field.

Founder John Hill saw himself and his employees as public relations counselors, much like lawyers. Instead of simply taking instructions from his clients and putting out press releases, he genuinely tried to advise them. If a company was getting bad publicity because of bad policy, Hill would advise that the policy be revised. He would routinely turn down clients if he felt they wanted "to shade the truth," explained George Worden, a Hill and Knowlton official, "He was a very moral man."

Robert Gray, on the other hand, didn't pay particular attention to ethical considerations. He wanted to be a player. And his first step was to create the illusion that he had already achieved that goal. One of his initial requirements was a limousine, not just for convenient transportation, but to enhance his image. His second, third, and fourth requirements: parties—going to the right ones, sometimes three a night, and hosting some of the more memorable events in the tedium of Washington night life.

In 1966, for instance, he gave a party at his home in suburban Virginia for the Saudi Arabian ambassador and his wife. "Visitors to the hillside home . . . were greeted by what appeared to be Arabs in full Arabic costume," reported the Omaha *World-Herald.* "[It] turned out they were mannequins. . . . But the ambassador, unlike the fixtures in their tarbooshes and other Arabian regalia, was wearing a conservative blue suit."

More important than the tableaux was the guest list. And on that count, Gray was cleverer than the average social climber. He found out who mattered in Washington, and then he called their wives. Mamie Eisenhower was just one of his grande dames. "He plays his social life smooth," former Nebraska Senator Carl Curtis says. "We've been to a lot of his parties and it would be filled with women old enough to be his grandmother. Wealthy [women]—he was the favorite escort of the oldest women." But they weren't just old. They were connected.

More contacts inevitably led to more clients. Before long, Gray provided services to accounts that included the American Petroleum Institute, Procter and Gamble, and the National Association of Broadcasters. Still, Washington power is a volatile thing, and Gray made his smartest move by looking ahead. By 1967 he'd joined a 50-member committee to elect his friend, Richard Nixon, to the White House. And when Nixon won, Gray became the big gun of Republican lobbyists.

How did he use his power? Consider one client who went away happy, El Paso Natural Gas. El Paso hired Hill and Knowlton to drum up support for legislation that would allow El Paso to buy out its competitor, Pacific Northwest Pipeline Company. (El Paso's earlier attempts to do so had been blocked by a Supreme Court decision on the grounds that it would have meant higher costs for consumers.)

Hill and Knowlton went to work on Warren Magnuson of Washington state, chairman of the Senate committee considering the legislation. The PR firm drafted a dummy, fill-in-blank resolution and distributed it to chambers of commerce in Magnuson's home state. Later, when the senator held hearings in Seattle, Hill and Knowlton helped provide witnesses, prepared testimony, and handled the press. It supplied background materials to state and local officials, as well as sample letters to send to Congress; it contacted newspaper editors with volumes of canned materials, and many of those editors wrote supporting editorials.

By the time El Paso got its way, it had paid Hill and Knowlton hundreds of thousands of dollars, a pittance compared to the cost of the $360 million buyout that the PR firm had made possible.

Get a Wife

A few more legislative coups like that one, and Bob Gray was king of the Hill. In 1980, he left Hill and Knowlton and set out on his own. In typical Gray style, he located his new offices, not on Capitol Hill, as many of the labor unions had done 20 years earlier, nor on K Street, in Washington's business and legal district, but in a beautiful old brick building on the canal in fashionable Georgetown. Gray paid $750,000 for the 19th-century building, a former power plant that once provided the energy for Washington's old street car system. With its towering but long-dormant smoke stack, Gray's new quarters were imposing. His gray and silver stationery read simply: "The Power House, Washington, D.C."

Gray's timing, as usual, was impeccable. This was the dawn of the Reagan era, and his was the perfect setting for carrying out the carefully crafted illusion of power, access, wealth, and influence, from the arched 25-foot windows to the blown-up photos of the Reagan inaugural. "[The] Power House was just a unique setting at the time. . . . " said Pate Felts, a Gray and Company senior vice president. "[It] was really a sexy place."

The illusion of power was also reflected in the names of those who occupied the offices. Gray had learned early on that Washington is a two-party town, and, in order to prosper, he had to create the appearance of access to both Republicans and Democrats. He lured Gary Hymel, who for years had worked as a top aide to House Speaker Tip O'Neill, and he snagged Bette Anderson, a former high-ranking Carter administration Treasury Department official. And to complete his power base, Gray revived a trick from his old dowager-cultivating days. Only this time, he didn't escort the wives-of to parties; he hired them.

There was Noreen Fuller, the first wife of Vice President Bush's former Chief of Staff Craig Fuller. There was Nancy Thurmond, wife of Senator Strom Thurmond, then chairman of the Senate Judiciary Committee. There was Washington socialite Joan Braden. Keeping the wives of the powerful happy was smart business. Not that they knew anything about lobbying, but they contributed to the illusion of access. "Need a favor from Henry Kissinger? Call Joan Braden," *The New York Times* wrote. "A prominent Washington hostess with many highly placed friends, she regularly counts Mr.Kissinger among her dinner guests."

The stars brought in clients from the Kennedy Center to Montgomery Ward. Yet perhaps the most crucial wife in Gray's roster didn't work for him at all—but Ursula Meese's husband would be one of his biggest catches.

"[Gray] was friends with the Reagans and all that, but he did not have a lot of contact with them," said Larry Speakes, Reagans's deputy press secretary in the early eighties. Ed Meese was a natural point of entry for the master of illusion.

Meese was the only one of Reagan's three top aides who was impressed by Gray. James Baker came from a rich, socially prominent family and had headed Gerald Ford's 1976 presidential campaign. He did not need any Washington introductions, either politically or socially. Michael Deaver, a skilled PR man himself, could see right through Gray's carefully crafted illusion of power and access. But Meese was new to Washington, had come with little money, and was vulnerable to offers of introductions to the "right" people, and to overtures of kindness and friendship during his times of trouble. He was just the type of person with whom Gray could ingratiate himself, and he had the kind of influence with Reagan that would make Gray's time and effort worthwhile.

The Meeses' financial difficulties were no secret. Meese's wife Ursula, *The Washington Post* wrote, "has worn borrowed evening clothes to fancy dinners because the family finances are tight." Gray knew an opportunity when he saw it; he had one of his clients create a job for Ursula. He convinced millionaire William Moss to create the William Moss Institute, a philanthropic foundation to poll Americans about their concerns for the future. It was associated with American University, another Gray client. Gray then recommended Ursula Meese for director of the institute at $40,000 a year, thereby increasing the Meese family income by about 66 percent. "Ursula Meese was hired only because she was married to the attorney general." a senior Gray and Company executive said. "I was there when she was hired and I remember the terms of the agreement and it was clear."

A few phone calls, and Gray had ensured that his White House calls would get returned. Buying influence was easy, and sometimes it was cheap. For example, Gray had known Caspar Weinberger for years, and it just happened that Weinberger's son needed a job. Gray paid Caspar Jr. $2,000 a month, and when Gray's clients needed something from the Pentagon, Gray and Company went right to the top.

Of course, keeping influence was sometimes trickier than getting it. Joan Braden's contacts, for instance, gave Gray and Company one of its most prestigious accounts—the government of Canada. But Canada also illustrated a problem with Gray's star system, as the big names often had no experience in PR.

Braden won the account through her friendship with Canada's then-Ambassador Allan Gotlieb. Once the account was secured, it was turned over to young, low-paid account executives, who saw it as a fat cow ready to be milked dry. "Everybody who could fancy the slightest reason for piling on, piled on," Joan Braden said in her memoir, *Just Enough Rope*. "Why were six people from the press department attending a conference in Ottawa?"

The Canada account ended with great public embarrassment. Gray and Company sent *The New York Times* a press release that misspelled the ambassador's name, the name of the reporter, and the name of the ambassador's guest at the luncheon the press release was promoting. The *Times* ran a story saying that Canada's publicists could not even spell the names correctly. Canada canceled the contract, and Joan Braden quit.

Presstidigitation

Still, Gray's business could survive, in part because, as the eighties progressed, the illusion-machine was on full power.

When Gray courted the media, he left nothing to chance, hiring personal aides or special assistants whose primary responsibilities were to get him favorable publicity. A mention in *The New York Times* and *The Washington Post* style sections could work wonders. High social visibility was encouraged, especially among top-tier people like Frank Mankiewicz, Alejandro Orfila, and Braden. The regular appearance of well-known Gray and Company stars at social and political functions and the drum beat in the press contributed to the firm's image as the most talented and well-connected in town.

When *The New York Times* wrote about Gray in 1982, he carefully orchestrated the interview as he had done so many times before. Clip files on Gray are filled with stories like this:

His hair is silver-gray, his suits are impeccably tailored, and he is always in a hurry. . . . "Get me Jim Baker," Mr. Gray calls to his secretary . . . Mr. Gray can get just about anyone in town on the telephone, maybe even the President now and then. . . . Just now, he is talking to Mr. Baker. "James!" he booms. "How are you doing?" . . . We want to help you anytime we can. . . . You know that." Then Mr. Gray brings up the real reason for the call: Mr. Reagan's minimum profits tax. . . . He hangs up the phone and telephones Robert B. Peabody, president of the American Iron and Steel Institute, one of his clients. "Bob," he says, "how're you doing? I just had a telephone call with Jim Baker on minimum profits . . ."

Illusion? By now, it was harder to tell. The get-it-while-you-can attitude of the Reagan years brought a steady stream of clients to the door of the Power House. But while business was thriving, it was also changing. As his Ursula Meese–style access-mongering began to work, Gray gravitated toward big contracts with clients a lot more questionable than the government of Canada. Gray and Company "was a company without a moral rudder," said Sheila Tate, a former Hill and Knowlton employee and later Nancy Reagan's press secretary, discussing the firm's controversial clientele; the only criterion Gray seemed to have in selecting his clients was the size of their wallets.

Most of Gray's international accounts were right-wing governments tied closely to the intelligence community or businessmen with the same connections. Gray represented Adnan Khashoggi, the "self-employed" Saudi Arabian businessman who was involved with Iran-contra. "Khashoggi was notorious for using us and not paying us," a senior Gray and Company employee said. Another questionable client was the government of Haiti during the reign of the murderous "Baby Doc" Duvalier. The Gray rationalization would have been dazzling if it weren't so appalling. Adonis Hoffman, a self-described liberal, was one of the executives who worked on the account: "The Haitian people were suffering. . . . We were working for the people in this hemisphere who have the lowest standard of living, who are entrenched in the deepest poverty." One of the reasons the Haitian people were so poor, of course, was the systematic pillaging of resources by the government Gray and Company represented. Baby Doc was using this devastatingly poor country's meager resources to pay, among other things, Washington's most expensive PR and lobbying firm to improve his image.

Domestically, one of the more notorious reputations Gray tried to sanitize was that of American fugitive Marc Rich. A billionaire, Rich fled to Switzerland in 1983 to avoid a 65-count criminal indictment. A year later his company, Marc Rich & Co., AG, pleaded guilty to 38 counts of tax evasion and paid a $150 million fine. Gray and Company turned the fine into a celebration—a media event. The deal was announced with great fanfare by New York's then-U.S. Attorney Rudolph Guliani, who accepted a huge, oversized check as if he had just won the Publisher's Clearinghouse Sweepstakes. This fine was publicized as one of the largest in American history. In reality, though, it was pocket change for Rich, who was charged with gouging the American taxpayers for as much as Charles Keating had with his savings and loan boondoggles.

Another Gray catch was the Teamsters Union. Jackie Presser, a former car thief and one of a long line of corrupt Teamster officials, saw in Gray not just an effective lobbyist but a man who could confer social and political acceptability. "That was the odd couple. . . Jackie just worshiped the ground Bob walked on. You know why? Because Bob was sort of the image of respectability and elegance and grace, and represented polite Washington society. And he accepted Jackie," said Mark Moran, a Gray and Company official.

Gray worked hard at maintaining the relationship. In Washington, he held a 50th birthday party for Presser at the Palm restaurant, known for the caricatures of famous people on its walls. At Gray's behest, Moran performed a service that typified the Gray touch: "I arranged to get Jackie's picture put up at The Palm. . . . We arranged for the table, and then we waited to see if Jackie picked it up. He didn't see it. . . . Then Bob showed it to him and Jackie went bananas. He thought that was the greatest thing," Moran remembered. "They put it next to the picture of Eugene McCarthy. . . . They couldn't have picked a better place."

Not all of Gray's efforts went so smoothly. One especially embarrassing incident involved the government of Morocco. Gray had pioneered a number of innovative PR techniques, such as "video news releases." The idea was to get television networks and local radio and television stations to air these advertisements as their own news stories. Gray and Company had started with a radio show called "Washington Spotlight." During these programs, the radio stations did not disclose that they were produced by Gray and Company or that Gray had been paid by clients to do them. But by 1984, "Washington Spotlight" was a big success: There were 656 subscribers to the "Gray and Company Network," and another 1,476 stations in the Mutual Broadcasting System and National Public Radio Network that received the program by satellite each month. Soon the program was being broadcast bi-weekly.

Riding this success, Gray decided to try the same idea on television. The company's PR packages began appearing on CNN as news stories: In March 1985, it sent by satellite "an exclusive interview" with King Hassan II, the autocratic ruler of Morocco. At the time, the king was being criticized for signing a treaty with Libyan leader Muammar Quaddafi. In a standup outside the palace, a Gray correspondent warned viewers that the West should not react harshly to the treaty and that any criticism of Morocco should be "tempered with the acknowledgment" of the country's strategic importance to the United States.

CNN and Channel 5 in Washington ran the story as if it were their own. At no time did either the network or the station disclose that Morocco was a

Gray client that was paying the firm a minimum of $360,000 to improve its image in the United States, or that Morocco had paid Gray and Company to produce the piece. Eventually, it ended in embarrassment after *The Washington Post* revealed that CNN was running videos made for clients of Gray and Company as news stories.

Clientitis

The obvious impetus to take on clients like Hassan was the huge fees Gray could collect. And the more money a client had, the more pressure there was internally to gouge him. "You'd see hours pop up any time a client had money," Carter Clews, a Gray and Company senior vice president explained. "I remember [one executive] pointed out that no phone call takes less than an hour. 'Always keep that in mind,' he said, 'once you pick up that phone, that's an hour. It doesn't matter how long you talk.' "

Another Gray and Company vice president remembered a client who was billed for expenses associated with a party to which he was not even invited. She said wine bought as Christmas gifts for clients was secretly included in their bills the following month. She maintained that even Gray's practice of taking clients' children to the circus each year, for which the company got credit in the press, was eventually charged back to the clients.

The urge to make the big bucks, combined with fiascos like Morocco's, impelled Gray to sell his firm in 1986. In true Gray fashion, he cut a sweetheart deal: In June 1986, JWT Group, Inc. agreed to buy Gray and Company and make it a part of its subsidiary, Hill and Knowlton. The merger agreement created an entirely new division of Hill and Knowlton called Hill and Knowlton Public Affairs Worldwide and put Gray in charge as its chairman. Hill and Knowlton returned Gray to its board of directors and made him chairman of its policy committee.

Gray Matter

But Gray's charm by the end of the eighties was wearing thin. The anything-goes Reagan era was over, and compounding Gray's poor judgment in clients was a growing public distrust of lobbying. Influence-peddling abuses were starting to surface, and Americans literally began to pay for them. The cozy relationships among the lobbyists, Congress, and the executive branch became publicly evident in one scandal after another. Members of Congress worked in tandem with lobbyists to generate "grass-roots" support for pet issues. The White House had recruited lobbyists to help with controversial appointees needing Senate confirmation. The very organizations designed to protect America from an abusive system had become part of the system, and Gray was predictably in the middle of it. Still, his connections were strong enough to keep his clients out of trouble.

In 1989, HUD investigators were looking into contributions made to a charity called Food for Africa by consultants and housing developers with whom Thomas T. Demery, the assistant secretary for housing, routinely worked. During the first 20 months after Demery assumed his HUD position, Food for Africa raised $546,000, more than half of which came from companies and individuals who had interests in HUD housing programs. In the nine months prior to that, Food for Africa had raised $34,000.

California Rep. Tom Lantos, whose government operations subcommittee had oversight of HUD programs, began hearings into influence-peddling at HUD in the spring of 1990. Just before Demery was scheduled to testify, he hired Hill and Knowlton to advise him on how best to make his case to the news media and Congress. Remarkably, Lantos announced at the hearing that the subcommittee was not going to investigate the relationship between Food for Africa and HUD contractors, a key portion of the inspector general's report that had started the HUD investigation in the first place.

Why not? Back in 1985, Lantos and Illinois Rep. John Porter had founded the Congressional Human Rights Foundation, and in 1988 Lantos had asked Gray to donate office space at Washington Harbour, one of the most expensive addresses in town, for the foundation. The Hill and Knowlton switchboard forwarded calls to the foundation. A private nonprofit organization, the foundation was dedicated to publicizing human rights abuses around the world. Ironically, it did not have to look much farther than its landlord's clients to find governments with poor human rights records—Haiti, Turkey, Indonesia, South Korea, Morocco, and China are some of the world's most egregious human rights abusers.

But even friends in the right places can do only so much to offset a string of bad publicity. Gray signed on the Church of Scientology, and later *Time* magazine ran a highly critical cover story titled, "Scientology—The Cult of Greed." He also signed a contract with the Catholic Church, agreeing to help change public attitudes toward abortion, a move that prompted severe public criticism as well as internal bickering at the firm. Other clients included the People's Republic of China—after the Tiananmen Square massacre. And then there was Citizens for a Free Kuwait, a client the company may never recover from.

In the wake of so much bad publicity, staffers began abandoning the firm for greener, and possibly cleaner, pastures. The biggest blow came in April 1991, when four top Hill and Knowlton executives publicly and abruptly left to start a competing firm, Capitoline. As more and more top executives left, morale dipped to an all-time low. From a staff of 250 during the Persian Gulf war, the office now had 90 people. Rows of offices sat empty, and Hill and Knowlton alumni could only laugh when they recalled the fights over who got the offices along the Potomac River.

In the fall of 1991, with Gray's contract due to expire, many expected him to retire. After all, he would be 70 years old. Had he finally taken one too many controversial clients, been implicated in one too many scandals? Was he ready to call it quits?

Of course not. Bob Gray signed on for another three years. And the illusion of power is certain to continue.

How much reality remains? A former Gray and Company executive gives an answer that goes to the heart of why Americans around the country have become so distrustful of Washington. "We were thought to be real because we were thought to have the influence and the access and the power and the understanding of how the system worked. It became almost a self-fulfilling kind of myth. The more people gave us credit for doing things, the more influential and effective we became. There is no answer to the question of was it real or was it just hype to protect [Gray's] own veneer. But the story is it didn't matter. It didn't matter to people here and it didn't matter to the clients and it didn't matter to the media, because everybody was playing the game."

THE MEDIA AND POLITICAL CONSULTANTS

Chapter
Three

The First Amendment's guarantee of freedom of the press both reflects and protects the political power of an institution that has always played an important role in the nation's politics. The publishers and pamphleteers of eighteenth-century America considered freedom of the press a natural liberty and acted accordingly. Their criticisms of British and colonial authorities helped to plant the revolutionary seed in the minds of the colonists. Colonial governors were aware of the dangers of a free press and sought unsuccessfully to control it by requiring government licenses for printing. Moreover, the authorities did not hesitate to bring charges of seditious libel against journalists who criticized the government.

The freedom of the press that was won in the eighteenth century created an environment in which political journalists could and did flourish. Although reporters could build successful careers by covering politics at state or national levels, Washington inevitably became the mecca for the political press.

By the time of the New Deal, the Washington press had become a firmly entrenched establishment force in the nation's capital. Jonathan Daniels, an experienced Washington hand who had served as President Franklin D. Roosevelt's press secretary, commented, "It would be difficult to find a body of men who more clearly represent Washington than the gentlemen of the press who report it. There are notions, carefully cultivated, that they are in Washington but not of it, and that they stand in scrutiny but also in separation. Actually, of course, they are probably more representative of the good and the bad on the Capital scene than any other body of bureaucrats. As they stay in Washington, which most of them hope to do, they are at least as remote from the country as the administrators are."[1]

The media are a powerful political force at all levels of the government. A century before the advent of radio and television, Alexis de Tocqueville pointed out that the diversity and power of the press is a major characteristic of democracy, particularly of a government such as that of the United States, which contains so many political subdivisions. "The extraordinary subdivision of administrator power," remarked Tocqueville, "has much more to do with the enormous number of American newspapers than the great political freedom of

[1]Jonathan Daniels, *Frontier on the Potomac* (New York: Macmillan, 1946), p. 159.

the country and the absolute liberty of the press."[2] Newspapers, concluded Tocqueville, can persuade large numbers of citizens to unite for a common cause. Moreover, "the more equal the conditions of men become and the less strong men individually are, the more easily they give way to the current of the multitude and the more difficult it is for them to adhere by themselves to an opinion which the multitude discard[s]. . . . The power of the newspaper press must therefore increase as the social conditions of men become more equal."[3]

The press has always attempted to create, in Tocqueville's terms, associations of citizens to back causes and candidates. The press attempts to be the king-maker for many of the ten thousand or more elected offices throughout the nation.

The growth of the electronic media, radio and television, added a new dimension to the traditional political role played by the press. While newspaper publishers and correspondents are free to express their political views, support-ing whatever candidates they choose, the electronic media are in an entirely different position. The airwaves used by the electronic media to communicate information are technically "owned" by the public. The government licenses broadcasting stations for a three-year period, after which it reviews the licensee's conduct in relation to statutory and administrative standards to determine whether or not the license is to be renewed.[4] One of the regulatory standards governing broadcasting requires impartiality in the "equal time" for the presen-tation of opposing opinions. Broadcasters, unlike publishers do not often endorse political candidates.

While broadcasting is supposed to be politically neutral, it is inevitably drawn into partisan politics. All news and public affairs programs have a slant, which indirectly shapes citizen attitudes on important issues. Statements about public policy are often made simply by the choice of subjects to be covered. The White House, which is so frequently the focus of media attention, complains constantly that it is not being treated fairly. Republicans attack the "Eastern liberal establishment" press, while Democrats always echo President Harry S Truman's lament: "I was sure that the American people would agree with me if they had all the facts. I knew, however, that the Republican-controlled press and radio would be against me, and my only remaining hope of communicating with the people was to get the message to the people in a personal way."[5]

However much they may criticize the media, politicians increasingly depend upon them to project their personalities and communicate their views to the electorate. Political consulting has become a major industry.[6] By 1952, 45

[2]Alexis de Tocqueville, *Democracy in America*, Vol. 2 (New York: Vintage Books 1954), p. 121. Tocqueville's volumes were first published in 1835.

[3]Ibid., p.122.

[4]In fact, almost all license renewals are automatic, making the licensees virtually permanent owners of their stations.

[5]Harry S Truman, *Memoirs*, Vol. 2 (Garden City, N.Y.: Doubleday, 1956), p. 175.

[6]See Larry J. Sabato, *The Rise of Political Consultants* (New York: Basic Books, 1981).

percent of households owned television sets; not surprisingly, that year marked the advent of political television in a big way in presidential campaigns.[7] General Eisenhower, portrayed as the simple and sincere man from Abilene, easily won over the sometimes acerbic but always witty Adlai Stevenson of Illinois. The Stevenson campaign spent only $77,000 on television compared to the Republican expenditure of $1.5 million on its media campaign. The use of media consultants and the expenditure of large sums of money for public relations has become de rigueur for almost all political campaigns, whether presidential, congressional, or at the state level, as television has evolved into the principal political medium. Media consultants are the new political gurus.

[7]Ibid., p. 113.

S UCCESSFUL CAMPAIGNING requires a broad array of skills. Electoral politics has become a big business because running for office is extraordinarily expensive, particularly at the national level. Successful House candidates spend an average of approximately $250,000 to $300,000 to be elected, while Senate races may cost as much as $5 or $6 million.

Candidates not only have to raise large amounts of money but also must deal with increasingly complex media. They must project a favorable image— one of a dynamic, energetic, and caring politician who takes the "right" stand on major issues.

Candidates cannot begin to run a successful campaign without political consultants, whom they have come to consider indispensable. Consultants themselves have become an important political force, shaping the electoral process and even influencing public policy formation through their access to office holders. As the following selection reveals, while candidates hire them to win elections, consultants are not simply hired guns, they often carefully select their candidate-clients to fulfill their own political objectives.

12 Larry J. Sabato
HOW POLITICAL CONSULTANTS CHOOSE CANDIDATES

There are several methods by which candidates are matched up with political consultants. The first is consultant solicitation. When the principals in Butcher-Forde Consulting, for instance, heard that there was no professional management team supporting Howard Jarvis's 1978 proposition 13 tax-cutting drive in California, they arranged a meeting with Jarvis, presented a plan of action, and hustled the extremely lucrative account. While solicitation is a common and necessary practice for lesser-known consultants, occasionally the national firms also seek the account of a campaign that has either great financial potential or a capacity to enhance their winning image and reputation. The D.M.I. polling firm systematically compiles a "druthers list" of the most desirable campaigns and contacts them in an attempt to sign them up (approaching political consultants working for the campaigns instead of the candidates on occasion).

Rarely in past times did consultants actually recruit an individual to make a race, but the practice is becoming disturbingly common due the expansion of ideological political action committees. A professional manager like Roy Day was once the exception in his role as Richard Nixon's original sponsor. Day, though, was also chairman of the Republican Central Committee of Los Angeles when he formed the Committee of One Hundred in 1946 to find an opponent for the Democratic incumbent U.S. congressman, Gerald Voorhis. Day placed advertisements on the front pages of twenty-six newspapers, and Nixon was one of the respondents. The future president was chosen to make his first race, launching his long political career. Today, however, consultants active in recruiting candidates have weak or nonexistent party credentials and sometimes are agents of party-rivaling political action committees, such as the committee for the Survival of a Free Congress or the National Committee for an Effective Congress.

Most major consultants do not bother to recruit because ideologically they are not very choosy and they have far more business than walks in the door unsolicited than they can possibly handle. In the vast proportion of client-consultant matchings, the original contact is made by the future client, and the odds are great that prominent consultants will not be interested or able to take them. Richard Viguerie claims to turn away 98 percent of all the people who come to him. David Garth reports that, while he took only five campaigns in 1978, he was approached by statewide candidates in thirty-nine states, and in twelve of those states (or twenty-eight—he cited different figures in two separately published interviews) he was offered both sides of the race.

It is little wonder that a few consultants are so swamped with requests. Candidates and their staffs usually know little about the national professionals or their campaign technologies and are likely to seize upon one of the periodic glowing press accounts of one or another consultant's miracles, after which the candidate or campaign manager issues the order to secure consultant X at any cost. A bit of campaign shopping could do wonders for a campaign budget, but there is astoundingly little of that. When it occurs, it is worth noting. U.S. Senator Birch Bayh's well-organized 1974 reelection effort, for example, arranged interviews with eight political pollsters. The two finalists, Peter Hart and Patrick Caddell, were not well known at the time. (After final interviews of one and a half hours each, Caddell was chosen over Hart.)

Demand for consultant services has so increased since 1974 that it is doubtful that any such carefully staged selection is possible today. Most potential clients would simply not be worth the preliminary investment of so much of a consultant's time. Regrettably, the consultant crunch at the first level is forcing candidates to solicit help from much less experienced and sometimes less scrupulous second- and third-level professionals. Many of the unethical practices in the consulting business find their origin there.

One other method of matching candidates and consultants should be mentioned. Candidates are frequently referred to a particular consulting firm by a third party. Sometimes a firm's previous candidate-clients who were satisfied by the services rendered will pass along the experience while offering advice to new candidates. A consultant who is too busy to sign the candidate on will sometimes suggest the names of friendly associates or some young, struggling firm with which he is acquainted. Many PACs have semipermanent relationships with certain consultants and will suggest a linking of arms to a candidate being supported with PAC money. Finally, the candidate's state or national political party committee may work on a regular basis with consultants, and a recommendation may be forthcoming from party officials. In some midwestern states, particularly in the Republican camp, a few consultants have done all of a party's major candidates for a number of years and are hired almost by habit.

For the most part, one problem candidates do not have to worry about is locating ideologically compatible consultants. While the professionals are not without political belief, they rarely let it overrule their business sense. For most consultants ideology is a surprisingly minor criterion in the selection of clients. Party affiliation plays a larger role for some, but usually because serving candidates of both parties is impractical and hurts business. (A significant minority of the professionals, however, are actively hostile to the parties—even to the very notion of a political system.) Political reporter David Broder connected the consultants' party links and lack of pronounced ideology to the credibility and professionalism required for success in their business: "I think the nonideological style they adopt is not dissimilar to that of political reporters, mainly that they try to really separate their own feelings and emotions so that they don't get in the way of making a professional judgment."

But the full explanation has a major financial component, as political consultant Sanford L. Weiner, addressing his peers, frankly surmised:

> We would all like to think we have worked for candidates we believed in, and who represented our own individual political thinking. . . . Unfortunately, as with any profession, economics enter the picture. We have all, from time to time, represented clients whom we didn't particularly love, but who could help us pay the overhead.

The businessman's profit motive is admittedly powerful, and when combined with most political professionals' disinterest in issues and the stuff of government, a remarkable tolerance results. Robert Goodman can say without blush, "I call myself a Jacob Javits Republican, but I can stretch to the conservative ends without a problem." His standard of judgment for potential clients is heroic, not ideological: "We see politics as theater, living theater, and it is classic theater. There is a hero and there is a villain. Now we won't knowingly take on a villain. We like to feel that our candidate has the potential of being the hero." Fellow Republican consultant John Deardourff has a less charitable assessment of the "heroic standard": "Bob Goodman doesn't care who he works for. He'll build a big, noisy campaign, with a forty-seven-piece band, around anyone."

As its literature notes, Deardourff's firm makes its services "available to candidates we wish to see in public office." His partner, Doug Bailey, identified two areas (civil rights and women's issues) where "unless we generally shared the candidate's philosophy, we would feel so uncomfortable it would be a nonproductive and unpleasant relationship." Yet he admits to working for candidates who have opposed the Equal Rights Amendment and racial balancing of school systems through busing. In 1978 the Bailey-Deardourff firm also handled at least three candidates with solid antiabortion records. Chuck Winner of California's Winner-Wagner organization proclaims insistently and forthrightly his undying resistance to his state's often-used initiative and referendum process: "I oppose the idea of law by mob rule. I oppose the idea of doing away with representative democracy. I oppose the idea of losing basic protections for the minority." But almost all of his lucrative political work is referendum- and initiative-related. (Someone has to do it, of course.)

Generalist consultant Hank Parkinson (who claims to have worked for both the Democratic and Republican national committees) explains his lack of issue orientation by calling himself "a technician, not an ideologue. . . . I have turned down extremists on both ends of the spectrum, but mostly because they simply can't win." Some professionals are addicted to sports analogies to communicate their love of the game and disinterest in the philosophy behind the plays. Others report that their ideological attachments are fading over time as their exposure to politics lengthens, and that ideological rigidity is part of the problem in the political system they observe. Says Patrick Caddell:

> I'm basically liberal, but also basically convinced that most of those answers aren't working either. Rigid ideological structures are helping to screw up what's going on in terms of our ability to solve our real problems. I've said to people who say, "How do you work for McGovern and work for Carter?" It's very simple. In both cases, I happen to think that they were the best people running for president at the time.

These comments would be an anathema to a small but growing band of political consultants who are more rigid in their ideological prerequisites for candidate-clients. Conservative Richard Viguerie has never been accused of ignoring his direct-mail firm's business interests, yet he carefully considers the ideology of all his prospective clients and organizational subordinates. The right-wing political action committees, which Viguerie often helps to coordinate, sometimes have prospective candidates fill out written ideological examinations. Paul Weyrich, executive director of the Committee for the Survival of a Free Congress, gives a seventy-part questionnaire on issues and ideology to each candidate who approaches the group for assistance, and the answers are crucial to chances for funding.

Perhaps because the contemporary United States is in a conservative-dominated political era and a period of retrenchment for liberals, most tests of ideological purity are administered on the right. But in a recent time more attuned to left-wing philosophy, the 1960s, the same degree of selectiveness by liberal political professionals existed. Only days before President Johnson withdrew from the 1968 presidential race, one of his campaign assistants was forced to tell Johnson that his staff had great difficulty finding a New York advertising agency willing to take him on "because they are all [Vietnam] 'doves.' "

Ideology is also at least one of a number of considerations for some consultants not at the liberal or conservative extremes of the spectrum. The direct-mail firm of Craver, Mathews, Smith, and Co. has been known to reject issue groups because they were philosophically in conflict with the partners' views. David Garth has his staff carefully research the records of his petitioners (because he has learned not to trust their own accounting of their voting histories), and he pays careful attention to views on a number of social issues. Generalist Walter De Vries eventually switched from the Republican to the Democratic party to accommodate his progressivism, although business needs entered into the decision. As he wryly noted, "If you work only for progressive Republicans, your market is getting pretty small." Regional media consultant Marvin Chernoff insists on working for "the most progressive or liberal candidate in the race," yet this carefully worded criterion often allows signing on a moderate or conservative.

Even consultants who put ideology on the back burner (or off the stove entirely) have some rock-bottom standards and very general prohibitive criteria. Joseph Cerrell will not work for anybody that he would "have trouble voting for." Pollster William Hamilton, a moderate-liberal Democrat who has worked for conservatives, had the opportunity to take one of George Wallace's presidential campaigns but refused it. Bob Goodman also rejected Wallace and did not respond to preliminary soundings from a U.S. Senate candidate from Virginia (who was eventually successful in his electoral bid) because he was "a guy who would have taken the rent from poor little Nellie and thrown her on the streets." He continued: "We will not handle people we don't like as human beings. We will not handle people we think are dangerous at either extreme. We could not handle a John Bircher, a racist."

It is a delicious commentary on the American system that some of the least ideological professionals take their chosen political party dead seriously, and anyone who cares about the party system can be grateful that they do. A few are fierce partisans, having had their political baptism as party functionaries and occasionally having had years of direct party employment. One of these, Robert Odell, is inclined to take on just about any Republican in his direct-mail firm because, "Democrats do little or nothing that I respect and Republicans do nearly everything I respect." Striking a rare pose for a private consultant, Odell declares, "The most important goal for me is to make the Republican party effective." Matt Reese holds the Democratic party in similar esteem, observing only half in jest that he is "a partisan without apology. I don't even like Republicans, except for Abraham Lincoln." And few professionals have shown as long and abiding a concern for a political party as Stuart Spencer and his partner, Bill Roberts, who both began their political careers as volunteers for the Republican party in California. Their consulting shop actually developed around the GOP and was encouraged by the party. Spencer explained that he and Roberts "wanted to be an extension of the party, a management tool that the party could use" and that they viewed each of their early consulting outings as "an opportunity for the Republican party." With the party's interests in mind, Spencer and Roberts gave Ronald Reagan an extended grilling when he approached them about his impending 1966 gubernatorial campaign in California. After a number of questions about his depth and experience, and whether he could win for the party or might instead become another Goldwater disaster, reportedly Reagan became exasperated and demanded: "Now, goddammit, I want to get some answers from you guys. Are you going to work for me or not?" The Spencer-Roberts agency finally did agree to handle him.

The greatest number of consultants, though, are simply not committed in any real sense to a political party. Michael Kaye, for instance, proclaims himself to be an Independent and the parties to be "bullshit." Revealingly, however, he still sensed that it was a mistake to work both sides of the street, comparing it to his practice while a product advertiser:

> People in political office, most of them are paranoid anyway. And I think it would make someone uncomfortable to think that I was working for a Republican at the same time I was working for a Democrat. That is why I work only for Democrats. I don't work for just Democrats because I think they are the only good pure people on this planet. It is the same reason that in the [product] advertising business I didn't work for two clients in the same business.

Yet for all of the danger supposedly involved in crossing party lines, consultants seem to yield frequently to the temptation. Democrat Peter Hart conducted Republican U.S. Senate nominee John Heinz's surveys in Pennsylvania in 1976 (and claimed he was told he could not take polls for Jimmy Carter as a consequence). David Garth has been "all over the lot," as one of his detractors termed his tendency to take moderate-to-liberal Democrats and Republicans indiscriminantly, and it was a surprise to no one in the profession when GOP Congressman John Anderson tapped Garth to help with his 1980 Independent presidential bid.

Another Democratic-leaning liberal firm, Craver, Mathews, Smith, and Co., took on Anderson's direct-mail program. The now-defunct firm of Baus and Ross in California secured the accounts of Richard Nixon, Barry Goldwater, and Edmund G. "Pat" Brown, Sr., within a few years of one another. The survey firm of D.M.I. not only once worked for both Democrats and Republicans, they actually polled both sides of the same congressional election district in 1966. Vincent Breglio, the D.M.I. vice president, took one side, and president Richard Wirthlin took the other. They ran the research independent of one another and provided consulting services to each side without crossing communications. Apparently the candidates were rather trusting souls who reportedly agreed to this outrageous arrangement (although it was quite a useful one for the firm's "win ratio"). D.M.I. converted permanently to Republicanism in 1967 when Michigan Governor George Romney asked the firm to join his presidential effort on the condition that they work only for the GOP. Convinced that the move was good for business, Wirthlin and Breglio made the switch over the objections of the Democratic members of the firm, who nevertheless stayed.

It is one thing to be apathetic about the party system and quite another to be hostile to it. The nonideological nature of American parties is the object of venomous rebuke by right-wing consultants such as Richard Viguerie and PAC leaders such as Paul Weyrich. Viguerie has flirted with a personal Independent candidacy and publicly expressed his hopes for a new conservative party to replace the GOP. Urging cross-party consulting for conservative candidates, Viguerie insisted that "conservatives must learn to disregard meaningless party labels." Weyrich's Committee for the Survival of a Free Congress practices Voguerie's preaching and has involved itself in party congressional primaries on both sides of the aisle, assisting the 1978 victories of the presidents of both the freshman Democratic and freshman Republican U.S. House classes. A "militant supporter" of Independent U.S. Senator Harry Byrd of Virginia, Weyrich believes that conservatives' "political victory will not come by the Republicans winning control but rather by a coalition of conservatives of both political parties getting together." The conservative Republican takeover of the U.S. Senate in 1980 may have given Weyrich second thoughts, but it hardly instilled in him any greater loyalty to the GOP. Barely had the votes been counted than Weyrich and other New Right leaders warned President-elect Ronald Reagan to hew closely to conservative ideology. Vice President-elect George Bush, suspected of moderate tendencies, was threatened in much stronger terms.

With the exception of the ideological PACs, party affiliation and ideology are by no means the only, or even the dominant, criteria for consultants in selecting their clients. The personal mesh between consultant and client seems to be of paramount importance, followed by the need for a balanced and economically rewarding program for the firm. There is a sort of ritualized mating dance when consultants and prospective clients meet, a mutual sizing-up and testing of one another that can sometimes be quite intense for all parties. Most consultants in preparing to meet with a candidate learn as much as possible about the individual ahead of time and request a full day of the candidate's time for the interview. They grill the candidate, peppering him with questions, many of them personal (in an attempt to ferret out scandal in advance). David Garth's interrogation is unusually issue-oriented: "How should the state or city be run? How should the money be distributed? What do you think about welfare?" Walter De Vries is particularly interested in the response to one query: " 'What makes you think you ought to be governor or United States senator?' And a lot of guys don't have very good answers. And if they haven't articulated in their own mind why they want to be governor, you can't do it for them." Matt Reese's mind is more directly on the prospects of winning when he confronts the candidate: "I ask how many people they've got and how much money. I know how to run a campaign with lots of people and little money. I know how to run a campaign with lots of money and few people. I love it when I've gots lots of money and lots of people. I don't know what to do when I don't have any money and any people." In his interview sessions, Pat Caddell tries above all to test character to find the "real patriots in the sense of really caring about the country. If I were to apply one single criterion, it would be whether the individual really gives a good damn about what happens to the United States. Large numbers of politicians, frankly, could care less as long as they stay in office."

The personal interviews are enormously useful, and normally essential, for both the candidate and the professional. Sometimes serious potential problems are exposed and explored so that all parties can anticipate the campaign ahead. Frequently a consultant encounters a reluctant candidate and after a rewarding session actively encourages his candidacy. On the other hand, as one consultant reported, "Many times what you find out is that person really shouldn' be running for office. Either they have problems or when you really get down to it they are running because somebody else wants them to run . . . or because they see a lot of glamour in it."

The interviews are not always revealing, of course, and many consultants (at least the ones who have sufficient clientele to afford the luxury of leisurely choice) often require a number of interviews over several weeks or months before an agreement is concluded. But even with multiple meetings, decisions on taking clients are always gambles. Media consultant Tony Schwartz asks rhetorically, "How well can you really know a guy? You get to know your wife better after you get married and your secretary better after you've hired her." Still, most professionals believe they can sense whether the client understands and appreciates what they do and whether the personal relationship in the campaign is likely to be a pleasant, satisfying, and effective one.

While the personal evaluation and relationship is the most crucial nonpartisan element in the selection process, at least half a dozen other factors are taken into consideration. The revenue-producing potential of a campaign is almost always at the top of the list. A major race that will contribute substantially to a firm's economic objectives is a good bet to be selected, and campaigns are scrutinized to determine the likelihood they will meet their projected budgets. Consultants also consider the stress that a campaign will add to their personal schedules. Most have a fairly fixed limit on the number of campaigns they will take in any year, and they often try to cluster them geographically, which saves traveling wear and tear. No consultant forgets about the overall batting average, either; a reputation that has been so lovingly nurtured must be protected with a sufficient quota of expected victories and upset wins. And a spirit of cooperation and an appreciation of the consultant's role must be manifested not only by the candidate but also by the spouse and the key internal campaign staff aides.

Some consultants are reluctant to take on campaigns at certain levels (usually local or presidential, although some firms refuse gubernatorial clients). At least until John Anderson came along, David Garth refused to consider presidential clients, saying, "I don't really have any great desire to elect a president. . . . The kind of physical and emotional expenditure it takes doesn't make sense for the company." Garth also claims to use a form of collegial decision making absent in most firms, wherein his staffers and associates participate fully in the client selection process rather than accept his dictation of choices.

The direct-mail firms have a number of specialized criteria peculiar to their technology. Vigueire's organization insists that candidates prove they can raise significant funds on their own, partially because of the huge initial costs involved in a direct-mail program. And some firms, such as Craver, Mathews, Smith, and Co., refuse a significant percentage of the candidates and organizations that approach them because direct mail is not an appropriate device in many cases and will not turn a profit for the company or the clients.

Each consultant applies these criteria quite differently, giving more emphasis to some than others, and consequently he can judge particular candidates differently than his peers. The case of Bill Bradley's 1978 bid for the Democratic U.S. Senate nomination in New Jersey will serve to illustrate. Bradley's personal charm and flattering appeal to Michael Kaye's professional pride won the consultant over:

> Bill saw my work for the first time. Apparently, as he tells me, he instantly realized I was the guy without a doubt. . . . I liked the fact that he genuinely wanted me. I told him I would give him a decision after the weekend, because I was still wondering if I really wanted to fly back and forth to New Jersey all the time. I said, "Bill, don't bother me until next Monday." The next morning, he calls me. He said, "Mike, I know I've broken the rules, but I just have to tell you how much I want you to do this campaign. Maybe I didn't get that point across

the other night, but I want you to know that we loved meeting you." That was very nice. Anyway, I did it and it was a marvelous year.

Kaye had not been Bradley's first choice, however; David Garth was. But Bradley's wooing of Garth had been much less successful, and Garth not only declined Bradley but signed on for Richard Leone, one of his opponents. Said Garth:

> I didn't like Bradley. I interviewed him. It was awful. I asked him five or six questions. I asked him questions about energy, housing, the kind of things I think as a candidate for the U.S. Senate from the state of New Jersey he ought to know. He didn't know anything. I didn't ask him any questions like "Do you want to win?" or "Will you change your clothes?" I don't like that. Dick Leone was a personal friend of ours. We had worked with him in several campaigns. He probably would have been the best qualified guy in that race. He was also an Italian and I felt there was a shortage, quite frankly, of Italians in office, that we need more because it's a group that really feels unrepresented, the same as the blacks do.

Garth's comments make obvious the fact that political consultants have become preselectors in the nominating process, encouraging and dissuading candidacies often with the mere announcements of their choices of clients in a race. In this respect and in others—slate balancing, for example, as in Garth's determination that more Italians should be in office—modern political consultants have substituted for the party bosses of old and make decisions today that should more properly be the prerogative of party leaders. Peter Hart sounds like a more grammatical version of Tammany Hall's George Washington Plunkitt when he relates this anecdote:

> I worked with [one candidate] in 1978 and came to the conclusion that he's a very, very bad human being and that I made a mistake. The person decided he'd seek office in 1980 and the guy made an appointment with me. I said, "I'm sorry to tell you, but I think you've got a character flaw. I'm sorry if nobody else has ever told you. I don't believe in you. I can't work to see that you get elected."

It is not that most political consultants look upon their preselector role cavalierly; some see it for what it is, a sobering responsibility. Sanford Weiner reminded his fellow consultants in a session of the American Association of Political Consultants that, in Watergate's wake, they had "a duty and a responsibility to screen would-be candidates more carefully than ever." But is it better for society to lodge this obligation with the political parties or with private individuals in the profit-making profession of consulting?

13

Ken Auletta
LOATHE THE MEDIA

The swarm of reporters hovered outside Blake's coffee shop in Manchester, New Hampshire, waiting for the candidate to appear. Suddenly Bill Clinton stepped out into the New England cold—not that you could see him, of course. What you could see were the boom microphones and TV cameras and tape recorders, all diving toward the dense center, reporters frantic to capture the moment—that *gotcha!* question, that gaffe—that would kill one candidate's quest for the presidency. What you felt was the competitive panic, the terror of missing the fatal moment. What you heard was the buzz of mindless questions shouted indolently, idiotically, at the dazed candidate: "Will you stay in the race if you lose the New Hampshire primary?" "Are you angry?" "Are you encouraged by the polls?" "Do you expect your opponents to pick on you in tomorrow's debate?"

It was mid-February, near the tail end of the Gennifer Flowers hysteria, and the questions had actually improved. Weeks earlier, usually-serious reporters were apologizing and then asking: "Did you ever sleep with Gennifer Flowers?" Clinton felt he needed to escape the incessant questions. To win, he realized he had to break away from the press gang and reach voters directly.

Leaving Blake's, Clinton sat in the front seat of a gray Chevy van, with his wife, Hillary, and an aide in the back. The entourage soon came to a halt a few blocks east, where the candidate was scheduled to talk to New Hampshire residents on the front porch of 83 Boyton Street. Instead, he ran into no fewer than 150 reporters camped on the lawn, their cameras and boom microphones and tape recorders poised to ambush him. Bemused, Clinton rolled down his window to see if he could spot some actual voters. When he finally spied a few, Clinton sighed. "These poor people don't have a chance."

As this tawdry campaign season nears its end, it's worth savoring the absurdity of that February day in New Hampshire and then rethinking why the electorate is so angry this year. It's a given that they're angry at politicians, but less noticed is why they're just as enraged at the press.

Only two decades ago, when the two parties allowed primaries and caucuses to replace the party elders in choosing candidates, the media was set to become the handmaiden to a new and exciting era of direct democracy. It was entrusted with screening the candidates, telling us about their character, their charisma, their competence, their skills, their electability. But as election day approaches, one thing is certain: The media is now significantly less pivotal a player in presidential politics than it was four years ago, less important even than it was on that February day in New Hampshire. This election may be remembered as one in which the much-heralded "boys on the bus" lost control of the political debate.

In retrospect, we reporters were ill-equipped to substitute for political parties. For all our power to select front-runners, we had too little shared history with the office seekers we chronicled. We were interested in probing their character but didn't know how to distinguish between what the public needed to know and what was best left private. We usually did not dwell on policy or on what candidates might actually do as president. We lacked the knowledge to do this, or were terrified of boring our readers and viewers. Maybe we didn't want to bore ourselves.

Too often, we feasted on politics as an end in itself. We defined news as what was fresh, which meant that we did not mine the candidates' basic themes because we had heard them a zillion times before. Instead, says the University of Pennsylvania's Kathleen Hall Jamieson, we treated the candidates "as performers, reporters as theatrical critics, the audience as spectators." We announced who staged the best events, who looked smooth, who sounded good, who was winning, who gave the best performance. So focused on form and entertainment value had we become that candidates spent more time devising ways to capture our attention than articulating a plan of presidential action. Days before the New Hampshire primary, Michael McCurry, senior adviser to Senator Bob Kerrey, described preparations for a debate: "We just spent two and one-half hours preparing for the debate tonight, and one-half hour of it was on substance and two hours was spent on coming up with snappy one-liners."

The result of all this positioning and counterpositioning, Joan Didion noted in 1988, is a political process "seen as so specialized that access to it is correctly limited to its own professionals . . . to that handful of insiders who invent, year in and year out, the narrative of public life."

The decline of the media's status in the public's eye has been more or less inversely proportional to our sense of self-importance. The rise of the talk-show media celebrity, who often tends to adopt an air of omniscience, further estranges the press from the public because reporters are supposed to *ask* questions, not make pronouncements. David Broder of *The Washington Post*, for one, believes that the chat- or shout-show phenomenon "cheapens journalism. It gives people the impression that what political reporters do is stand around and holler at each other."

Hollering is also at the center of another dubious institution: the media stampede that follows any whiff of scandal. Reporters have always succumbed to frenzies, of course. But this year's were different. They were not occasioned by the reputable *Wall Street Journal*, which pursued Geraldine Ferraro's family finances in 1984, or by the *Miami Herald*, which staked out Gary Hart's home in 1987. No, this year the *Star*, shows like "A Current

Affair" and "Hard Copy," tabloid newspapers, and local TV news jostled to the forefront and were able to pressure the established media to follow their dubious lead.

The media's mistakes led to a startling transformation in the role of the press. One can divide the campaign into two acts: pre-Perot and post-Perot. In Act One, the media largely maintained its role as a filter between candidate and public. After Perot appeared on "Larry King Live" in mid-February, Act Two began; soon George Bush and Bill Clinton aggressively began to bypass the media and reach voters directly.

This transformation did not occur in a vacuum. The diminution of the media's importance is linked to a broader trend toward the elimination of elites and middlemen, including decentralized government, more responsive corporations, and direct access. It happened in Eastern Europe. It's happened with TV clickers and multiple channel choices that permit viewers to avoid the big three networks and program for themselves. It's happened with mail-order catalogues and computers that allow customers to shop and bank at home. It's happened with chain stores like Wal-Mart and the Gap. It's happened with corporations that shed layers of management so that workers are closer to their product. And so this year it happened when candidates and citizens alike rebelled against the media middleman. This year they decoded—perhaps forever—the insider game once dominated by the boys on the bus.

The press had promised to behave this year, to be less reactive, more thoughtful and substantive than it was in 1988. This time most news organizations began planning their campaign coverage early, determined to downplay the too-familiar horse race and play up the real issues.

In 1988 the Bush campaign skillfully captured the agenda with clever photo opportunities and almost daily assaults on Dukakis. This year, says *The Washington Post*'s Dan Balz, the newspaper tried to stray more from the campaign bus, to supply readers with more context and a more in-depth look at the candidates. "Motion and thought tend to be enemies," says Ron Brownstein of the *Los Angeles Times*, explaining why he often stayed off the bus and broadened his bank of sources to include academics and "people of thought."

But other factors intruded, at least initially. Partly because of the recession, partly because of the ascendancy of the accountants, and partly because politics smells like fish to most consumers, less time and space was devoted to the campaign this year—the networks earmarked 58 percent less coverage from Labor Day 1991 through January 1992 than they did four years earlier, according to one report. The networks often relied instead on pictures from the increasingly influential local stations.

The emergence of local television opened a door for the candidates. Starting with President Bush in January, the candidates used satellites to conduct live interviews with local stations around the country. During the

1992 primary season, the Freedom Forum Media Studies Center at Columbia University found that twice as many local stations used satellite interviews as they did in 1988; and partly to save money, one in ten local stations now accepted video news releases produced by candidates—a threefold increase over 1988—with half failing "to reveal the source of this material to viewers."

Still, pre-Perot, the media continued to dominate the dissemination of the candidates' messages. By November 1991, the insiders of the press had decided that Bob Kerrey was probably too unfocused, too existential a character to be president. So in mid-November, when Kerrey whispered what he thought was a private (if lame) joke about Jerry Brown into a live microphone, the established media pounced on this gaffe as a metaphor for the "aimless" Kerrey campaign.

While reporters limned Kerry's joke for all its news potential, they virtually ignored a major Clinton economic-policy speech, proving what Bush adviser Roger Ailes has called his orchestra-pit theory of politics: "If you have two guys on a stage and one guy says, 'I have a solution to the Middle East problem,' and the other guy falls in the orchestra pit, who do you think is going to be on the evening news?"

Still, the tone of the pre–New Hampshire campaign this year was surprisingly elevated, thanks in no small measure to the substantive questions asked by actual voters when they encountered the candidates. But with a month to go before the February 18 New Hampshire primary, the boys on the bus were restless. They had heard the set speeches of the candidates so many times that they no longer took notes.

To them, news was what was *new*, and from the candidates they heard little that qualified as fresh. Under the pressure of deadlines, constant worries about getting beat, and too little time to reflect, and with cellular telephones allowing reporters to file stories instantly, reporters are easily seduced by a flap or, better, the prospect of a scandal, no matter how flimsy its provenance.

Something new finally happened on January 23. That's the day the *Star*, a racy supermarket tabloid, paid an undetermined sum of cash to publish Gennifer Flowers's claim that she had carried on a twelve-year affair with Bill Clinton. Although Flowers had a year earlier denied the allegation and even threatened to sue a Little Rock, Arkansas, radio station if it broadcast the story, the *Star* said it had tapes of conversations between Clinton and Flowers.

Clinton was confronted by the same type of media hysteria that drove Gary Hart to abandon his campaign in 1987. With one big difference: The Hart story was based on an actual sighting and a picture of Hart and Donna Rice together, as well as on a pattern of undisciplined behavior on the part of a presidential candidate; the Flowers story was still just an allegation. At first, says Gwen Ifill, who covers Clinton for *The New York Times*, "I thought it was a tabloid story. Yet when we arrived in Nashua for a candidates' forum, there were one hundred reporters there. There was an amazing frenzy."

Ifill remembers how she and the other reporters on the bus "compared notes" that Thursday. "We had done no independent reporting," says Ifill, assuming this sensible journalistic test was adequate. Even if it were true that Clinton had had an affair with Flowers, as many reporters suspected, since Clinton was not pretending his had been a perfect marriage, why was it important? Dan Balz bumped into the candidate late Thursday night and remembers how he and Clinton silently looked at each other for a long moment before a pensive Clinton said, "This is not why you or I got into this business."

For the first three days of the scandal, the traditional news outlets, to their credit, tried to resist the story. In effect, they were telling the public: *Eat your spinach!* But the story attracted such "critical mass," says the *Baltimore Sun*'s Jack Germond, "that it became a spectacle that you could no more ignore than a huge purple elephant standing in a room." An estimated 21 million viewers, for instance, watched Flowers sing "Stand by Your Man" on "A Current Affair," where the reporter thought to ask: "On a scale of one to ten, how was Clinton as a lover?"

The once-marginal tabloid press was now in the saddle, and the establishment press was partly to blame. Not without reason, the public tends to confuse the trash news programs with the ostensibly serious ones. Programs like "Hard Copy" or "Geraldo" are, after all, broadcast on network-owned stations; Diane Sawyer did ask Marla Maples, "Was it the best sex you ever had?" *People* magazine and the newsweeklies have relied on mere hearsay to peek into, say, the marriage of Princess Di and Prince Charles. Docudramas now appear regularly on television, mixing fact and fiction. As the editor of the *Star* had noted gleefully, it was the *Times* and NBC News, not the *Star*, that identified William Kennedy Smith's alleged rape victim.

The editor of the *Star* was being disingenuous, of course. The *Times* and NBC do not regularly descend to tabloid level. But too few reporters bothered to follow *Newsweek*'s lead in probing Flower's credibility. "The press just reported what the *Star* said she said," says Everette Dennis of the Freedom Forum Media Studies Center.

Clinton made a fateful decision to appear with Hillary on "60 Minutes" three days after the revelation—Super Bowl Sunday—which licensed even mainstream reporters to treat the Gennifer Flowers press conference the next day as a momentous event. Hillary Clinton remembers watching CNN that day and thinking, when the regular newscast was interrupted, "I thought it would be a story like we were invading Iraq!"

Hundreds of reporters packed the Jade Room at the Waldorf Astoria to inspect the bleached blonde in the fire-engine-red jacket who sat beside her attorney and the editor of the *Star*, just beneath a large poster reproduction of the *Star*'s front page: MY TWELVE-YEAR AFFAIR WITH BILL CLINTON. Those who watched this event live on CNN, or saw large chunks of it as it led that evening's newscasts on all three networks, had their stereotypes of reporters comically confirmed. They saw Dick Kaplan, editor of the *Star*, suddenly transformed into Mr. Responsibility—"Please, please, please!"—as he tried to calm the hive of photographers pushing forward to get a better shot. They heard the question from Stuttering John of "The Howard Stern Show," who wanted to know: "Gennifer, do you plan to sleep with any other presidential candidates?"

"January 27 ought to be a black day in American journalism," Paul Begala of the Clinton campaign says of the Flowers press conference. "They ought to fly the flag at half-staff at all journalism schools."

But the story was out there, and it did affect Clinton's standing in the polls. Clinton did, stupidly, violate his own stricture not to discuss his marriage. Flowers had been placed on the state payroll, she did have tape-recorded conversations with Clinton, which suggested a certain intimacy, and he did acknowledge that it was his voice when he later apologized to Governor Cuomo for something he had said on the tapes.

Nevertheless, despite the seminars and critiques of sometimes sensationalist and mindless press coverage of prior campaigns, despite the media's desire to focus on issues, ABC executive producer Paul Friedman admits, "With the best of intentions, we got swept up." An astonishing 46 percent of more than four hundred journalists surveyed by the Times Mirror poll in May 1992 concluded that Clinton's character was the most important issue of the contest, and 20 percent said Gennifer Flowers's press conference was the most significant event of the campaign to date.

The Flowers incident was significant not only in itself but also for the less-than-salutary civics lesson it taught: Conflict sells. By February, the Democratic contenders were pummeling one another, and Republican contender Patrick Buchanan was flailing away at Bush. And before this campaign would end, the Bush team would savage Democrats as godless supporters of homosexuality, and Hillary Clinton as favoring the right of all children to sue their parents. Clinton's team would pummel Republicans as crypto-Nazis and boast that campaign aides like James Carville were every bit as mad-dog mean as Lee Atwater or James Baker. The voters, apparently, found all of this "hardball" tedious and off-putting, perhaps sensing that their political system was being hijacked by a bunch of political and media insiders. Throughout the first eighteen primaries, only 30 percentof those who were eligible actually bothered to go to the polls.

Which brings us to Act Two of the 1992 campaign: the citizens' revolt. The date the public first froze the attention of the press and the candidates was February 20, the night H. Ross Perot appeared on CNN's "Larry King Live" and pleged that he would run for president if citizens in the fifty states put him on the ballot. In return, he vowed he would "not sell out to anybody but the American people" (an ironic statement in retrospect).

Perot was treating citizens as participants, not spectators, much as FDR did with his fireside radio chats in the Thirties. Perot had recognized that he could use the power of technology to bypass the networks and the boys on the bus. One day, Perot knew, citizens would be able to vote at home. If he were elected president, Perot said, the first thing he would do is create a direct democracy through electronic town halls.

In the rush of excitement over his scoop, Larry King did not ask how such a direct democracy squared with the concept of representative government embedded in our constitution. Wasn't our system of checks and balances intended to allow elected officials or appointed judges to resist the momentary demands of a majority? Wasn't it meant to frustrate the accretion of power in any one branch of government? Wasn't the Bill of Rights designed to protect individuals from any plebiscite? King did not ask whether, if there were no press filter, candidates might not misstate facts to voters and get away with it, as happened when David Duke appeared on King's show while running for governor of Louisiana and falsely claimed he possessed letters from huge corporations professing eagerness to relocate to Louisiana if he were elected. King did not ask whether an electronic town hall would actually make our sound-bite politics worse, eradicating ambiguity by reducing complicated questions to yes or no responses. He did not ask whether the combination of money and technology might produce a Robocandidate who lives in his own control room.

Despite the tidal wave of support generated by Perot's appearance, reporters continued to intrude with pointless personal questions, believing they were searching for clues to character. ABC's Sam Donaldson put on his sheriff's badge during a March 2 interview with Bob Kerrey on "This Week with David Brinkley." "Did you ever use drugs?" he asked Kerrey.

"No," responded Kerrey.

"Ever use marijuana?"

"No."

"Ever use cocaine?"

"No."

Donaldson thanked Kerrey for his "candid" responses, yet one wishes Kerrey had told him: *None of your business! You're just fishing for a headline. You've done no reporting. You're imitating Joe McCarthy asking, "Are you now or were you ever a communist?"*

Had Kerrey refused to answer, however, a press hive might have formed, buzzing about what he was hiding. *Gotcha!* may be a game, but it's one a candidate can't win. He either gets hurt for being candid or hurt for covering up. Even more ridiculous, candidates were now expected to respond not only to questions about their private lives but also to rumors that could be printed with the excuse that their mere existence had an impact on the campaign. As George Stephanopoulos, Clinton's communications director, told *Vanity Fair*, "It's not enough to dispute the rumor—you have to *disprove* it."

In New York, a local TV reporter made headlines when she asked Clinton whether he had smoked, but not inhaled, marijuana while a student at Oxford. It was the same media mindlessness that prompted *USA Today* to think it had a scoop when it revealed that former tennis star Arthur Ashe has AIDS; the same mindlessness that whipped up a local and national press frenzy about a House banking "scandal" in March, even though no public funds had been stolen; the same conformity one witnesses every time a Clinton or Bush handler stops to chat with a couple of reporters. Within seconds a hive surrounds them, fearful of missing some vital spin from the candidate. Once, after a Clinton/Brown debate in New York, Dan Balz played for a colleague in the NBC lobby a tape of what Clinton had said to reporters that morning about the military draft. Although they could barely hear it, dozens of reporters stuck their tape recorders out without knowing what it was they were listening to.

It wasn't just the mindlessness, it was the impression of arrogance that proved offensive to voters. Bob Kerrey recalls one new Hampshire debate in which some questions asked by moderator Cokie Roberts were designed more, he felt, to snare a good story than to gather useful information. This was particularly so, Kerrey says, when she asked: "As president, would you sign New Jersey's welfare-reform bill?" "That's not a question people care a damn about," says Kerrey. "The question was asked incorrectly. It wasn't asked in a way to allow us to debate welfare. The right question is: 'What's wrong with welfare?' Or: 'Why are so many black children born out of wedlock?' "

By the time Clinton made an appearance on "Donahue" on April 1, it was clear that public sentiment had turned against the media. Donahue prowled the stage with a microphone, asking Clinton: "Have you ever had an affair?" "Have you and Hillary ever separated?" Then the sheepish host had his microphone gently taken by a female member of the audience who exclaimed, "Given the pathetic state of the United States at this point— medicare, education, everything else—I can't believe you spent half an hour of airtime attacking this man's chracter. I'm not even a Bill Clinton supporter, but I think this is ridiculous!"

Donahue was humbled by a ferocious burst of applause. He was smart and gracious enough to allow the show to be taken out of his hands. So he allowed his audience to pose questions, none of which concerned Clinton's marriage.

When Clinton won the New York primary six days later, he had managed to transform his victory over Brown into a victory over the media as well. The entire establishment media structure "is coming unglued," wrote Jonathan Alter in *Washington Monthly*. "We are witnessing the dawning of a new media order."

Although Jerry Brown's 800-number had already netted $5 million from a whopping 250,000 contributors, no one was better at manipulating this new order than Ross Perot. Through Perot's success, the other candidates gleaned a better appreciation of how political communication had become decentralized. Clinton wore bebop sunglasses and played his saxophone on "The Arsenio Hall Show," fielded questions from young viewers on MTV, and, demonstrating that he was not averse to baring his private life if it helped, posed with his wife for the cover of *People* in July. The morning network shows gave over one or two hours for live call-ins between voters and Clinton or Perot, actually enlarging the regular viewing audience. Although Bush pointedly said it was unpresidential to appear on MTV or "Donahue," he did belatedly consent to an interview with Barbara Walters on ABC's "20/20" to "CBS This Morning," and to CNN and public television's "MacNeil/Lehrer Newshour." Vice-President Dan Quayle sat for an hour with public television's Charlie Rose. Quayle also appeared on the daily Rush Limbaugh national call-in radio show, which reaches nearly 12 million listeners.

By the end of July, the usually accessible Clinton had gone a full three weeks without talking to the boys on the bus. "The new communication works," he told me in Dallas. "Real voters don't ask me—as you journalists always do—about the political process and polls. They ask how their lives are going to be changed."

The media was getting the message. By June, ABC executive producer Paul Friedman was telling *Variety*, "I don't know why, but we really missed the amount of frustration and anger out there." He scheduled a week-long series of reports on voter alienation. Erik Sorenson, executive producer of "CBS Evening News," announced in early July that except in special circumstances, all quotes from candidates must be at least thirty seconds. This would allow CBS to meet "what seems to be a real yearning for information" from the voters (the network ended its experiment in September, however, terming it "a success"). By the first week of July, NBC News was running two-minute snippets of the candidates' speeches, an innovation soon adopted by CBS. The idea, Connie Chung explained on air, was to give viewers "an unfiltered sense" of the candidates.

When candidates did go through the traditional press, their gaffes seemed to wound them less. Perot appeared on "Meet the Press" in May, where moderator Timothy J. Russert pressed him to explain exactly how he would balance the federal budget, as he had vaguely promised to do. Perot sounded uninformed and ridiculously accused Russert of trying to trap him. Yet the appearance was deemed a success, because Perot had presumably stood down the media goons. "Anytime there's confrontation, the phone circuits blow away," Perot told *The New Yorker*.

The Perot technique of bypassing reporters was taken a step further in California, where candidates were ignoring voters as well. Congressman

Mel Levine, who sought the Democratic Senate nod, shunned bumper stickers and buttons and shook few hands as he made only about twelve public appearances between March and the June 2 primary. Instead, Levine spent his days "dialing for dollars," with the $5 million he collected earmarked for TV ads. Levine explained to *The New York Times*, "Talking to people is just spinning our wheels." Levine may well be a harbinger of the future of political discourse, but it is by no means certain that this Brave New World has arrived. After all, media criticism of Levine's arrogant campaign led to his defeat.

The media's ability to frame the news, or gather into a powerful pack, was not yet history. In May, when Quayle made a thirty-three-minute speech on the importance of family values, the media latched on to a single sentence in that speech in which he criticized the television show "Murphy Brown." The resulting press tumult prompted President Bush to turn to Canadian prime minister Brian Mulroney, who was visiting the White House, and mock the reporters by whispering to his fellow government head during a press conference, "I told you what the issue was. You thought I was kidding."

President Bush in late July and August would suffer from the media mind-set that he was a loser—as Bill Clinton had in June when the press hive was convinced that he could never overcome the character issue and was persuaded that Perot's presence in the race would devastate the Democrat. As happened to Clinton earlier—or Dukakis in 1988 or Ford in 1976—Bush was overwhelmed by the media's sense that his candidacy was terminal. We had our narrative. One negative story fed another. Then, as happened to Clinton in January, a tabloid story (in this case, in the *New York Post*) alleging a Bush extramarital affair unleashed a new insect attack.

The August front-page headline was triggered by a thirty-one-line footnote in a new book, *The Power House*, by Susan B. Trento. The footnote leans on an interview (by someone else) with a former American arms-control negotiator (now dead) who shared his (non-tape-recorded) impression that vice-president Bush had had a 1986 tryst in Geneva (the source admitted he couldn't be sure). The author also couldn't be sure, which is why she buried this on page 413.

The *Post* seized on the footnote as a welcome excuse to be first in print with a decade-old rumor about which there have been no direct witnesses or facts. The insects were sent into a higher state of excitement by CNN White House reporter Mary Tillotson, who startled Bush at a press conference by asking about the *Post* story. Bush called the question "sleazy."

When Tillotson was telephoned later so she could be asked why a serious journalist would heave such a live grenade, this lion of the fourth estate meekly had her calls intercepted by a CNN spokesman, who said, "Mary's not doing interviews."

By forcing Bush to respond in public, Tillotson had made the rumor a media fact. So, that night Stone Phillips asked Bush on "Dateline NBC" if he had ever had an affair. Bush responded, "You're perpetuating the sleaze by even asking the question." Phillips coolly defended himself, insisting that the question "goes to the point of character."

Phillips never returned my calls either, but an NBC spokeswoman, Tory Beilinson, did say it was "a double standard" for Bush to promote "family values and then say it is sleazy when you are asked about one of those values, which is marital fidelity." A nice rationalization, but not very convincing given the flimsy factual basis for the story. And even if the facts were true, is this value crucial to being a good president? And if it is crucial, don't we have to learn more about all public marriages? Where do we stop?

So how'd the press do overall? "Campaign coverage is better and worse this year," concludes David Maraniss of *The Washington Post*. Through mid-September, the press could boast of having paid more attention to substance and to monitoring the misleading TV ads of the candidates; reporters did probe the implications of, say, the federal deficit. (It was the candidates who ducked the issue.) There was, said Republican operative Roger Ailes before the Republicans began attacking the media, "more evenhanded coverage—they are picking on Democrats as well as Republicans."

The public was treated to some fine reportage. This year no media organization fielded a better first team than *The Washington Post*. "God, do they have a bench," says the *Baltimore Sun's* Germond. Captained by David Broder and Dan Balz, the bench included E.J. Dionne and Thomas B. Edsall, both of whom wrote books that this year were required political reading. Also notable was the sparkling writing or digging of Maraniss, Anne Devroy, David Von Drehle, Maralee Schwartz, and Lloyd Grove.

The feeling was widespread among the candidates' handlers and the scribes that *The Wall Street Journal* also had a good year, largely on the strength of its series on the issues and David Shribman's luminous profiles. Joe Klein of *New York* magazine (now of *Newsweek*) writes with verve and spotted Clinton early, though there was some snickering that he was too much of a booster. Still, "his columns drove the coverage," says Stephanopoulos. Ron Brownstein of the *Los Angeles Times* is singled out for focusing on government and substance and not just on politics, and Tom Rosensteil's media reporting turned heads. Because they weren't afraid to bore viewers, CNN and the "MacNeil/Lehrer Newshour" and C-SPAN often enthralled them; NBC anchor Tom Brokaw fielded the conventions like a Gold Glove shortstop. Charlie Rose did extraordinary interviews with the candidates on public television. *The Boston Globe*, particularly Curtis Wilkie, was dazzling in New Hampshire. John King of the Associated Press and Matthew Cooper of *U.S. News & World Report* were singled out as two younger and much-respected reporters. And even as they tended to disparage the campaign coverage of *The New York Times* as sluggish and slow off the mark, colleagues eagerly awaited Maureen Dowd's vivid profiles.

Another plus this year was the democratization of media; the public received more information from more sources than ever before. "That's an improvement over 1988 and 1984," says David Broder, "when the only thing the public saw from the winning candidate was what the candidate chose to put on the air himself." Of course, as Broder shared his thoughts in the lobby of New York's Intercontinental Hotel during July's Democratic convention, candidate Bill Clinton entered the lobby and was immediately ambushed by shouted questions about some abortion protesters who had tried to hand him a dead fetus that morning. "Governor, what did you think of that fetus?"

In a way, this scene captures the essential weakness of the press hive. As smart and as much fun as the press is to pal around with, its protean nature is often at war with reality's complexity. We offer saturation coverage, say, of the L.A. riots, but not sustained coverage of inner cities. What coverage we get tends to squeeze reality into a Left/Right continuum—either racism or the breakdown of order is the villain. Liberals blame a lack of resources, conservatives an absence of values. In fact, both can be true.

Yet the form of journalism—gimme a headline, gimme a sharp lead, gimme a vivid picture or sound bite, and do it fast—too often shapes the content. "Sometimes I stand in a pack of reporters and I'm embarrassed that my relatives might see me on C-SPAN," says one reporter.

Although we reporters like to think of ourselves as individualists, the process often imposes conformity. We love to harp, say, on the "political impact" of the latest Clinton draft "scandal." We shy away from ambiguity. We too rarely report on each other. We adopt an all-knowing posture, which creates a conventional wisdom that has been so wrong this year—from Bush is a shoo-in (September 1991) to Cuomo is the one (November) to no third-party candidate stands a chance (winter) to Clinton cannot win (spring) to Perot may win (June) to Bush is dead (preconvention) to Baker may save Bush (September).

As in any gang, peer pressure plays a role. "When the press goes after you is when they think you have a chance to be president," observes Clinton strategist James Carville. The press's desire to demonstrate independence sometimes leads us to adopt an in-your-face, antiestablishment pose. Roger Ailes, the master of the negative campaign, who chose to play a much smaller role in Bush's campaign in 1992 than he did in 1988, told me earlier this year that "if my primary time is spent trying to keep a guy from falling down the stairs or saying something stupid because that's going to be a headline, then we are getting nowhere. . . . I can't do it anymore. I mean, it's just bullshit! It becomes a game of trying to swing the pictures and make the other guys make mistakes and you stay on offense. I mean, that's the game. Meanwhile, the political consultants and the media are intertwined in a conspiracy to avoid issues, and the candidates . . . don't have to make a statement that they have to defend later."

Our political coverage is often either personality driven, like a soap opera with an ongoing narrative, or ephemeral, like "the beam of a searchlight," as Walter Lippman once wrote. Following the success of Theodore H. White's pioneering *The Making of the President* series, which began in 1960, the press has been largely preoccupied with drama and personalities. We ask: Who's winning? Or: Is it new? We *should* ask: Is it important? Reporters pursue surface questions for many reasons, not the least being that it is easier to maintain objectivity by reporting who wins or loses than by reporting who's right or wrong. By judging the quality of a candidate's ideas, we risk being seen as partisans, a view that would drain the press of what credibility it retains.

No doubt we will learn from some of the mistakes we made in 1992. But while we learn, so have voters and the candidates. One day history may say of this contest that it represents the end of the power of the boys on the bus and the start of something new.

That something new may be the opportunity to campaign for president in a wholly different, and perhaps dangerous, way. In the future, a candidate could ignore not just the press but his own party, as Bob Kerrey predicted over breakfast the day before his party nominated Bill Clinton. If he were masterminding a campaign, Kerrey says, "I would advise my candidate: 'Don't seek the nomination of the Democratic party, because what you must do to get the nomination denies you the ability to get a consensus.' "

Instead, Kerrey would follow Jerry Brown's example and raise money through an 800-number and then "use the Ross Perot method and get on the ballot" as an independent. He would ignore all the questionnaires from public-spirited organizations and special interests and reporters, all the questions that reduce choices to checklists. Unlike Ross Perot, who was driven from the race partly because of good and tough reporting, a candidate like Senator Bill Bradley—or Bob Kerrey—would be able to hedge on details because he already has a public record to run on. "The reason Ross Perot couldn't get away with it," he says, "is that he didn't know the answers. But if you're Bill Bradley, they know you know the answer." And in the end, such an independent candidate would have a mandate to seek change, a mandate that would compel the Democrats and Republicans to cooperate.

The future? "Another Ross Perot will come along, and the next time he'll have a sense of history and be informed," says Kerrey, leaving the impression he just might want to be that man, the one who finally learns how to bypass the political insiders and the insects of the press.

SUCCESSFUL POLITICAL CANDIDATES learn to deal with the media from the day they run for office until they retire. The grist of the reporter's mill is information—and sometimes misinformation. Reporters follow political candidates like hawks stalking their prey, hoping that in one fell swoop they will be able to capture information that will command a front-page headline or a spot on the nightly television news. At least that is the view of the press held by many politicians.

The most intense press attention focuses, understandably, on presidential politics, on both running and governing.

Before Richard Nixon boarded over the indoor White House pool to make a press-briefing room, presidential aides going to their offices in the West Wing walked through a press lounge. There, one White House aide told the author, the "piranha" eagerly waited to devour White House staffers. In the paranoiac atmosphere that so frequently pervades politics, the press is always the enemy unless it is controlled. Every president in the modern era, from Franklin D. Roosevelt to Ronald Reagan, has attempted to manage the news. William Safire defines managed news as "information generated and distributed by the government in such a way as to give government interest priority over candor."[1]

The media are, to use the phrase of Douglass Cater, the fourth branch of the government.[2] The press, which now includes the electronic as well as the print media, has appointed itself guardian of the public interest. Although many members of the press have a cozy relationship with public officials, upon whom they depend for valuable information, the theory of the press that is taught in journalism schools requires reporters to distance themselves personally from the subjects of their stories. The adversary relationship between investigative reporters and the government enables a reporter to ferret out the facts no matter how unpleasant they may be.

Although the Washington press includes reporters like Bob Woodward and Carl Bernstein, whose investigations of the Nixon White House's coverup of the break-in at the Democratic National Headquarters in the Watergate office complex led to impeachment proceedings against the president and to his resignation, these reporters are exceptions and not the rule. Understandably, the seductive Washington environment, in which power and status mean everything, has co-opted many. The press has become part of the Washington establishment because it has learned to play the game of power politics itself. The Gridiron Club, an old and exclusive organization of newspaper people, symbolizes the press elite. Annually it invites members of the political establishment to join it in a fun-filled session of humor and satire. The spirit of camaraderie that prevails at such a gathering can be appreciated by those on the inside. President and Mrs. Reagan were the highlights of the club's meeting in 1982, as the first lady skillfully performed a skit that satirized the prevailing press view of her activities.

[1]William Safire, *Safire's Political Dictionary* (New York: Random House, 1978), p. 397.

[2]Douglass Cater, *The Fourth Branch of the Government* (Boston: Houghton Miflin, 1959).

119

The Gridiron Club may roast politicians, but its members recognize that the press and the politicians are in the same broader club of the politically powerful. Washington reporters recognize that to be at the top of the newspaper profession they must have access to the top of the political world. The linkage between success and power often softens the adversary stance of the press.

Washington's political centers of power recognize that the press is an important fourth branch of the government. Presidents, members of Congress, and even Supreme Court justices know that managing the news will buttress their power and may even be a key to survival. Presidents, especially during their first few years in office, feel besieged by a press that they consider hostile and unfair. Even before he became president,

John F. Kennedy went out of his way to warn an aide about the press. "Always remember that their interests and ours ultimately conflict."[3]

Kennedy cultivated political reporters, and his good press relations not only helped him to win the presidential election in 1960 but also buttressed his presidency. Richard Nixon blamed his 1960 defeat on an unfair press, an attitude that was intensified after he lost his race for the California governorship in 1963. Nixon understandably put managing the news at the top of his agenda when he became president.

This desire to manage the news gives, in the view of Jimmy Carter's press secretary Jody Powell in the following selection, the White House the right to lie when national security is at stake.

14   Jody Powell THE RIGHT TO LIE

Since the day the first reporter asked the first tough question of a government official, there has been an ongoing debate about whether government has the right to lie.

The debate took on its present form one day in 1963, when then Pentagon spokesman Arthur Sylvester, for reasons known only to himself, responded to the question officially and honestly. "Yes," he said, "under certain circumstances I think government does have the right to lie."

The resulting furor has made every sitting press secretary and senior government official leery of the question from that day since. Like all my predecessors, I was always careful not to give a direct response. It was one of

"The Right to Lie," from *The Other Side of the Story*, by Jody Powell, William Morrow & Company, New York, 1984. Copyright © 1984 by Jody Powell. By permission of William Morrow & Company, Inc.

[3]William Safire, *Safire's Political Dictionary*, p. 397.

those questions for which you prepare and keep on file a standard evasion. But Sylvester, of course, was right. In certain circumstances, government has not only the right but a positive obligation to lie. For me, that right-obligation flows directly from two other principles:

First, that government has a legitimate right to secrecy in certain matters because the welfare of the nation requires it. In other cases, individuals, even public figures, have a certain right to privacy because common decency demands it.

Secondly, the press has a right to print what it knows within very broad limits, without prior restraint, because the survival of democratic government depends on it.

Those two principles are often in conflict. Fortunately, the confrontation is not usually irreconcilable. Questions can be evaded. Answers can be devised that may mislead, but do not directly misrepresent. A "no comment" can sometimes be used without its being taken as a confirmation. Or the reporter can be sworn to secrecy himself and told why it is that certain information would be terribly damaging if published.

That is usually the case, but not always. Occasionally, the conflict is so sharp and the matter involved so important that there is no way to slide off the point. There is simply no answer that is both true and responsible. In such cases, the only decent thing to do is to lie and, I would argue, to make it the most convincing lie you can devise.

In my four years in the White House, I was only faced with that type of situation twice. The first involved a question from a so-called reporter who was noted for trading in gossip and personal scandal, and who worked for a publication that had an even worse reputation in that regard.

The question involved the personal life of a colleague and that of his family. To have responded with what I believed to be the truth would have resulted in great pain and embarrassment for a number of perfectly innocent people. Beyond that, I could see no reason why the matter should be of public interest.

I had little doubt that an evasion or "no comment" would be taken as more than adequate confirmation by this particular writer, and no doubt whatsoever that there was no hope of successfully appealing to a sense of compassion and fair play. So I lied.

I did not just deny the allegation, but went to some trouble to construct a convincing argument as to what I suspected to be the case. Apparently, it worked, probably because others who were asked responded in much the same way I did. In any case, the story never appeared in print anywhere that I know of.

I have absolutely no regrets for what I did, and can say without hesitation that I would do the same thing again if similar circumstances arose. Quite simply, it seems to me that to the extent journalism insists upon the right to probe into matters that can destroy families and ruin careers, but which in no way involve a breach of public trust, it must also grant the right to those who become targets to defend themselves by the only means available.

Moreover, there will inevitably be a disputed area between journalists and public figures over what is, and what is not, a legitimate matter of public interest. In some cases, the answer may not be clear, even to the most unbiased observer, except in retrospect. And it hardly needs to be said that a *post hoc* decision that a personal matter should have remained private is of absolutely no benefit to those who have been hurt by its publication.

The other situation in which I believed, and still believe, that I had an obligation to lie occurred in April of 1980.

Following the collapse of the first of two attempts to negotiate an agreement with the Iranian government to secure the release of our hostages, because those nominally in positions of authority either could not or would not live up to their promises, the president began to look more seriously at a military rescue operation.

He had given orders for work to begin on such an option as soon as the hostages were seized. At that time, there seemed to be no feasible way to go about it with a decent chance of success. In the intervening months, as the Pentagon studied, planned, and trained, and as we learned more about the situation in the embassy compound through intelligence operations and the news media, the chances for a successful attempt began to increase.

Although I knew the work was being done, I knew nothing about its specifics, and indeed did not want to know, until March 22, 1980. In a meeting at Camp David to review our options following the disintegration of the first agreement, Secretary of Defense Brown and Joint Chiefs of Staff Chairman General David Jones presented a full briefing on their plans for a rescue operation.

It was impressive, both because of the work that had gone into it and the intelligence that we had managed to gather, and because the detailed consideration of such an option inevitably has a powerfully sobering effect on anyone with a say in whether or not it will be implemented.

Still, no one seemed to feel that this was the correct choice at the time. There were some questions raised about whether some aspects of what was necessarily a complex plan could not be simplified. More important in the decision not to go ahead then was the willingness, although reluctant, to give diplomacy one last chance. No one doubted that there would be American casualties, even in a successful operation. One Israeli soldier and three hostages had been killed at Entebbe, and the problems that faced our planners, and would face the strike force, were many times more difficult than anything the Israelis had confronted. There had also been messages from our intermediaries, and indirectly from Iranian officials, almost begging for a chance to put the negotiated agreement back on track.

Even though no one argued that day that we should choose the rescue option, I left the meeting feeling that we were heading down a road that would soon bring us to that choice unless the Iranians suddenly came to their senses. Despite my agreement with the decision to try the diplomatic approach again, I had to admit to myself that the odds seemed to be against the Iranians' implementing the agreement they had already reneged on once.

On the morning of April 11, shortly after that second diplomatic effort had indeed collapsed, the president called me into his office a few minutes before the regular Friday morning foreign-policy breakfast was to begin. During most of the administration, I had not attended these breakfasts on a regular basis. When the president felt that the agenda required my presence, he would let me know. Occasionally, I would ask to be included if I had a point I wanted to raise, or if I felt the need to listen to the discussion on a particular topic.

Once the hostage crisis began, however, I asked to attend on a regular basis, so that I could keep abreast of the latest thinking by the decision makers, as well as the often fast-breaking events. The president readily agreed. So I was somewhat surprised that morning when he said that he wanted to talk to me about whether I should attend the breakfast.

Then he explained that one of the topics, not included on the written agenda, was the rescue mission. I could tell, or thought I could, by his tone of voice and expression that this had now become a serious option for him.

Was this something I would rather not know about? the president asked. Would it make my job easier if down the road I could honestly claim to have had no knowledge of this option?

I replied that I had given some thought to the matter since the Camp David session. It seemed to me that if he decided to go ahead with the rescue option, we would need an aggressive effort to protect its secrecy. That might involve purposely misleading or even lying to the press. If it did, I was the person to do it. And if I did it, I wanted to have the information necessary to make my effort successful. Since I was also being asked about the Iran crisis almost every day, I said, there was a chance that I might inadvertently compromise the mission unless I knew exactly what activities were the most sensitive.

The president said he had expected that would be my response, and he agreed with it, but he had wanted to hear it from me.

Then he added with a hint of a smile, "If you have to lie to the press, I may have to fire you when this is all over, you know. I'm not sure I can have a press secretary who won't tell the truth to the press."

"That," I said, "would be doing me a real favor."

"And an even bigger one for the country," said the president with what I hoped was a smile, as he turned to walk to the Cabinet room, where his foreign policy team was waiting.

The briefing, on which I took no notes, was much the same as the earlier session at Camp David. Maps and charts were positioned on an easel and occasionally spread on the table for closer examination. The questions and suggestions from three weeks earlier had been taken into account, and the military planners had come up with a few new wrinkles on their own.

By the time it was over, I sensed that the men around the table, including the president, were leaning strongly toward ordering the plan to be implemented. The comments that followed confirmed my hunch. I added my endorsement, and emphasized again my feeling that we would need to give some thought to cover stories and an aggressive effort to protect the secrecy of the mission if the president decided to go ahead.

The only partial demurral came from Deputy Secretary of State Warren Christopher. Although he was inclined to recommend that the president order the mission, as he made clear later, he did not know how Secretary of State Vance (who was taking a brief and well-earned vacation) would react and did not feel that he should express a personal opinion.

The president said he was tentatively inclined to proceed with the mission, but would defer a final decision until he had discussed it with Vance.

As we got up to leave the room, I found myself standing next to Harold Brown. "Mr. Secretary," I said, "the president is going to go with this thing, I can sense it. If we can bring our people out of there, it will do more good for this country than anything that has happened in twenty years."

"Yes," said Brown, "and if we fail, that will be the end of the Carter presidency."

"Be we really don't have much choice, do we?"

The Secretary shook his head no as we walked out the door.

A moment later, Helen Thomas, of UPI, walked around the corner from the press room on the way to my office.

"Big meeting, huh?" she called down the short corridor. "You guys decide to nuke 'em?"

Brown and I both nodded yes, and I offered to let Helen and her colleagues know in plenty of time to be on the scene when the warheads struck.

If she only knew, I thought.

In fact, one of the problems we faced, once the president made his final decision four days later, was the number of press people in Teheran. As part of his objections, Cyrus Vance had warned that the Iranians might seize some of the several hundred Americans still in Teheran, thus leaving us with more hostages to worry about, even if the mission was a success. A fair number of this group were journalists.

I told the president that I saw no way for us to make the reporters come home, short of telling the news organizations what was about to happen, and that was clearly out of the question. Still, he felt an obligation to try. The president's first inclination was to order them home. I argued against this. There was no way to enforce the order, and I suspected that the attempt would so enrage the news executives that they would insist on keeping people there who might have been planning to come back anyway.

"Some of them are so ornery that they might just send an extra correspondent over to prove they can do it," I said.

In the end, we decided to use the increasingly volatile situation in Iran as an excuse to try to get journalists and other Americans to come home.

At a news conference on April 17, the president announced that he was prohibiting all financial transactions between Iranians and Americans and barring all imports from Iran. Then he stated that "to protect American citizens," he was banning all travel to Iran.

These steps, he said, would "not *now* be used to interfere with the right of the press to gather news."

"However," he continued, speaking slowly and precisely, "it is my responsibility and my obligation, given the situation in Iran, to call on American journalists and newsgathering organizations to minimize, as severely as possible, their presence and their activities in Iran."

As we had feared, the only effect was to provoke angry calls, particularly from the networks. After listening to Washington bureau chiefs and presidents of news divisions berate us for trying to repeal the First Amendment and stifle news coverage for political ends, I finally lost my temper with Sandy Socolow of CBS.

"Look Sandy," I said, "the president told you what he thinks you ought to do, and I have nothing to add to it. I warned him that you people would get on a high horse, but he wanted to do it anyway. I personally don't give a good goddamn what you people do. If I had my way, I'd ask the fucking Ayatollah to keep fifty reporters and give us our diplomats back. Then you people who have all the answers could figure out how to get them out."

As soon as I hung up the phone, I regretted having lost my temper. Not because I feared that I had hurt Socolow's feelings—he is not an overly sensitive fellow—but because I was worried that my angry response might have implied that something dramatic was about to happen. I had come that close to saying that he would have to accept the consequences for what happened if he ignored the president's warning, but had caught myself in time. I vowed to keep my temper in check, at least until this operation was complete.

The president's statement of April 17, in addition to being a futile attempt to get Americans out of Teheran, also fit into our cover story. By announcing additional sanctions, he implied that there would be a period of time during which we would wait and see if they would work before any other actions were taken. I, and others who knew what was actually afoot, strengthened this impression with background briefings.

We also suggested that if we were forced to consider any sort of military option, it would be something like a blockade or mining of harbors. This was the cover story we had devised for the military movements necessary to prepare for the rescue mission. On several occasions I speculated with reporters off the record about the relative merits of a blockade as opposed to mining.

We had, in fact, ruled out both of these options. They were unlikely to force the Iranians to yield, and once attempted would have to be followed up by an escalation of military force if no response was forthcoming. We would thus be starting down a road the end of which no one could see. We also believed that once any sort of military move was made, the Iranians as part of any general reaction might tighten security around the embassy, which we knew to be extremely lax, or disperse the hostages, thus denying us the rescue option.

The problems associated with the blockade were much the same as those associated with bombing power stations or other valuable targets in Iran— ideas that were being advanced by several columnists and commentators. I had suggested to the president earlier that what he ought to do was "bomb the hell out of every dam and power station in Iran. Let the Ayatollah shoot two hostages and call on the Russians for help, then turn the whole thing over to Agronsky and Company to handle."

His response is not printable.

By the week of April 20 it was becoming clear that our cover story was working too well. All the talk about mining and blockades was making some people nervous and everyone curious. That presented a problem. We did not want anyone, even on the White House staff, snooping around in an effort to find out what was going on. They just might stumble on something. In addition, once the staff begins to talk a great deal about anything, it is only a short time before the press gets interested, too.

But this also presented us with an opportunity to reinforce our cover story. On Tuesday, April 22, little more than forty-eight hours before the Delta Team would enter Iranian air space, Hamilton called a staff meeting to address the concerns that were buzzing about the staff. He assured them all that we had no plans, at the moment, for mining or blockading. When asked about a rescue mission, he lied.

As soon as I heard what had taken place, I began to prepare for a press call. It came less than ninety minutes after the meeting ended. Jack Nelson, bureau chief of the *Los Angeles Times*, wanted to talk to me about something he had heard from a "pretty interesting staff meeting you people had this morning." I said I had not been there but would check with Hamilton.

I then called Hamilton to tell him what I was about to do. I hated to do it to Nelson, who was one of the more decent journalists that I had gotten to know since coming to Washington, and one who would become a good friend once the administration was over. But I did not feel that I had any choice. I knew what he wanted to talk about. It was an opportunity to reinforce the web of deception we had constructed to protect the rescue mission.

When I called Nelson back, he said he had heard that some staffers had expressed concern that we were about to take some action that might "involve us in a war." I confirmed this report and repeated Hamilton's assurances that we were planning no military action whatsoever, and certainly nothing like a rescue mission.

Later that day, Nelson came by my office to continue our discussion. Toward the end of that conversation, he asked, "You people really aren't thinking about doing anything drastic like launching a rescue mission, are you?"

This was the moment of truth, or, more accurately, of deception. Up to this point, I had only repeated false statements made by others, an admittedly fine distinction, but a distinction nevertheless. Now I was faced with a direct question. With a swallow that I hoped was not noticeable, I began to recite all the reasons why a rescue operation would not make any sense. They were familiar because they were exactly the ones that it had taken four months to figure out how to overcome.

"If and when we are forced to move militarily, I suspect it will be something like a blockade," I said, "but that decision is a step or two down the road."

I made a mental note to be sure to call Jack and apologize once the operation was completed, hoping he would understand.

The result was a story in the *Los Angeles Times* reporting Hamilton's assurances to the staff that no military action was in the offing, and that a rescue operation was still considered to be impractical.

When I read it the next day, I remember hoping that some Iranian student at Berkeley had enough loyalty to the Ayatollah to phone it in to Teheran.

Two days later the hostage rescue attempt ended in disaster. Nelson, to his credit, seemed to understand what I had done, even though he could not explicitly condone it. Most other reporters reacted in similar fashion when the story of my deception came out. A few even stopped by to say privately that they would have done the same thing in my position. A few others were quoted, anonymously, as saying that I had destroyed my credibility and ought to resign.

The issue quickly faded as we dealt with the spectacle of Iranian leaders boasting over the bodies of American servicemen, the tortured but eventually successful efforts to secure their return, and the ceremonies honoring their courage and dedication to duty.

There were a few attempts to exploit the situation for political purposes: Stories were planted with reporters that the mission had been discovered by the Soviets and a call from Brezhnev had brought about the cancellation, and that the military commanders had wanted to go ahead after the loss of three helicopters but the president had lost his nerve and ordered them to turn back. These attempts at disinformation were largely unsuccessful. Later, . . . those responsible for these efforts were able to find journalists whose indifference or incompetence made them useful political tools.

In October of 1983, . . . controversy flared again between the White House and the press over the relative rights and responsibilities of the two institutions. The occasion was the American invasion of Grenada, and there were several reasonably separate issues involved.

The first was the same one that I had dealt with three and a half years prior: the right of government to lie. On the afternoon before American forces landed in Grenada, CBS White House correspondent Bill Plante learned from a reliable source that an invasion would take place at sunrise the next morning. He checked with the White House Press Office and got a flat denial. "Preposterous," said spokesman Larry Speakes. Other reporters got the same response from other government officials.

The decision by the Reagan administration to deceive journalists rather than risk the possibility that the invasion plans would be disclosed seemed to me to be eminently defensible.

When I asked Plante later what he would have done if the White House had confirmed the invasion plans, his response was "I don't know; we would have tried to find some way to use what we knew without endangering the operation."

That in itself would seem to confirm the wisdom of the White House judgment. You cannot expect government to leave such questions in the hands of the fourth estate. The consequences of an error are too severe.

Moreover, given the extent of eavesdropping capabilities in Washington, it would be an unacceptable risk to have Mr. Plante and others at CBS chatting at some length over open telephone lines about how they would use the information. By the time their decision was made it most likely would be moot.

Some journalists were willing to agree privately that this situation was one of those in which there was no other choice but to lie. Most, however, were unwilling to endorse publicly the idea that lying could be condoned under any circumstances, feeling that government does enough lying as it is without any encouragement from them.

They make the very valid point that once you step away from the categorical, there is no easily discernible place to draw the line.

Still the essential dilemma remains. What about those situations where an evasion simply will not work, where a "no comment" is almost certain to be taken as a confirmation? If, at the same time, the information to be protected is of sufficient importance, if lives are at stake for example, a lie becomes in my estimation the lesser evil of the choices available. It is ludicrous to argue that soldiers may be sent off to fight and die, but a spokesman may not, under any circumstances, be asked to lie to make sure that the casualties are fewer and not in vain.

Churchill made the point with his usual flair in 1943. "In wartime," he said, "truth is so precious that she should be attended by a bodyguard of lies."

Unfortunately, once one steps onto the slippery slope of relativism, firm footing cannot be established, even on the basis of "wartime" or "lives at stake." There are other dilemmas that can and do arise, where calculated deception might be appropriate.

Although I never faced it personally, the protection of an important intelligence source or method, even in peacetime, might be one.

And what about the protection of an important diplomatic initiative? I almost faced such a situation at Camp David when reports of bad blood between Sadat and Begin arose and when there were leaks about Sadat's threat to break off the talks. . . . I was able to deal with those problems without telling a bald-face lie, but that was mostly a matter of luck.

In the midst of the Grenada controversy, a columnist revealed that the premature publication by Jack Anderson of a story about Henry Kissinger's secret diplomatic initiatives had damaged, although not fatally, the movement toward normalization of relations with China. That initiative became arguably the most significant strategic event since the Second World War. Would lying have been appropriate in an effort to keep it on track?

In the early months of the Carter administration the *Washington Post* published accounts of secret payments through the CIA to King Hussein of Jordan. The story appeared on the day that Secretary of State Vance arrived in Aman to discuss a Middle East peace initiative with Hussein. Needless to say, the result was a less than positive environment for the talks.

In that case, we had chosen to be candid with the *Post* and appeal to their sense of responsibility. From our point of view the effort was a failure. Although we had not asked them not to publish the story, feeling that such a request would be futile, we had requested a delay. When it came out at the most unfortunate of all possible times, we felt the *Post* was guilty of bad faith. The *Post* maintained that the timing was a result of a misunderstanding.

In any case, the question remains. In our judgment the *Post* had enough information to go with the story whatever we said. But what if we had concluded that it was possible to kill the story with a lie, would we have been justified in doing so?

To take another step down the slope, what degree of deception would be acceptable from a Justice Department official trying to protect the rights of an innocent person whose name had cropped up in an investigation?

Or what about a spokesman at Treasury attempting to avoid the premature disclosure of information on a financial decision that could lead to severe damage to innocent parties and great profits for those in a position to take advantage of the leak?

The problem becomes, as noted above, where precisely to draw the line. There is no convenient place. About the best one can do is to argue that it must be drawn very tightly, for practical as well as moral considerations. Distinctions may be difficult at the margins, but we can all tell the difference between mountains and molehills. If government does have the right to lie in certain situations, that right is as precious as the truth it attends. It must not be squandered on matters of less than overriding importance.

Which brings us to another issue in the Grenada controversy. Many correspondents said that the exchange between Speakes and CBS was not the cause but the catalyst for their outrage. They charged that the administration had repeatedly lied to them on matters that were in no way vital to national security or the protection of lives. They listed examples that ranged from the dates of resignations to travel plans to attempts to square the facts with some off-the-cuff presidential remark.

They also pointed to a history of efforts to curtail the flow of information from the screening of calls to White House officials from reporters by the communications and press offices to proposals for the review of anything written by thousands of government officials after they leave office. (At this writing, Congress had wisely blocked this last absurdity, but the administration has vowed not to give up).

That attitude was not unanimous, but it was clearly shared by a large number of White House correspondents. And that is a dangerous set of circumstances for the administration and potentially for the nation. The danger for the administration is that it will find itself lacking credibility across the board, that no explanation will be accepted at face value and every action will be subject to the most unflattering interpretation.

For the nation, the danger lies in the fact that an administration that is generally believed to be dishonest will not command the respect necessary to protect legitimate secrets. There are many cases in which truths less vital than the timing and objective of military operations are protected by successful appeals to reporters not to publish. The full and exact reasons for such requests cannot always be disclosed, because they too may be quite sensitive. Needless to say, such appeals—which amount to a request to "trust me"—can only be effective in a climate of mutual trust.

To the extent that this climate was placed in jeopardy following the Grenada controversy, the problem was not primarily a conflict over government's right to lie about issues of ultimate importance, but a perceived pattern of deception solely for the sake of convenience—of lies designed to protect and promote nothing more precious than someone's political backside.

Even during the Grenada operation, there were lies from the government that were difficult to justify by any reasonable standard. Claims that coverage was curtailed, after the invasion had begun, because of concern for the safety of reporters were poppycock. Even experienced spokesmen had a hard time making that argument with a straight face.

Similarly, attempts to blame the decision to restrict coverage on "military commanders" were deceptive and cowardly and dangerous. There is no doubt that many uniformed military officers hold the press in less than great esteem or that the restricted coverage was completely in line with their preferences. But that is not the point. Such decisions are always subject to White House review. And they were repeatedly brought to the attention of White House officials. If the preferences of the military commanders were honored, it was because the president and his men agreed with them.

This refusal to accept responsibility for one's own actions was dangerous in this case because it served to exacerbate tensions between the military and the fourth estate, to heighten mutual distrust on both sides. These tensions are already high enough and that problem is going to be with us for the indefinite future. Already it works against responsible and accurate reporting of national security issues. It also promotes an unreasoning distrust of all things military in our society. There is, in my view, no excuse for an administration's hiding behind the armed forces simply to avoid facing ticklish questions.

A related issue has to do with how much the White House press secretary should be told in situations such as this. It very quickly became clear in this particular case that the press secretary and the press office had been kept in the dark until the invasion was under way. Mr. Speakes and his people were not intentionally lying themselves when they denied the reports from Plante and other newsmen; they were merely passing on what they had been told by members of the National Security Council staff.

This quickly became a bone of contention within the White House. Mr. Speakes and his people were none too happy about the way they had been treated. One deputy resigned as a result. However, more senior White House officials declared themselves well pleased with the procedure and stated that they would handle things the same way if similar situations arose in the future.

Mr. Speakes made it clear that if a lie was required and he was to be sent out to tell it, he wanted to know what was at stake. And he was exactly right. Keeping the press secretary in the dark can create serious problems.

First, it inevitably erodes the press secretary's effectiveness. It costs him in prestige and status, factors that may mean more than they should in Washington, but still cannot be ignored. The press secretary's job is tough enough as it is; he deserves every break his colleagues can give him. Putting the guy whose business is information in a position that makes him appear to be uninformed, out of touch, and not trusted makes no sense over the long haul.

Beyond that, if a secret is worth lying about to protect, it makes sense to come up with the most effective lie possible. Most sensitive operations are accompanied by a cover story, designed to provide an innocent explanation for bits and pieces that might leak out. Since the first group of people that such a story must convince is the press, having the press secretary involved in designing the story is not a bad idea. He more than anyone else is likely to know what will be convincing and what will not.

Furthermore, the use of the story, if it ever becomes necessary, is likely to be more effective if the person who puts it out knows exactly what he is trying to do. Dealing with the press, particularly in ticklish situations, is very much an art. You cannot treat the press secretary like a robot and then expect him to perform like an artist.

Another danger in keeping the press secretary uninformed comes from the way in which a press office operates. When a new question arises or an issue looks like it is going to get hot, the press office begins to function very much like a news organization. Deputy and assistant and deputy assistant press secretaries immediately get to work calling all over the government to try to find out what is really going on and where it may lead.

As information is gathered, it is often passed on to the reporter who has made the query in bits and pieces as part of a continuing exchange of information and ideas. Needless to say, if there is something highly sensitive that has to be protected, the press secretary needs to know about it. Otherwise, this process could stumble into and lead to the uncovering of information that should be kept secret.

In matters large and small, keeping the press secretary in the dark is risky business. If he cannot be trusted with sensitive information, he should be replaced. Failing that, he ought to be given the information he needs to do his job effectively.

Having said all that, however, I suspect that the most important lesson from this episode is to be found in the fact that the press was a clear loser in its fight with the administration over Grenada. It lost in the court in which such matters will eventually be decided—the court of public opinion. In the immediate aftermath of Grenada it was sometimes difficult to tell which the American people enjoyed more, seeing the president kick hell out of the Cubans or the press.

And the reasons the fourth estate lost were to a large extent its own fault.

The strength of the public reaction in favor of the administration's policy of denying access to the press was a shock to many Washington journalists. The more thoughtful were concerned as well as surprised.

It is true that the press is particularly vulnerable among our major institutions because it is so often the bearer of sad tidings, the forum for criticism of ideas, individuals, and institutions that Americans hold dear. It is also true, as journalists are fond of pointing out, that their job is not to win popularity contests. But the vocal and sometimes vicious public reaction against the press in the wake of Grenada was more than just some sort of "shoot the messenger" syndrome.

In part it sprang from the way the fourth estate handled the terrorist bombing of our marine headquarters in Beirut, which occurred just prior to the Grenada operation. The behavior of some news organizations was not the sort that would inspire public confidence in their judgment or self-restraint.

There was, for example, the repugnant spectacle of CBS camped ghoulishly at the home of parents awaiting word on the fate of their marine son in Beirut. And they hit the jackpot. The boy was dead. So they got to film the arrival of the casualty officer and the chaplain bringing the tragic news to the parents.

The tragic scene, for which every standard of good taste and decency demanded privacy, was then offered up to satisfy the voyeurism of the worst segments of the American television audience and the demands for the higher ratings that are believed, with some justification, to come with sensationalism.

Nor was this sort of gross insensitivity confined to television. A few days after the Beirut bombing, readers of the *Washington Post* were treated to the incredibly insensitive comments of a *Newsweek* executive describing at some length what a wonderful thing the tragedy was for his magazine: "We are exhilarated by this. It's the sort of thing *Newsweek* does best—react to a big story in a big way. We'll be pulling out all the stops. . . . one hell of a story . . . pursuing a variety of angles . . . expect lot of competition, it's the biggest story of the year."

If the tasteless coverage of the Beirut tragedy was a factor in the public's reaction to Grenada, it was by no means the whole of it. The attitudes reflected did not develop over a few days or weeks.

If the government has in this and other instances been guilty of excess in the exercise of what I believe to be its legitimate right to mislead and even deceive on matters of vital import, the fourth estate has also been guilty of excess in its cavalier insistence on the right to do as it pleases with little regard for good judgment, good taste, or the consequences of its actions—and the American people know it.

One consequence of the information explosion has been that more and more Americans have had the opportunity to see news coverage of incidents they knew something about. And they have come away disillusioned, and sometimes angry, because of the wide gap that too often existed between what they knew to be the case and what was reported.

And if they were foolish enough to try to set the record straight by appealing for a correction, they also ran head on into that determination never to admit a mistake, much less do anything about it.

The public's reaction to Grenada ought to be a danger signal for journalism. The question . . . is how the fourth estate will react. The greatest danger is that the reaction will be defensive, a renewed determination to pretend that nothing is wrong except the shortsightedness and lack of sophistication of the American public.

THE PRESIDENCY

Chapter
Four

The administrations of Lyndon B. Johnson and Richard M. Nixon changed the perspective of many Americans about the presidency. In spite of the bitter partisanship that precedes presidential elections, the office of the presidency before Lyndon B. Johnson had always been treated with great reverence, which often extended to the person who occupied the White House. This is not to suggest by any means that presidents had always been extolled for their virtues and placed on a kingly throne, for anyone familiar with American history knows that there have always been personal attacks on presidents by a wide assortment of critics. And these presidential critics were not above calling their prey "mentally unbalanced." Nevertheless, most presidential biographies concentrated on the heroic and not the neurotic qualities of their subjects. An eloquent illustration of this is Carl Sandburg's biographical volumes on Abraham Lincoln as well as more recent books on presidents by such authors as James David Barber or Doris Kearns, not to mention Bob Woodward and Carl Bernstein, whose work reveals the major differences between past and present approaches to assessing presidents.[1]

Although the administration of Lyndon B. Johnson seemed rational to his supporters, other persons, particularly critics of the Vietnam War, believed the president to have relentlessly, single-mindedly, and more importantly *irrationally* embarked on a highly destructive policy. David Halberstam began an extensive study of the history of the war to determine how the United States became involved. His best-selling book *The Best and the Brightest*, published in 1972, emphasized the role of personalities, not so much of the president himself as of his top-level advisers, in making the critical decisions committing the country to the war.[2] In the same year, political scientist James David Barber published his ground-breaking book *The Presidential Character*, in which he made personality profiles of a variety of presidents to assess the effect of presidential character on performance. With the publication of Barber's book, psychopolitics came of age.

James Barber attempted a complex classification of different character types and came to the conclusion that the best presidents were what he termed "active-positive." The active-positive president is achievement-oriented and productive and has well-defined goals. He is rational, "using his brain to move

[1]See James David Barber, *The Presidential Character* (Englewood Cliffs, N.J.: Prentice-Hall, 1972); Doris Kearns, *Lyndon Johnson and the American Dream* (New York: Harper & Row, 1976); Bob Woodward and Carl Bernstein, *The Final Days* (New York: Simon & Schuster, 1976).

[2]David Halberstam, *The Best and the Brightest* (New York: Random House, 1972).

his feet." Above all, he is flexible; he can change his goals and methods as he perceives reasons for altering his course of action. He has a sense of humor about the world and, more importantly, about himself. John F. Kennedy was, according to Barber, an ideal active-positive president.

Perhaps even more significant than the active-positive presidents are the "active-negative" presidents. These are the presidents that may do irreparable damage, according to Barber. They have a compulsive need to work because of personal problems and a misguided "Puritan ethic." They are ambitious and power-hungry but lack goals beyond that of rising to power. They tend to be politically amoral, as was Richard Nixon, but may take on false and misleading goals, such as making the world safe for democracy, as did Woodrow Wilson. The great energy of the active-negative type is frequently directed in irrational ways, and once set on a course of action the active-negative president surrounds himself with yes-men in order to fortify him in confrontation with the hostile world outside. What is suggested by Barber's portraits of various active-negative presidents, including Richard Nixon, when taken in conjunction with the portrait of President Nixon in Bob Woodward and Carl Bernstein's *Final Days*, is truly frightening, Because of the enormous power that presidents possess, it is especially important to examine their characters and styles, which set the tone of presidential administrations.

The selections in this chapter illustrate various dimensions of presidential personality and, what is frequently overlooked, the way in which the personalities and styles of the president's staff can influence the political process.

I N THE FOLLOWING SELECTION, political scientist James David Barber presents this thesis: The total character of the person who occupies the White House is the determinant of presidential performance. "The presidency," he states, "is much more than an institution." It is not only the focus of the emotional involvement of most people in politics but also is occupied by a person whose emotions inevitably affect his or her conduct. How presidents are able to come to grips with their feelings and emotions often shapes their orientation toward issues and the way in which they make decisions. Particularly important is the way in which presidents cope with their staffs in an era when the presidency is more institutional than personal. The president's character and style remain the most important influence upon operations in the White House.

15 James David Barber
PRESIDENTIAL CHARACTER, STYLE, AND PERFORMANCE

When a citizen votes for a presidential candidate he makes, in effect, a prediction. He chooses from among the contenders the one he thinks (or feels, or guesses) would be the best president. He operates in a situation of immense uncertainty. If he has a long voting history, he can recall time and time again when he guessed wrong. He listens to the commentators, the politicians, and his friends, then adds it all up in some rough way to produce his prediction and his vote. Earlier in the game, his anticipations have been taken into account, either directly in the polls and primaries or indirectly in the minds of politicians who want to nominate someone he will like. But he must choose in the midst of a cloud of confusion, a rain of phony advertising, a storm of sermons, a hail of complex issues, a fog of charisma and boredom, and a thunder of accusation and defense. In the face of this chaos, a great many citizens fall back on the past, vote their old allegiances, and let it go at that. Nevertheless, the citizen's vote says that on balance he [or she] expects Mr. X would outshine Mr. Y in the presidency.

This [book] is meant to help citizens and those who advise them cut through the confusion and get at some clear criteria for choosing presidents. To understand what actual presidents do and what potential presidents might do, the first need is to see the man whole—not as some abstract embodiment of civic virtue, some scorecard of issue stands, or some reflection of a faction, but as a human being like the rest of us, a person trying to cope with a difficult environment. To that task he brings his own character, his own view of the world, his own political style. None of that is new for him. If we can see the pattern he has set for his political life we can, I contend, estimate much better his pattern as he confronts the stresses and chances of the presidency.

The presidency is a peculiar office. The founding fathers left it extraordinarily loose in definition, partly because they trusted George Washington to invent a tradition as he went along. It is an institution made a piece at a time by successive men in the White House. Jefferson reached out to Congress to put together the beginnings of political parties; Jackson's dramatic force extended electoral partisanship to its mass base; Lincoln vastly expanded the administrative reach of the office; Wilson and the Roosevelts showed its rhetorical possibilities—in fact every president's mind and demeanor has left its mark on a heritage still in lively development.

But the presidency is much more than an institution. It is a focus of feelings. In general, popular feelings about politics are low-key, shallow, casual. For example, the vast majority of Americans knows virtually nothing of what Congress is doing and cares less. The presidency is different. The presidency is the focus for the most intense and persistent emotions in the American polity. The president is a symbolic leader, the one figure who draws together the people's hopes and fears for the political future. On top of all his routine duties, he has to carry that off—or fail.

Our emotional attachment to presidents shows up when one dies in office. People were not just disappointed or worried when President Kennedy was killed; people wept at the loss of a man most had never even met. Kennedy was young and charismatic—but history shows that whenever a president dies in office, heroic Lincoln or debased Harding, McKinley or Garfield, the same wave of deep emotion sweeps across the country. On the other hand, the death of an ex-president brings forth no such intense emotional reaction.

The president is the first political figure children are aware of (later they add Congress, the Court, and others, as "helpers" of the president). With some exceptions among children in deprived circumstances, the president is seen as a "benevolent leader," one who nurtures, sustains, and inspires the citizenry. Presidents regularly show up among "most admired" contemporaries and forebears, and the president is the "best known" (in the sense of sheer name recognition) person in the country. At inauguration time, even presidents elected by close margins are supported by much larger majorities than the election returns show, for people rally round as he actually assumes office. There is a similar reaction when the people see their president threatened by crisis: if he takes action, there is a favorable spurt in the Gallup poll whether he succeeds or fails.

Obviously the president gets more attention in schoolbooks, press, and television than any other politician. He is one of very few who can make news by doing good things. His emotional state is a matter of continual public commentary, as is the manner in which his personal and official families conduct themselves. The media bring across the president not as some neutral administrator or corporate executive to be assessed by his production, but as a special being with mysterious dimensions.

We have no king. The sentiments English children—and adults—direct to the Queen have no place to go in our system but to the president. Whatever his talents—Coolidge-type or Roosevelt-type—the president is the only available object for such national-religious-monarchial sentiments as Americans possess.

The president helps people make sense of politics. Congress is a tangle of committees, the bureaucracy is a maze of agencies. The president is one man trying to do a job—a picture much more understandable to the mass of people who find themselves in the same boat. Furthermore, he is the top man. He ought to know what is going on and set it right. So when the economy goes sour, or war drags on, or domestic violence erupts, the president is available to take the blame. Then when things go right, it seems the president must have had a hand in it. Indeed, the flow of political life is marked off by presidents: the "Eisenhower Era," the "Kennedy Years."

What all this means is that the president's *main* responsibilities reach far beyond administering the executive branch or commanding the armed forces. The White House is first and foremost a place of public leadership. That inevitably brings to bear on the president intense moral, sentimental, and quasi-religious pressures which can, if he lets them, distort his own thinking and feeling. If there is such a thing as extraordinary sanity, it is needed nowhere so much as in the White House.

Who the president is at a given time can make a profound difference in the whole thrust and direction of national politics. Since we have only one president at a time, we can never prove this by comparison, but even the most superficial speculation confirms the common sense view that the man himself weighs heavily among other historical factors. A Wilson reelected in 1920, a Hoover in 1932, a John F. Kennedy in 1964 would, it seems very likely, have guided the body politic along rather different paths from those their actual successors chose. Or try to imagine a Theodore Roosevelt ensconced behind today's "bully pulpit" of a presidency, or Lyndon Johnson as president in the age of McKinley. Only someone mesmerized by the lures of historical inevitability can suppose that it would have made little or no difference to government policy had Alf Landon replaced FDR in 1936, had Dewey beaten Truman in 1948, or Adlai Stevenson reigned through the 1950s. Not only would these alternative presidents have advocated different policies—they would have approached the office from very different psychological angles. It stretches credibility to think that Eugene McCarthy would have run the institution the way Lyndon Johnson did.

The burden of this book is that crucial differences can be anticipated by an understanding of a potential president's character, his world view, and his style. This kind of prediction is not easy; well-informed observers often have guessed wrong as they watched a man step toward the White House. One thinks of Woodrow Wilson, the scholar who would bring reason to politics; of Herbert Hoover, the Great Engineer who would organize chaos into progress; of Franklin D. Roosevelt, the champion of the balanced budget; of Harry Truman, whom the office would surely overwhelm; of Dwight D. Eisenhower, militant crusader; of John F. Kennedy, who would lead beyond moralisms to achievements; of Lyndon B. Johnson, the southern conservative; and of Richard M. Nixon, conciliator. Spotting the errors is easy. Predicting with even approximate accuracy is going to require some sharp tools and close attention in their use. But the experiment is worth it because the question is critical and because it lends itself to correction by evidence.

My argument comes in layers.

First, a president's personality is an important shaper of his presidential behavior on nontrivial matters.

Second, presidential personality is patterned. His character, world view, and style fit together in a dynamic package understandable in psychological terms.

Third, a president's personality interacts with the power situation he faces and the national "climate of expectations" dominant at the time he serves. The tuning, the resonance—or lack of it—between these external factors and his personality sets in motion the dynamics of his presidency.

Fourth, the best way to predict a president's character, world view, and style is to see how they were put together in the first place. That happened in his early life, culminating in his first independent political success.

But the core of the argument . . . is that presidential character—the basic stance a man takes toward his presidential experience—comes in four varieties. The most important thing to know about a president or candidate is where he fits among these types, defined according to (a) how active he is and (b) whether or not he gives the impression he enjoys his political life.

Let me spell out these concepts briefly before getting down to cases.

Personality Shapes Performance

I am not about to argue that once you know a president's personality you know everything. But as the cases will demonstrate, the degree and quality of a president's emotional involvement in an issue are powerful influences on how he defines the issue itself, how much attention he pays to it, which facts and persons he sees as relevant to its resolution, and, finally, what principles and purposes he associates with the issue. Every story of presidential decision making is really two stories: an outer one in which a rational man calculates and an inner one in which an emotional man feels. The two are forever connected. Any real president is one whole man and his deeds reflect his wholeness.

As for personality, it is a matter of tendencies. It is not that one president "has" some basic characteristic that another president does not "have." That old way of treating a trait as a possession, like a rock in a basket, ignores the universality of aggressiveness, compliancy, detachment, and other human drives. We all have all of them, but in different amounts and in different combinations.

The Pattern of Character, World View, and Style

The most visible part of the pattern is style. *Style is the president's habitual way of performing his three political roles: rhetoric, personal relations, and homework.* Not to be confused with "stylishness," charisma, or appearance, style is how the president goes about doing what the office requires him to do—to speak, directly or through media, to large audiences; to deal face to face with other politicians, individually and in small, relatively private groups; and to read, write, and calculate by himself in order to manage the endless flow of details that stream onto his desk. No president can escape doing at least some of each. But there are marked differences in stylistic emphasis from president to president. The *balance* among the three style elements varies; one president may put most of himself into rhetoric, another may stress close, informal dealing, while still another may devote his energies mainly to study and cogitation. Beyond the balance, we want to see each president's peculiar habits of style, his mode of coping with and adapting to these presidential demands. For example, I think both Calvin Coolidge and John F. Kennedy were primarily rhetoricians, but they went about it in contrasting ways.

A president's *world view consists of his primary, politically relevant beliefs, particularly his conceptions of social causality, human nature, and the central moral conflicts of the time.* This is how he sees the world and his lasting opinions about what he sees. Style is his way of acting; world view is his way of seeing. Like the rest of us, a president develops over a lifetime certain conceptions of reality—how things work in politics, what people are like, what the main purposes are. These assumptions or conceptions help him make sense of his world, give some semblance of order to the chaos of existence. Perhaps most important: a man's world view affects what he pays attention to, and a great deal of politics is about paying attention. The name of the game for many politicians is not so much "Do this, do that" as it is "Look here!"

"Character" comes from the Greek word for engraving; in one sense it is what life has marked into a man's being. As used here, *character is the way the president orients himself toward life*—not for the moment, but enduringly. Character is the person's stance as he confronts experience. And at the core of character, a man confronts himself. The president's fundamental self-esteem is his prime personal resource; to defend and advance that, he will sacrifice much else he values. Down there in the privacy of his heart, does he find himself superb, or ordinary, or debased, or in some intermediate range? No president has been utterly paralyzed by self-doubt and none has been utterly free of midnight self-mockery. In between, the real presidents move out on life from positions of relative strength or weakness. Equally important are the criteria by which they judge themselves. A president who rates himself by the standard of achievement, for instance, may be little affected by losses of affection.

Character, world view, and style are abstractions from the reality of the whole individual. In every case they form an integrated pattern: the man develops a combination which makes psychological sense for him, a dynamic arrangement of motives, beliefs, and habits in the service of his need for self-esteem.

The Power Situation and "Climate of Expectations"

Presidential character resonates with the political situation the president faces. It adapts him as he tries to adapt it. The support he has from the public and interest groups, the party balance in Congress, the thrust of Supreme Court opinion together set the basic power situation he must deal with. An activist president may run smack into a brick wall of resistance, then pull back and wait for a better moment. On the other hand, a president who sees himself as a quiet caretaker may not try to exploit even the most favorable power situation. So it is the relationship between president and the political configuration that makes the system tick.

Even before public opinion polls, the president's real or supposed popularity was a large factor in his performance. Besides the power mix in Washington, the president has to deal with a national climate of expectations, the predominant needs thrust up to him by the people. There are at least three recurrent themes around which these needs are focused.

People look to the president for *reassurance*, a feeling that things will be all right, that the president will take care of his people. The psychological request is for a surcease of anxiety. Obviously, modern life in America involves considerable doses of fear, tension, anxiety, worry; from time to time, the public mood calls for a rest, a time of peace, a breathing space, a "return to normalcy."

Another theme is the demand for *a sense of progress and action*. The president ought to do something to direct the nation's course—or at least be in there pitching for the people. The president is looked to as a take-charge man, a doer, a turner of the wheels, a producer of progress—even if that means some sacrifice of serenity.

A third type of climate of expectations is the public need for a sense of *legitimacy* from, and in, the presidency. The president should be a master politician who is above politics. He should have a right to his place and a rightful way of acting in it. The respectability—even religiosity—of the office has to be protected by a man who presents himself as defender of the faith. There is more to this than dignity, more than propriety. The president is expected to personify our betterness in an inspiring way, to express in what he does and is (not just in what he says) a moral idealism which, in much of the public mind, is the very opposite of "politics."

Over time the climate of expectations shifts and changes. Wars, depressions, and other national events contribute to that change, but there also is a rough cycle, from an emphasis on action (which begins to look too "political") to an emphasis on legitimacy (the moral uplift of which creates its own strains) to an emphasis on legitimacy (the moral uplift of which creates its own strains) to an emphasis on reassurance and rest (which comes to seem like drift) and back to action again. One need not be astrological about it. The point is that the climate of expectations at any given time is the political air the president has to breathe. Relating to this climate is a large part of his task.

Predicting Presidents

The best way to predict a president's character, world view, and style is to see how he constructed them in the first place. Especially in the early stages, life is experimental; consciously or not, a person tries out various ways of defining and maintaining and raising self-esteem. He looks to his environment for clues as to who he is and how well he is doing. These lessons of life slowly sink in; certain self-images and evaluations, certain ways of looking at the world, certain styles of action get confirmed by his experience and he gradually adopts them as his own. If we can see that process of development, we can understand the product. The features to note are those bearing on presidential performance.

Experimental development continues all the way to death; we will not blind ourselves to midlife changes, particularly in the full-scale prediction case, that of Richard Nixon. But it is often much easier to see the basic patterns in early life histories. Later on a whole host of distractions—especially the image-making all politicians learn to practice—clouds the picture.

In general, character has its *main* development in childhood, world view in adolescence, style in early adulthood. The stance toward life I call character grows out of the child's experiments in relating to parents, brothers and sisters, and peers at play and in school, as well as to his own body and the objects around it. Slowly the child defines an orientation toward experience; once established, that tends to last despite much subsequent contradiction. By adolescence, the child has been hearing and seeing how people make their worlds meaningful, and now he is moved to relate himself—his own meanings—to those around him. His focus of attention shifts toward the future; he senses that decisions about his fate are coming and he looks into the premises for those decisions. Thoughts about the way the world works and how one might work in it, about what people are like and how one might be like them or not, and about the values people share and how one might share in them too—these are typical concerns for the post-child, pre-adult mind of the adolescent.

These themes come together strongly in early adulthood, when the person moves from contemplation to responsible action and adopts a style. In most biographical accounts this period stands out in stark clarity—the time of emergence, the time the young man found himself. I call it his first independent political success. It was then he moved beyond the detailed guidance of his family; then his self-esteem was dramatically boosted; then he came forth as a person to be reckoned with by other people. The *way* he did that is profoundly important to him. Typically he grasps that style and hangs onto it. Much later, coming into the presidency, something in him remembers this earlier victory and reemphasizes the style that made it happen.

Character provides the main thrust and broad direction—but it does not *determine*, in any fixed sense, world view and style. The story of development does not end with the end of childhood. Thereafter, the culture one grows in and the ways that culture is translated by parents and peers shape the meanings one makes of his character. The going world view gets learned and that learning helps channel character forces. Thus it will not necessarily be true that compulsive characters have reactionary beliefs, or that compliant characters believe in compromise. Similarly for style: historical accidents play a large part in furnishing special opportunities for action—and in blocking off alternatives. For example, however much anger a young man may feel, that anger will not be expressed in rhetoric unless his life situation provides a platform and an audience. Style thus has a stature and independence of its own. Those who would reduce all explanation to character neglect these highly significant later channelings. For beyond the root is the branch, above the foundation the superstructure, and starts do not prescribe finishes.

Four Types of Presidential Character

The five concepts—character, world view, style, power situation, and climate of expectations—run through the accounts of presidents in [later chapters of Barber's book], which cluster the presidents since Theodore Roosevelt into four types. This is the fundamental scheme of the study. It offers a way to move past the complexities to the main contrasts and comparisons.

The first baseline in defining presidential types is *activity-passitivity*. How much energy does the man invest in his presidency? Lyndon Johnson went at his day like a human cyclone, coming to rest long after the sun went down. Calvin Coolidge often slept eleven hours a night and still needed a nap in the middle of the day. In between the presidents array themselves on the high or low side of the activity line.

The second baseline is *positive-negative affect* toward one's activity—that is, how he feels about what he does. Relatively speaking, does he seem to experience his political life as happy or sad, enjoyable or discouraging, positive or negative in its main effect. The feeling I am after here is not grim satisfaction in a job well done, not some philosophical conclusion. The idea is this; is he someone who, on the surfaces we can see, gives forth the feeling that he has *fun* in political life? Franklin Roosevelt's Secretary of War, Henry L. Stimson, wrote that the Roosevelts "not only understood the *use* of power, they knew the *enjoyment* of power, too. . . . Whether a man is burdened by power or enjoys power; whether he is trapped by responsibility or made free by it; whether he is moved by other people and outer forces or moves them—that is the essence of leadership."

The positive-negative baseline, then, is a general symptom of the fit between the man and his experience, a kind of register of *felt* satisfaction.

Why might we expect these two simple dimensions to outline the main character types? Because they stand for two central features of anyone's orientation toward life. In nearly every study of personality, some form of the active-passive contrast is critical; the general tendency to act or be acted upon is evident in such concepts as dominancy-submission, extraversion-introversion, aggression-timidity, attack-defense, fight-flight, engagement-withdrawal, approach-avoidance. In everyday life we sense quickly the general energy output of the people we deal with. Similarly we catch on fairly quickly to the affect dimension—whether the person seems to be optimistic or pessimistic, hopeful or skeptical, happy or sad. The two baselines are clear and they are also independent of one another: all of us know people who are very active but seem discouraged, others who are quite passive but seem happy, and so forth. The activity baseline refers to what one does, the affect baseline to how one feels about what one does.

Both are crude clues to character. They are leads into four basic character patterns long familiar in psychological research. In summary form, these are the main configurations.

Active-positive. There is a congruence, a consistency, between much activity and the enjoyment of it, indicating relatively high self-esteem and relative success in relating to the environment. The man shows an orientation toward productiveness as a value and an ability to use his styles flexibly, adaptively, suiting the dance to the music. He sees himself as developing over time toward relatively well-defined personal goals—growing toward his image of himself as he might yet be. There is an emphasis on rational mastery, on using the brain to move the feet. This may get him into trouble; he may fail to take account of the irrational in politics. Not everyone he deals with sees things his way and he may find it hard to understand why.

Active-negative.   The contradiction here is between relatively intense effort and relatively low emotional reward for that effort. The activity has a compulsive quality, as if the man were trying to make up for something or to escape from anxiety into hard work. He seems ambitious, striving upward, power-seeking. His stance toward the environment is aggressive and he has a persistent problem in managing his aggressive feelings. His self-image is vague and discontinuous. Life is a hard struggle to achieve and hold power, hampered by the condemnations of a perfectionistic conscience. Active-negative types pour energy into the political system, but it is an energy distorted from within.

Passive-positive.   This is the receptive, complaint, other-directed character whose life is a search for affection as a reward for being agreeable and cooperative rather than personally assertive. The contradiction is between low self-esteem (on grounds of being unlovable, unattractive) and a superficial optimism. A hopeful attitude helps dispel doubt and elicits encouragement from others. Passive-positive types help soften the harsh edges of politics. But their dependence and the fragility of their hopes and enjoyments make disappointment in politics likely.

Passive-negative.   The factors are consistent—but how are we to account for the man's *political* role-taking? Why is someone who does little in politics and enjoys it less there at all? The answer lies in the passive-negative's character-rooted orientation toward doing dutiful service; this compensates for low self-esteem based on a sense of uselessness. Passive-negative types are in politics because they think they ought to be. They may be well adapted to certain nonpolitical roles, but they lack the experience and flexibility to perform effectively as political leaders. Their tendency is to withdraw, to escape from the conflict and uncertainty of politics by emphasizing vague principles (especially prohibitions) and procedural arrangements. They become guardians of the right and proper way, above the sordid politicking of lesser men.

Active-positive presidents want most to achieve results. Active-negatives aim to get and keep power. Passive-positives are after love. Passive-negatives emphasize their civic virtue. The relation of activity to enjoyment in a president thus tends to outline a cluster of characteristics, to set apart the adapted from the compulsive, compliant, and withdrawn types.

The first four presidents of the United States, conveniently, ran through this gamut of character types. (Remember, we are talking about tendencies, broad directions; no individual man exactly fits a category.) George Washington—clearly the most important president in the pantheon—established the fundamental legitimacy of an American government at a time when this was a matter in considerable question. Washington's dignity, judiciousness, his aloof air of reserve and dedication to duty fit the passive-negative or withdrawing type best. Washington did not seek innovation, he sought stability. He longed to retire to Mount Vernon but fortunately was persuaded to stay on through a second term, in which, by rising above the political conflict between Hamilton and Jefferson and inspiring confidence in his own integrity, he gave the nation time to develop the organized means for peaceful change.

John Adams followed, a dour New England Puritan, much given to work and worry, an impatient and irascible man—an active-negative president, a compulsive type. Adams was far more partisan than Washington; the survival of the system through his presidency demonstrated that the nation could tolerate, for a time, domination by one of its nascent political parties. As president, an angry Adams brought the United States to the brink of war with France and presided over the new nation's first experiment in political repression: the Alien and Sedition Acts, forbidding, among other things, unlawful combinations "with intent to oppose any measure or measures of the government of the United States," or "any false, scandalous, and malicious writing or writings against the United States, or the president of the United States, with intent to defame . . . or to bring them or either of them, into contempt or disrepute."

Then came Jefferson. He too had his troubles and failures—in the design of national defense, for example. As for his presidential character (only one element in success or failure), Jefferson was clearly active-positive. A child of the Enlightenment, he applied his reason to organizing connections with Congress aimed at strengthening the more popular forces. A man of catholic interests and delightful humor, Jefferson combined a clear and open vision of what the country could be with a profound political sense, expressed in his famous phrase, "Every difference of opinion is not a difference of principle."

The fourth president was James Madison, "Little Jemmy," the constitutional philosopher thrown into the White House at a time of great international turmoil. Madison comes closest to the passive-positive, or compliant, type; he suffered from irresolution, tried to compromise his way out, and gave in too readily to the "warhawks" urging combat with Britain. The nation drifted into war, and Madison wound up ineptly commanding his collection of amateur generals in the streets of Washington. General Jackson's victory at New Orleans saved the Madison administration's historical reputation; but he left the presidency with the United States close to bankruptcy and secession.

These four presidents—like all presidents—were persons trying to cope with the roles they had won by using the equipment they had built over a lifetime. The president is not some shapeless organism in a flood of novelties, but a man with a memory in a system with a history. Like all of us, he draws on his past to shape his future. The pathetic hope that the White House will turn a Caligula into a Marcus Aurelius is as naive as the fear that ultimate power inevitably corrupts. The problem is to understand—and to state understandably—what in the personal past foreshadows the presidential future. . . .

H IGH HOPES ACCOMPANIED president Bill Clinton's inauguration on January 20, 1993. His stunningly successful presidential campaign amazed his friends and adversaries alike. But campaigning and governing require different talents. The following selection examines Clinton's style in handling the relationships that determine presidential performance.

16 Michael Kelly and Maureen Dowd
THE COMPANY
HE KEEPS

We're in a reaching out sort of mood this Inauguration. We're connecting. We're opening up. We're celebrating diversity and embracing wholeness. We're on an odyssey of self-discovery. We're thinking communitarian, New Covenant, a Government that looks like America, inclusive not exclusive, omnicultural. We're having Renaissance Weekends, wearing our names strung around our necks on pieces of colored yarn and talking about renewal of nation and self. We've released our inner children and are looking for nannies for them. We're feeling a little weepy, but that's O.K. (and you're O.K., too, although your family's dysfunctional). We're wearing clothes that look like the Summer of Love, only a lot more expensive, and the designer gives part of the profit to Friends of the Earth. We're not buttoned down and monogrammed anymore: We have a President named Bill, a First Lady named Hillary, a First Daughter named Chelsea . . . We're hugging trees. We're hugging each other. We're hugging each other's trees.

The Co-Dependent White House is upon us. The President likes to talk of his family's two generations of compulsions (stepfather an abusive alcoholic, mother a gambler, brother a recovering cocaine addict, himself a fast-food addict.) He has admitted to marital problems and has been through family therapy for his brother's addiction.

Vice President-elect Gore also became involved in family therapy as his son was recovering from near-fatal injuries sustained in 1989 after he was hit by a car. In the ensuing years, Gore developed into something akin to the nation's first Senator-Shrink. He enjoyed weekly visits from a therapist in his Senate office, once conducted a group seminar on dysfunctional families and, in the wake of Anita Hill, was host of a consciousness-raising "gender dynamics" seminar for Slow-to-Get-It Senators and their spouses. He decries "physic numbness," quotes John (*Healing the Shame That Binds You*) Bradshaw, and has written a book mixing ecology and psychology in sentences like ". . . just as the unwritten rules in a dysfunctional family create and maintain a conspiracy of silence about the rules themselves, even as the family is driven toward successive crises, many of the unwritten rules of our dysfunctional civilization encourage silent acquiescence in our patterns of destructive behavior toward the natural world."

With their Iron John election-night clinch, Bill and Al struck a blow not only against psychic numbness but also against the unwritten political ban on male full-body contact—strictly observed since the famous Richard Nixon–Sammy Davis Jr. hug in 1972 bruised the reputations of both men.

What it all comes down to is, we're relating again.

Of course, there are relationships and there are relationships. The word covers a lot of territory. Tristan and Isolde had a relationship. But so did Bonnie and Clyde. Scott and Zelda. Michael Dukakis and Jesse Jackson. George Bush and Ross Perot. David Letterman and NBC. John F. Kennedy and libido. Richard Nixon and bile.

Washington, never mistaken for Sunnybrook Farm, is, on the whole, more comfortable with the darker side of the relationship picture, preferring sharp elbows to Buscaglian embraces. As power transfers from George Bush to Bill Clinton, from the Republicans to the Democrats, the nation's capital is busy with the sort of relating it knows best: conniving and maneuvering, tossing and turning at 2 A.M. thinking about what jobs are available and whose back has to be climbed over, polishing the old brass knuckles and shining up the shiv. There's so much looking over shoulders that the entire city is practically pirouetting.

Here, then, in the spirit of new-age—and age-old—relationships, we offer six to watch as the Administration gets under way. How these liaisons, dangerous and otherwise, play out over the next four years will determine the essential character—and success—of the Clinton Presidency.

Bill and Al: The Incredible Shrinking Vice President

The scene is a familiar one. The new President is at the podium. He is talking on, in that Washington way, at length and about himself. A couple of steps back, tucked in the shadow of his right shoulder, stands the helpmeet, listening and smiling, with an occasional widening of the eyes to mark an especially orotund piece or rhetoric.

But with Bill Clinton, the adoring one standing in his shadow is not his wife, Hillary. (She is probably busy in a smokeless back room, vetting Supreme Court candidates.) It is Al Gore.

Like every marriage, the private relationship between Clinton and Gore is more complicated than the public one. The delicate tension of this uncommon partnership was revealed during the Vice Presidential debate in October, a night expected to be a cakewalk for an A-student over the class clown.

Instead, as Bill Clinton watched in growing frustration, Al Gore failed, time after time, to answer directly Dan Quayle's repeated charge that the Arkansas Governor did not have the integrity and character to be President. "Why the hell isn't Al defending Bill more?" one top campaign adviser asked another. Clinton aides muttered darkly that Al had missed five shots to stand by his man.

Afterward, Gore called a friend. "Do you think I should have responded more to the attacks on Bill?" he asked. "Some people are saying that, but I don't think that's fair."

To a few close friends, Gore confided that he had gone about as far as he thought he could in sticking up for Clinton. Famously straight-arrow, Gore was uncomfortable in the role of character witness to a man who has not always lived a life as careful and disciplined as his own, whose evasiveness was a problem throughout the campaign.

"He felt an inner constraint," says one Gore confidant. "He could not push himself to say something that would sound preposterous. As he said to me, 'There are certain things you can say and certain things you cannot.' "

When they next met on the campaign trail, the two men patched things up. Each recognized that theirs was a beautiful political friendship, not to be risked over misunderstandings, and for the rest of the campaign, Gore went to great lengths to defend Clinton's character. On election night, he delivered a long and sugary encomium to his boss: "He asked for your vote by challenging you to make America better. Where I come from, we have a name for that. It's called character."

For years before the 1992 campaign, the two Southern politicians had circled each other warily. One from the political aristocracy, one a charmed son of the meritocracy, each saw in the other an unswerving ambition, a sense of generational entitlement to the Presidency.

But these political siblings had their weaknesses. Gore, who had tried and failed to reach the White House on his own, was a man of such starchy manner and deliberate speaking style that he seemed, as the writer Michael Kinsley once noted, "an older person's idea of a young person."

In private, there was a playful side. Gore amused friends by balancing spoons and quarters on his nose and he repeated jokes at his own expense. (He told friends that one perk of the Vice President's job would be free medical care from the Forest Service: "They'll send over a tree doctor.") But his public demeanor was numbingly earnest, even by the standards of Washington, where the Senator had been known to show up at dinner parties with charts and graphs to illustrate a lecture on the fate of the ecosystem.

Clinton, by contrast, was a man of too many faces, all of them smiling. Beset by accusations of marital infidelity and draft dodging, his easy charm and seductive expressions smacked of the actor's artifice.

In their campaign symbiosis, each man helped diminish the other's flaws.

Gore benefited from the reflected warmth of Clinton's social skills. More important, Clinton received from Gore a dowry, not of geographical balance or political supporters, but of image. With the square-jawed Dudley Doright from Tennessee by his side, Slick Willie from Arkansas did not seem quite so slippery. Having a Vietnam veteran as his running mate helped shield Clinton as he defended his own troubled war history. And with the openly affectionate Gores holding hands beside them, the Clintons were able to sidestep some old baggage, the appearance that their union was less a romance than an arrangement between two calculating souls. "It was like a gestalt theory—the whole was greater than the sum of the parts," says Tipper Gore.

The two men campaigned together less like the top and bottom of a ticket than like two sides. They both had healthy egos. Clinton was, in the psychological jargon he favors, outer-directed; he craved the adulation he drew from crowds, so much so that he felt compelled to plunge into every rope line he saw, no matter how late the hour, and to keep talking even when audiences grew restless and reporters chanted "Get in the car!" Gore seemed curiously inner-directed for a politician, a man who was nothing so much as his own reflection. It was as though there were two Albert Gores on stage: one a Victorian maiden high on a pedestal; the other at the base looking up in admiration and wonder.

Having come to the relationship bearing a great gift, Gore was always determined to be treated with appropriate respect. He made the point in the Governor's mansion, the morning of July 9, as he and Clinton were rehearsing for the joint news conference they would soon hold to announce that Gore was joining the ticket. An aide, acting as reporter, threw out a question accusing Gore of being an environmental extremist.

Gore answered, but then Clinton cautioned, "We don't want to come off like a bunch of Greenpeace warriors."

Gore, the author of a best-selling psycho-environmental polemic, *Earth in the Balance*, shot back: "What do you mean *we*, kemo sabe?"

After a tense moment, Clinton began to laugh, then everyone else did, too. From that day on, Clinton and Gore appeared as the Alphonse and Gaston of politics, handing off the microphone to each other on stage, picking up each other's points. Except for some Southern focus groups' grumping that the two looked like a couple of yuppies with cellular phones and Rolexes, the act went over big. While George Bush campaigned with rarely a mention of Dan Quayle's name, Clinton used Gore to great advantage, employing him to lead the attack on the Bush Administration's prewar coziness with Saddam Hussein, and to serve as ambassador to Jewish and environmental groups.

Gore used Clinton to achieve true national celebrity, glomming great gulps of time at their joint appearances, grabbing the microphone to interrupt Clinton in midsentence. Campaign insiders said that the words Clinton most feared were, "I'd like to add something to that."

But that was then. That was back when Clinton had to put up with all sorts of things. He doesn't now. He is President. And Gore is not. Clinton no longer needs Gore to rescue him, because when reporters ask Presidents questions about affairs, they mean foreign and domestic—not extramarital. And those sorts of questions Clinton can handle on his own.

Those familiar with Vice Presidential territory say the job is always difficult for two reasons: The No. 2 has to try to use a largely ceremonial office to polish his reputation so he can someday run for No. 1, and the natural rivalry between the President's and the Vice President's staffs tends to magnify slights and miscues.

The supremely confident Clinton does seem prepared to give Gore a certain amount of influence and a good deal of attention. Gore's power was evident in the transition, as Clinton included him among the handful of people with a final say on Cabinet appointments. "At the table in the Governor's mansion, there were only five people present on a regular basis," says Mark Gearan, the Clinton aide who ran the Gore campaign. "Bill Clinton, Hillary Clinton, Warren Christopher, Bruce Lindsey and Al Gore."

Gore's first big play was to block the selection of the former Vermont Governor Madeleine Kunin as Environmental Protection Agency chief. He preferred that the post go to Carol Browner, his 37-year-old former Senate aide who had most recently served as the Secretary of Environmental Regulation in Florida.

But Gore's ambition may outstrip Clinton's largess. Gore told friends during the transition that he expected to have serious say in at least three or four Cabinet appointments. Instead, a friend says, Gore was told, in essence, "'Look, you can have Environment.' Then they give him the gift of letting him sit at the table." Gore was also disappointed when his two best Congressional friends, former Colorado Senator Tim Wirth and former New York Representative Tom Downey, were passed over for Cabinet seats.

During the transition, two top Gore staff members sat in the main dining room of the Capital Hotel in Little Rock and talked for an hour over breakfast about who might get the job of Clinton's chief of staff. "We've got to get someone in there who is going to look out for Al and not just Bill," one said.

But Clinton soon made it clear that he does not intend to gear his White House to protect Gore's interests. He chose the candidate most likely to give total loyalty to *him*—his oldest friend, the Arkansas businessman Thomas F. McLarty 3d.

Another unfortunate omen for Gore came during Clinton's first press conference as President-elect, when he invited his Vice President to join him on stage, but made no opening for him to say anything. Gore stood silently, staring somewhat vacantly into the middle distance with his arms straight at his side. He looked, said William Kristol, Vice President Quayle's chief of staff, "like an environmentally correct wooden Native American outside a cigar store." The humorist Calvin Trillin later memorialized it in a poem for

The Nation, asking "What's that, behind the President-elect—/That manlike object stiff from head to toe?"

No one knows better than Gore that he looks awkward hovering in his boss's shadow, and his friends worry that he might take Quayle's place as the favorite target of late-night comedians. "He's getting more and more stiff because he's cognizant of the fact that, as the Administration expands, his power contracts," says one Gore friend.

In response, Gore developed a tendency to overcompensate. That was embarrassingly clear at the first really big show of the incoming Administration, the 19-hour talkathon in Little Rock on the economy. Clinton impressed many in the audience at the two-day forum with his knowledge of what he called "megaissues and metaissues"—macro- and micropolicy, human infrastructure and information infrastructure and techonological infrastructure and just plain old infrastructure. Gore chimed in from time to time, trying to show off his own command of policy arcana. But it came across as the class salutatorian trying to keep up with the valedictorian.

Gore also faces one nearly insurmountable obstacle to gaining real power in the new Administration. "Al Gore hasn't yet realized there is going to be a co-Presidency, but he's not going to be part of the *co*," says one Republican lobbyist, paying backhanded homage to the clout of Hillary Clinton. During the transition, Susan Thomases, Clinton's scheduler and a close friend of Mrs. Clinton's, told associates that Gore did not understand that, once the Administration got under way, he would have to adjust to a smaller role. He could make it easy, Thomases said, or he could make it hard. (Gore had had run-ins with Thomases and other Clinton staff members during the campaign; he wanted more bus tours with Clinton and more visibility in the campaign commercials, and he wanted to make more major speeches.)

One other sign of possible trouble ahead for Gore comes in a story told by a close friend. When the Vice President-elect and his wife did not show up on the invitation list for the highly publicized dinner party for the Clintons at the Georgetown home of the Washington Post Company chairwoman, Katharine Graham, Tipper Gore had to ask Hillary Clinton if that was what she really had intended. Mrs. Clinton said no and instructed a staff member to rectify the oversight. Meanwhile, Graham, who had originally intended to have a separate party for the Gores, had decided on her own to add them to the list. But the Gores blamed the Machiavellian work of Clinton staff members for not making sure they were invited in the first place.

It was for Al Gore a particularly pointed lesson in Vice Presidential humility.

Bill and Hillary: From Policy Maker to Cookie Baker and Back

The first fib was always that 1600 Pennsylvania was the only household in America where the wife had no say over what the husband did.

Even in the face of strong First Ladies like Abigail Adams, Mary Todd Lincoln, Edith Wilson, Eleanor Roosevelt, Rosalynn Carter, Nancy Reagan and Barbara Bush, that fiction about Presidential domestic life persisted.

The Clintons hewed to the hoary "Father Knows Best" script long enough to win the Presidency, and then quickly put to rest the notion that East Wing never meets West. After the election, when he was asked who he wanted in the room when he makes his big decisions, Bill Clinton replied "Hillary"— shattering, with a single word, 200 years of Presidential protocol.

"If we disagree and I think I'm right," he told *Time* magazine, "I just go on and do what I think is right. And then she tells me, 'I told you so.' "

Those who try to Balkanize the influence of the new First Lady—Is she responsible for the liberal Cabinet appointments? The number of women chosen for top spots?—are underestimating her. "You can't disentangle the two," says one Democrat who has known the Clintons for years. Hillary Rodham and Bill Clinton both came east to the Ivy League to remake themselves, and they ended up doing it together. Those who forecast marital tensions as Hillary, the liberal, tugs Bill, the centrist, to the left also misread the pair. "He's a hell of a lot more liberal than people understand" says their Democratic friend. "But he's guileful and he moves crablike, with certain kinds of conservative cover. Part of their initial attraction was that they are both very political people, and there's not a terrific ideological difference between them."

In the end, the ideological truth about the Clintons is like Poe's purloined letter—so obvious that no one notices it, even though the couple point it out themselves. "It's rare that I think he's wrong," she said in one interview. "We think so much alike and our values are so much alike."

Both Clintons are committed believers in the liberal religion of the 60's college days, the promise that Government activism and central planning could solve the problems of private lives. But far from being liberal senti- mentalists, they are political pragmatists. Both husband and wife were chastened by the lesson of Clinton's 1980 defeat in Arkansas: that the public does not like politicians who surround themselves with the kind of people George Orwell once described as "that dreary tribe of high-minded women and sandal-wearers and bearded fruit-juice drinkers who come flocking towards the smell of 'progress,' like bluebottles to a dead cat."

The real tensions in the Clinton marriage have been personal, not political. The focus was intensified by the role Hillary Clinton played in saving her husband's campaign. When she stood beside him, after he euphemistically confessed to past marital "problems," she was endorsing the idea that their marriage was real. As their poll taker, Stan Greenberg, conceded at the time, voters would reject Bill Clinton if they thought that he did not have the imprimatur of his wife, or if they thought the union was a phony arrangement fueled only by ambition.

Some friends say that the Clintons can be affectionate in front of others;

campaign insiders say that, offstage, the candidate kissed his wife whenever he came into a room. Other friends, perhaps wishful thinkers, even see the strains in the marriage as evidence of its authenticity. As one dryly notes: "You couldn't sustain that level of irritation if it were an arrangement."

Yet the campaign image of their marriage was, in many ways, contrived. Last April, several of their top strategists sent the Clintons a long memo with suggestions on ways of making their relationship seem more affectionate and Hillary more traditional and maternal.

"More than Nancy Reagan, she is seen as 'running the show,'" the memo said. "The absence of affection, children and family and the preoccupation with career and power only reinforces the political problem evident from the beginning." The remarkably detailed course of action recommended for Mrs. Clinton included "joint appearances with her friends where Hillary can laugh, do her mimicry," a family vacation (preferably to Disneyland) and "events where Bill and Hillary can go on dates with the American people."

But whatever romance was dished up for public consumption, and whatever painful patches they have gone through in private over the years, the Clintons have a political partnership so tight that, as one former Carter Administration official puts it, "they make Jimmy and Rosalynn Carter look like strangers."

"I don't doubt that she's probably wanted to kill him sometimes—and with good reason," says a lawyer who is a close friend of Hillary Clinton's. "But this relationship is more than a cold, practical bargain. They like each other immensely."

More than most Presidential marriages, the Clintons' will need to have a happy public face. The image of the incoming President as a honest, decent man depends on the carefully cultivated idea that though he may have sinned, he has been redeemed. "He can't play J.F.K.," says a top Democrat. "If he does, it would be a killer. All bets would be off."

Bill Clinton told his family long ago that he didn't want to marry a beauty queen. Rather, he wanted to marry the smartest girl in the class. When they met at Yale Law School, he was immediately drawn to her ambition, discipline and love of liberal causes, and since then he has never shown any desire to diminish her—except when, as in the 1992 campaign, it was politically expedient to do so.

When George Bush decided to run for President, there were suggestions that Barbara Bush spruce herself up. "I'll do anything you want," she told Roger Ailes, the campaign media adviser, "but I won't dye my hair, change my wardrobe or lose weight."

By contrast, Hillary Clinton, supposedly far more independent, transformed her looks from plain to glamorous, from campus radical frump to blond Junior Leaguer with velvet headband—a curtsy to the mainstream. After her husband's 1980 gubernatorial defeat, she also gave up her surname, Rodham, a sacrifice to prove she wasn't an uppity Northern feminist, and took the name Clinton.

But the R-word was always hovering, just out of sight. Even at the height of the campaign controversy over her crack that she could have just stayed home baking cookies and having teas, and even when she was in a tremendous rush, she always made sure to sign autographs Hillary Rodham Clinton, the same way she signed her tax returns. Staff members refer to her as H.R.C., which is also the magic-marker monogram on her bulging file boxes.

Other First Ladies perpetrated the myth that they would never think of talking to the President about anything as *serious* and *complicated* as foreign affairs, but they might whisper to him about some White House staff member who was overstepping bounds. The new one isn't playing that game.

The real Hillary Clinton, superseded for much of the 1992 campaign by a quiet, smiling baker of cookies, popped back up in an interview with Ted Koppel broadcast on Election Day. The Clintons sat side by side in their airplane seats, and twice, as Koppel directed questions to Bill, Hillary answered for him. Her husband did not seem to mind, nor even particularly to notice.

Mrs. Clinton also sat in on her husband's "Man of the Year" interview with *Time*, boldly answering questions about policy and politics and speaking not of "he" but of "we." That idea is beginning to sink in. Even the Rev. Billy Graham, who will deliver the Inaugural invocation, recently said that Bill and Hillary "will make a unique team to help lead America and the Western world at this period of history."

Clinton staff members are just as scared of offending Her as Him (the Clintons both have a temper with aides if something is not done to their liking), and they know that if She tells them to do something a certain way, they don't have to double-check with Him.

They don't argue about it, either. During the transition, Clinton's staff worked out the usual arrangement by which the President-elect is always covered by a small pool of journalists. One afternoon during their New Year's vacation in Hilton Head, S.C., the Clintons decided to go for a bicycle ride on the hard-packed sandy beach. As they were leaving the house, Mrs. Clinton noticed two pickup trucks, carrying the journalists, getting in position to accompany them on the ride. "No trucks," she said abruptly to the Secret Service agent in charge. And so in a second, because the next First Lady wanted more privacy, the agreement made by her husband's staff was broken.

With the possible exception of Dan Rather, no public figure is the recipient of more unsolicited advise than the President's wife. And the advice is often unpleasantly personal. How the First Lady dresses, how she decorates, what she spends money on, her social manners, the way she raises her children, the way she treats her husband—these are all subjects the nation has felt utterly free to weigh in on.

Washington, a city prone to devour those who ignore its tribal rules, has always regarded First Ladies as particularly appetizing subjects. Presidential wives who have shown an independent turn of mind have quickly found themselves cast in the role of First Lady Macbeth.

"My sense is that Hillary will get brushed back a little bit," says Edward Rollins, the Republican strategist. "She's got to be careful not to overexpose herself or to play bad cop to Bill's good cop. She can't overshadow him or be perceived as manipulating him."

Sheila Tate, who saw the worst of what can happen to a First Lady's image when she worked as Nancy Reagan's press secretary, agrees: "No matter how careful the Clinton people are to point out how qualified Hillary is, there could be trouble. People don't like the wife mucking about in the husband's affairs. She wasn't elected and they just don't like it."

Mrs. Reagan has told friends that she empathizes with Mrs. Clinton's bumpy press coverage. "They were after me before I even got to Washington too," she told one confidante, and added this about Hillary Clinton's negative publicity: "It's not fair."

One night during the campaign, at a small dinner in a revolving restaurant atop a hotel in Covington, Ky., Mrs. Clinton wondered why Americans treated the First Lady's office as though it were Miss Havisham's dining room, circumscribed by the cobwebs of the past and great expectations for the future. She did not understand why people cared whether Rosalynn Carter attended Cabinet meetings. She did not see why she could not behave in the White House just as she had in Arkansas—shepherding some legislation in areas of interest to her (education, for example), helping her husband choose who would run departments, being as deeply involved in policy as he.

Hillary Clinton's friends say she does understand, however, that as First Lady she will have to thread her way through at least three sets of demands—feminists urging her to smash the mold, liberal interest groups wanting to coalesce around her and conservatives complaining she wasn't elected to anything. Like Anita Hill, she will undoubtedly come to serve as the canvas on which others, warring over the shifting role of women in American society, may paint their individual passions. She is clearly a First Lady with her own agenda and power base. What she cannot yet fully know is what structural tensions with the West Wing may surface, and whether she will be able to control the forces that seek to use her name and influence.

"Hillary feels like she's walking into Washington with her arms wide open and smiling, but she's watching on both sides," says Linda Bloodworth-Thomason, the Arkansas-bred television producer of "Designing Women," "Evening Shade" and "Hearts Afire" who has known the Clintons for years. "She's not a fool. She knows that Washington is treacherous." But unlike her husband, Hillary is not someone, Bloodworth-Thomason says, who "feels the overwhelming need to be understood and validated by everyone. She will do everything she can not to be misunderstood. Then she will be who she is and let the chips fall where they may."

But, as Mrs. Clinton has shown through much of her public life and particularly during the transition, she does not intend to jeopardize her husband's efforts to move his party toward the center—efforts that are at the very heart of his political success.

The Clintons have been careful to keep a strategic mix of liberal and conservative in their Democratic appointments so far. And Mrs. Clinton shares with her husband an ability not only to look for compromise but also to keep both eyes on the prize. When two campaign honchos, Susan Thomases and Mickey Kantor, both "Hillary people," crossed swords with political advisers during the campaign and transition, they were the ones who were forced to back down.

"Hillary is willingly taking on the freight of a lot of liberal groups," says one prominent Southern Democrat who knows the Clintons. "But she is not a little high priestess of idealism, either." The Democrat points out that while Mrs. Clinton served on the board of the liberal-activist Legal Services Corporation, she also served on the board of Wal-Mart and has been a corporate litigator for the Rose Law Firm, one of Arkansas's three largest.

Mrs. Clinton is still struggling to figure out how to bring her role into modern times. She has speculated with friends about the possibility of a job outside the White House, teaching law part-time perhaps. She does not know to what extent she should formalize her position in the new Administration. Should she be in the paper loop of critical documents, or should she just wait until evening to look at them? Should she have office space in the West Wing, to be closer to the action? She still feels she was burned during the campaign by her husband's open talk of giving her a Cabinet post and by the use of the motto, "Buy one get one free." She wants to tread more gingerly now.

But there are signs that the new First Lady has little patience for what is conventionally expected of the attentive political wife. At the end of the Clintons' Hilton Head bike ride, he stopped to play a game of touch football with their daughter, Chelsea, and 40 or 50 others, in front of a cordon of cameras eager for a happy-family-at-play shot. Hillary Clinton never paused in her pedaling but sailed serenly on, without a backward glance at the scene behind her.

Bill and His Enemies: The Top 10, Even Before He Takes Office

Clinton's friends like to say that he cannot hold a grudge. And indeed, the President-elect's instinct for consensus is so strong, going back to his earliest days as a playground glad-hander, that his chronic conciliator does seem incapable of personal vendetta. But that hardly matters. Bill Clinton's closest advisers, beginning with his wife, are more than capable of making up any shortfall.

Even before Inauguration Day, the Clinton enemies list is longer than George Bush's was after four years. Herewith, the Top 10 at the moment:

- John Major, Prime Minister of Great Britian, for sending Conservative Party strategists to Washington to advise Bush's campaign on how to beat Clinton.
- Jerry Brown, for being relentlessly annoying, for not knowing when to quit and go home, for just generally being Jerry Brown.
- Representative Charles Rangel of New York, for unhelpfully pointing out, again and again, how little time Clinton was spending in poor black neighborhoods.
- The Democratic Governor of Maryland, William Donald Schaefer, for, amazingly, endorsing Bush.
- Clifford Jackson, a former Oxford Friend of Bill's turned enemy, for his unceasing peddling of dodge-the-draft stories.
- Republican Representative Robert K. Dornan of California, for being the architect of the McCarthyite assault to depict Clinton as the last pinko.
- The former Republican Representative from Michigan Guy Vander Jagt, for holding a news conference two days before the election to accuse Clinton of having carried on a campaign-trail affair—without a scintilla of evidence.
- Marilyn Quayle, Rich Bond, Bob Novak and anyone else who ever said, implied or even thought anything mean about Hillary.
- NBC (the Nail Bill Clinton network, staff members called it), especially the correspondent Lisa Myers and the magazine program "Dateline: NBC," for its long piece during the primaries examining whether, as Governor of Arkansas, Clinton had sought to cover up two allegedly fatal mistakes by his mother as a nurse-anesthesiologist.
- Mary Matalin, the acid-tongued Bush deputy campaign manager, who once insinuated that Clinton was a "philandering, pot-smoking draft dodger." Yet Matalin gets a special Presidential pardon on the grounds that she is already undergoing the punishment of writing a "he said, she said" campaign memoir with her lover-political foe, James Carville, sentencing herself to relive her mistakes and his shrewd moves.

Aside from those whom Bill Clinton has reason to dislike, there is another growing list of people who have reason to bear him ill will. Heading that list at the moment are former Senator Wirth, former Governor Kunin and the Washington lawyer Brooksley Born, the one-time leading candidates to head up, respectively, the Department of Energy, the Environmental Protection Agency and the Justice Department. They all came away from talks with Clinton believing they had been chosen, only to lose out at the last minute.

How many enemies a politician makes is not much help in forecasting how he will fare. Richard Nixon stumbled with an extremely long list and George Bush stumbled with an extremely short one. All his life Bill Clinton has tried to avoid having any enemies at all. But the President-elect seems to offend as many people by making them think he agrees with them as he would if only he let them know that he didn't.

Bill and His Friends: It's Payback Time

For the first Democratic President in 12 years, enemies are not the biggest problem. It's his friends that Bill Clinton has to worry about.

Not his real friends, but his professional ones, the organizers and members of Democratic interest groups. Each faction, from Act Up to Zero Population Growth, holds itself responsible for at least a piece of Democratic victory, and each wants at least a piece of the President in return.

With his oft-repeated campaign promise of "a government that looks like America," Clinton had fed the expectations of all. But there was only so much pie to go around, and, by halfway through the transition, some of the President-elect's constituencies were turning on him, and on each other.

"Lesbians to Clinton: Why no Dykes in the Cabinet?" asked a news release from the homosexual activist group Queer Nation.

"Department Secretaries Named to Date: Total: Male 3, Female 1; White 3, African-American 1," counted the Coalition for Women's Appointments during the selection process.

"Dear Mr. President-elect, environmentalists worked very hard to help you achieve victory in November," wrote the Sierra Club and the League of Conservation Voters. They were trying to bring Clinton back to the fold after he had selected Hazel O'Leary (black and female) as Secretary of Energy over Tim Wirth (a white-but-environmentally-correct male).

Responding to all the pressures, Clinton complained, calling the feminist pressure groups "bean counters" who were "playing quota games and math games." Some said the outburst was calculated to distance himself from the feminist lobby and to send a warning signal to all the pressure groups to back off. That may have been the case, but Clinton did seem genuinely outraged, his face red, his voice edged with sharp anger.

His feminist friends shrugged the scolding off. "Right now, he's just starting to squirm a little," says Patricia Ireland, the president of the National Organization for Women.

It boggles the mind, but Bill Clinton may have even more friends than George Bush. The President-elect, one of the great Rolodexers of modern times, has been networking and cultivating the rest of the human race on a vast scale since childhood. Is there a city in America that doesn't boast at least a few people who call themselves F.O.B's? The sheer volume of these friends, with their cacophony of points of view and competing desires for White House access, can mean trouble down the road for the new President.

Republicans eagerly anticipate a four-year siege of Bill's friends trying to push him this way and that. "If this continues," says Dan Quayle's speech writer, Lisa Schiffren, "those of us who are packing up our offices now will be packing up to move back in again in four years."

Bill and His Diet: The President as Omnivore

When Barbara Bush began living at the White House, she worried about all the elaborate meals she was about to be served and how they would affect her weight problem. But when the White House waiters began putting plates in front of her, she noticed something strange: the portions were puny. "Why aren't they feeding us?" she wondered, telling the story later to friends.

Then Mrs. Bush realized what the problem was: the chefs had been instructed by Nancy Reagan to serve social X-ray portions. But Mrs. Bush decided not to reverse the policy of less-than-normal-size meals. "She figured it was good for her and the President to just ask for seconds and thirds," says a friend of Mrs. Bush.

If Hillary Clinton also adheres to Nancy Reagan's Lean Cuisine regime, expect the local Domino's Pizza to be getting plenty of 3 A.M. calls from the White House.

We have seen the President as communicator, the President as warrior and the President as healer. Now comes the President as omnivore.

"He eats like a Tasmanian devil—Dunkin' Donuts, McDonald's, tin cans," says Mort Engleberg, a Hollywood producer ("Smokey and the Bandit") and occasional Clinton adviser who shares Clinton's accordion appetite. "You'll never find this guy asking for a splash more coffee. He's not a nervous eater. He enjoys it."

Engleberg claims that during the campaign, Clinton had a special radar for finding a Dunkin' Donuts in the middle of the night in small towns. "He'd say, 'Let's just get a cup of coffee,' but then he'd end up eating donuts and soup and broccoli with cheese."

Clinton is not the only President who tends to get, as he likes to put it, "fat as a wood tick." The first thing William Howard Taft did after his Inauguration was to flop his 300 pounds onto a White House sofa, just to prove he was President and could bust any spring he liked.

George Bush eats like a teenager, gobbling down nachos, steaks and egg rolls with equal gusto, and once ingested the most disgusting breakfast in Presidential history: oatmeal with a Butterfinger bar crumbled on top.

Clinton eats like a teenager, too. Linda Bloodworth-Thomason laughs about her old pal's habit of reaching over and spearing something on a companion's plate, noting, "You don't want that, do you?"

Bill Clinton's favorite foods include chicken enchiladas, tacos, barbecued ribs, cheeseburgers, lemon chess pie, peach pie, beef tenders marinated in Italian dressing and his mom's sweet-potato casserole. (Take 6 pounds of mashed sweet potatoes. Add 1 pound of brown sugar, 3 eggs, half a pound of butter and a pound and a half of sweetened condensed milk. Flavor with nutmeg, cinnamon, vanilla, ginger, allspice and nuts. Top with 10 ounces of melted marshmallow miniatures.)

His weight fluctuates by about 40 pounds, beginning at a minimum of 190 and going up to 226. One of his more embarrassing food moments on the road came when a customer at a Taco Bell greeted Clinton by reminding him that they had met before—at a Pizza Hut.

James Carville, Clinton's wiry chief political strategist, recalls eating many an awful plane meal with Clinton. A former heavyweight himself, Carville marveled at the candidate's cheerfully gluttonous feeding patterns. "We would get warmed-over lasagna and two-day-old salad, the worst stuff I had since the Marines, and I never did see him complain," he says. "I suspect if they give it to him, he'll eat it. If the White House chef comes down with an elaborate duck à l'orange, he'll eat that, too."

Clinton's eating habits have already turned into something of a national joke. Political cartoonists have portrayed him with his cheeks swallowing up his eyes, while comics and esthetes alike have begged him to stop wearing short shorts while jogging. "Saturday Night Live" depicted the President-elect in a sketch ending a 30-foot run at a McDonald's, where he foraged through the room snatching burgers and fries from startled customers. Jay Leno asserted that Clinton needs to appoint "a Thighmaster General," pointing out that Vice President-elect Gore is "just a Big Mac away from the Presidency."

Warning that the well-upholstered Clinton and Gore might, should their padding increase, become known as "the Blubber Bubbas," the writer and noted eater Calvin Trillin envisioned mud-throwing Republicans questioning whether "men who order the cottage-cheese-and-fruit salad and then pick at a companion's double order of cheese French fries to the point at which the plate requires no washing are really the sort of men you want making life-and-death decisions for this nation."

Even Clinton's press secretary, Dee Dee Myers, said at a recent political dinner in Washington that those who were skeptical when Clinton said he "didn't inhale" had clearly never been to a McDonald's with him.

But girth is no laughing matter to the gastronomically correct. A group of chefs led by Alice Waters of Chez Panisse, the exceedingly cutting-edge Berkely, Calif., restaurant, sent the President-elect a snippety letter urging him to appoint a White House chef who would serve food that shows "care for our waters and pastures."

Clinton, reasonably enough, did not feel the need to respond personally to a dietary tract that included among its signatories Paul Prudhomme, the New Orleans chef who had singlehandedly refuted the poet John Donne's contention that no man is an island.

But will the new President continue to flout the social conventions of a nation of Stairmasterers? Calvin Trillin respects Clinton for going beyond what he disdainfully calls the "show eating" of George Bush—who used pork rinds as a political statement—and defended the Clinton sweet-potato-casserole recipe as "not as bad as Tricia Nixon's Chicken Divan."

"I'm not so sure how deep into society this whole calorie-counting, cholesterol-watching, stair-stepping sickness ever really went," Trillin says. "The Clinton Administration could be like the Day the Fat People Invaded. This sort of eating may very well be the secret of Clinton's appeal, his link to the common man."

Bill and the Camera: Are They Spending Too Much Time Together?

It was about halfway between Election Day and Inauguration Day that it began to dawn on people that there was simply no escaping Bill Clinton.

It had become almost impossible to turn on a television set without seeing the President-elect talking or waiting for his turn to talk while someone else talked to him. C-Span had come to resemble some sort of 24-hour Clinton channel: "All Bill. All the time."

The deluge reached biblical proportions at the Little Rock economic conference, a made-for-television event featuring more than 300 people talking for 19 solid hours. Clinton, clearly in his element, had never seemed happier.

"And so the specific question I wanted to ask is in this whole idea of redirecting the $15 billion," he told one participant in a discussion on defense conversion. "Do you think we ought to do it through the Defense Advanced Research Products Agency, through a new agency, through expanding that mission? And how, as a practical matter, based on your own experience in this area—how much dual-use technology can we really do that will benefit, truly benefit both the commercial sector and the defense sector that we're not doing now?"

When it came time on the second day of the conference to break for lunch, Clinton demurred. "I'm not going to have a break for lunch, " he said to his fellow gasbags, "This is too interesting." (He also actually referred to a chart at one point as "moving.")

The participant in the conference seemed equally enthralled; never before had so many been allowed to talk so long about so much that was so boring. "Mr. President, words fail me in describing what an extraordinary event this is," said the economic columnist Robert Kuttner.

Clinton replied, "I hope that doesn't mean it's all downhill from here."

It could be. Clinton, the only man in America who would actually pay for C-Span if it became a premium channel, has promised to numb the nation with further colloquia on such topics as health care, welfare reform and the environment. He has hinted as well at further getting-out-among-my-people bus trips, conjuring up the frightening image of the Presidency as nightmare combination of Greyhound tour and "G.E. College Bowl"—with Clinton leading a caravan of eggheads endlessly through the heartland, touching down periodically for 20 hours or so of stimulating conversation.

In the 1980's everyone had their 15 minutes of fame; in the 1990's, it looks as though everyone will have 15 minutes on air with Bill Clinton—especially now that the President will have access to 500 cable channels.

Clinton's never-ending conversation with the American public is going over big now, because, after four years of George Bush's headmasterish style of governing, Americans are starved to have a voice in their own political affairs. But there is a precedent from which it is possible to gauge just how long voters can be expected to tolerate all this listening, and it does not augur well for Clinton.

Jimmy Carter, like Bill Clinton, began his Presidency with an extravaganza of populism. He update F.D.R.'s fireside chats for television, hosted a telephone call-in show to the White House, held a "town hall" in the town of Clinton, Mass., and traveled around the country visiting with "average Americans." The act palled quickly. By the time Carter ran unsuccessfully for reelection, his strategists were advising him that his best hope lay in staying home, out of the public eye.

Ronald Reagan's advisers, having studied Carter's approach, sharply limited the President's visibility. "The more you expose yourself, the more you expose yourself to trivialization." says Michael Deaver, the Washington public relations executive who was Reagan's chief imagist. "And if things start not working, people are going to say, 'Get off your rear, quit talking and do something about it.' "

At the moment, however, the Clinton camp appears not to be able to conceive of a world in which their chatty boss could be overexposed.

"I think you'll see a lot of town halls, of the sort we did in the campaign," says one Clinton official, his enthusiasm rising as he contemplates the future. "Maybe one every couple of months. Also, bus tours, of course. We have to keep doing those, but no so many, maybe one every six months or once a year. And maybe we could do the old capital-for-a-day bit too. You know, move the White House and the entire Cabinet to some place like Bismarck, N.D., one morning and make it the capital of the whole country for a day. Wouldn't that be great?"

William Jefferson Clinton becomes the 42d President of the United States three days from now an oddly unknown man. He has succeeded remarkably well in being many things to many people, but that leaves the question of who he really is.

Is he the New Democrat, or the same old thing? Will he only tell people what they want to hear, or will he be able to say no to important constituencies? Will he continue to act as though the solutions to the country's problems are painless, or will he explain what sacrifices need to be made?

There is a fundamental tension in Bill Clinton between the glib politician and the dedicated student of public policy, the man always looking for approval and the man who knows that wrenching changes are required to put the country on a new course.

In the end, the most important relationship to be sorted out in the next four years is between Bill and Bill.

17

James M. Perry and Jeffery H. Birnbaum
"WE" THE
PRESIDENT

Bill Clinton may be having trouble hitting the ground running. But there are no such fears about Hillary Rodham Clinton.

No sooner had she been named by her husband to head a national task force on health care than she was working the phones. She tracked down Sen. Donald Riegle, chairman of a Senate health-care subcommittee, at his home in McLean, Va., where he was watching the conclusion of a Detroit Pistons basketball game.

The people she contacted all dropped whatever they were doing to talk to a woman who gives every indication of becoming the most powerful—and perhaps the most controversial—First Lady in American history. When Hillary Rodham Clinton calls, people listen. She inspires respect—even fear.

"From what I hear she's got both hands on the throttle," says Democratic Rep. Dan Rostenkowski of Illinois, whom she had called earlier.

She starts her work in the White House with strong support from the public. The latest *Wall Street Journal*/NBC News poll shows a positive rating of 57%, up from 46% in December. On the question of whether she is or isn't a positive role model, 74% say she is. Only 15% say she isn't.

But on a key question—whether she should or should not be involved in developing major policy decisions—respondents split straight down the middle, with 47% saying she should and 45% saying she shouldn't.

And on a cultural and symbolic issue—what name she wants to be called—she is bucking public opinion. Respondents, 62% to 6%, say she should stick to Hillary Clinton, instead of the name she now prefers, Hillary Rodham Clinton, while 28% say it doesn't matter, she should use whatever name she wants.

Americans have always been curious about the wives of their presidents—the family living in the White House is as close as this country gets to a royal family living in a palace—but there rarely, if ever, has been anything approaching the intensity of the nation's interest in this First Lady.

"I'm rah-rah-rah for Hillary," says Myrtle Yomas, a 70-year-old retiree who lives outside Baltimore. "I'm so glad to see those young people there. Maybe that's what we need, some new thoughts."

Voters seem to sense that Mrs. Clinton is going to be a daring high-wire act, and they already are holding their collective breath as the drama begins to unfold. Democratic strategists pray she can pull it off, while Republican operatives look for signs of her losing her balance.

"It has every potential for disaster," says Vince Breglio, a GOP pollster.

She shatters all the precedents. She goes to work in a small room at the center of the second-floor work space in the West Wing of the White House, surrounded not by social secretaries but by the largely anonymous policy experts who will lay out the new administration's domestic programs. She will be the voice most of them listen to most respectfully most of the time. (The previous occupant of the office was Janet Mullins, who, in a twist of fate, is being investigated for her alleged role in a pre-election search of Mr. Clinton's passport files.)

On the question of Mrs. Clinton and her staff moving into larger quarters—taking over space now used as a press room for White House reporters—the respondents to the *Journal*/NBC poll say, by the modest margin, that she and her aides should stay where they are. It is probably less a ringing endorsement of the press than a feeling Mrs. Clinton shouldn't be building a personal bureaucracy.

Donna Shalala, the new secretary of Health and Human Services, calls the political risk of putting Mrs. Clinton in such a high-visibility role "huge." But Mrs. Clinton "represents a different generational experience," says Ms. Shalala. "She's on the cutting edge of that and it's very tricky, because she's on the borderline between a more traditional role and this new role for women. Twenty years from now we won't think twice."

Mrs. Clinton has friends and old associates scattered through the upper ranks of the entire federal bureaucracy. When they want something done, they will go—they already go—to Mrs. Clinton. "You can be sure," says Ms. Shalala, "that if I and every other Cabinet officer think she can be helpful on something specific, like trying to recruit the best person in the country, we're going to call her and say please help us recruit this person."

Old-line politicians like Mr. Rostenkowski may feel uncomfortable with her assignment. Is it a good thing, he is asked. "That remains to be seen." he replies. "I don't know that Hillary will have the same amount of exposure as an elected official."

Rep. Pete Stark, a California Democrat, says he's a little "miffed." President Clinton had led the lawmaker to believe that he, the president, would take the lead on health care. "He changed his mind," Rep. Stark says. But miffed or not, he says, "I'm happy. I'll be happy to negotiate with his wife, anytime."

"More Focused"

What is off-putting to traditional politicians, and perhaps to many Americans who are still trying to grapple with this kind of partnership, is the self-confidence Mrs. Clinton exudes and the brain power she unleashes.

"She's as smart as a treeful of owls," says Charles Murphy Jr., a former chairman of the Arkansas Business Council and chairman of Murphy Oil Co., one of Arkansas' largest concerns.

"She's more focused" than her husband, says Betsey Wright, former chief of staff to Mr. Clinton when he was governor. When it comes to reaching a solution to a problem, Ms. Wright says, "it doesn't take her near as long to get there" as it does for him.

Mrs. Clinton also is unabashed about the professional partnership she has formed with her husband, and often uses the term "we" to describe presidential actions. When she spoke to Rep. Rostenkowski, he says, she thanked him for sending policy memoranda to her husband, which she said they both had read. "You've been a real friend," he says she added. "We hope you can help us."

Ms. Shalala bridles at the suggestion that she and others in the administration are "Hillary people."

"We think of ourselves as Clinton people," she says. "Both of them will have very strong roles" in developing and promoting health-care overhaul.

The curious thing about what is sometimes called the "Billary" partnership is that folks in Arkansas, not always portrayed as one of the nation's New Age outposts, seem less worried about Mrs. Clinton's role than people here in Washington. They have become accustomed to it.

Popular There

By almost every account she remains a popular figure in her adopted state. Dick Morris is now a Republican pollster—he switched allegiances in 1988—but he worked for Mr. Clinton through his last campaign for governor, in 1990, and still advises him. He says that in all the Arkansas polls he has taken in which he measured Mrs. Clinton's popularity, the favorable rating has never been less than three to one.

Mr. Morris attributes this to her role in pushing through education reform, as her husband's partner, in 1983. "People in Arkansas saw her as the lead person on that, and it wasn't because she advocated smaller classroom size or more pay for teachers," he says. "It was because the program she developed as head of the Arkansas Education Standards Committee required competence testing for teachers. She took on the establishment, the Arkansas Education Association—the union—and she won. That was widely seen in Arkansas as something well outside the liberal prism into which people had tried to place her."

It is, of course, as a liberal that her opponents are trying to condemn her. It gets pretty rough. One book, *Hillarious,* by George Grant, ties her to the Democratic Party's "abortion battlements of feminazi, sensitivity-or-else crowd." *Spy* magazine put her on its cover in leather and chains, holding a whip.

Inviting Attention

Like Eleanor Roosevelt, Mrs. Clinton will be in the eye of the storm—critized for her own actions and singled out as the most vulnerable target for hurting her husband. She sometimes seems to invite the attention, as when she said she could have "stayed at home, baked cookies and had teas" instead of becoming a successful lawyer and key adviser to her husband. She invites attention now by insisting that she be called Hillary Rodham Clinton. She had previously changed her name to Hillary Clinton from Hillary Rodham after her husband was defeated for re-election as Arkansas governor in 1980.

"There are all these connotations about Hillary," says conservative GOP strategist Donald Devine. "The name business, her association with the Children's Defense Fund, which we see as a radical organization. She's very handy for the right."

The question for Republicans is whether to begin attacking Mrs. Clinton now, as a way of getting at her husband, or allow her enough time to do damage herself. Speakers at the GOP national convention—Patrick Buchanan and Marilyn Quayle chief among them—tried attacking Mrs. Clinton as a kind of superliberal feminist who would seek to change the role of the traditional American family. It didn't work. And so, many GOP strategists are reluctant to try it again, not quite yet anyway. "These right-wing attacks are counter-productive," says Mr. Breglio, the GOP pollster. "Politicians are most frequently hoisted by their own petards, and that's where she's going to end up, I suspect."

Mrs. Clinton's boosters say it is the Arkansas model the nation should watch. In the White House, says Lisa Caputo, her spokeswoman, Mrs. Clinton "will be an adviser to the president on matter of domestic policy. It will be parallel to what happened in Arkansas." Mrs. Clinton declined to be interviewed for this story.

She did take on a challenging task in Arkansas—education reform—and she pulled it off. When she reported her findings to the state legislature late in 1983, talking for more than an hour without notes, she won a standing ovation from lawmakers who had been skeptical about where she wanted to take them. She then toured the state and the sold voters on the plan.

But Arkansas is not Washington, and education reform in that state is not health-care reform for the whole country. This is an immense challenge, and if Mrs. Clinton—for whom there are such high expectations—fails to meet it, there will be serious political consequences for her husband's administration.

THE FOLLOWING SELECTION depicts how one president, John F. Kennedy, handled the most serious major power confrontation since World War II—the October 1962 Cuban missile crisis. The piece reveals how Kennedy's character and style defined his performance in the White House as he brought the world to the brink but ultimately saved it from a nuclear holocaust.

18   Tom Morganthau
AT THE BRINK
OF DISASTER

Even today, 30 years after the fact, the Cuban missile crisis ranks as the climactic moment of the cold war—a superpower morality play in which courage and candor triumphed and low cunning and dark purposes were defeated. The missile crisis pitted a popular and charismatic American president, John F. Kennedy, against a wily and bellicose Soviet leader, Nikita Sergeyevich Khrushchev. It involved—it was fundamentally *about*—the most lethal weapons of mass destruction then known, and it was played out in full view of millions upon millions of ordinary citizens the world over. Most of all, it ended happily—which is to say, without nuclear war.

Few who lived through that period, Oct. 14–28, 1962, will ever forget the drama that unfolded day by day. There was Kennedy's somber television speech to the nation on Oct. 22. Two days later, on Oct. 24 came news that Soviet ships approaching the U.S. Navy's mid-Atlantic quarantine line had stopped dead in the water. "We're eyeball to eyeball," Secretary of State Dean Rusk said laconically, "and I think the other fellow just blinked." On the 25th, Adlai Stevenson stunned the United Nations and flummoxed Soviet Ambassador Valerian Zorin with dramatic U-2 photographs of the missiles themselves. Finally, on Oct. 28, there was Radio Moscow's announcement that Krushchev had ordered the missiles removed from Cuba. Americans everywhere stood and cheered.

But the newsreel version of the Cuban missile crisis is distorted—a cartoon rendition of a complex series of actions, some intended and some not, that took the world much closer to war than most Americans ever knew. Kennedy, to be sure, conducted himself with distinction throughout the crisis, and the whole episode is rightly studied as a textbook case of presidential leadership in a time of acute international tension. But the real history of the missile crisis has been coming out bit by bit for years, partly from Soviet sources and now from secret U.S. documents released by the CIA. Taken as a whole, that history is far less reassuring than the more familiar version. It is a story of blunder, miscalculation and dumb luck. It is also the story of remarkable dedication and competence within the U.S. intelligence community and the stunning contribution of an almost forgotten Soviet traitor.

The missile crisis had its origins in the Bay of Pigs invasion and the superpower arms race. The Bay of Pigs debacle, 20 months earlier, convinced Khrushchev that Kennedy would buckle under pressure, and it may have led him to believe Cuba needed Soviet protection against another U.S. invasion. But his essential motive for the missile gambit was strategic. Despite Khrushchev's bluster, both sides knew the Soviet Union was far behind the United States in missiles, bombers and deliverable nuclear warheads. U.S. analysts now believe the Soviets had no more than 44 operational intercontinental missiles and 155 long-range bombers in 1962— while the United States had 156 ICBMs, 144 sub-launched Polaris missiles and 1,300 strategic bombers.

Deploying medium-range missiles in Cuba gave Soviet forces a significant increase in the number of warheads that could reach the United States—though it is unlikely that Khrushchev had nuclear war in mind. Khrushchev was a believer in atomic diplomacy. Obsessed by the Soviet Union's strategic inferiority, he "was looking for any way to talk to the Americans equally," says Aleksandr Alekseyev, who was Soviet ambassador to Cuba during the crisis. The Cuban gamble was a quick and easy way to redress the nuclear balance, and the Castro regime was more than willing. In early May, Alekseyev was summoned to the Kremlin and briefed on Khrushchev's plan. If the deployment was kept secret until after the U.S. elections in November, Khrushchev said, Kennedy would not risk war to force them out. No one asked whether the Americans might find other ways to force a Soviet retreat.

Almost no one in Washington believed that Khrushchev would try it. True, the CIA had thousands of alarming reports of Soviet missile activity in Cuba—but these reports, most of which came from Cuban refugees arriving in Miami, were invariably wrong. True, the CIA knew the Soviets had begun a considerable military buildup to defend the Castro government and that Soviet "technicians" were building a chain of SAM-2 missile batteries from one end of the island to the other. But the SAM-2 was an antiaircraft missile: it didn't carry a nuclear warhead and it couldn't even reach Key West. Consequently, the agency took a skeptical view of the many missile sightings contained in the refugee reports: to a civilian, a 35-foot-long SAM would look like a monster missile.

In a national intelligence estimate prepared for Kennedy on Aug. 1, the CIA and other U.S. intelligence agencies maintained that the Soviet buildup on Cuba would almost certainly be limited to defensive weapons. That judgment, appallingly wrong, was reaffirmed in a second special estimate on Sept. 19—the day *after* the CIA received a top-secret report from an agent inside Cuba identifying the precise area, about 50 miles southwest of Havana, where the Soviets were building a base for their SS-4 ballistic missiles. The agent's report, written in invisible ink and sent to a mail drop outside Cuba, has now been released by the CIA. It warned that Soviet troops had blocked off a large area of Pínar del Rio province around the town of San Cristóbal, and that very secret work, probably involving missiles, was taking place on the *finca* (ranch) of a Dr. Cortina. CIA headquarters skeptically noted that "it is doubtful that ground forces could effectively control . . . a zone as large as the one cited above."

But they had—and in mid-October the first SS-4s arrived at San Cristóbal. By that point, CIA Director John McCone had won a narrow victory in his clash with Rusk on the need to send U-2 spy planes to reconnoiter the Soviet buildup. Almost alone in the U.S. intelligence community, McCone was certain Khrushchev would send offensive missiles to Cuba; his reasoning was that the SAM-2 network was a sign the Soviets were up to something big. Rusk, equally adamant, was worried that the U-2s would be shot down by the SAMs, just as Francis Gary Powers's plane had been shot down over the Soviet Union in 1960. This impasse, compounded by rainy weather over Cuba, prevented U.S. reconnaissance for more than a month—but on Oct. 14, an air force U-2 flew directly over San Cristóbal at 72,500 feet with its camera rolling.

The San Cristóbal imagery was stunning: it showed SS-4s at two different sites in a hilly, wooded area outside town. *Those rotten bastards*, thought Vincent DiRenzo, the CIA photo interpreter who made the call. DiRenzo told his boss, Dino Brugioni, and the photo team checked its conclusions against "the black book." The black book contained the CIA's best information on Soviet strategic weapons. Some of it was fragmentary and some of it was wrong—but the book was dead accurate about the SS-4. It said the SS-4 had a range of 1,020 nautical miles—enough to reach Washington from San Cristóbal—and that it carried a one- or three-megaton nuclear warhead. The book contained remarkably specific information on SS-4 launching operations and a detailed perspective drawing of a typical launch site that showed the missile erector, the control cabling and the missile-ready tents. Everything matched.

This mother lode of Soviet missile secrets was code-named "Ironbark" and was arguably the most spectacular Western espionage coup of the cold war. Ironbark was the work of one man, an embittered Soviet colonel named Oleg Penkovsky—a senior agent in the GRU, Soviet military intelligence, and the son-in-law of a Soviet Army marshal. His story has now been retold by Jerrold L. Schecter and Peter S. Deriabin in *The Spy Who Saved the World*, a book that relies heavily on CIA sources. Penkovsky was arrested on Oct. 22 and executed in 1963. But he had already provided the West with invaluable political and strategic intelligence from the top echelons of the Soviet military hierarchy. The SS-4 data, microfilmed from the manual of a Soviet officers' school, was crucial. "It was possible to look at the diagram and tell just how far along they were and how soon the missiles would be ready to fire," says former CIA director Richard Helms. "This was extremely important in the management of the crisis."

The U-2 imagery galvanized the Kennedy administration. Photo reconnaissance was stepped up: navy and air force jets, screaming over Cuba at 300 to 500 feet, provided a day-by-day record of the Soviets' frenzied efforts to prepare the missile sites. How soon would they be ready? Kennedy wanted to know. Five to six days, said CIA missile expert Albert Wheelon. Are you sure? JFK demanded. *You bet your ass*, Wheelon thought—then, remembering where he was, said, "Yes, sir." More SS-4s were found at Sagua La Grande, 150 miles east of Havana. Two new sites, one just west of Havana and one 185 miles to the east, were identified as launch areas for an entirely different missile, the SS-5. The SS-5 carried a larger warhead and had a range of 2,200 nautical miles—enough to reach most major cities in the continental United States. (The SS-5s, on Soviet ships that turned back when the United States imposed its naval quarantine, never reached Cuba.)

The combination of Penkovsky's material and intensive photo reconnaissance gave Kennedy two priceless advantages in the crisis: certainty and time. Time was crucial: it gave diplomacy a chance. Were the missiles being prepared for a Soviet first strike? It seemed unlikely, but no one knew for sure. The SS-5s in particular posed a threat to U.S.-based strategic bombers and missiles, and the Joint Chiefs of Staff were alarmed. The chiefs debated an array of military options ranging from bombing Cuba (OPLAN 312), 18 days of bombing followed by invasion (OPLAN 314) and five days of bombing followed by invasion (OPLAN 316, a so-called quick-reaction variant). Administration officials also discussed surgical strikes on the missiles, but the JCS thought that wouldn't work.

Kennedy and his top advisers—the "ExComm," or executive committee of the National Security Council—weighed the options and settled on a public warning to Khrushchev backed by a naval quarantine of Cuba. The blockade was firm action that stopped short of bombing or invasion. Throughout the crisis, Kennedy fended off pressure to use military force; his calm restraint was the measure of true leadership. The CIA, meanwhile, was desperately trying to figure out if the SS-4s had nuclear warheads. Field agents used neutron detectors, a device like a Geiger counter, to check for radiation coming from Soviet planes and ships en route to Cuba. Dino Brugioni, now retired from the CIA, has written an ambitious history of the crisis (*Eyeball to Eyeball: The Inside Story of the Cuban Missile Crisis*). He says the warheads were already on the sites—in specially equipped vans the photo experts had overlooked. The SS-4s and their nuclear payloads could be ready for launch within hours.

Kennedy waited four days for Khrushchev to respond. In Cuba, Soviet troops finished work on the SS-4 sites around San Cristóbal and Sagua La

Grande; in Washington, the Joint Chiefs of Staff pressed for tougher action—probably OPLAN 316, the quick-reaction plan. But Moscow was silent—and even now, former Soviet officials give sharply contradictory accounts of Khrushchev's decision process. Oleg Troyanovsky, a career Soviet diplomat who in 1962 was Khrushchev's translator, says Khrushchev did not seem alarmed by Kennedy's Oct. 22 speech or the U.S. quarantine. One of the six Soviet deputy commanders in Cuba, Gen. Leonid Garbuz, says Khrushchev gave orders to Soviet forces on the island to resist any American attack on Oct. 22, Oct. 25 and again—"categorically"—on Oct. 27. Garbuz, interviewed in Moscow by *Newsweek's* Dorinda Elliot, also says Khrushchev was emphatic that no nuclear weapons could be used.

Garbuz's account may shed new light on Khrushchev's thinking as the crisis approached it finale. Garbuz confirms that Khrushchev did not order the SAM launch that shot down an air force U-2 on Oct. 27; a Soviet commander in Cuba did that. But Khrushchev's repeated orders to his commanders to resist an American attack suggest that he was prepared to risk a shooting war as late as Oct. 27.

Kennedy was still maneuvering to resolve the crisis peacefully. Khrushchev on Oct. 26 had sent a long, impassioned letter that seemed to promise the missiles' withdrawal. On Oct. 27, however, Khrushchev sent a second letter demanding that Kennedy remove U.S. Jupiter missiles from Turkey in exchange for the SS-4s. The U-2 shootdown that same day seemed to underscore this new demand with the threat of further hostilities. Transcripts of the ExComm's deliberations show that many of Kennedy's advisers expected rapid escalation. The Joint Chiefs, unwilling to tolerate further attacks on U.S. reconnaisance planes, pushed for prompt approval of OPLAN 316.

Still, Kennedy played for time. He sent Robert Kennedy to see Anatoly Dobrynin, the Soviet ambassador in Washington, with a last message to Khrushchev. While accounts differ, the message seems to have been half stick and half carrot. The Jupitors would be withdrawn, so long as this concession was never linked publicly to the SS-4s—but all hell would break loose over Cuba unless Khrushchev replied within 24 hours. Again, the American side waited—and on Sunday, after a meeting with his inner circle at a government dacha outside Moscow, Khrushchev accepted the deal. The crisis was over. But the cold war and the arms race continued for 27 more years—and the lesson for presidents, looking back at the harrowing days of October '62, is to ensure that we never come so close to the brink again.

THE WORLD OF THE WHITE House staffer is unique. In the rarefied atmosphere of the West Wing of the White House, the president's press secretary, national security adviser, top personal assistants and troubleshooters, and other staffers who are particularly close to the president work near the Oval Office. Occupying physical space that is near the president is of enormous symbolic significance, being generally taken to reflect a close relationship with the president himself. Not all of the White House staff works in the West Wing; many occupy offices in the old and new executive office buildings, which are respectively adjacent to and directly across Pennsylvania Avenue from the White House. The formal executive office building overlooks the West Wing. President Carter moved Vice President Walter Mondale into an office in the West Wing to symbolize a close presidential–vice presidential relationship (the former vice president's office is occasionally used for ceremonial functions and stands ready to receive vice presidents in the future).

The White House staff is a relatively new institution; President Roosevelt created it in 1939 as part of his reorganization plan establishing the executive office of the president. The White House staff, however, did not come into its own as an independent force until much later. Although it always included powerful and influential persons, its original purpose was best expressed by Harry Truman: "The presidency is so tremendous that it is necessary for a president to delegate authority. To be able to do so safely, however, he must have around him people who can be trusted not to arrogate authority to themselves."[1] Truman continued, "Eventually I succeeded in surrounding myself with associates who would not overstep the bounds of that delegated authority, and they were people I could trust. This is policy on the highest level: it is the operation of the government by the Chief Executive under laws. That is what it amounts to, and when that ceases to be, chaos exists."[2]

President John F. Kennedy put together a dynamic and forceful staff that was later inherited by Lydon B. Johnson and described as "the best and the brightest" by journalist David Halberstam.[3] Halberstam argued persuasively that major White House decisions escalating the Vietnam War during the Johnson administration could be traced directly to powerful White House staffers such as Walt Rostow, McGeorge Bundy, and Robert McNamara (who later changed from hawk to dove and resigned his position as secretary of defense to become president of the World Bank).

It was during the Nixon years that the White House staff, controlled by H. R. (Bob) Haldeman and John Ehrlichman, arrogantly wielded power around Washington in the name of the president. The White House staff was dubbed the "Palace Guard," because of its reputation for preventing direct access to the president by cabinet officers and other top officials. Like Truman, Nixon recognized the need to delegate power, but unlike Truman, he

[1] Harry S Truman, *Memoirs: Volume 1, Year of Decisions* (Garden City, N.Y.: Doubleday, 1955), p. 228.

[2] Ibid.

[3] David Halberstam, *The Best and the Brightest* (New York: Random House, 1972).

did not recognize the critical importance of retaining absolute control over his own staff. Many of the acute embarrassments to the White House that occurred during the Nixon administration, including possibly the Watergate break-in itself, might have been avoided had the president been less optimistic about the system of broad delegation of powers that he established in the White House.

Regardless of who is president, the tendency of those on the White House staff is to aggrandize their personal power. White House staffers continually seek to be in the good graces of the president, which not only may involve back-room intrigue among different individuals and groups of staffers, but also tends to mute honest criticism of the president if he embarks on what an ambitious staffer feels to be the wrong course of action. In the following selection,

George Reedy, a longtime associate of Lyndon B. Johnson, both on Capitol Hill and in the White House, provides a succinct personal account of the way in which the institution of the presidency affects staffers. Reedy was Lyndon Johnson's press secretary in 1964–1965, after which he returned to private life, only to be summoned back to the White House in 1968 as a special adviser to the president on domestic matters. When Johnson was in the Senate, Reedy served him at various times, both as a staffer on the committees Johnson chaired and as a member of the senator's personal staff. Reedy's thesis is that the atmosphere of the White House tends to breed "blind ambition," to borrow John Dean's phrase on the part of staffers, even though their personalities might not have revealed this trait before they entered the White House.

19   George E. Reedy
THE WHITE HOUSE STAFF: A PERSONAL ACCOUNT

The most frequently asked question of any former presidential assistant is whether he misses the White House. My answer is a heartfelt no!

It is an institution which can be regarded with a far higher degree of approbation from the outside—where reverence softens the harsh lines of reality—than from the inside. Like any impressionistic painting, it improves with distance. . . . The factor that I have missed in most of the works on the presidency I have read is the impact of the institution on individuals. The literature on the subject seems to assume that the White House somehow molds the man and his assistants into finer forms and that the major problem of government is to assure channels through which these forms will have full expression. It is virtually taken for granted that the proper objective of a study of our chief executive is to identify those inhibiting factors which frustrate his efforts to resolve national problems and to devise mechanisms which will remove those frustrations. This is a type of study which should be continued on a priority basis. The frustrations are many and could be catastrophic.

But the analysis is inadequate. It ignores that fundamental reality of society, which is that institutions are manned by individual human beings and that government—regardless of the managerial flow charts produced by the behavioral scientists—is still a question of decisions that are made by people. The basic question is not whether we have devised structures with inadequate authority for the decision-making process. The question is whether the structures have created an environment in which men cannot function in any kind of a decent and humane relationship to the people whom they are supposed to lead. I am afraid—and on this point I am a pessimist—that we have devised that kind of a system.

To explain this, I must start with a highly personal reaction. The trouble with the White House—for anyone who is a part of it—is that when he picks up a telephone and tells people to do something, they usually do it. They may sabotage the project, after they have hung up the phone. They may stall, hoping that "the old son of a bitch" will forget about it. They may respond with an avalanche of statistics and briefing papers in which the original purpose will be lost and life will continue as before. But the heel click at the other end of the wire will be audible and the response—however invalid—will be prompt. There will be no delay in assurance, however protracted may be performance.

This is an unhealthy environment for men and women whose essential business is to deal with people in large numbers. It is soothing to the ego, but it fosters illusions about humanity. It comforts the weary assistant who may have gone round the clock in his search for a solution to an insoluble problem, but it paves the way for massive disillusionment. And for the very young, the process is demoralizing. It creates a picture of the world which is ill adapted to that which they will face once the days of glory come to an end. There should be a flat rule that no one be permitted to enter the gates of the White House until he is at least forty and has suffered major disappointments in life.

My own heart is back in the Senate, where I spent so many years of my adult life either as a newspaperman or a staff assistant. This is not because the people at the other end of Pennsylvania Avenue are any better in terms of character, wisdom, or goals. It is simply that their egos must face daily clashes with similarly strong egos who stand on a par and who do not feel any sense of subordination. In the Senate, no course stands the remotest chance of adoption unless a minimum of fifty-one egotistical men are persuaded of its wisdom, and in some cases the minimum is sixty-seven. These are preconditions under which even the most neurotic of personalities must make some obeisance to reality.

The inner life of the White House is essentially the life of the barnyard, as set forth so graphically in the study of the pecking order among chickens which every freshman sociology student must read. It is a question of who has the right to peck whom and who must submit to being pecked. There are only two important differences. The first is that the pecking order is determined by the individual strength and forcefulness of each chicken, whereas in the White House it depends upon the relationship to the barnyard keeper. The second is that no one outside the barnyard glorifies the chickens and expects them to order the affairs of mankind. They are destined for the frying pan and that is that.

The White House does not provide an atmosphere in which idealism and devotion can flourish. Below the president is a mass of intrigue, posturing, strutting, cringing, and pious "commitment" to irrelevant windbaggery. It is designed as the perfect setting for the conspiracy of mediocrity—that all too frequently successful collection of the untalented, the unpassionate, and the insincere seeking to convince the public that it is brilliant, compassionate, and dedicated.

There are, of course, men who see the inwardly over this affront to human dignity—most of whom either go smash or leave quietly, their muscles set rigidly to contain an indescribable agony. There are, of course, the warm and relaxed permanent White House staff members, secure in their mastery of the essential housekeeping machinery of the mansion and watching with wry amusement and some sympathy the frenetic efforts to shine forth boldly of those who have only four years out of all eternity to grab the brass ring. But the men of outrage are few and for some reason avoid each other after they slip out the side door. There are experiences which should not be shared. A reunion would lead only to a collective shriek.

It is not that the people who compose the menage are any worse than any other collection of human beings. It is rather that the White House is an ideal cloak for intrigue, pomposity, and ambition. No nation of free men should ever permit itself to be governed from a hallowed shrine where the meanest lust for power can be sanctified and the dullest wit greeted with reverential awe. Government should be vulgar, sweaty, plebeian, operating in an environment where a fool can be called a fool and the motivations of ideological pimpery duly observed and noted. In a democracy, meanness, dullness, and corruption are entitled to representation because they are part of the human spirit; they are not entitled to protection from the harsh and rude challenges that such qualities must face in the real world.

It is not enough to say that the White House need not be like this if it is occupied by another set of personalities. It is not enough to point out that I may subconsciously be exaggerating the conditions which I describe in overreacting to the reverence that has characterized most studies of the presidency. The fact remains that the institution provides camouflage for all that is petty and nasty in human beings, and enables a clown or a knave to pose as Galahad and be treated with deference.

Is my reaction purely personal disappointment or shaped by service in a specific White House in a specific administration? Obviously, no man can be truly objective about an experience so central to his life and so vital to all his goals and his aspirations. All I can say is that I am fully aware of the treacherous nature of one's sensory mechanisms in surveying the immediately surrounding universe. I have taken this factor into account and tried to allow for it in every possible way. . . . I believe that what I am saying is more than the conclusion of one man in a unique set of circumstances.

The thirty years I have spent in Washington have been punctuated with a number of telltale incidents. I have observed, for example, that former White House assistants are reticent about their experiences. When pressed for a description they invariably resort to words like "richly rewarding" and "fulfilling"—the clichés that men always use when they wish to conceal, rather than to convey, thought. And their congratulations to newly appointed assistants begin always with perfunctory "best wishes" and then shift to heartfelt friendly tips on how to survive. Only once have I felt a genuine flash of fire. It came from one of the top "assistants with a passion for anonymity" of the Roosevelt days. I described to him White House life as I saw it and his response—which was passionate—was: "Don't worry! That's the way it has always been and that's the way it will always be!"

I have a feeling that Camelot was not a very happy place. Even the gentle language of Malory does not fully cloak hints of intrigue, corruption, and distrust—reaching as high as Guinevere. And the "Table Round" seems better adapted to boozing in a vain effort to drown disappointment than to knightly discourse on chivalrous deeds and weighty matters of state.

In fact, Malory makes virtually no effort to describe Camelot as a seat of government. King Arthur was presumably beloved by his subjects because he was wise and valiant. But how did he handle road building, public charity, or the administration of justice? Such questions had to wait several hundred years for the advent of Mark Twain, whose entirely fictitious (and wholly irreverent) account was probably much closer to the reality than that produced by the original sources.

It is this aspect that gives cause for concern. The psychological ease of those who reside in Camelot does not matter except to the individuals themselves. But the type of government that Camelot produces affects every individual and, ultimately, can determine the character of the society in which we all must live.

It is my highly pessimistic view that Camelot will no longer suffice—however effective it may have been in the past. As a rallying point for men who would beat off dragons and ogres, it was superb. As a devise to lead us through the stresses of modern life, it is wholly inadequate, And one of the few historical principles in which I still retain faith is that an inadequate government will either fall or resort to repression.

There is no reason to believe that the United States is exempt from the forces of history. We have no special writ from the Almightly which will substitute for normal human wisdom. There is no evidence that such wisdom is being applied effectively to the overwhelming problems that beset us nor is there any light on the horizon. And while it may seem premature at this point, we may well be witnessing the first lengthening of the shadows that will become the twilight of the presidency.

20

David Von Drehle
BRUCE LINDSEY, BASKING IN ANONYMITY

The Washington Power Game is an indoor sport: You must be in the room to play. Nowadays, Bruce Lindsey is always in the room. Nowadays, you see, "the room" is wherever President Clinton happens to be making decisions. "The room" is Clinton's innermost circle. Lindsey is always there, a trusted adviser on all manner of subjects.

And because he is in the room, Lindsey—a mild-looking Arkansas lawyer and behind-the-scenes pol—may have influence second only to Hillary Clinton's, though most Americans have scarcely heard his name.

Tough, smart, loyal, well-to-do, unassuming to the verge of anonymity, Lindsey was "the one indispensable person" in Clinton's campaign. Clinton said so himself, to Arkansas Sen. David Pryor.

He comes to Washington with the wide-ranging powers of a "senior adviser" to Clinton and head of the White House Office of Personnel. He will be a riddle, in this town where the backslapping, name-dropping, press hound former ambassador Robert Strauss is a quintessential man of influence. Lindsey is so deeply, self-effacingly devoted to Clinton that he borders on invisible.

"Washington has never seen a guy like Bruce," says Pryor, who once leaned on Lindsey as heavily as Clinton now does. "There is no Bruce Lindsey agenda, and that's what makes him fascinating. He has only the best interests of Bill Clinton in mind."

Imagine how precious that must be to Clinton, whose universe is choked with people, from Medford to Murmansk, who have favors to ask or axes to grind. "Or they have a grievance, or some advantage they want to get for their little bit of inside information," says Clinton communications director George Stephanopoulos.

By contrast, according to old Arkansas friends and campaign veterans, Lindsey appears to want nothing more than to advance, protect and serve his old friend. Clinton trusts him "completely. More than completely," Stephanopoulos says.

No job title can capture the range of Lindsey's service to Clinton; his roles have included being Clinton's pal, his lawyer, his bludgeon, his stiletto, his brake and his conscience.

When candidate Clinton was too jazzed to sleep, Lindsey stayed up half the night playing hearts with him, a sly and cunning counterpoint to Clinton's bold shoot-the-moon style.

When a damaging story appeared in *The New York Times* after the Florida primary, one close aide recalls, Lindsey tracked the leak to a campaign consultant and "ripped his head off."

When Clinton's national organization was at odds with a group of Georgia volunteers, Lindsey sliced through the bureaucracy to clean up the debacle.

Insiders call him "The Enforcer," "The Attorney," "The Truth-Teller," "The Loyalist" and most precisely, perhaps, "The *Consiglieri*," borrowing the underworld term for a Mafia don's closest, most reliable counselor.

Consider this little story, related by a high-level campaign aide:

Back in autumn of 1991, the entire Clinton juggernaut consisted of Bruce and Bill, two drawling 40-somethings from little ol' Little Rock, flying commercial and plotting the defeat of a wildly popular incumbent.

They had a chance to hire a whiz from Capitol Hill as deputy campaign manager. At the end of the young man's interview, Clinton asked Lindsey, Why should I hire a deputy when we don't even have a campaign manager yet?

"Because," Lindsey said, "you need to hire George Stephanopoulos." That was the young man's name. Lindsey's pick turned out to be one of the campaign's brightest stars.

Lindsey, however, was never a star. He likes his profile low. In his conservative spectacles and tidy gray suits, he looks as innocuous as a bank examiner.

He refuses all requests for interviews; asked to talk for this article, he groaned, "Oh, no!" Lindsey is so publicity-shy that his colleagues were surprised to see him strutting after TV's "McLaughlin Group" named him "the second most powerful person" in the Clinton White House.

Then the Clinton camp realized what made him so proud. It was another assessment on the show, from *Newsweek's* Eleanor Clift: "Bruce Lindsey will never be a good source."

The idea of power being exercised behind closed doors by little-known figures makes many Americans uncomfortable. But his friends—and even some people who might be expected to be enemies—say there is nothing to fear from Lindsey.

One reason is Lindsey's upbringing. He's the son of the late Bob Lindsey, which in Little Rock is like saying he was born on Olympus. Bob Lindsey was one of Arkansas' most important lawyers and a pillar of the Presbyterian Church. Bob Lindsey "told his clients what the right thing to do was, then he made them do it," a protege recalls.

As a young man, Bruce was told repeatedly not to expect a place at his father's firm. When Bruce eventually applied to join, Bob Lindsey refused to recommend his son to his partners.

"Mr. Lindsey told Bruce he should never abuse a special relationship," says Bruce Lindsey's wife, Bev.

Like his father, Bruce Lindsey made a lucrative practice of defending corporations in labor disputes. Nevertheless, even John T. Lavey, perhaps Little Rock's most rock-ribbed pro-labor lawyer, speaks highly of his frequent adversary. "Bruce gives it to you straight," he says. "He never sandbagged a case on me, and the end would never justify the means for him."

The difference between the Lindseys was politics; The father had little interest; the son caught the bug. After graduating from Rhodes College in Memphis, Lindsey went to work for former Democratic senator William J. Fulbright. In Fulbright's office, in 1968, he met the young Bill Clinton.

A couple of years later, Lindsey began his right-hand-man relationship with Pryor, foreshadowing his service to Clinton. He was Pryor's legal counsel in the governor's mansion, then Pryor's top legislative aide in the Senate.

"He has a mind that is very, very useful," says Pryor. "If I were to call Bruce today and ask him how I voted on some little State Department bill back in 1979, he would close his eyes and spew out the vote and then tell me why I was for or against."

Pryor also remembers Lindsey as "wonderful company"; clearly Clinton feels the same, because Lindsey is his constant traveling companion. "I always remember the time we were flying around Arkansas attending Fourth of July events." Pryor says. "Well, the National Guard landed us in the wrong town and we wound up hitchhiking 20 miles in the back of a watermelon truck. Even in that truck, Bruce managed to look dignified.

"You might not tell by looking, but Bruce loves combat," says Pryor. "He just doesn't want to be the general."

Since 1980, he has been in Clinton's unofficial, unpaid service. It's a very close relationship. Bev Lindsey, a formidable pol in her own right, has worked on Clinton's paid staff. The Lindsey's two daughters are friends of Chelsea Clinton.

They are a lot alike, Bruce at 44 and Bill at 46. Clinton blows the saxophone; Lindsey plays the piano. A mutual friend tells of a ride through the Arkansas countryside when the pair matched their prodigious memories by recalling vote totals from past elections in each precinct they crossed.

Both understand that politics is in the details: Late one recent night, Lindsey found—deep in a USA Today profile of a football coach in East St. Louis—a brief mention of the fact that the coach had been photographed with Clinton but never received a print. Lindsey woke the staff photographer and directed him to find the negatives and print one for the coach.

But where Clinton hopes to please everyone, Lindsey is more likely to let people know what he thinks of them. He reads nearly everything written about Clinton, then dishes out soft but stern complaints to reporters and darts to loose-lipped staff members.

And where Clinton, and his wife, Hillary, love to bat around policy ideas, Lindsey focuses on political pragmatics. "He tends to be pessimistic, to expect the worst," says Arkansas state legislator David Matthews. "That's a good balance, because Bill tends to be optimistic."

Doug Buford has been in many legal and political strategy sessions with Lindsey. "Someone can come in and blow everybody away with a great-sounding proposal. But you look over at Bruce and he has a troubled look on his face. He can see down the road further than most people. "It's a little like chess," he says. "Bruce is in his endgame when the rest of us are in the middle."

A senior campaign aide tells this story: Very late in the campaign, Clinton was stumping in Oregon, where he was sure to win. An antihomosexual measure was on the ballot. Several Clinton strategists urged him not to make a speech against the initiative, saying there was nothing to gain in Oregon and plenty to lose in closely contested conservative states.

Lindsey was in the room. After all the arguments had been put forth, Lindsey made his brief comment. "Why do you want to be president if you can't stand up for what you believe?" the source recalls him saying.

Clinton made the forthright speech.

T HE EMOLUMENTS OF HIGH political office include an array of perquisites (or perks, as they are more commonly called) that are often unknown to but would dazzle the average citizen. The criticism of perks paid by taxpayers is a favorite media sport, and even politicians themselves find that they can profit by attacking the perks of government officeholders. The president and his staff enjoy the most extensive perks in government, as the following selection describes.

21 Christopher Georges
EXECUTIVE
SWEET

"Imagine what it's like to fly first class on the best airline," says one Bush aide. "Well, think of one level better; now you're getting close to what White House travel is like." Bragging perhaps, but the sad truth is that he's right. And the perks don't just come at 20,000 feet; back on earth there's the White House Mess, the 29-car limo fleet, the health care benefits, the free gym, and more. How could this be, you ask? Didn't they clamp down on all those White House freebies back when they put the House bank out of business? Not a chance. Despite the podium pounding and the mea culpas from congressional and White House big wigs over perks, the dirty little secret on West Executive Drive is that as far as White House goodies go, it's business as usual.

And quite a business it is. The White House employs a staff of nearly 100 butlers, doormen, maids, drivers, chefs, waiters, "gift analyzers," florists (four of them), and calligraphers (five). Travel costs for the president and his staff come to more than $100 million annually. The total budget for White House expenses? About $150 million. The real cost of presidential perks, however, can't be measured in dollars, but by the attitude it engenders among the president's top aides. Eating lunch, for example, means a short walk down to the Mess where the waiter (who has been your personal waiter for the past two years) sits you down (at the table with an engraved pewter ingot that bears your name), and serves you a drink (which you didn't have to order because he already knows what you like). After that kind of treatment, you might just feel a little grander than the average person.

Of course, with the arrival of Bill Clinton, there's some hope that this may change. After all, central to his anointment was his ability to convince people that he does in fact empathize with the average American; that he's as likely to lunch at a Northeast McDonald's as at the West Wing Mess. But there's no guarantee that the Clintonites won't rely on the same arguments as have administrations before them to preserve their special status—namely that the perks make them more efficient and the freebies are no grander than those enjoyed by, say, business leaders or high priced lawyers.

Care, Free

That, of course, may be true, but it's also true that their private sector counterparts don't make policy for the rest of America. Which is why the issue of perks can't simply be dismissed, as it often is, as a matter of a few harmless goodies that make life just a little bit easier for hard working White House staffers. Consider the health care perk, which is arguably the most damaging of them all, as it can easily blind top policymakers to the urgency of the nation's problem. White House big shots not only automatically receive the very best of health insurance plans (for just $100 per month), but have access to some of the best doctors and most sophisticated medical facilities in the nation. The White House medical unit, led by the president's personal physician, is on call 24 hours a day to care for any medical emergencies that any White House brass or Cabinet members may encounter. And while the nation's first doctor and his staff won't offer regular checkups, the office does work as a referral service. "We'll make sure you get into the best location at the best price," said President Bush's physician Dr. Burton Lee III. If such solicitous service were not a given at the presidential mansion, we might today be debating how to improve on our universal health care plan instead of still trying to create one.

At the other end of Pennsylvania Avenue, Congress, although still clinging to some of its perks—such as free parking in and around the Capitol and at airports, amnesty from parking tickets in D.C., and limousine privileges—has at least cut out some of its freebies. Gone are the discount gym, car wash, and haircuts, free flowers, bargain gift shop, and House bank, It wouldn't hurt for the Clinton administration to pick up where Congress left off. No one, of course, wants our government leaders to go without health insurance or be forced to walk to lunch in the rain, but as Clinton's top aides find themselves drawn into the presidential bubble, one way they can keep their feet on the same ground as—and their ears attuned to the problems of—the rest of America, is to close the gap between the way the White House staff and the rest of us live.

And just what sacrifices would that entail? For one, it would mean making travel with the president a little less regal. Here's a sketch of what it's now like to be a part of the president's travelling entourage:

About the only strain is getting yourself and your bags to your White House office. Once there, a member of the trip crew will ferry your personal belongings to the plane. A limousine or helicopter will be waiting outside the White House to rush you to Andrews Air Force Base, where you'll board Air Force One. Once in your seat (and every seat is first class caliber), you'll most likely be served—even though you didn't place an order for—your favorite drink in a crystal glass. "The stewards make it a point to know what each of us likes," explains one White House frequent traveller. "And from then on, the flow of food and service is endless"—which helps explain the $40,000 per hour cost of maintaining the plane. Perhaps you need to conduct some business? Secretarial support is at the ready to place a call or take a memo. "It's what I call 'low impact travel,' " explains one Bush aide. "High impact travel is lugging your bags to the airport, standing in line, and arguing when you can't get a seat. None of that here."

Once you've touched down, the presidential party is led to the waiting motorcade, which is where perk-mongering can get competitive. The goal is to land yourself a seat in one of the frontmost cars, known as the "secure package"—the group of limos that carry the president, his most trusted advisors, their aides, and various other hangers-on. Why the pressure to get in (aside from the glee of inciting the envy of your co-workers)? The secure package takes you from the airport to the most convenient of disembarking points, perhaps a special entrance to the hotel. The rest of the president's court will be unceremoniously dropped off perhaps a few yards away from the hotel entrance and face the humiliation of hoofing it to the lobby from the curb.

Once at the hotel, you can keep your Ramada Reward card in your wallet. Accommodations are almost always first class (the Four Seasons in Beverly Hills—at about $300 per night for a single room—and the Marriott in Century City—at about $200 per night—were two of Bush's West Coast favorites). Inside, staff escorts will be waiting to take you to your room. (In fact, during the trip, you'll never have to deal with anyone but federal employees.) No mad scramble to the check-in counter here. Your room is preselected and your bags (remember, the last we saw them was in the White House) are there waiting.

For those annoying cases when your escort forgets which room is yours, you're still in good shape. Staffers' names are written in calligraphy on cards placed on their room doors. And if you're worried about drawing a room with, say, the Simpsons next door, no sweat. Presidential parties don't reserve rooms, but floors. The big shots, such as the Bakers and Scowcrofts, will get suites while the rest will have to make do with singles. To soften the blow, however, each staffer will be greeted with a basket of fresh fruit and a cheery note from the manager.

But but before taking a bite out of that mango, check the phone to see how you're doing in the White House pecking order. If you're a bigfoot, your phone will have already been rewired so that it is part of the White House system back in D.C. No need to trouble yourself hitting that nasty eight key to place a long distance call. But pick up the phone and get the hotel operator, and you'll know you're still not in the upper echelons of the White House staff.

And what's it like when it's time to leave the hotel? Consider the eight day, May 1989 presidential trip from D.C. to Rome, Brussels, Bonn, and London, which cost taxpayers more than $1.5 million to move and house 107 staffers (including, among others, an assortment of assistant press secretaries, scheduling secretaries, and personal aides to the First Lady). For one 15-minute drive down London's Downing Street to attend a reception hosted by Prime Minister Margaret Thatcher, a few dozen staffers were ferried by a caravan of 18 vehicles. The first four held the president, a British dignitary, and secret service. The next held John Sununu, followed by cars carrying Marlin Fitzwater and James Baker. In the middle cars were Brent Scowcroft, Margaret Tutwiler, Andrew Card, and the White House chief of protocol. Then came various aides, empty follow-up vehicles, a camera car, police cars, ambulances and, last and least, the press van.

Eventually, of course, the entourage comes home, and while life isn't nearly as cushy, no one's griping about the comfort level at 1600 Pennsylvania. Perhaps the most coveted of White House perks is the right to dine in the White House Mess—which is to lunch what Steuben is to glass. "The beauty is not the room or the food," explains one Bush aide, "but the prestige. It's the ultimate invitation."

How so? Executive Mess rights are the precious privilege of about 30 of the president's top aides, including Cabinet secretaries, assistants and deputy assistants to the president. "Many will call, but few are chosen," explains one aide with a seat in the Mess. (It's called the Mess because it's operated by the Navy.) That seat entitles him to breakfast or lunch (no dinner is served there) in the tastefully appointed room—seven tables, wood paneled walls adorned with pictures of Navy carriers, upholstered seats—located in the White House basement.

Upon arriving for lunch at the Mess, you're greeted at the door by a Navy steward who, of course, knows your name and where you like to sit, which is likely to impress even the most cynical of guests. On the way over to the table, chances are good you'll pass by the president. While the meals are not extravagant, the food is top quality, similar to what you might find at a small, fine restaurant. The menu changes daily and there's always a fresh fish of the day, as well as an assortment of salads. (Thursday—Tex/Mex day—is especially popular, staffers eagerly volunteer, as is Friday—crab cake day.)

Of course, the food's not free, but none of those I talked to knew the price of the meals. Why not? Everything goes on a monthly tab. But, they assured me, the costs were about 25 percent cheaper than what you'd find in a comparable restaurant in the outside world.

For those who don't make it into the top 30, you can watch with envy, but in sufficient comfort, from the Staff Mess located next door. Hardly a booby prize, Staff Mess privileges are doled out to about 100 White House workers, mostly commissioned officers to the president. The main difference is basically prestige, as the kitchen is shared, but the walls are there so the big shots don't have to rub elbows with the lower echelons of the staff.

Limousine Conservatives

If you do decide to take your lunch—or any excursion—outside the compound, you can show off your special status by making use of the White House's limo service. Simply call down for a car and a Chrysler New Yorker (equipped with a car phone) will be at the ready to ferry you three blocks or 30 miles. For most staffers, the only place the cars won't take you is home. That perk, known as portal to portal, is reserved for Cabinet secretaries, deputy Cabinet secretaries, and any six aides the president chooses. In the past, portal to portal privileges have gone to the chief of staff, the chief economic advisor, the national security advisor, the budget director, and the chief of protocol.

Other goodies, such as free parking on West Executive Drive just outside the White House, certainly make life easier for the staff, but ultimately drive a wedge between the leaders and the led. White House biggies also have access to the president's private tennis court, located on the South Lawn. (It's a single, hard surface court that one staffer complained "is on a slant.") For rainy days, there's the private gym in the basement of the Old Executive Office Building, complete with weights, a treadmill, exercise bike, nautilus machines, sauna, jacuzzi, and shower. (The swimming pool, bowling alley, and movie theater are reserved only for the president, his family and guests.) And about 100 of the top staff can sign up to use the presidential box at the Kennedy Center, which seats up to twelve. (Use of this perk, however, was frowned upon in the Bush White House. "They made us jump through hoops to get them," groaned one aide.)

While the Bushies may have been forced to rely on some savvy to cash in the free tickets, it's a far cry from the attitude in the Carter White House, which marked the last time there was any attempt to keep a lid on the perks. Carter perhaps took too personal a role in restricting perks (as when he insisted that he personally monitor the list of who was using the White House tennis courts), but his heart was in the right place. When he closed down the Executive Mess (which Regan later restored) and insisted that Kennedy Center tickets be issued only as rewards for exemplary work, he knew he was not only sending a signal to America that White House staff are no more special than the rest of us, but a message to his team not to forget whence they came.

Bill Clinton can't rely on Congress to send that message to his staff. (While there is currently a bill pending Congress dealing with White House expenses, the furthest it goes is requiring the White House to disclose exactly how it spends its operating budget.) Only the president can set the tone.

If he doesn't, he'll be faced with the same kind of attitude expressed by one senior level Bush White House aide, who remarked that "It is not important to me that Brent Scowcroft knows the price of peanut butter, but it is important that he knows what's going on in Somalia." Scowcroft is, no doubt, a smart guy. There's no reason why he—or whoever fills his office in the White House—shouldn't know both.

THE CONGRESS

Chapter
Five

Congress is a fascinating amalgam of individual characters, personalities, and styles, which help to shape the institution. Personality is particularly important, as it affects congressional leadership, both of party leaders and of committee chairpersons. Different personality types in positions of power within Congress develop contrasting styles that influence the way Congress operates. For example, the Senate under the majority leadership of Lyndon B. Johnson operated very differently than it did under Mike Mansfield. Johnson's active-negative character was as evident in the Senate as in the White House. His personality compelled him to seek control over the Senate, which he managed to achieve through knowledge of the strengths, weaknesses, and needs of his colleagues; skill in manipulation of institutional procedures; and an extraordinary ability to persuade others. Each senator became a challenge to Johnson, who sought personal loyalty above all else. The aggressive and dominating style of Lyndon Johnson as majority leader of the Senate was similar to but much more flamboyant than that of his mentor, House Speaker Sam Rayburn, and it stemmed from different personal needs.

In sharp contrast to Johnson's style was that of Mike Mansfield, who was elected majority leader in January 1961 and served until his retirement at the end of the nintey-fourth Congress in 1976. Mansfield's style was, to say the least, more muted than Johnson's. He treated each senator with great respect and as an equal. No attempt at a personal cult of leadership was evident during Mansfield's tenure. Johnson was highly effective as a personal leader, whereas Mansfield's effectiveness was as a team player. The contrasting personalities of Johnson and Mansfield go a long way toward explaining differences in Senate operation during their periods of leadership. Under Mansfield, senators were far freer to pursue their own legislative interests without fear of retaliation if they happened to disagree with the majority leader. Mansfield's style became the model for his successor, Robert Byrd. Howard Baker, too, led by consensus, not by command, in a Senate that would no longer tolerate Johnson's system of unilateral control.

Personality is as important in the House as in the Senate in determining who runs for positions of party leadership and what their styles of leadership will be. Sam Rayburn, Speaker of the House for 17 years, enforced discipline. Like Lyndon Johnson in the Senate, Sam Rayburn knew every member of the House, their constituencies, and their needs and aspirations. He was able to use this information to consolidate his power as Speaker. Again like Johnson, Rayburn operated on a highly personal basis. The House was his constituency, as the Senate was Johnson's, and he did not hesitate to involve Republicans as well as

Democrats in his decisions. The election of John McCormack as Speaker of the House in 1962 brought profound changes, primarily because of the contrasting personalities of Rayburn and McCormack. Robert L. Peabody says:

> Peaceful succession brings on more incremental change, but the impact of such *different personalities* as Rayburn and McCormack on the Office of the Speaker was considerable. McCormack's style was both more institutional and partisan than Rayburn's. He called more meetings to discuss legislative strategy and involved the Majority Leader and Whip to a much greater extent than Rayburn did. . . .
>
> The telephone was one of McCormack's most effective weapons—"I'd call the devil if I thought it would do any good." In contrast, Rayburn operated on a more independent and personal basis. He preferred the intimacy and informality of after-the-season gatherings of the "Board of Education." The Whip organization was used less frequently and Rayburn almost never called a party caucus beyond the opening meeting.[1]

Both Rayburn and McCormack, although differing in their personalities and styles, provided effective leadership to the House. In contrast, Carl Albert of Oklahoma, who became Speaker in 1971, displayed a personality and style critics denounced as weak and ineffective. Peabody points out that "one reason he easily advanced to the speakership was summed up in a widely affirmed statement—'Nobody's mad at Carl.' "[2] Being a "nice guy" is usually a reflection of the inability to make hard decisions that inevitably antagonize others.

After an extensive analysis of congressional leadership, Peabody concluded:

> Of the twenty variables highlighted in this analysis, the most pervasive and continuing influence upon leadership's selection for party office has been exerted by the personality and skill of the candidate and, especially, of the incumbent. Every leader in Congress, as in other organizations, brings to office a unique set of characteristics: age, ambition, education, health, personal skills, prior political and professional experience—in sum, a personality. Not only does this personality affect the opportunities he may have to obtain a leadership position, they also, in part, influence the extent to which he can maintain office and perhaps even alter the scope and potential of a given party position. A leader's personality, his strengths and liabilities, also is the single most important variable that affects his ability to withstand or succumb to a challenge.[3]

Personality is also a factor in the selection of committees and in the functioning of the committee chairmen. The Senate Government Operations Committee (renamed the Governmental Affairs Committee in 1977) under the chairmanship of Senator Joseph McCarthy from 1953 until 1955 operated very

[1]Robert L. Peabody, *Leadership in Congress* (Boston: Little, Brown, 1976), p. 309. Italics added.

[2]Ibid., p. 155.

[3]Ibid., p. 498.

differently than it has at any other time because of the senator's distinctive personality and style. Likewise, the Senate Foreign Relations Committee underwent notable changes after Senator John Sparkman of Alabama became chairman; following Senator William J. Fulbright's long tenure from 1959 until his defeat in 1974.

South Carolina Republican Strom Thurmond ran the Senate Judiciary Committee from 1984 to 1986 in an entirely different way than did both his predecessor, Massachusetts Senator Edward Kennedy, and his successor, Delaware Senator Joe Biden, who took charge in 1987.

Weak chairmen, strong chairmen, chairmen who seek the limelight, and those who use chairmanships for "grandstanding," all have contrasting personalities and styles. The committee system is an important institution of Congress, and the way it functions largely depends on the personalities of committee members. Committees are used to advance the goals of their heads and key members, who are attempting to gain power and status within and outside of Congress. Thus, the legislative work of committees is often undertaken as much to serve personal ambition as to respond to constituents' needs; legislators use the committee hearing and investigation process for personal aggrandizement as well as for legislation.

Beyond Capitol Hill, personality is also a key factor in determining the way in which representatives and senators relate to their constituents. Personal choice and preferences determine the amount and kinds of electoral responsibilities that will be delegated to staff, how much time a candidate will spend in his or her district, the nature of constituent contacts—whether in large or small groups or one-on-one—and what type of media will be emphasized. Political campaigning always reflects the character and style of the candidate.

POLITICAL SCIENTIST RICHARD F. Fenno, Jr., lists three incentives that guide, to varying degrees, the behavior of members of Congress: (1) reelection; (2) power and influence *within* Congress; (3) good public policy.[1]

Goals are not mutually exclusive, but members usually do pursue one more than the others. Junior House members, for example, who have not yet secured their electoral bases, devote more time, energy, and resources to winning reelection than to climbing the congressional ladder of power. But once members of Congress can count on electoral support, which House members usually do after they have served several terms, they can devote more time to their Washington careers. A House member in his second term observed, "I haven't been a congressman yet. The first two years, I spent all of my time getting myself reelected. So I won't be a congressman until next year."[2] Being a congressman means to most members being free to pursue internal power and influence without having to worry about constituency pressures.

Members of the House and the Senate can take either the *committee* or *party and leadership* routes to power. The first involves seeking the most prestigious committees, such as the House Ways and Means, Appropriations, and Rules committees, or the Senate Foreign Relations, Judiciary, Finance, and Appropriations committees. It is difficult and sometimes impossible for junior congresspersons and senators to obtain seats on these committees. They often have to wait years before they can get on the panels of their choice.

Moreover, junior members may prefer what are called *reelection committees*, such as Agriculture, Interior, and Insular Affairs, which have jurisdiction over matters of more direct and special concern to their districts. Of course, members of Congress can and have used their positions on the more prestigious committees, particularly Appropriations, Finance, and Ways and Means, to boost their reelection prospects by tending to constituency interests and claiming credit for benefits flowing to their districts. But these and other influential committees represent and serve the broader memberships of the House and the Senate, diminishing the capacity of any single committee member to give priority in committee deliberations to interests of his or her district.

Although most members seeking internal power take the committee route, a select few rise to the top through service to their congressional parties. House members who set their sights particularly high aim to become Speaker, which is one of the most powerful positions not only in Congress but in the entire government. It is a long journey to the speakership. The majority party, which determines who will fill the position, chooses only someone who has performed effectively in lower-party leadership posts. The House majority leader often succeeds to the speakership, having been elected by the party to the next highest position. The party caucus chairman and the chief whip then may compete to become majority leader. The chairman of the Rules Committee, who occupies what is essentially a party leadership po-

[1] See Richard F. Fenno, Jr., *Congressmen in Committees* (Boston: Little, Brown, 1973) and *Homestyle* (Boston: Little, Brown, 1978).

[2] Fenno, *Homestyle*, p. 215.

sition, may also join the fray if he or she is particularly ambitious. Of course, no one is excluded from running for party posts, although generally the party leadership track is confined to those who have chosen it over the committee route to power.

The following selection portrays one of the most powerful members of the House of Representatives, who took the committee route to power and influence. Woodrow Wilson, in his famous book entitled *Congressional Government* (1885), called committee chairman the "feudal barons" of Congress who wield absolute power over their committee fiefdoms. More than one hundred years later, Hedrick Smith, one of the most astute observers of the Washington political scene, labeled committee chairmen the "prime ministers" of our government.[3] There is little doubt that the subject of the following study, Michigan Congressman John Dingell, is one of the prime ministers of Capitol Hill.

22   David Rogers
MAN OF
CAPITOL

Most members of Congress tax, spend and borrow. John Dingell muscles, questions and regulates.

As the chairman of the Energy and Commerce Committee, Mr. Dingell can be both advocate and arbiter in disputes between the Baby Bells and American Telephone & Telegraph, hospitals insurers, stockbrokers and banks. Because of its historic role in creating agencies such as the Securities and Exchange Commission [SEC], the panel that he heads reaches into executive-branch decision-making in a fashion matched by few others. That authority, bolstered by the fact that Mr. Dingell also personally leads the committee's Investiations and Oversight Panel, gives him a hunting license to probe much of corporate America—oil, rails, securities, communications, science—and he is the legislative switchman on the freightlines of commerce.

"Talk to me," invites the burly Michigan Democrat, but before the words are out, his arm settles on his target's shoulder with the weight of a 4 × 4 post—pressure treated. "We have a very good friendship," says Rep. Edward Madigan, an Illinois Republican and senior member of Energy and Commerce. "I think I'm high on his list—after General Motors, Ford, Chrysler and Detroit Edison."

[3]Hedrick Smith, *The Power Game: How Washington Works* (New York: Random House, 1988).

Behind his restless, bullying energy, the 63-year-old Mr. Dingell is a study in power—and a study in Congress itself as the institution seeks to regain direction in a new decade. For more than a half century, the Dingell family has held a seat in the House, and few lawmakers are more identified with the entrenched legislative government that endures as presidents come and go.

Growing Up in Congress

"Let's go back home," Mr. Dingell tells an aide upon leaving the White House for the Capitol. As a boy, he walked the stone-tiled halls with his father. As a chairman, his love of procedure and iron hand emulate Sam Rayburn, who ran the Commerce Comittee early in the New Deal before becoming Speaker.

"You have given me no reason to undo what my father and Sam Rayburn did," Mr. Dingell once told an executive seeking to weaken a 1930s public-utility holding-company law.

Like a modern Judge Roy Bean, Mr. Dingell uses his dominating personality to pressure witnesses—and force action—even without any specific legislation.

He snorts at the "whole helluva mess of bonuses" paid before Drexel Burnham Lambert Inc.'s demise—and letters go out to the SEC demanding an accounting. (SEC Chairman Richard Breeden said . . . that the SEC is looking into Drexel's payment of $260 million of bonuses in cash and stock to its employees.)

In full-page newspaper ads, Bolar Pharmaceutical Co. blasted him last fall for creating a "climate of fear" in the generic-drug industry. Months later, the New York company was embarrassed when its outside counsel acknowledged that the company had submitted false documents to the Food and Drug Administration.

No Man to Con

"You don't try to con John Dingell," says Sen. Ted Stevens, an Alaska Republican whose own legislative style also tends to the Sam Peckinpah school. "I don't think at the moment he has a peer as chairman of an oversight committee," Speaker Thomas Foley says.

"I am first among equals; I am not the boss," Mr. Dingell says with a laugh, explaining himself to Polish Solidarity leaders here to learn about committe procedure. His voice quavers as he—the great-grandson of a Polish immigrant—becomes a teacher for the new parliament. "They are a model of strength and endurance and courage and dedication," he says later. "I'd rather see a lot more of that kind of thing around me."

Mr. Dingell longs for a more activist federal government even as he senses that his own democratic institution—Congress—may be faltering. In the past year, scandal has swept away old leadership allies, and he himself has come to symbolize the parochialism that often characterizes Congress and his party.

Mr. Dingell's alliance with the auto industry—and reluctant pursuit of a new clean-air law—strains the patience of liberal friends. He provoked a bitter fight by insisting on acting on a business-backed product-liability bill before the 1988 elections. His aggressive investigative style brought embarrassment last year when an aide—since dismissed—was found to have authorized secret tapings of phone conversations in a securities-industry probe.

"I'm not a big power; I *hold* big power," Mr. Dingell says. But power draws him into a Washington establishment far removed from his political heritage. Before becoming a congressman, Mr. Dingell's father was a jack-of-all-trades, pipeline supervisor, beef dealer and news printer—the consummate little guy who overcame poor health to fight for medical care for others. Describing the capital's lobbyists in 1936, he said, "There are altogether too many cheap lawyers here whose practice is about on a par with petit larceny, who would starve to death anywhere but in Washington."

Today, Mr. Dingell hunts with and befriends the same lobbying corps. Although organized labor remains his largest single source of political funds, corporate political action committees [PACs] gave the lion's share of more than $1 million received by the chairman's organization over the past three election campaigns. The issues that Energy and Commerce deals with tend less to pit unions against business than to pit industry against industry—making the committee the leading magnet for special-interest money in the House.

PACs have contributed an estimated $25 million or more to current committee members in the past three election campaigns, and special-interest money has become a form of patronage within the panel. In the last Congress, for example, Mr. Dingell overrode caucus rules and pushed through a change in how members are assigned to subcommittees. That single stroke cut the power of rival subcommittee chairmen and helped his younger allies win lucrative assignments to panels with jurisdiction over cash-rich industries able to give large amounts.

His Many Roles

In the bloody fight over his product-liability measure—a crucial issue to Michigan powers Ford Motor and Upjohn—Mr. Dingell was unsparing in his anger over opposition from trial lawyers. In other cases, as in a fight between television networks and producers over whether the networks can share program-syndication rights, Mr. Dingell can seem to dance with both sides. At one point, he supported the networks on a critical procedural motion, then gave the producers a bill barring the Federal Communications Commission from acting in favor of the networks.

Mr. Dingell's aggressive expansion of his jurisdiction is near-legendary, but the reaction of his fellow chairmen is more complex than it first appears. Former House Banking Committee Chairman Fernand St. Germain once yielded jurisdiction to Mr. Dingell, knowning that Energy and Commerce would slow down a bill Mr. St. Germain feared was moving too fast in his own panel. Similarly, Mr. Dingell, in a celebrated jurisdictional battle with the House Public Works Committee in 1987, had strong support among his fellow chairmen but lost largely because of GOP opposition to his increased power.

"Power is a tool . . . like a hammer or a saw or a wrench," Mr. Dingell says. Standing 6 foot 3 inches, this blacksmith's grandson prefers the hammer. He pounds witnesses with rapid-fire questions, often accompanied by abrasive commentary that puts his target at a disadvantage. "One of the things I have found with rascals is they generally tend to try to retreat into a state of blissful ignorance," said Mr. Dingell in an aside aimed at Safeway executive Walter Schoendorf in a 1987 hearing. "He just dominates," says Mr. Schoendorf, laughing about the experience today. "There's not much give-and-take."

Rooted in New Deal

Others find it harder to laugh, and after 35 years in Congress, Mr. Dingell can seem less a lawmaker than a law unto himself. His roots remain in New Deal liberalism, but he mostly divides his world between friends and enemies. Scientists complain that his aggressive investigations of alleged research fraud cast a chilling effect over future inquiry.

Environmentalists are baffled at what they see as changes in a man once perceived at the forefront of their movement. With a few exceptions, Mr. Dingell says enviornmental leaders are "fishy friends: They tend to be very, very ungrateful." Reviewing Mr. Dingell's environmental voting score, the Audubon Society's Brock Evans calculates "50 out of 100. That's not bad if he was from Alabama."

As chairman today, Mr. Dingell speaks of respect for authority, but in the past he himself has been quick to challenge the leadership. In 1985, he almost single-handedly frustrated an effort by now-Speaker Foley to better organize House Rules. He regularly harassed the first Commerce Committee chairman he served under, Oren Harris of Arkansas, and helped weaken the last one, West Virginia's Harley Staggers, before gaining the job himself. In frustration, former House Speaker Thomas O'Neill once considered sending a bill to Mr. Dingell's committee for only 36 hours.

But beneath this hard-boiled image is a complex, even romantic man. When Mr. Dingell's first marriage collapsed in the 1970s, he raised the four children—one as young as two—himself. When beleaguered then-Speaker James Wright broke into tears at a heated news conference last year, Mr. Dingell gave his friend time to regain his composure before the TV cameras by setting off a round of applause.

Mr. Dingell was slow to embrace the Equal Rights Amendment for women but, in 1964, risked his career by actively supporting in floor debate the Civil Rights Act during a tough Democratic primary. In recent years, when a black staffer ran for the Harvard board of overseers on an anti-apartheid divestment platform, Mr. Dingell made telephone calls—without notice—on her behalf.

Strong Desire to Win

What is most consistent is Mr. Dingell's desire to win and dominate. He has no use for what he sees as the unelected elites who intrude on his party—his turf. "I used to say I support the platform. I haven't said that for years," he says. He denounces Ralph Nader as an "unmitigated scoundrel." (The consumer activist has said worse about Mr. Dingell.)

In fact, Mr. Dingell's oversight subcommittee amounts to his own Dingell's Raiders, and, despite his scorn for many environmentalists, he is a naturalist who has sketched wildlife and spells accurately the Latin name— oreamnos—of the mountain sheep in a painting on his wall.

Above all, Mr. Dingell is a government man. For him, regulation has enduring value, and the sweep of Energy and Commerce's jurisdiction— from steel leghold animal traps to heart values to golden parachutes—suits his purposes. Asked to name two failures of Congress, he cites Vietnam and the swine flu liability debacle of the late 1970s.

To get the answers he needs, Mr. Dingell brings the government to bear. Energy and Commerce's annual budget of more than $5.1 million for investigations and studies surpasses any in the House. Recent records of the General Accounting Office, Congress's investigative arm, show that it commits more personnel and spends more travel money in support of Mr. Dingell's panel than it does for the Armed Services and Ways and Means Committees combined.

"It would be fair to say I love Congress," says Mr. Dingell, and, as with the Capitol itself, there is about him a sense of constancy amid the changing seasons and sessions of lawmaking. In 1964, during the civil-rights fight, he remembers early press reports saying he would lose his primary. Today, a young woman who worked in his Washington office then and was the niece of his campaign manager is the wife of Speaker Foley. A seven-year-old son, Christopher Dingell, is now a tall Michigan state senator and potential successor, but the father isn't yet ready to yield.

"I am not drunk on power, I am not getting rich in this goddamn place, I can assure you of that," John Dingell says. "I do view this as a place where I serve."

R EELECTION, THE QUEST FOR personal power on Capitol Hill, and "good public policy" are the principal incentives guiding members of Congress, according to congressional scholar Richard F. Fenno.[1] Personal power can be achieved on many levels and in different ways. The principal routes to power are through committees or congressional parties; members must choose whether they want to become committee chairmen or party leaders. House minority party members face a particularly difficult task in fulfilling their chosen goals, as the following portrayal of the colorful Georgia Republican Newt Gingrich illustrates.

23   Adam Clymer
HOUSE REVOLUTIONARY

A room full of three dozen clean-cut college juniors who are spending their summer as volunteers at the Republican National Committee might seem like an unlikely place to recruit revolutionaries. Not to Newt Gingrich.

The House Republican whip rushed over to the Capitol Hill Club, a Republican watering hole, one afternoon last month between critical meetings on enterprise zone bills and speeches assailing Democrats. In a 20-minute break from his war on Congress, he told them the welfare state was strangling their dreams. "We will not make it through your lifetime without radical change," he said. "You're either going to force the changes, or your generation is going to suffer a long, steady decline in the quality of life.

"I am essentially a revolutionary," he told them. And like any good revolutionary, he identified enemies: bureaucrats who run city governments for their own comfort and not the public's; senior faculty members out of touch with reality, and, above, all the Democrats. Occasionally, he said, virtuous Democrats do come to Congress, but they are quickly told by their leaders: "If you ever want to get on a decent committee, you better learn to sell out." To whom? To the Democrats' basic elements, "a coalition of big-city machines, trial lawyers, union leaders, left-wing activists and political incumbents."

Although Gingrich tends to say so many words so fast that his high voice gets chirpy, like a tape recorder on fast-forward, the volunteers were captivated. They smiled, asked a few respectful questions and applauded as

[1] Richard F. Fenno, Jr., *Congressmen in Committees* (Boston: Little, Brown, 1973), Chapter 1.

he exhorted them: "Real revolutions are made by the young. They are made by the energetic. They are made by the risk-takers." Then he dashed back to vote against a Democratic bid to kill Vice President Dan Quayle's White House Council on Competitiveness.

Newton Leroy Gingrich, at age 49, is no longer young, but he is an energetic risk-taker. He leads one of the least-noticed but potentially most far-reaching campaigns of this bizarre political year. Gingrich is trying to use voters' anger at government to end 38 years of Democratic control of the House. Outright Republican control would require winning 52 more seats, an awesome electoral swing, but picking up an attainable 30 or so would enable Republicans to dominate the House in alliance with conservative Democrats. The Republicans now hold 166 seats out of 435. Gingrich says the odds are "better than even that we will be above 200 for the first time since 1956. The odds are very, very good."

Gingrich pursues that goal of Republican control in the well of the House, taunting Democrats as corrupt and despotic. He works at it in Capitol back rooms, hammering out policy statements so that Republicans can argue they stand for change. He nourishes it in the office of his political action committee, Gopac, with telephone hookups that enable dozens of Republican challengers around the country to tie their strategies to his. And he travels the country raising money for Republicans by preaching a gospel of lower taxes as the route to economic growth and more prisons and longer sentences as the path to domestic order.

Largely because of his efforts, the Republican campaign for House seats is more organized than it has been in years, unlike the uncertain Bush campaign. For months, Gingrich has argued openly that the President needed to do more to define his campaign goals, to call for radical change, to sound more like, well, like Gingrich. Relations with the White House have been bumpy as a result.

Yet for all the interest Gingrich claims to have in public policy issues like medical care or better schools, in his 14 years in the House he has spent most of his energy going after one colleague after another on ethical grounds. He says his motives were not partisan, but all but one of his targets have been Democrats. His biggest scalp was Jim Wright's; he brought down the Speaker of the House in 1989, accusing him of circumventing the rules by accepting payoffs and selling a pseudo-book.

He portrays himself as forced by knowledge of evil he has acquired to pursue such charges or become an accomplice. "I don't think I'm a Savanarola," the Baptist lawmaker said in an interview in May in his PAC office. "I don't think I have any great interest in running around and finding sin." But he plays very rough. He insists that one of his own aides who worked against Wright was falsely accused of spreading the rumor in 1989 that incoming Speaker Thomas S. Foley was a homosexual. The reporter who accused her, Lars-Erik Nelson of *The Daily News*, insists that his article was accurate and says Gingrich sent a letter to his editor, on Congressional stationery, demanding he be fired. Nor does he confine his attacks to colleagues who can fight back. He outraged Foley and many Republicans with a charge they thought farfetched by saying a Foley aide might have participated in a coverup of corruption in the House post office.

His most strenuous campaign has been on the House bank, coaching and encouraging a group of seven Republican freshmen who made a national scandal out of a peculiar, terribly run, financial institution in which some members' deposits covered their colleagues' sometimes spectacular over-drafts. No taxpayers' money was involved, though Gingrich said the practices reflected "systemic, institutional corruption." But the growing scandal became political dynamite through a combination of Republican attacks, the inability of Speaker Foley to sense political danger and insistent newspaper and radio talk-show arguments that the dubious checks symbol-ized how remote Congress was from real life. That argument, however distant from the hard work, education and honesty that actually character-izes Congress today, took hold in an environment in which nothing is getting done about health care or schools or crime.

Gingrich argues that Foley's inability to recognize a "tidal wave" of public opinion caused the damage. But a tidal wave is a natural phenomenon; this was more like a forest fire, and Gingrich was there when it started, with gasoline.

His hairsbreadth victory in a July 22 Georgia Republican primary is both the best evidence of his claim to be a revolutionary, ready to take great risks, and of the potency of the enmity he has unleashed. His own 22 overdrafts, including a $9,463 check to the Internal Revenue Service, were the heaviest weapons against him in an anti-incumbent campaign waged by an underfi-nanced former state senator. After lavishing $1.1 million on the race, Gingrich survived, by 980 votes, and the district is so Republican that he seems a shoo-in in November. If anti-incumbency campaigns like the one waged against him defeat enough Democrats, he may someday achieve his ambition of becoming Speaker of the House. It is a goal he has nourished since his teens, when his stepfather, a combat infantryman, was transferred from Germany to Fort Benning and a bookish Newt entered politics by running a successful high-school student council campaign.

But as his own close call demonstrated, incumbent Republicans are at risk, too. The man he calls "my closest friend in the House," Representative Vin Weber of Minnesota, announced plans to retire after disclosures of 125 overdrafts. Gingrich sounds pained about Weber's decision, though Weber says Gingrich has never told him of his sorrow. "He has no desire to do me any political harm," Weber observes and adds, "Newt's sense of the cause that he's pursuing outweighs all other causes in his mind."

Republicans often follow Gingrich out of frustration with Democratic rule. As Representative Henry J. Hyde, an Illinois Republican and hardly one of Gingrich's leading supporters, argues, House Republicans find themselves in a "legislative ghetto" where they are barely tolerated. "That can be infuriating," he says. "Even a bunny rabbit, when cornered, will fight back."

Gingrich has prodded his traditionally more accommodating boss, Representative Robert H. Michel of Illinois, the minority leader, to complain about such indignities as the fact that Democrats hog the committee staff jobs, with an average of 5.3 staffers compared with 2.6 for each Republican, and regularly write floor procedures to keep the Republicans from even offering amendments.

The fractious Democrats need those advantages, because their rank and file appear to want an organizational free lunch, complaining of weak leadership but unable to follow with any discipline. Thus, the Democrats are often barely able to find a consensus in their own party, and they don't dare risk letting a skillfully drawn amendment shatter it. Representative Frank D. Riggs of California, one of Gingrich's noisy freshmen, says he came to Congress to deal with housing and education and got into reform issues only after finding that "the legislative process is effectively closed to constructive minority input."

In all this, the House is quite different from the Senate. There, nothing gets done without bipartisan cooperation whether it is by Robert J. Dole breaking a logjam on unemployment compensation or John C. Danforth working with Edward M. Kennedy and overcoming the Bush Administration's opposition to a civil rights bill. The Senate's rules and, even more, its traditions dictate respect for the minority. The best lawmakers there, like Kennedy and Dole and Lloyd Bentsen, know how to find allies across party lines.

But in the House, the Democrats seem oblivious to G.O.P. unhappiness. It is Gingrich who makes that cauldron of irritability boil over. As Norman Ornstein of the American Enterprise Institute says, "Newt and a handful of allies can take a polarized situation and make it 10 times worse."

As befits a revolutionary, Gingrich cuts a rumpled figure as he races to keep appointments and catch planes. He dresses like the assistant professor he once was, carrying more books and papers than conveniently fit under his arm. His distinctive helmet of gray hair provides a low-maintenance signature; it's cut these days at Great Clips of Marietta, Ga., and dries naturally after his morning shower. His airplane reading tends to be heavy stuff. *Lincoln and the Radicals* by T. Harry Williams, *The Conservative Party from Peel to Churchill* by Robert Blake.

On the road, he stops to call his wife, Marianne, several times a day. If he finds the time, he visits local zoos. (He used speaking fees that exceeded what House rules allowed him to help the Atlanta zoo buy two baby rhinoceroses, Bo and Rosie, who have delighted his nieces, Susan and Emmy.)

He has two married daughters from his first marriage, to his high-school math teacher, whom he followed after graduation to Emory University and wed. They were divorced soon after he got to Congress, with her campaign help. He married Marianne, an urban planner whom he met on a political trip to Ohio, in 1981. They live quietly in a town house in Marietta; they have a one-bedroom apartment on Capitol Hill.

The family has been little in the public eye, but last month one of the daughters, Kathy Gingrich Lubbers, made news with an abortion-rights appeal. Gingrich firmly opposes abortion and does not quarrel with his party's staunch stand against it, but Lubbers came to Washington from her home in Greensboro, N.C., where she is opening a coffee-bean roasting company, to tell a news conference sponsored by the National Republican Coalition for Choice: "If the Republican Party is to appeal to young people in general and specifically to women, we must throw off the stranglehold that the anti-choice movement has on the appartus of the party."

She said that her father had never tried to silence her and that "our family is big enough to encompass both sides of this issue." For his part, Gingrich said, "Both my family and my party are strong enough to have healthy, spirited debates."

Gingrich came to the House from the campus of West Georgia College, where he taught history, environmental studies and a course on the future. He won his first election in 1978, on his third try, at age 35. In his speeches, he praises the college for a program it started to encourage third-graders to read by paying them $2 for every book they read and explained to an adult. He says the program shows children that reading is profitable and that adults care about it, lessons he says billions in Federal aid have never taught. He does not say that he financed the program for its first few years, from excess speaking fees.

But the Gingrich revolution is not about endowing zoos, or even reading programs. This is how he defined it in a speech he gave in the House on Jan. 3; the chamber was all but empty, but he was facing the C-Span camera and its dedicated following of a couple of hundred thousand Congress addicts, an audience he has played to with after-session speeches since he arrived:

> Taking the streets back from violent crime and drugs, so local TV news is no longer a death watch, would be a revolution in every major American city. Replacing welfare with workfare and ending a process by which teenage mothers have children outside marriage with ignorant, irresponsible male children who have sex but are not fathers would be a revolution. Having schools that are disciplined, require homework and beat the Japanese in math and science would be a revolution. Replacing the most expensive, red tape-ridden litigious health-care system in the world with a revitalized, health-oriented private system we can afford, and that would be available to everyone, would be a revolution. Having government bureaucracies that are

lean, efficient, courteous and customer-service oriented would be a revolution. Having a tax code that favored work, savings and investment, that helped create more and better jobs; greater productivity and higher take-home pay to make us the fastest growing industrial economy in the world would be a revolution.

Everything on that list, except probably teenage pregnancy, is something the Federal Government might be able to do something about. Ideas of this sort were Gingrich's passion in his first few years in Congress. With Vin Weber, he founded the Conservative Opportunity Society, and he performed for the C-Span audience, even if he didn't know anyone out there who was watching except some junior Reagan White House staffers.

That sort of follow-through and hard work have not been much in evidence lately. An 11-month effort to write a health-care bill that emphasizes private insurance and individual efforts to cut costs is about the only recent effort in the domain of ideas that he has been a part of. He has taken no action at all on the one concrete promise in his Jan. 3 speech, a commitment to find money and land for prisons so that violent offenders can be kept locked up and not turned loose because of overcrowding. Gingrich asserts he would rather work on ideas and win elections on them. But, he said in an interview in his Gopac office—in a bland office building near the Capitol where aides prepared for that night's hookup with challengers—building a consensus on ideas "is a backbreaking, slow, difficult process."

Nor does he think an all-out effort to spell out revolutionary ideas would help Republicans right away with the public. Such efforts, he says, would not get press attention. "It is much easier to communicate, in the current generation of news media, about scandal than about substance," he says. Moreover, conservative ideas have not been much use to House Republicans lately. After winning 192 seats with Ronald Regan in 1980, a dozen years of supporting two of the most conservative Administrations in history have not led to further gains. Indeed, the Republicans have never won more than 182 seats since. Today's 166 leave them 52 short of a majority, only 7 ahead of where they were the morning of Reagan's election.

No one on Capitol Hill doubts that November's elections will produce more House Republicans. Reapportionment following the census has shifted seats to Republican parts of the country. The subsequent process of drawing the new district maps has helped the G.O.P., too, as Republican appointments to the Federal courts produced rulings at least neutral and sometimes friendly to Republicans when legislatures and governors could not agree.

But there is more to this year's G.O.P. hopes for the House. Active recruiting by the National Republican Congressional Committee and by Gingrich's Gopac has produced 941 Republican hopefuls, half again as many as sought nominations two years ago. Gopac's most important effort now is to find them money, not by giving it to them directly but by finding donors. In direct gifts, it can lawfully give only $10,000 to each candidate. But there is no limit to how much it can steer their way. Its goal is finding 100 donors, or people promising to raise $1,000, for each of 170 nonincumbent Republicans.

That goal will not be reached. Political money is short this year. But because of Gopac, quite a few Republican challengers will get more money than they otherwise would have. Indeed, a Federal Election Commission report this month showed that 208 Republican hopefuls had raised $50,000 by June 30, up from 114 two years ago. One who wasn't there yet, Steve Stockman, went to a lunch atop a Houston bank building where Gingrich was drumming up backing from businessmen and developers. After the pasta salad and speeches, Stockman approached one guest, former Treasury Secretary John B. Connally, and told him he was running against Jack Brooks, the formidable Galveston lawmaker who is finishing his 20th term in the House and heads the Judiciary Committee. Connally gripped his hand and said, "Give me your card and I'll send you $1,000." That night in Irvine, Calif., Gingrich's gospel of Gopac and "revolution" enlisted 35 volunteers to raise or give $1,000 from a crowd of about 400 Republicans.

Money isn't all Gingrich offers. Each Thursday night, he gets on a telephone hookup with 60 to 90 Republican challengers, offering them commentary on recent events and advice about how to campaign. Just after the Los Angeles riots, he warned them to be sure to denounce "racism, police brutality and violence," and not to forget any of the three. Then, once a month, Gingrich stages a press conference in Washington with telephone hookups to their campaign headquarters, so challengers can identify themselves with, or even claim credit for, legislative proposals like the Republican health-care plan or a bill to limit the number of years someone can receive Aid to Families with Dependent Children.

Campaigning on scandal alone may not be enough for Republican challengers if they ignore national problems, Gingrich believes. Or, as he put it in a brief appearance at a candidates' training session just before the April lunch in Houston: "Don't focus in only on scandal[s] on the Hill. They're interesting. They're great soap opera. They're important. But they have to be attached to people's lives." To do this, he said, challengers should list the problems the Democratic Congress is not solving, like health care or jobs, and then say: "And by the way, the guys who are failing you on every front can't manage the Capitol. So they have managed to both screw up the Capitol and screw up your lives and it's their fault."

Gingrich is offering advice to others he hasn't followed himself, for his House career has been continually confrontational. And he has brought the House minority leader, Michel, along—to a degree. They still offer something of a good cop, bad cop routine, with Michel as the genial veteran who can sit down and talk with Foley and Gingrich as the tough guy who boasts that polls now show only a fifth of the public approves of how Congress is doing its job. "We've accommodated pretty well to each other's different traits," Michel says. He adds that when Gingrich won his position as whip by two votes over a Michel ally in 1989, he had feared constant friction between them. He also worried that Gingrich would not attend to the basic duty of "whipping" Republicans into agreement on how to vote. "Some of the earlier concerns I had have dissipated," Michel says. "Quite frankly, we complement one another." He says he hopes that in 1993 he will be Speaker, "being credible and being respected and having a fair and even hand," while Gingrich could be the Republican majority leader "who gives the opposition fits."

That might be a relief for the next Bush Administration, if there is one, for in between his fights with Democrats, Gingrich has tangled with the President and his aides. In 1990, he took on President Bush and the rest of the Republican leadership in both houses over that year's budget agreement, which violated G.O.P. orthodoxy and Bush's own campaign promises by imposing tax increases to accompany spending cuts. In 1991 he harassed the President into asking Congress to pass capital-gains tax cuts instead of adjourning, which made Bush look silly.

But most of the time, he has assaulted Democrats, and on issues of character, not policy. In 1984, he was speaking to an empty House and a C-Span camera, attacking one Democrat after another for supposedly unpatriotic sympathies for the Sandinistas. Speaker Thomas P. (Tip) O'Neill Jr. was enraged when he heard about it, and ordered the cameras to pan to show the empty chamber. Then, O'Neill took the House floor to denounce Gingrich, saying "My personal opinion is that you deliberately stood in the well before an empty House and you challenged their patriotism, and it is the lowest thing that I have ever seen in my 32 years in the House." Gingrich won that round, when the Speaker suffered the remarkable rebuke of being ruled out of order for using unparliamentary language.

He went on to other battles, pushing the Ethics Committee or the whole House into stiffer sanctions against various Democrats and one Republican, Representative Dan Crane of Illinois, who was censured for having sex with a House page. He put less formal pressure on two other backbench Republicans to resign.

Gingrich's two-year confrontation with Wright over the propriety of the Speaker's money-making schemes had the air of a vendetta. Gingrich was outraged at Wright's personal effort to negotiate a political settlement in Nicaragua. Wright resigned after the Ethics Committee decided there were dozens of charges against him worth pursuing. Soon after, the committee rejected a counterattack from Wright's backers. They had charged that businessmen concealed campaign contributions to Gingrich with $5,000 investments in a book he wrote in 1984. They lost their money when the book did not sell.

His support among Republicans in the House is solid, stronger than when he squeaked through to the whip's job in 1989. A Connecticut moderate like Nancy Johnson sings his praises, recalling how he helped her devise parliamentary tactics to push abortion rights even though he disagreed with her aim. Scott Klug of Wisconsin, one of his freshman followers, found him encouraging on the House bank issue when many senior members were not. Gingrich told them: "If you guys think this is right, go for it." He worries some Republicans, like his friend Weber, who is troubled by the emphasis on personal attacks even as he hails Gingrich as a rare Representative who thinks about politics on a grand scale, beyond the next election or the next amendment.

Some Republicans who will not talk for attribution see him as a destructive force. They agree with Representative David R. Obey, a senior Wisconsin Democrat whom Gingrich says he respects for his diligence and trustworthiness. Obey says he sometimes sees "the ghost of Joe McCarthy" in Gingrich. "Newt enjoys smearing people's character," he says. "He contributes to the destruction of the body politic."

For years, Democrats have said his tactics amount to a desire to burn the House down, in the expectation that since it has a Democratic majority, more Democrats than Republicans will suffer and new Republicans will take their places.

That view of him is now spreading on both sides of the House. One lawmaker after another agrees with the notion that Gingrich is the political equivalent of the Air Force major in a famous interview amid the rubble of Ben Tre in South Vietnam. It was just after the Tet offensive in 1968, and the major explained, "It became necessary to destroy the town in order to save it."

P OLITICAL PUNDITS AND CON-
gressional scholars alike have
long asserted that reelection is
the major incentive guiding most members of Congress. But at the same time
they are pursuing reelection, members of
Congress are also seeking to establish
personal power on Capitol Hill and to
build their Washington careers. How to
balance reelection activities with the pursuit of power in Congress is a dilemma
that all representatives and senators confront. A failure to attend to constituent
needs spells certain defeat for members
of the House, as the following selection
illustrates.

24 Alison Mitchell
FOR ONE LAWMAKER, ALLURE OF CAPITOL
HAD DOUBLE EDGE

He was one of the brash, bold reformers who swept into Congress 18 years
ago on a wave of popular revulsion over Watergate and the Vietnam War.
Elected at age 25, he was so boyish that he was carded in bars and mistaken
for a Congressional page. And no one really begrudged him when, with an
immature charm, he researched whether he could be called the youngest
person ever to enter the Congress.

Representative Thomas J. Downey of Amityville literally grew up in the
marble corridors of the Capitol. He married during his tenure in Washington
and made a home with his wife and children in a Capitol Hill townhouse.

"Lost Touch" with Voters

But as the years passed, voters in Long Island's Second Congressional
District began to wonder if he had drifted away from his roots and from the
people who had elected him. And last week, they resoundingly defeated
Mr. Downey in favor of someone who was remarkably reminisicent of the
Tom Downey of old: a young Turk from the Suffolk County Legislature who
said the incumbent had become too high and mighty and distant.

Mr. Downey, whose only adult job outside government was a brief stint
in the personnel department of Macy's, was devastated. "I did not have any
sense that I had lost touch with the community," he said, but he admitted
that his opponent had fatally wounded him with that charge. "Sadly it stuck
and had nothing to do with reality."

Some members of Congress now see Mr. Downey's defeat as a cautionary tale of how the power and the prerequisites of Washington can seduce them all; of how even the brightest star of the post-Watergate era could eventually seem to the voters as too much like the insiders as he once scorned.

And in Suffolk County, some wonder whether the voters had turned on Mr. Downey precisely because they had once loved him so, mothers and grandmothers cooing over the boy Congressman, with the Paul McCartneyesque cap of brown hair.

"That kind of—it may be too strong to say adoration—that kind of feeling for him, love for him, may have dissipated as he climbed up the ladder," said Dominic J. Baranello, the Suffolk County Democratic leader.

Mr. Downey first went to Washington on a tidal wave of voter revolt against the Nixon presidency and the Watergate scandal. Campaigning door to door and undaunted by the seeming futility of being an anti-war liberal running in a district that had given Richard M. Nixon 72 percent of the vote just two years earlier, Mr. Downey prevailed over the incumbent Republican Representative, James. R. Grover. The next day's papers had pictures of the young Congressman-elect playing basketball with his 11-year-old brother.

Symbol of His Time

In his youth, fervor and brashness, Mr. Downey was symbolic of his time. The elections of 1974 sent 75 freshmen into the House of Representatives, Mr. Downey the youngest among them. They were righteous, idealistic, ready to change the world, and they promptly ran a minor revolution in the tradition-bound House by toppling three committee chairmen. Mr. Downey did his part on the House Armed Services Committee, where he helped depose the aging chairman, Representative Edward Herbert of Louisiana.

Mr. Downey quickly became one of the leaders of the Democratic newcomers, a tight-knit circle who shared anti-establishment political views and played ferocious basketball in the House gym. Along with Al Gore, who came to the House two years later, he made himself into one of Washington's select coterie of arms control experts.

His colleagues remember his utter confidence. "He would be announcing, 'We're going to do this. We're going to that,' " recalled Representative George Miller, a California Democrat. "We'd say that the Speaker won't like that and he'd say it didn't matter."

Mr. Downey also emerged as one of the Democrats' most articulate—and vitriolic—polemicists, a role that left him with enemies on the Republican side of the aisle. "If he had a weakness as a speaker, it was that he'd leave you no quarter. He'd cut you off at the knees and take a second swipe at you," Mr. Miller said. "That would cause you problems in the Congress because members of Congress weren't used to being devastated publicly."

Serving the Voters

As he became an ever larger presence in Washington, Mr. Downey remained a model of the constituent-oriented Congressman. He invited thousands of voters to his parents' home in West Islip to talk issues. He made a van into a mobile office to move about the sprawling South Shore district. Former Representative Geraldine A. Ferraro of Queens, who entered Congress in 1978, remembers that Mr. Downey was so successful that he was asked to address freshmen on how to serve their districts.

In 1980, with the birth of his first child, Lauren, Mr. Downey and his wife, Chris, who had been an elementary school teacher in Dix Hills, were faced with the choice all members of Congress must wrestle with, how to mix the demands of family and politics. They moved to Washington so that Mr. Downey could spend more time with his daughter and later, with his second child, Theodore. On weekends, the Congressman would commute back to Long Island.

The Downey home in Washington eventually grew into a social center for a small circle of House Democrats. Once a week, Chris would cook dinner for a group that could include Marty Russo of Illinois and Leon E. Panetta, Barbara Boxer, Nancy Pelosi and Mr. Miller, all of California.

In hindsight, several of Mr. Downey's colleagues said that his relocation to Washington might have set the stage for his defeat. "I really think that matters," said one representative, who spoke on the condition of anonymity. "You by nature stay in touch more if you live in your district. You live in Washington, you just get sucked into Washington."

In fact, it was sometime in the mid-1980's that Frank R. Jones, a Republican official who is now supervisor of Islip, first began hearing complaints about Mr. Downey. "He had good constituent service, he absolutely did—for the first 10 or 12 years," he said. "After that, real or perceived, it began to fall off. I had a fellow, a staunch Democrat, who said to me, 'You know, I've had innumerable meetings with Congressman Downey and he was always late.' "

By the late 1980's, Mr. Downey had reached the height of his legislative powers as an influential member of [the] Ways and Means Committee and the Select Committee on Aging.

"Vulnerable This Year"

He also became acting-chairman of the Ways and Means Subcommittee on Human Resources after Representative Harold E. Ford, a Tennessee Democrat, fell under the cloud of an indictment. And there he became one of the lead legislators in the Congress on welfare policy and child care. On an issue of key concern to Long Island, he also led the effort that prolonged the life of Grumman's F-14 fighter plane for three years.

But in 1990, just before an election, Mr. Downey was one of many members of the Ways and Means Committee caught by hidden cameras on ABC's "Prime Time Live" at a junket in Barbados, jet-skiing in a bathing suit and playing football on a beach. He apologized to his constituents and said he had made a mistake. And he was re-elected.

But Republicans noted that he had won with only 56 percent of the vote against a weak opponent. It was, said Suffolk Republican leader Howard C. DeMartini, "the early warning signal that Downey would be vulnerable this year."

Mr. Downey also saw the trouble signs. "I had a sense that things were very wrong in 1990," he said in an interview, "I have all these diary notes about this: You've got to get to work. You've got to work a little harder." He said he started serving his district with renewed vigor, returning to Long Island one out of every three days in 1991 and every other day in 1992.

Then the House bank scandal struck at a time when Long Island was in deep recession. It was bad enough that Mr. Downey had overdrafts on 151 checks totaling $83,000. It was worse still that Mrs. Downey, who had a patronage job working for the House sergeant-at-arms, had been hired on a budget line that listed her job title as auditor of the House bank.

Rick Lazio, a 34-year-old two-term Suffolk County legislator, built his campaign against Mr. Downey around the bank scandal and Barbados trip, in a race that was strikingly reminiscent to Mr. Downey's own battle 18 years ago against an entrenched incumbent.

Anger Toward Congress

Mr. Lazio sent out a last-minute blitz of direct mail playing on the popular resentment of Congress. One flier offered "Tom Downey's Limousine Liberal guide to surviving the recession," a 10-point primer.

"Tough times on Long Island getting you down?" it asked. "Move to Washington. Rent out your multiple-family Long Island home (one of three homes he owns); put your children in private school in Virginia." That was just point No. 1.

Mr. Downey was thrown on the defensive, forced to invite voters to drop by his two-family house in Amityville to prove he still had a place to live on Long Island. "I live on Long Island, I have lived here all my life," he said in a televised debate. "If you have any doubt, come to 155 Cedar Street, where I have lived for 13 years."

Mr. Lazio, a moderate pro-choice Republican, offered a refreshing gee-whiz quality, as evidenced in his reflections on the race a few days after victory. "There's something bigger than how powerful you are, how many powerful people you know and whether you get invited to powerful cocktail parties," he said. Of the voters, he added, "what they want is to say, 'I know him. He goes to the same diner I go to.'"

Election Day was bittersweet. The Democrats had recaptured the White House and Washington hung on the threshold of generational change. Mr. Downey's close friend, Al Gore, had become Vice President-elect. It should have been Mr. Downey's time; he still so young at just 43 and yet with nearly two decades of Congressional seniority.

But instead, he spent election night consoling his children about his defeat and telling them they should be happy for the victory of Bill Clinton. The next day he drove back to Washington and strove to put the best face on things. "This has been—all losers must have this sense—this has been a wonderful 18 years," he said. "That's how I'd prefer to remember it."

He showed a small hint of his old sharp tongue, when asked if he had the feeling that he had been beaten by a new Tom Downey, "I know Tom Downey, and he's no Tom Downey," he said of Mr. Lazio. "I'm sure there's some irony in all of this, but it's lost on me at the moment."

Across the country, Mr. Downey's House colleagues raged that Long Island's voters had not appreciated Mr. Downey as they had. "This is a person who is extremely bright, very talented in knowing the possibilities of government," said Representative Pelosi. "He was masterful at shaping legislation and he was very respected." She added, "It's hard to understand why there wasn't a recognition of his value in his district."

But at the West Islip firehouse, near Mr. Downey's campaign headquarters, the dispatcher, Mel Lauber, said he had voted against Mr. Downey although he had supported him in the past. "I didn't like the idea of rubber checks," he said, "and I didn't like the idea of him parading around on vacation on taxpayers' money." All that puzzled him was why so few other Congressional incumbents had fallen: "I thought they wanted a clean Congress."

THE "INCUMBENCY EFFECT" usually makes it very difficult for outside challengers to win congressional elections. Typically, over 90 percent of House incumbents who choose to run win victory margins ranging from 58 to 80 percent of the vote. Incumbent senators, who are more likely to be challenged because of the high visibility of their offices and the much sought-after political prize of their seats, typically win more than 80 percent of their reelection contests. Nevertheless, campaigns against incumbents, although usually quixotic, are always fun for candidates and staffers who enjoy the political game. And, as the following account of such a campaign illustrates, challengers never give up the hope, however slight, that they can win.

25

Mark G. Michaelsen
MY LIFE AS A CONGRESSIONAL CANDIDATE

It was quite late and I was in bed, just drifting off to sleep, when the telephone rang. The caller identified herself as working for the *New Republic*.

I snapped to attention. The *New Republic!* As the Republican candidate for Congress in Wisconsin's Seventh District in 1984, I was accustomed to late-night calls from journalists, usually wire-service reporters racing to meet a deadline. But never had I received a call from such an important publication.

I told her what a fine magazine I thought the *New Republic* was and how much I had enjoyed a recent article on Sandinista human rights abuses. At the same time, my mind raced ahead: How did I come to their attention? Was it my stand on family issues or defense? The quixotic campaign of a 26-year-old neophyte against an entrenched seven-term liberal incumbent Democrat? My skillful exploitation of the resentment of northern Wisconsin sportsmen toward an agreement to let American Indians ignore fish and game laws?

What would the article say, I wondered. Would it be favorable or unfavorable? It didn't really matter. Regardless of tone, a *New Republic* article mentioning my candidacy would surely unlock a torrent of political action committee contributions, instantly transforming my campaign from amateur shoestring effort to formidable, well-financed juggernaut. Big Mo was just around the corner; I could taste it.

What could I do for the caller, I asked.

"We've noticed we haven't received your subscription renewal," she

"My Life as a Congressional Candidate," by Mark G. Michaelsen. From *The American Spectator*, November 1989. Reprinted by permission.

said. "If this is just an oversight, we'll be happy to continue sending you the *New Republic* until we receive your check."

My dreams popped like a big soap bubble. This wasn't a reporter, it was a telephone solicitor!

On election night, 1984, I was blown out by incumbent David R. Obey, who received 61 percent of the vote. That same night, President Ronald Reagan trounced Walter Mondale in one of history's great landslides. In Wisconsin's Seventh Congressional District, Reagan beat Mondale 53 percent to 46 percent. So much for coattails.

The obvious question is *why*. Why would a 26-year-old kid with no name identification challenge the formidable 49-year-old chairman of the Joint Economic Committee, who had served in Congress since 1969, when former Rep. Melvin R. Laird vacated the seat to become Nixon's defense secretary?

The answer: almost by accident. I didn't mean to be the candidate. A native of central Wisconsin, I was working at Hillsdale College in Michigan in early 1984, when I learned that Wisconsin state senator Walter John Chilsen was mulling a run against Obey. Obey had edged the former senate majority leader in the 1969 special election to fill Laird's seat. There had been no rematch. I let Chilsen know that I was interested in helping him oust Obey. He put me in touch with his Washington consultant, who suggested I become campaign finance director.

I pored over district vote totals and read whatever I could find about district demographics, funding-raising, issues, Obey's voting record, and public speaking. It would be tough, but with a strong coattail effect from Reagan's re-election, a ton of money spent on advertising and mail, and a little bit of luck, Chilsen could win in November. I was excited by the possibilities.

When Chilsen opted not to vacate a safe seat in the state senate to challenge Obey, I was disappointed. Election after election, Seventh District Republicans had fielded token challengers with little financial support—retired vacuum cleaner salesmen, bankrupt mobile-home moguls, a fellow named Burger who campaigned wearing a chef's hat and a white apron, and so on. None had received more than 38 percent of the vote.

I stepped forward. I had the energy, the knowledge of national issues, the speaking skills, and the fund-raising prowess to be the candidate. I had a deep love for, and knowledge of, the towns and cities, forests and dairy farms of the Wisconsin Seventh District, which sprawls across all or part of eighteen of the state's central and northwest counties. I cared deeply about America's future and was a dedicated conservative. I had some connections in the conservative movement in Washington. Those were my strengths.

But I had weaknesses, too. Almost no one outside my hometown had ever heard of me. I didn't hold public office. I wasn't rich. I hadn't lived in Wisconsin for years. And my name was really hard to pronounce, an alliterative tongue-twister which confounded broadcasters, statesmen, and voters.

I figured these weaknesses could be overcome with an advertising campaign which started with a spot where people mispronounced my name, perhaps ending with a tag line such as "It doesn't matter how you say it. Mark Michaelsen for Congress." With name identification established, spots clobbering the incumbent on issues would follow. The media campaign would end with warm, sentimental spots about shared values and dreams for a better future, loaded up with pretty Wisconsin pictures: "It's morning again in north-central Wisconsin."

With pride and gratitude, I accepted the unanimous endorsement of Seventh District Republicans. On the advice of Chilsen's consultant, I procured a promise from district Republican leaders to raise a hefty amount of start-up cash. That money would be necessary to hire a talented campaign manager and finance director, and to get started raising big money and enlisting an army of volunteers for what would be the strongest challenge ever to Obey. I packed my belongings in a U-Haul trailer to head home for Wisconsin.

The months flew by, an endless stream of parades, speeches, fundraisers, and county fairs. Cows were admired, good deeds were praised, and hands were shaken.

"I'm Mark Michaelsen," I said, dratting the troublesome moniker, and offering a handshake. "I want to work for you in Washington."

"You've got an uphill road ahead of you," nodded the object of my greeting.

"I'm Mark Michaelsen," I said, extending my hand. "I want to be your congressman."

"Ah, you've got a tough row to hoe," observed my new acquaintance.

Maybe it was the Ogema Christmas Tree Festival. Or the Spooner Rodeo. Or the Central Wisconsin State Fair.

"I'm Mark Michaelsen," I said, similing and proffering my calloused mitt. "I'm running against Dave Obey."

"You've got a tough, uphill road to hoe," said the voter.

Exactly! This unintentional mixed metaphor perfectly described my plight. Imagine a man using a garden implement to try to dislodge asphalt from a road running almost straight uphill, like one of Hercules's mythological labors. That was me.

The money trickled, not poured in. The promised Republican cash never materialized. The PACs, seeing no "viability" (their word for a snowball's chance in hell) in my election, weren't about to invest in my race. I faced the American campaign Catch 22: I couldn't raise money until I showed momentum, I couldn't show momentum until I raised money.

Top consultants were hired, then fired. My campaign manager quit; he said he was homesick for Chicago. And, worst of all, my opponent ignored me—ignored my stinging press releases, critical of his votes on school prayer, national security, and federal spending; ignored my call for debates throughout the district; ignored my very existence as a candidate.

At least I had the van.

A small group of hometown supporters had purchased an aging Ford Econoline, painted it red, white, and blue, and outfitted it with a bed and desk. But most impressive was the public address system, which allowed me to blare Sousa marches at deafening volumes while I greeted voters along parade routes.

One day I was late for an interview at a television station in one of the District's remote cities and I couldn't find a place to park. Desperate, I left the van in a parking ramp near the studio. After the interview, I was leaving the ramp when I noticed how low the ceiling was getting. Suddenly I heard a sickening crunch. My roof loudspeakers crashed to the ground.

I retrieved them and continued my progress toward the exit. Headroom continued to shrink. Twenty feet from the exit the van's roof began to scrape on the concrete ceiling. I had to let nearly all the air out of the tires to finally escape. Behind me, a dozen cars were lined up, their egress blocked by my embarassing plight.

What kind of idiot was causing their delay, I could feel them wondering. "Michaelsen for Congress," answered my van in eight-inch letters.

As the grand finale to a candidate training school sponsored by the National Republican Congressional Committee, would-be GOP congressmen were herded into [the] Gold Room of the White House to be photographed with the President and Vice President.

I was somewhat nervous and tongue-tied when I met the Leader of the Free World. I should have said, "Mr. President, dairy farmers of northern Wisconsin are concerned about your agriculture policy" or implored him to come campaign on my behalf. Instead, I mumbled something about having worked for Hillsdale, which he had visited and praised. President Reagan grinned genially, and we sat. He hadn't heard a word; I'd spoken in his bad ear.

As we sat in the ornate chairs by the fireplace, cameras whirring, he cocked his head and said, "Wisconsin. That's just north of my old stomping ground in Illinois." He leaned forward and put his hand on the arm of my chair. He was a nice man.

We shook hands and I left, to be replaced by another candidate. I was already kicking myself for being such a book with President Reagan. I fared better with the Vice President.

I'd met George Bush twice before, during the 1980 Wisconsin presidential primary. I inquired about one of his sons whom I'd also met in 1980. He became quite animated. His son and daughter-in-law were expecting their first child any day.

Newcomers to my current office see my pictures with Ronald Reagan and George Bush and assume the photographs are clever forgeries purchased from an arcade.

Election night found me in a local watering hole, appropriately named

The End of the Line, watching returns and swilling something strong with a few of my friends. As the returns came in it was clear I had lost, and lost big. For most of my acquaintances from campaign school, the night would end similarly. That night only thirteen GOP candidates would unseat Democratic opponents despite the avalanche of support for President Reagan at the top of the ticket.

For me, it could have been even worse. Although Obey outspent me nearly five to one, my 92,507 votes were both the highest total and highest percentage of votes cast against Dave Obey since he was elected in 1969. I won one northern county and lost another by only five votes. I won my hometown by a landslide, but lost my home county. My campaign treasury finished with a slight surplus; I owed no creditors. The worst possible result would have been to amass a huge debt, come very close, and lose; that might have tempted me to run again in 1986. At least now I would never have to wonder what I could have done differently to put me over the top.

EDWARD M. KENNEDY AND Robert C. Byrd have fundamentally different personalities, which have shaped their respective Senate careers. Each, like most of his colleagues, has sought power and status on Capitol Hill. But the route to power each has selected reflects a different background, character, and style. Kennedy is a star and has embraced an individualistic style; through the astute use of the committees he chairs he has sought to put the Kennedy imprint upon legislation, investigations, and committee reports. Kennedy's style represents the "new Senate," in which individual senators are more independent of their colleagues. They seek power not so much through the traditional emphasis upon collegial cooperation but by gaining personal recognition among colleagues for hard work on committees, specialized knowledge, and legislative accomplishments. There remains an important collegial aspect to these efforts, but in the modern Senate an increasing number of members tend to focus on the separate worlds of their committees more than upon the collective demands of the institution.

Robert Byrd, in contrast to Kennedy, adopted a collegial style of operation; he sought positions of leadership in the Senate body rather than emphasize his individual power through committees. Because of his service to fellow senators, Byrd was elected majority whip and majority leader. His personality was more muted than that of Kennedy, his style less flamboyant and aggressive. As the following selection makes clear, each has made an important contribution to the Senate.

26 Laurence Leamer
ROBERT BYRD AND EDWARD KENNEDY: TWO STORIES OF THE SENATE

The Capitol is the greatest public building in America. Visitors can sit in the House and Senate galleries, climb the broad staircases, roam the marble halls, and ride the elevators. They can go almost anywhere they choose. Yet hidden within the Capitol are offices and nooks and gathering places that are private. On the House side of the Capitol, down a back staircase from the House floor, stands an unmarked door. Behind the door is a dark room shrouded in drapes, with an old desk and a few chairs casually arranged. Here Speaker Sam Rayburn's "Board of Education" used to meet each afternoon over bourbon and water to talk politics. Fifteen years after Rayburn's death the star of Texas is still there, painted in ornate style on the far wall.

On the Senate side of the Capitol there are fifty-four private rooms used

Excerpt from *Playing for Keeps in Washington* by Laurence Leamer. Copyright © 1977 by Laurence Leamer. Reprinted by permission of Doubleday, a division of Bantam Doubleday Dell Publishing Group, Inc.

by senators. Some are no more than rude accumulations of government-issue desks, chairs, and paintings. Others are exquisitely decorated with antiques, political memorabilia, ornate telephones. The largest office is a three-room suite that can be reached by going down a narrow staircase just off the main corridor. These are the offices out of which Bobby Baker, the assistant to Senate majority leader Lyndon Johnson, operated. Baker had worked there until he was convicted of abusing his position and sent to prison.

These are the rooms that Edward "Ted" Kennedy of Massachusetts claimed as his own in 1969 when he was elected Democratic whip, the number-two position in the Democratic leadership. Then the offices had all the sweaty urgency of a political boiler room. The suite was full of Kennedy people. The phones rang constantly. Journalists hurried in and out. Now and again Kennedy came bursting in for a few minutes before rushing off somewhere else. There was always something happening. There had never been anything quite like it in the Senate.

In 1971 Robert C. Byrd of West Virginia defeated Kennedy and took over the suite. From all appearances, Byrd did not think the suite a grand prize but more a gift kept for occasional use. The doors might stay locked for days. Byrd decorated the rooms with just enough pictures and artifacts so that the suite became indisputably his. On the wall he put mounted whips that Senator Joseph Montoya of New Mexico had given him and a copy of a *Parade* magazine story about himself ("Senate Whip Bob Byrd: From Poverty to Power").

On the wall of the outer office hung pictures of the fourteen men who had served as Democratic whip. From Jay Hamilton to Hubert Humphrey, from Morris Sheppard to Russell Long, from Lister Hill to Lyndon Johnson, the first twelve faces looked forth with the fleshy, canny confidence of the professional politician. But Kennedy and Byrd were different. Kennedy's picture had the perfect looks of a Hollywood publicity glossy. Byrd, for his part, looked half-embarrassed, as if in the act of allowing himself to be photographed he was giving away something that he did not want to give away.

As much as Kennedy and Byrd were different in appearance from the twelve men who preceded them, so were they different from each other. They were two of the most powerful men in Washington. They did not like each other. They did not like each other's politics. In their distinct ways they symbolized what power had become in the modern Senate.

Senator Robert Byrd walked down the main corridor of the Capitol, down a narrow staircase, and unlocked the door to the whip's office. Many senators travel with a flotilla of aides, but Byrd almost always walks alone. He is a little man with a chalk-white face and black-and-white streaked hair swept back in a high pompadour. He looks like a wary sparrow, with a face that could be found up most any hollow in Appalachia, the face of a man who had missed some basic nutrient. It belonged to the man who was on the verge of becoming the Senate majority leader—the most powerful and prestigious position in Congress.

Byrd is a man of religious intensity, both public and private, the personification of the self-made man, a man of deep, unfathomable ambition, beyond perhaps anyone else's in the Senate. He sought power, wooed power, lived with and for power. . . .

The Senate that Byrd was sworn into in January 1959 was still dominated by Southerners like Lyndon Johnson of Texas and Richard Russell of Georgia. A conservative might believe that a certain lassitude and the petty corruption of privilege were merely the exhaust fumes given off by the Senate as it made its stately way through history. Senator Thomas Dodd of Connecticut, for instance, had an elderly retainer known as the "judge" who slept blissfully at a desk outside the senator's office.

The Senate had not yet spread out into the nearly completed New Senate Office Building. Donald R. Matthews, an academician, was finishing work on a book on the Senate, *U.S. Senators and Their World.* He broke Senate offices down into two general types: the bureaucratic and the individualistic. In the bureaucratic offices, "the senator has delegated considerable nonroute responsibilities to his staff, established a fairly clear-cut division of labor and chain of command." The individualistic officers were "vest pocket operations in which the senator has delegated only routine tasks and in which the staff has little influence and less authority."

Byrd was arriving in the Senate as it was going through a profound evolution. The old Senate, the Senate of "individualistic" offices, had just been portrayed in *Citadel: The Story of the United States Senate*, a book by William S. White. White wrote of the U.S. Senate as "an institution that lives in an unending yesterday where the past is never gone, the present never quite decisive, and the future rarely quite visible. It has its good moments and its bad moments, but to the United States it symbolizes, if nothing else at all, the integrity of continuity and wholeness." This Senate was an institution where, when a man was sworn in, he assumed a mantle of dignity and honor. It was honor enough for any man to be in this body.

When the *Citadel* came out, Senator J. William Fulbright noticed that for a few days some of his colleagues attempted to play senator, walking the halls of Congress as if they were wearing togas. On January 15, 1957, Lyndon B. Johnson had a luncheon for the six new Democratic senators. He gave the six freshmen autographed copies of *Citadel* and he told them that they should think of the book as a kind of McGuffey's *Reader*.

Johnson knew that White's Senate was not his, but he may have found a certain comfort in that mythical body. To White, the Senate was a great conservative body, the naysayer and watchman of democracy. But what gave the Senate its greatness were individual senators with individual ideas.

They worked in the body of Congress to transform their ideas into legislation that would affect the nation. When Johnson had come to Washington,
George Norris of Nebraska was still in the Senate. For years Norris had
studied how to protect the land and the people. He had prepared his bill for
the Tennessee Valley Authority, and he had defended it as if it were a part of
his very being, which in a sense it was. Robert Wagner of New York was in
the Senate too. For years he worked on the great legislation of the New Deal,
including the labor bill that bears his name. Bob La Follette and Robert Taft
were also in the Senate in those years. What these senators had in common
was an organic relationship between what they believed, the people they
served, and what they did and said to achieve their ends.

When Robert Byrd entered the Senate, he accepted the life of the Senate
as the central reality of his being. "Over the years he has cloaked himself in
what he perceives to be senatorial dignity and aura," said one of Byrd's
former aides, "but even when he arrived, there really was very little dignity
left and the aura was gone."

Byrd allied himself with Lyndon Johnson of Texas and more closely yet
with Richard Russell of Georgia. Those who watched Byrd often thought
him great only in petty things. But to a man who revered the Senate as much
as Byrd, there were no petty duties. In 1960, during an all-night civil rights
filibuster, Byrd talked for a record twenty-one hours. Five years later in
another filibuster, he talked for fifteen hours. Byrd was always ready to
volunteer for the KP duty of legislative life. The Senate was based on rules
and precedents. And Robert Byrd, alone of his generation, was willing to
learn the rules and the precedents. He studied them until he knew them as
did no one else and then he studied them some more.

Byrd performed duties, great and small, for senators of every persuasion,
North and South, Democrat and Republican. He helped colleagues whenever he could. When he had helped, he sent them notes saying that he had
been glad to be of service. These he filed away. In 1967 he was elected
Secretary of the Democratic Conference, the number-three position in the
Senate Democratic leadership. Four years later he defeated Ted Kennedy
and became Senate whip, the number-two position in the Senate Democratic leadership.

As a Senate leader, Byrd worked even harder. He knew the Bible, the
book of Senate rules and the book of precedents, and these were just about
the only books he figured he would ever have to know. He had read the
900-page collection of precedents cover to cover, two times, and late at night
at home he was reading it for the third. When the Senate was planning to go
into closed session on matters of national security, he would go over Rule 35
once again. When there was going to be a vote on cloture, he would read the
rule on cloture. Byrd knew the rules and he knew the precedents and could
make them turn upside down and dance on the heads. It was *his* Senate
now, and he left the floor rarely.

The Washington Monument splits the window of his vast inner office in the Capitol. Senator Byrd speaks quietly, the twang of the hills in his voice: "The Senate is a forest. There are ninety-nine animals. They're all lions. There's a waterhole in the forest. I'm the waterhole. They all have to come to the waterhole. I don't have power but I have knowledge of the rules. I have knowledge of the precedents. I have knowledge of the schedule. So I'm in a position to do things for others.

"Now the majority leader is the dispatcher, the engineer, the fellow at the head of the engine who's looking out from the dark night at the headlight down the railway, pulling on the throttle a little harder, pushing on the throttle a little, or leveling off a little, moving it along. Or he determines to move over on this sidetrack or that sidetrack. This legislative organism, with its power, has to have direction. It has to have a leader, but he doesn't have the power. He's the umpire, the referee. He doesn't have any more of that raw power than any other senator has.

"The president, he has power. He's the chief executive of this country. The presidency of the United States should in reality seek the man. Someone said that. That's the way it ought to be. People ought not to be persuaded by a person's pretty teeth, by his smile, or by the way he cuts his hair—by his charisma. That's misleading. That's not to say that a person with pretty teeth and a pretty smile and a handsome build and charisma may not have the ability. But they don't necessarily go together either."

Talking about pretty teeth and a pretty smile and the cut of a man's hair, Robert Byrd could have been sketching a caricature of Edward Kennedy. Byrd and Kennedy were the two Janus faces of the Senate, Byrd often looking backward to a past that had never been, Kennedy looking forward to a future that might never arrive. They approached their work as differently as two men in the same profession possibly could. They also had different conceptions of power and how to use it.

Edward Moore Kennedy walked down the center aisle of the Senate to be sworn in as the junior senator from Massachusetts on January 9, 1963. He had the accent and bearing of the Kennedys, but was a big, brawny fellow with a rousing, friendly manner that suggested an Irish politician of a half century past. He was the scion of a family that seemed destined to dominate American political life in the last decades of the twentieth century as had the Adams family in the first decades of the nation's history. . . .

Kennedy fit unobtrusively into the traditional role of the freshman senator. One morning he went around to see Senator James Eastland of Mississippi, chairman of the Judiciary Committee and champion of the old Senate. He drank bourbon with the senior senator and Eastland discovered that the Kennedys were not all alike. He went around to see Senator Richard Russell of Georgia, Robert Byrd's patron, and he went to the Senate prayer breakfast, too—once at least—and led his colleagues in prayer.

While Kennedy might act out such old-fashioned rituals of the Senate, he was still the most modern of freshmen. A decade later, James Macgregor Burns, a biographer of Kennedy, would call him a "presidential senator." Kennedy was a presidential senator not only in the sense that he had become the sole bearer of the Kennedy legacy and heir apparent to the White House. He was presidential in the way he went about being a senator. He launched a frenetic, permanent presidential-like campaign within the very Senate.

In the favored analogy of his staff, Senator Kennedy stood at the center of a circle of aides who flowed in and around him. The Kennedys had always had a special talent for acquiring and using people whose talents met the needs of the moment. They attracted members of that natural aristocracy of the able and the ambitious. These aides were perhaps no more talented than those around other contenders for the ultimate prize in American politics. But in the livery of the Kennedys, they seemed to serve with extraordinary energy and devotion, and in the end they were, in one way or another, rewarded in kind.

One of those who was there when Kennedy entered the Senate was Milton Gwirtzman, now a Washington lawyer.

"From the beginning Kennedy knew how to use his staff," Gwirtzman observed. "Even in his first term he had that lineup outside his office. There were perhaps six professionals then and Kennedy used them as a multiplier." To a Borah or Taft or Wagner, the idea of a senatorial multiplier would have been absurd. It would, indeed, have been impossible, for until the Legislative Reorganization Act of 1946, most senators had only a clerk and a secretary.

Kennedy was one of the first senators to employ his staff so systematically that he helped create a new definition of "senator." Kennedy not only used the half dozen or so aides who were his natural due, but he subsidized two others. Gwirtzman, for one, left the staff in 1964 but for the next six years was paid $18,000 a year by the Park Agency, a Kennedy family conduit, for speeches and advice. Kennedy, moreover, had a press secretary. That itself was a relatively new position on the Hill: a media-savvy specialist who measured success in newsprint and television time, not merely in a product called legislation.

Kennedy understood how to develop his staff so that they would serve him. He did not want any one Super Aide around him who might become for him what Ted Sorensen had been for Jack. He did not want an alter ego. What he did want was a group of people who could work on their own, self-motivated young men ambitious for themselves and for him, men whose competitiveness with one another might sometimes spill over into jealousies, but whose energies and ideals could be channeled into furthering Senator Ted Kennedy and his career.

In those first years in office, Kennedy did not draw on his name. He did not use his power in ways that were memorable or important. He had a quotation from Machiavelli as his maxim: "power not used is power saved." Machiavelli, however, was writing about power that had once been used. Kennedy was hoarding a commodity whose worth he could not know until he used it. He was acting as if even he accepted the common definition of himself as the last and the least of the Kennedys—the kid brother.

During the day Kennedy abided by all the rituals of egalitarianism: bantering with aides, employing the ersatz intimacy of first names. However, if an aide stepped over a certain line, visible only to Kennedy, that aide learned to regret it. By day they might be members of a team but not in the evening. It was simply understood that if you worked for Ted Kennedy you did not go to social gatherings that he attended. You learned to treat his family in a special way. An aide had taken a phone call from Rose Kennedy in Hyannisport one day. "Your mother called," the aide said when Kennedy returned to the office. "You mean *you* talked to *my* mother?" Kennedy said. If politics was one world, and social life another, then the family was yet a third and the most exalted of Kennedy's worlds. Here the subordinates were not allowed to trespass, even for a moment.

On that November afternoon in 1963 when President John F. Kennedy was assassinated in Dallas, Ted Kennedy was performing that most thankless of tasks foisted on the freshman: presiding over a nearly empty Senate. When he learned of the shooting and he finally reached his brother on the telephone, Robert Kennedy told him, "You'd better call your mother and your sisters." In their division of the duties of mourning, it fell to Ted Kennedy to comfort the family.

By the next June, Kennedy had prepared his public face. His party back in Massachusetts was preparing to nominate him for his first full term in office. Kennedy, however, was still on the floor of the Senate waiting to vote on the civil rights bill. It was so typical of his life to have a dozen people, a dozen decisions, a dozen proposals backed up waiting for him.

Kennedy finally left Washington for Massachusetts by private plane, accompanied by Senator Birch Bayh of Indiana and his wife Marvella, and aide Ed Moss. It was no kind of weather to be flying in a private plane, but Kennedy lived in a world of days that were scheduled too tight, cars that were driven too fast, planes that were flown when they shouldn't have been. On the approach to the airport outside Springfield, the plane crashed. The Bayhs were injured, the pilot was dead, Moss would die soon afterward, and Kennedy had cracked ribs, a punctured lung, and three damaged vertebrae.

Kennedy spent the next six months in bed. . . .

While still in the hospital, Kennedy won reelection in Massachusetts with 74.4 percent of the votes. In New York, his brother Bob defeated Kenneth Keating for a Senate seat by a much closer margin. Afterward his brother had come up to visit in the hospital. The two Kennedys had posed for the photographers. "Step back a little, you're casting a shadow on Ted," one of the photographers said to Bob Kennedy.

"It'll be the same in Washington," Ted Kennedy said laughing.

During the nearly four years that the two Kennedys served together in the Senate, Ted Kennedy largely deferred to his brother and to his leadership. In 1965 he took over the chairmanship of the Subcommittee on Refugees and Escapees. This was his first chairmanship, the natural legacy of the seniority system. It was a moribund subcommittee concerned largely with refugees who had fled Communist Europe. But it represented more staff and an area that he could now legitimately make his own.

Ted took the subcommittee and expanded its mandate to the refugees of Southeast Asia. He used it as his ticket of admission to the issue of Vietnam. He went to Vietnam and the papers were full of the poignant testimony of human suffering. . . .

It was not until after the murder of his brother Bob in 1968 that Ted Kennedy, the senator, began to fully emerge. In his time of mourning he had gone sailing for days on end, and drinking, and carousing. Then in August in Worcester he had given a speech important enough to be televised nationally. He told his audience that he had been at sea. But he said, "There is no safety in hiding. Not for me, not for any of us here today . . . like my brothers before me, I pick up a fallen standard." He went on to talk about the Vietnam war and all it had cost in money and blood. He proposed that the United States unconditionally end the bombing and negotiate a peace. . . .

The next office Kennedy did seek was one that his brothers would never have considered. In January he defeated Russell Long, that son of Louisiana, and son of oil, to become majority whip. The whip had a series of thankless bureaucratic duties such as rounding up senators and arranging schedules. He was, nonetheless, the number-two leader in the Senate. Kennedy set out to make the whip more than that. He brought in some of his own academic and other expert advisors to forge a cohesive policy for the Democrats. Senators, however, are a jealous and self-protective group. A hundred different policies were better than one, if the one came stamped with the mark of a particular senator. Worse yet, Kennedy simply did not perform the mundane, pesky tasks of the whip as they were supposed to be. Bored by them, he foisted such chores as he could onto his staff.

Kennedy was drinking heavily. At times his face had the florid look that showed him a full-blooded member of the race of Irish drinkers. Then in July on vacation he had gone over to Chappaquiddick Island to attend a party for some of Bobby Kennedy's "boiler-room girls." He had left with one of them, Mary Jo Kopechne, and the next morning the police had found her body in Kennedy's overturned Oldsmobile off a bridge on a dirt road on Chappaquiddick Island.

Kennedy, according to his own statement, had dived down to try to get her out and then he had left and gone back to his friends to get help. He had not contacted the police until the next morning. The Kennedys, whatever else one said about them, had always showed the grace under pressure that Hemingway had called the mark of courage, the mark of a man. The private Kennedy had failed that night, as those around him failed. "It was in part a failure of staffing," one of his aides said. "He had no one with him to tell him he was crazy."

Within hours Kennedy had left the island. He retreated into that flimsy story; he made a televised public statement prepared by Ted Sorensen, Gwirtzman, Richard Goodwin, and Burke Marshall and then backed into legal refuges, the power of wealth and position, and the sympathy that people of Massachusetts had for him and for his family. . . .

Until that night at Chappaquiddick, Kennedy had appeared an inevitable choice for the 1972 presidential nomination. But that was all over. When Kennedy returned to the Senate, Mike Mansfield, the majority leader, as goodhearted a man as was to be found in that body, noticed Kennedy pausing for a moment in the cloakroom. "Come here," Mansfield said encouragingly. "Come here, right back where you belong." To the last of the Kennedys, it was a phrase not without its ironies. . . .

RARELY DOES A POWERFUL congressional party leader give up his post to become a committee chairman. However, when the committee is one of the most powerful in the body, such as the Senate Appropriations Committee, an effective chair not only can serve constitutents better than a party leader but also can continue to be a powerful force in the body. The following selection reveals how former Senate Majority Leader Robert Byrd (D-W. Va.) maintained and perhaps enhanced his power on Capitol Hill when he stepped down as party chief to head the Appropriations Committee.

Jackie Calmes

27 FROM MAJORITY LEADER TO COMMITTEE CHAIRMAN: HOW ROBERT BYRD WIELDS POWER IN THE SENATE

Some of those close to the Senate Appropriations Committee like to quip that Robert C. Byrd would be the strongest chairman in years if only because he came to the coveted job before age had sapped his health and senses. Even Byrd is in on the macabre joke. He quotes South Carolina's Deomcratic senator: "Fritz Hollings one day said, 'We have a real, live chairman now!' "

But the verdict on Byrd goes well beyond simple vitality: After one year on the job, the West Virginia Democrat is emerging as the most powerful Appropriations chief in a generation. It's sweet praise for the proud man who gave up the Senate's top spot, the majority leadership, after years of sniping about his style.

"I would say that he is the strongest leader in that role of chairman that I have served under," says Oregon's Mark O. Hatfield, the committee's senior Republican and the only other recent chairman (1981–87) not enfeebled by age.

At 72, after spending 22 of his 31 Senate years in its leadership circle, Byrd says his new post is the one he always wanted. Some observers say it is the one for which he is best suited.

Byrd was often criticized during his tenure as Democratic leader for being too stilted and old-fashioned to represent his party in the TV age. But in the insiders' world of Appropriations, he is succeeding in the model of the 1950s-era committee chairmen, the benevolent dictators he watched as a new senator. "He embraces power," says Sen. Thad Cochran, R-Miss. "He doesn't shirk from it."

"From Majority Leader to Committee Chairman: How Robert Byrd Wields Power in the Senate," by Jackie Calmes. From *Congressional Quarterly Weekly Report*, December 9, 1989, pp. 3354–3359. Copyright © 1989 by Congressional Quarterly, Inc. Reprinted by permission.

As majority leader, Byrd at best was first among equals on the Senate floor, subject by its wide-open rules to the whims of the most junior members, and beholden for his job to his demanding fellow Democrats. But in the ornate Capitol committee room, he gavels away with the security of one who leads by right of seniority, without fear of the filibusters and non-germane amendments that stymie floor action for a majority leader.

No longer under party pressure to be a media-smart political visionary, Byrd now is judged and respected for his devotion to institutional and legislative detail. He is compared to a technically competent plant manager, a conductor who runs the trains on time.

"He's done a good job, a very good job," says Sen. Pete V. Domenici, R-N.M. "As difficult as things are, given the budget constraints, he's led."

When the full committee met, it approved the allocation of funds in record time. Some past sessions had taken days and multiple roll-call votes.

Similarly, Byrd unveiled his September counter proposal to President Bush's call for higher anti-drug funding only after consulting with the subcommittee heads and Hatfield. His proposal, which became the basis of a compromise after much wrangling with Republicans and the administration, provided a bigger increase, allocated more money to treatment efforts to balance Bush's emphasis on prisons, and made small, across-the-board cuts in the 1990 appropriations bills to offset the extra funding.

Awaiting His Turn

Byrd tried to lead in his former role, and often did. The 100th Congress, his last term as majority leader, was among the most productive in years.

But his dozen years as Democratic chief were filled with enough disappointments that by early 1988 Byrd announced he would not seek the job again. Half of those years were spent as minority leader—"a purgatory if not worse"—and in that time he was challenged twice from within his own ranks, reflecting Democrats' longing for a telegenic foil to Ronald Reagan.

Byrd's fallback was an enviable one. In 1989, he inherited both the Appropriations chairmanship and the post of president pro tempore, a ceremonial job for the Senate's senior majority member that satisfies Byrd's love of parliamentary ritual.

"If I had had the opportunity to be Appropriations chairman before this year, I would have taken it. It is the position I always wanted since I went on the committee 31 years ago," Byrd says. "But I had to take my turn."

Seven men—six Democrats and Hatfield—held the job in that period. The Democrats included some of the Senate's major postwar figures—Carl T. Hayden of Arizona, Richard B. Russell of Georgia, Allen J. Ellender of Louisiana, John L. McClellan of Arkansas and Warren G. Magnuson of Washington—but most were aged and near the end of their careers by the time they assumed the chair.

Five of the six Democrats were ailing, and three died in office. Byrd succeeds John C. Stennis of Mississippi, a revered 41-year Senate veteran who retired at age 87 in ill health after a single term at Appropriations.

At the House Appropriations Committee, where senators in general and Byrd in particular have never been popular, a top aide said recently that any grumbling about Byrd "just reflects the thinking of people who aren't used to having a leader as Senate Appropriations chairman."

A Style Suited to the Job

By all accounts, it is the job rather than the man that has changed. In fact, some of the praise reflects a measure of relief that he is no longer majority leader.

"He transferred the same style of leadership to the committee . . . a very sober-type, serious, no-monkey-business, all-business type of leadership, with a knowledge of exactly how he wanted to get from point A to point B," Hatfield says.

But Hatfield and others agree that Byrd's style has worked better in the committee than it did on the floor. The panel's membership is smaller (29), its rules tighter and partisanship rare as members swap support to steer federal dollars to their home states.

Looking back over his first year as chairman, Byrd said, "I used the same approach that I always used as majority leader and minority leader. My approach was to counsel others, and work individually with senators . . . to develop a consensus. I think as time went on, I developed a pretty good level of unity in my party, and I've done the same at Appropriations."

Byrd says his consultation with the subcommittee chairmen "makes them feel that they're part of the team." Members do credit Byrd for consulting them, though there is some feeling that he actually is informing the senators about decisions that he and his staff already have worked out.

Also, by meeting with senators one-on-one, Byrd's own power is enhanced. He can pick off members' support individually until he has the votes to assure the outcome he wants. The approach suits Byrd not only politically, but personally. An intensely private, insular man, he has never been comfortable in clubby situations.

As majority leader, a former aide recalls, "Byrd was not particularly fond of large group settings, particularly when a great deal of power was collected in one room. [In a small group] he felt he was more in control, [that there was] less possibility of a spontaneous revolution."

A Man Apart

For a man who loves the Senate as his home, Byrd has never been close to other members of the family. As he said in an extraordinary, angry moment on the Senate floor in 1987, "I understand that I am not very well-liked around here."

He spends off-hours not socializing or relaxing but educating himself—reading histories, Shakespeare, the Bible, even the dictionary, and writing his own Senate history series—in a drive for self-improvement that has consumed him since his days as an orphan in West Virginia's coal fields. A box in his office reads, "Secret of Success," and opens to say, "Work."

Sen. Wyche Fowler Jr., D-Ga., recalls that when Sen. Frank R. Lautenberg, D-N.J., asked Byrd how he'd spent the August recess, Byrd said he'd reread a multivolume history of England. After Lautenberg quipped that he hoped Byrd had his kings straight, Byrd recited each one in order.

At Appropriations, it is said privately that members follow Byrd not because they like him, but because they fear him.

"I've heard that very frequently," Hatfield says. "I suppose it's one of those situations where there's a careful line drawn between respect and affection—a lot of respect but not a great deal of affection. And I think that's too bad."

Amid their general praise for Byrd's stewardship, members and staff do complain about the bang of his gavel—the symbol of his obsession with quick and orderly action. "The gavel probably could be struck a little less loudly and still command respect," Cochran says.

He has embarrassed his equally proud colleagues by admonishing them in public sessions, or summarily gaveling their requests out of order. "I am a grown man, and this is not a grade school," one senator said.

But while Byrd clearly runs the show at Appropriations, he defers to the subcommittee heads in matters under their jurisdiction. Byrd himself remains chairman of one subcommittee, with broad responsibility for the Interior Department, national parks, mines, Indian affairs and the arts.

"The committee is run with a firm hand, but the subcommittee chairmen still have quite a bit of autonomy," says Warren B. Rudman, N.H., senior Republican on the subcommittee for the Commerce, Justice and State departments and the judiciary. "I haven't seen a lot of interference at all. He just likes to keep the trains running on time."

One feud that did break into the open involved Rudman's Democratic counterpart, Commerce Subcommittee Chairman Ernest F. Hollings.

The September morning after Byrd unveiled his anti-drug funding proposal at a Capitol press conference, Hollings led his panel to approve what he and Rudman called a better alternative. It provided a smaller increase, all for the law enforcement programs covered in Hollings' subcommittee bill, and a smaller offsetting cut in other programs.

Just as Hollings finished describing the plan, Byrd entered, huddled with him for a brief and audibly testy exchange, then abruptly left. Until the matter was resolved, Byrd refused to schedule full committee action on Hollings' subcommittee bill.

Committee members dismiss the incident as a misunderstanding between two proud senators with a history of strained relations. In the last decade, when Byrd was Democratic whip and heir apparent to retiring

Majority Leader Mike Mansfield, Hollings had considered challenging the West Virginian.

Wielding Power . . .

The same drug-funding issue also soured Byrd's relations with the Bush White House, and particularly with budget director Richard G. Darman.

Those relations "went very, very well up to the drug package," Hatfield says. "Then there was a time when he just did not respond to their telephone calls, to their offers to meet with him. He felt they had invaded and overplayed their indirect role in the legislative process, and therefore challenged the role of the House and Senate. He told me, 'You're the [Republican] spokesman, and I take your word and your position for these things as representing the administration.' "

By contrast, during the spring Byrd had successfully joined with the administration to oppose a major $822 million drug-funding boost that the House included in the 1989 supplement appropriations bill. That angered many congressional Democrats, who wanted to make a party stand against drugs, but Byrd was intent on avoiding the threatened veto of his first bill as chairman.

"I felt there ought to be more [anti-drug] money, but there was a time to get that money and we were two or three months ahead of that point," he recalls. "It was the wrong time, and I had a supplemental appropriations bill that I felt would be lost entirely if we took on an additional issue."

Some Appropriations sources suggest that Byrd's stance would have been different as majority leader, the party point man. Byrd himself notes the change in his role: As Appropriations chairman, his responsibility is to his committee's work, he says, while "the party leader has to protect the party's program. . . . One is apt to be cast into controversial roles."

But would he have acted differently on the supplemental bill had he still been majority leader? "I can't stay," Byrd replies after a pause.

His later fight for higher drug funding in September, during action on the 1990 appropriations, combined the roles of both committee and party leader. As Appropriations chairman, Byrd was delivering on his spring promise that more money would be provided in regular appropriations for 1990, and devising a way to pay for the increase that would be least painful to other programs. As a senior Democrat, he was trying to put a party stamp on a matter of widespread voter concern. In the House, which jealously guards its prerogatives as the originator of the annual appropriations bills, Byrd's take-charge operation of the Senate committee has required some getting used to.

"Previously we'd deal with our own Senate [subcommittee] counterparts one-on-one. Now there's the overriding presence of Bob Byrd," says Rep.

William Lehman, D-Fla., chairman of the House Appropriations Committee's Transportation Subcommittee.

At year's end, for example, Byrd stepped in to break an impasse between House and Senate subcommittees negotiating the agriculture bill. Sen. Dale Bumpers, D-Ark., was holding out against Jamie L. Whitten, D-Miss., Chairman of both House Appropriations and its Agriculture Subcommittee, to get a $1.1 million grant for a home-state firm providing chemicals information to farmers.

Byrd offered to find money elsewhere, in the Interior appropriations. That did not please Byrd's opposite number at the House's Interior panel, Chairman Sidney R. Yates, D-Ill.

Inevitably there has been institutional rivalry—notably during the supplemental bill debate. On a personal level, many House members have long considered Byrd cold and stubborn, the epitome of the pompous senator. In years past, they occasionally would block West Virginia projects out of spite.

That makes the latest praise all the more surprising: House appropriators have been impressed by Byrd's command of his panel and his ability to move bills through the Senate. In September, spending bills were moving from subcommittee to full committee and floor passage in as few as two or three days.

"He's done an outstanding job," says Rep. John Murtha, D-Pa., chairman of House Appropriations' Defense Subcommittee.

Outside his committee, Byrd has assiduously guarded its turf against others in Congress and the White House, reclaiming some of the panel's prestige that eroded under the budget changes of recent years. Always a stickler for parliamentary rules and procedure, he now channels that zeal to protect Appropriations' right to determine spending levels.

The turf fights inevitably have aggravated lawmakers off the committee, just as Byrd's quick gavel and occasional disciplinarian-like lectures have irritated those who are on it.

In a powerplay this fall, he revived a long-dormant rule and successfully battled the Senate Foreign Relations Committee's practice of mandating minimum amounts of funding for certain foreign aid programs.

In Congress' final hours last month, a $100 million provision for social service block grants to the states was stripped from a major deficit-reduction package and passed separately—after Byrd objected that non-appropriations bills were not the place for spending proposals.

Also at his behest, Senate negotiators on a bill (HR 3611) authorizing drug-fighting aid to South American nations forced the House to drop a number of provisions specifying how money would be spent. Though Byrd was not on the conference committee, its statement on the final compromise pointedly noted that the House earmarks were dropped "at the insistence of the chairman of the Senate Appropriations Committee."

Byrd's protectiveness of his turf extends outside Congress. Enraged by a lobbying firm's efforts to steer federal money to its clients, Byrd used his Interior Appropriations bill to shepherd into law new disclosure requirements. They require recipients of federal funds to report the names and pay of lobbyists hired to obtain those funds, and bar the use of federal money for lobbying costs.

. . . And Delivering

Byrd's anti-lobbying campaign began when he learned that the firm was taking credit for securing an $18 million research center for West Virginia University. That struck at Byrd's pride in his own renowned ability to get the pork for his state.

Because of his reputation, few took Byrd seriously in 1988 when he said he was forgoing another bid for majority leader because he could do more for West Virginia at Appropriations.

But he moved immediately to live up to his vow. The 1989 supplemental spending bill included $75 million to rebuild a radio telescope at the National Radio Astronomy Observatory in Green Bank, W.Va., and $6.6 million for rural-airport subsidies on which his state depends. The subsidies got another $30.7 million in the 1990 transportation bill this fall—less than the Senate provided but much more than the urban-oriented House wanted.

Byrd's own list shows that he secured more than $400 million for West Virginia projects in the 1990 appropriations bills. That sum does not include millions of dollars more for the state's share of programs for which Byrd is a leading proponent, including Economic Development Administration funds, rural-airport subsidies, coal-research efforts and unspecified flood-control projects.

The Interior measure was predictably generous to West Virginia. As Byrd notes, just the $11.7 billion for fisheries and wildlife projects is more than the president requested for the entire country. The Bureau of Mines got $34 million more than Bush sought, mostly for health and safety programs important to Byrd's state.

According to a House aide, Whitten joked last spring that the supplemental conference was delayed "because Byrd discovered there was one West Virginia county he had not taken care of." But, the aide added, "Byrd's no more parochial than anyone else, particularly anyone in his high position."

"Where I Want to Be"

Byrd's transition to that position seemed smooth from the start this year, though few doubted that it was difficult for him to forfeit the majority leadership.

"I think that having the dual role of president pro tem of the Senate and the chairmanship of the committee has probably helped," Hatfield says. "As president pro tem, he is still able to occupy a very important role in Senate proceedings."

The job entitles Byrd to preside over his cherished Senate whenever he chooses, and he has done so more than any predecessor in memory. "I'm a very active president pro tem," Byrd says. "I put more work into it."

He also has put more money into it. The office received $296,000 for 1990, nearly double the 1989 appropriations. Byrd says funding had not kept pace with inflation or the office's responsibilities to oversee Senate organizations. The staff also helps on Byrd's history project.

That labor of love has eased his transition, too. Now at work on the second book, Byrd recently checked out 44 volumes of the *Congressional Record* from the Senate Library for one weekend's research.

"I think the man's just been keeping so busy that probably in some way he's relieved of not having the nitty-gritty, everyday activity leadership to worry about,' Hatfield says.

Whether staring down from the Senate presiding officer's chair, or managing his Appropriations Committee's legislation, Byrd takes pride that he has not interfered with his successor, Majority Leader George J. Mitchell, D-Me.

"Extraordinary kudos go to Byrd," says Fowler, a member of Mitchell's circle. "He has not second-guessed Mitchell, except when Mitchell asks. He walked away and held his peace."

"I severed my ties with that responsibility," Byrd says simply. "I had it many years, I walked away from it, I don't want it again. I am where I want to be and doing what I want to do."

WEST VIRGINIA SENATOR Robert Byrd's junior colleague John D. Rockefeller IV seems to have taken a leaf from Byrd's book on how to achieve power in the Senate, as he too has gained prestige in the body by paying careful attention to its norms and customs. Unlike Byrd, the native son of a coal miner, Rockefeller, the scion of a dynasty, moved to West Virginia in 1964 to work in a poverty program. He stayed and was elected to the state legislature in 1966, where he served one term. Then, in 1968, he successfully ran for the statewide office of West Virginia Secretary of State. After a brief stint as a college president in the 1970s, he became governor of West Virginia in 1977 and was reelected in 1980, serving the two terms allowed by the state constitution. Although Rockefeller has presidential ambitions, he has achieved Senate power not by grandstanding and seeking high visibility but in the "old-fashioned" way—by hard work, respect for colleagues, and developing a reputation for policy expertise—as the following account of his Senate career illustrates.

28 Julie Rovner
ROCKEFELLER'S PATH TO SENATE POWER

In an era of new-age, sound-bite, press-release politics, John D. Rockefeller IV has chosen a decidedly old-fashioned path to power in the Senate.

Rockefeller, D-W.Va., whose very name commands attention, spent his first years in the Senate firmly on the back benches, learning the chamber's folkways, attending to committee work and familiarizing himself with the issues.

That was a marked contrast to some other members of the Class of 1984, such as Senators Al Gore, D-Tenn., Phil Gramm, R–Tex., and Tom Harkin, D–Iowa, who sought and won high visibility. And it surprised pundits who had been touting Rockefeller as presidential timber from the day he entered politics.

But Rockefeller's slow, steady course is paying off. Through labor and luck, he is heading into his first re-election campaign as an emerging Senate power. He commands the respect of Senate leaders and is wielding influence in his committees. As the spotlight he has shunned seeks him more often, talk of presidential possibilities could resurface.

Rockefeller has made his mark most clearly in health policy. Last year, his first as chairman of the Finance Subcommittee on Medicare and Long-Term

Care, he was credited with pushing to fruition a far-reaching overhaul of the way Medicare pays doctors.

Now, as chairman of the Pepper Commission, a bipartisan, bicameral group of health policy makers, he is facing a tougher challenge—one that could either polish his reputation as a political heavyweight or tarnish it before it gains much luster.

The commission is to make recommendations by March 1 on how to pay for long-term care for the elderly and how to ensure access to health services for the estimated 31 million Americans who lack health insurance. Both questions have defied piecemeal attempts to address them, and both divide policy makers and health-industry experts.

Rockefeller, a relative novice at health policy, has his hands full in seeking a consensus among 15 strongwilled commission members, nearly all of whom have more expertise.

Because it includes virtually all of the health experts in Congress, the commission will have a head start on legislative action for its recommendations—assuming it can agree on some. But unless Rockefeller, as chairman, can sell the commission's product to a wider audience, he will glean little political benefit from it. And that is an area where he remains untested.

Physician-Payment Reform

In a world where professional talkers abound, Rockefeller has made a specialty of listening.

"You know what he did the first year or so? All he did was listen," says Dave Durenberger, R-Minn., a Finance colleague and one of four Pepper Commission vice chairmen. "And he still does; that's his style."

Rockefeller's most striking achievement to date was his unexpected success in winning enactment last fall of an overhaul of Medicare's physician-payment system.

As part of budget-reconciliation legislation (HR 3299), both chambers passed legislation to shift Medicare to a new fee schedule that pays doctors based on the relative work, training and expenses required to provide a given treatment of service. The bills differed in several important ways, including their provisions to gain control over the volume of services that doctors provide.

Rockefeller and Durenberger, the subcommittee's ranking Republican, set out to forge a compromise.

Rockefeller and his staff "got everybody together—they consulted early and often with both House subcommittee chairmen and interest groups," says one lobbyist who was involved in the process. "They went the extra mile to involve everybody in the takeoff so they would all be there at the landing. . . . It was a textbook case of the right way to do it.' "

Despite their efforts, however, the plan nearly died. By Nov. 17, House and Senate negotiators had agreed on most health-related elements of the reconciliation package—but not on physician-payment reform.

At that point, Rockefeller says, "I was told it was dead and lay off it"—an order from Finance Chairman Lloyd Bentsen, D-Tex., that he chose to defy. "I wasn't going to stand for it. It was stupid" to let something so important die so close to the finish line.

Instead, Rockefeller set up a meeting for the following day—a Saturday—which he practically begged leading conferees to attend.

Henry A. Waxman, D-Calif., author of one of the competing House plans, was at synagogue that morning. But when he got home, he says, "there were half a dozen messages on my answering machine from Jay asking me to come to the meeting." He went.

"He's not an easy man to say 'no' to," says Rep. Bill Gradison, Ohio, ranking Republican on the Ways and Means Subcommittee on Health.

Durenberger says, "There's a genuineness in his interest in your opinion that makes it difficult when he says, 'Yes, but. . . .' It's pretty hard when he's been nice to you not to be nice to him."

After hours of hard bargaining, then and on subsequent days, a compromise was reached, with Rockefeller pushing the whole way. Gradison says, "The last rites were being administered when he came along. . . . Clearly, he deserves credit for saving it."

Bentsen, too, praises Rockefeller's accomplishment: "He never gave up. He was very tenacious."

Tougher Going Ahead

Although Rockefeller bucked his elders on the question of when to quit, he has been slower to venture his views on points of policy.

Because he has considerably less expertise in health matters than most of those he works with, Rockefeller sees himself primarily as a mediator. "I come at everything with the idea of, 'Is there a way of solving this, and can we do it together?' I'm bipartisan by my nature and I think that helps and I think Republicans respond to that."

Some say Rockefeller can be too accommodating. "Jay doesn't want to offend anybody," says Rep. Pete Stark, D-Calif., chairman of the Ways and Means Health Subcommittee and a Pepper Commission vice chairman. "But at some point you've got to decide where the winners and losers are."

That time may be at hand with the Pepper Commission, where things so far are not running very smoothly. Two days of closed meetings in Annapolis, Md., this month failed to produce a consensus. Although the group is scheduled to meet again Feb. 5, Rockefeller has already moved back the deadline for decision making.

There also have been complaints about the secrecy surrounding the proceedings. Rockefeller refused to release his own working proposal, and in some cases, commission members have been given documents at meetings only to have them taken back at meetings' end.

"There's been no other choice," says Rockefeller. "The secret to the Pepper Commission is that I have caused people to come out with what they really think . . . and you can't do that in public. You can't embarrass or put on the spot senior people like that."

Minding P's and Q's

Rockefeller's deference to "senior people" is part and parcel of his old-fashioned approach to building a Senate power base.

Instead of going for the headlines, he chose, when he first arrived, what he calls "the Bradley model," after fellow Finance Committee Democrat Bill Bradley, N.J., another nose-to-the-grindstone senator who figures prominently in presidential speculation.

"I used to talk about it with Bill Bradley," Rockefeller says. "Don't say much, work hard, learn stuff, and when you have, then go get it."

Indeed, Rockefeller remembers being invited to join "a classic early 'let's get on TV [junket]' with a group of nameless senators . . . who went roaring down to Central America within seven minutes of getting sworn in. And instinctively, I knew the answer was no."

His low-key approach also "reflects somewhat my way of doing things," says Rockefeller, who "can't wait to open up and start reading" briefing books for hearings, and who color-codes his highlighting. "There's a certain element of personality in there."

Democrat Robert C. Byrd, his senior West Virginia colleague and chairman of the Appropriations Committee, has encouraged Rockefeller.

"The way to become influential in this body is to know your subject well, and the other people will start to listen to you. . . . Senator Rockefeller is doing that," Byrd says. "He doesn't want to get ahead on his name. He wants to be judged on his merit."

Seizing Opportunities

Of course, being in the right place at the right time hasn't hurt.

"If Claude Pepper hadn't died, he wouldn't be chairman of this commission," says Waxman, chairman of the Energy and Commerce Subcommittee on Health and the Environment.

Rockefeller agrees, noting that but for George J. Mitchell's ascent to majority leader, he also would not be chairman of a Finance subcommittee.

But he has not been shy about taking advantage of opportunities when they arise. "He begged me to let him be chairman when Claude died. He loves this stuff," Stark says. "This is not something he didn't go after. He was not a blushing, bashful virgin bride dragged to the altar by his hair."

Still, Rockefeller seems considerably less drawn to the limelight than some of his colleagues.

"That old line about workhorses and show horses is really true," Majority Leader Mitchell, D-Maine, said in an interview. "The senators know who does that work."

Mitchell and Bentsen have given Rockefeller more than mere accolades.

Bentsen wrote 1987 legislation creating the National Commission on Children, a 36-member group assigned to develop policies to promote the health and well-being of children. He saw to it that Rockefeller was appointed to the commission and supported his selection as chairman. The commission, whose members include comedian Bill Cosby and pediatrician T. Berry Brazleton, is scheduled to complete deliberations in 1991.

Bentsen also split the former Health Subcommittee, headed by Mitchell in the 100th Congress, into two panels so that Rockefeller could be a subcommittee chairman.

"I thought he would be effective," Bentsen says. "He's fulfilled my expectations."

Mitchell, whom Rockefeller supported for majority leader in 1988, appointed Rockefeller to replace him on the high-visibility Pepper Commission. Rockefeller became chairman last June, after the death of the man for whom the commission was named, Rep. Claude Pepper, D-Fla.

Now, even though he originally intended to specialize in trade on the Finance Committee, Rockefeller has become captivated with health policy, much as Mitchell was before him.

"It's sort of replaced defense at center stage," Rockefeller says, "except defense only ruined the national budget. Health ruins the family, corporate and national budgets and destroys people right and left and leaves out people right and left."

Rockefeller says he plans to keep his primary focus on health.

"I can't think of anything more useful that I could be doing in the Senate than working on that. For my state, for the country and for my own sense of satisfaction."

The Future Is Now?

If Rockefeller's emergence into the Senate spotlight thrusts him into the presidential sweepstakes speculation, it won't be the first time.

In 1968, *The Wall Street Journal*—in a story headlined "Will Rockefeller Be President in 1976?"—touted the 30-year-old's bright political future on the strength of no more than his primary-election nomination to be West Virginia's secretary of state.

Two years later, when Secretary of State Rockefeller helped engineer the primary-election defeat of several sitting state senators, *The New York Times* took up the chorus. "In a party that is searching desperately for younger national leaders, Mr. Rockefeller is often mentioned as a future presidential or vice presidential possibility," wrote *Times* political correspondent R. W. Appler Jr.

Rockefeller's 1972 loss to Republican Arch A. Moore Jr. in his first race for governor dimmed his star somewhat. But he came back to win the governorship in 1976, and in 1983, as he was finishing his second term as chief executive, the presidential talk was raised again, this time by *People* magazine, which called him "one heir apparent" in the "early line on the 1988 presidential race."

So is he tired of being asked when he will run for president?

"Politicians don't get tired of that," he says, smiling, then quickly denying that anything is imminent. "I'm not without ambition, but there's no sense of pressure within me to respond to that ambition now because I'm so thoroughly happy with what I'm doing."

And he insists that people shouldn't read anything into the fact that in 1989 he made his first "road" speech as senator outside West Virginia in the ever-important presidential primary state of New Hampshire.

He used the opportunity to chide his audience about the acid-rain problem from the perspective of a coal-state politician. "I got no applause during the speech, but boy, did they listen," he says.

Country Roads

The incident was typical. Although known for his self-deprecating humor, Rockefeller is serious about his adopted state.

"My eyes are squarely on West Virginia," he says, noting that he keeps a third of his staff at home working on more than 14,000 constituent cases. "I really work hard on the state."

Rockefeller's road to West Virginia began in Washington nearly 30 years ago. R. Sargent Shriver, President John F. Kennedy's brother-in-law and first director of the Peace Corps, enlisted him as his assistant in 1961. Although Rockefeller had voted for Kennedy, he was a registered Republican at the time.

"I grew up in a Republican family," he says, noting that his uncle Nelson had sought the 1960 GOP presidential nomination.

But Jay Rockefeller, like countless others his age, was swept up in the Kennedy allure.

"It was a time in Washington that was just indescribable," he says. "It was so idealistic, and government was terrific and public service was the best thing to be in."

His becoming a Democrat, he says, "just clearly had to be. . . . And what's odd is that literally 80 percent of my generation" in the Rockefeller family "are Democrats. And serious Democrats; participating, activist, liberals."

Besides becoming a Democrat, Rockefeller abandoned his early specialty in the Far East, and in 1964 joined the Peace Corps' new domestic counterpart, VISTA, as a volunteer.

"I didn't go to West Virginia to do politics. I went to West Virginia to do VISTA," he says. He decided to stay "because it was so direct. It was direct action. It wasn't sitting there writing books about Japan. . . . And that led to politics."

Characteristically, he started at the bottom and worked his way up.

First came two years in the West Virginia House of Delegates, followed by a term as secretary of state, then the failed run for governor, after which he briefly served as president of West Virginia Wesleyan College.

In 1976 Rockefeller won the governorship, and in 1980 he was re-elected, defeating 1972 victor Moore, who was seeking to make a comeback.

The $12 million in personal funds Rockefeller spent on the 1980 race, which included buying television time in the Washington, D.C., and Pittsburgh markets to reach West Virginia voters, gave rise to the ubiquitous "Make Him Spend It All, Arch!" bumper stickers.

Unable to serve more than two consecutive terms, Rockefeller, to no one's surprise, ran for the Senate in 1984, when Jennings Randolph (1958–85) retired.

But during his second term as governor, the state "really got bombed by the recession," as Rockefeller put it. As governor, he took much of the blame. "Presiding over 21 percent unemployment is not exactly exhilarating," he says.

Indeed, it took another $12 million campaign to beat political neophyte John Raese, and even then, Rockefeller won with only 52 percent of the votes. Polls also showed he had a disturbingly high 40 percent negative rating.

"When he went to Washington, the political advice he got to cut down on that negative rating was just to stay quiet," says Dick Grimes, political editor of the *Charleston Daily Mail*.

Rockefeller concedes that was part of the reason for his early low profile. "I wanted to be sure that my own people in West Virginia didn't think I was coming up here to showboat or run for the presidency; that I really cared about the job, which I do."

But that was not the only reason. "I think that what counts around here is that you have a collegial relationship with your colleagues; that you're known to be serious; that you're known to work hard," Rockefeller says.

The Name

Rockefeller is not eager to embarrass himself, either. He is acutely conscious of the benefits and the responsibilities that go with his name.

"It is not exactly a heavy burden," Rockefeller says. "If you can think of five minuses, I can think of 100 pluses. I'm very proud to be that and very happy to be that, and it's allowed me to do a lot of things in my life that I otherwise probably could not or would not have done."

Not that others don't tease him about it. During Senate consideration Nov. 7 of legislation to increase the federal debt ceiling, Rockefeller wanted to offer an amendment to ensure continued funding of health benefits for retired coal miners.

Gramm quipped, "I am tempted to say to my dear colleague from West Virginia that if he wants to offer that amendment so bad, maybe he could float the national debt for a few days."

Rockefeller rejects suggestions from some critics that he could have put his name and fortune to better use faster.

For example, when Sen. Robert F. Kennedy, D-N.Y., was assassinated in 1968, Nelson Rockefeller, then governor of New York, wanted to appoint Jay to replace him.

The younger Rockefeller refused. "That would have been one of the worst exercises of judgment, both moral and political, that I could think of. . . . I turned it down because I was in West Virginia; I was committed to West Virginia and running for secretary of state in West Virginia."

Among other things, he says, "I was not ready to be in the Senate" in 1968. By taking his time, he says, "I really know West Virginia intimately. In 20 years in state politics, it's hard to explain in Washington, D.C., but it gives me a grounding, some practical sense."

Now, he says, "There's a lot of things I know that a lot of other folks here don't. Those of us who have been governors, who have come up through state politics, have dealt with people intimately."

THE SUPREME COURT

Chapter Six

Character, personality, and style help to shape the judiciary at all levels. A true picture of the judicial process would not be complete without a personality profile of the actors that are involved, including judges, prosecuting attorneys, lawyers for the defense, plaintiffs and defendants, and, in some cases, jurors. At the trial level, the drama of the courtroom is shaped by all of the personalities who take part. The full-fledged and celebrated criminal trial is, however, a rarity, and personality usually affects the judicial process outside the public view.

The character of judges inevitably has a profound effect on the judicial process. At the trial court level, their personalities determine the way in which they run their courts. At the appellate level, and particularly on the Supreme Court, their personalities and styles determine the effect they will have on colleagues. The character of judges has been molded long before they reach the bench. Certainly it would be profitable to apply James Barber's character classification of presidents to judges. An active-positive judge would deal with cases quite differently than would an active-negative judge. The value system of the former would be better developed and more likely to affect opinions but would not be rigid. An active-negative judge would be opportunistic on the bench and, particularly below the Supreme Court, would always be keeping an eye out for the possiblity of higher judicial or political office. The character of some judges will cause them to seek the emulation of colleagues, and others will exhibit a strongly independent and iconoclastic streak. Some judges will attempt to control everything that goes on in their courts and will protect the rights of defendants who they feel deserve a break. The character of every courtroom reflects the personality and style of the presiding judge.

The Supreme Court is unique, not only because its decisions are far-reaching, but also because it is affected more by group dynamics among the justices than other courts are. Coalitions are formed, and pressures are used to change minds. The effectiveness of the chief justice and the influence of other justices largely depend on their personalities. A strong and persuasive personality can often change colleagues' minds. Potentially an important leader, the chief justice presides over the weekly, secret conferences of the justices, gives his or her opinion first, and votes last. Voting with the majority determines which majority justice will write the opinion. A forceful chief justice can bring unity to a divided Court and, in some cases, bring about unanimity on politically crucial decisions, such as the desegregation decision in *Brown v. Board of Education,* decided in October 1953. After the *Brown* case has been taken up by the Court, Earl Warren used his considerable powers of persuasion and his highly personal leadership style to bring unanimity to a highly divided Court.[1]

Judicial decision making, at both Supreme Court and lower levels, is a far more fluid process than is commonly known. In commenting on Supreme Court decisions in the decade that ended with the Brown decision, one scholar concluded on the basis of the private papers of Supreme Court justices that "hardly any major decision in this decade was free of significant alteration of vote and language before announcement to the public."[2] Justices often change their minds regardless of their seeming ideological commitment. Group pressure has its effects on Supreme Court justices as on ordinary human beings. The "freshman effect" causes instability in voting patterns among new justices to the Supreme Court.[3] Freshman justices may follow rather than lead their colleagues during their initial period of assimilation into the Court, although this certainly was not true of Chief Justice Earl Warren, who was a pivotal justice from the time he was appointed in 1953.

Most Supreme Court justices have had little or no prior judicial experience before joining the Court, and almost without exception those justices ranked as great or near-great have been more "political" than "judicial" in their styles.[4] Many of the most effective justices, from John Marshall to Earl Warren, held elected or appointed political offices and often were highly partisan politicians. This political experience helped to shape their style of operation once on the Court. The Court was viewed as a political arena, in which pressure and persuasion could be used to change the minds of colleagues on cases that had far-reaching ramifications.

Although the Supreme Court is somewhat more cloistered than the other branches of the government, the justices do not remain in isolation from each other or from Congress, the president, and administrative officials. Conflicts between the Court and other branches are often smoothed through personal contacts. While the Court was turning down much of Roosevelt's New Deal legislation, Justice Harlan F. Stone, at an informal party, gave Frances Perkins, FDR's secretary of labor, the idea to use the taxing and spending authority of

---

[1] See S. Sidney Ulmer, "Earl Warren and the Brown Decision," *Journal of Politics* 33 (1971): 689–702.

[2] J. Woodford Howard, Jr., "On the Fluidity of Judicial Choice," *The American Political Science Review* 52 (March 1968): 43–56, at p. 44.

[3] Ibid., p. 45.

[4] An interesting rating of Supreme Court justices by law school deans and professors of law, history, and political science, undertaken in 1970, may be found in Henry J. Abraham, *Justices and Presidents* (New York: Oxford University Press, 1974), pp. 289–290. Holmes and Cardozo were notable exceptions to the usual lack of prior judicial experience among justices ranked as great.

Article 1 to support the Social Security Act.[5] The Court is not supposed to give advisory opinions, but nothing prevents a justice from informally communicating his ideas to the president or member of the administration. Justice Felix Frankfurter remained a close personal friend of Franklin Roosevelt after he was appointed to the Court, and Abe Fortas was a constant political adviser to President Lyndon B. Johnson. Hugo Black, who wrote the majority opinion in the 1952 *Steel Seizure* case, which held that President Truman did not have independent constitutional authority to seize the steel mills, invited President Truman to dinner to help keep the president and the Court on good terms with each other. Justice William O. Douglas, who was present, described the incident in his autobiography as follows:

> Hugo loved company and long conversations. His spacious garden in his exquisite Alexandria home was ideal for that purpose during spring and summer. He loved to entertain there; and when, during the Korean War, the Court held on June 2, 1952, that Truman's seizure of the steel mills was unconstitutional, Hugo asked me what I thought of his idea of inviting Truman to his home for an evening after the decision came down. I thought it a capital idea. So in two weeks Hugo extended the invitation and Truman accepted. It was stag dinner, and only Truman and members of the Court were present. Truman was gracious though a bit testy at the beginning of the evening. But after the bourbon and canapes were passed, he turned to Hugo and said, "Hugo, I don't much care for your law, but, by golly, this bourbon is good." The evening was [a] great step foward in human relations, and to Hugo Black, good human relations were the secret of successful government.[6]

As this anecdote shows, the personalities and styles of the justices affect external as well as internal relationships.

[5]Frances Perkins, *The Roosevelt I Knew* (New York: Viking, 1946), p. 286.

[6]William O. Douglas, *Go East Young Man* (New York: Random House, 1974), p. 450.

NOWHERE IN GOVERNMENT is the impact of character and personality more important than on the Supreme Court. Each week while the Court is in session, the justices meet secretly in conference to deliberate their decisions on cases involving some of the important issues that confront our government, such as discrimination, freedom of speech and press, the death penalty, the busing of schoolchildren, executive privilege, the separation of church and state, and abortion. The decisions of the Court take precedence over those of the president, the Congress, and the state legislatures, and the actions of the Court are unreviewable.

The scales of justice are supposed to be balanced through a rational, deliberative process that carefully and objectively ascertains the facts of individual cases and applies the law. However, the law is not readily defined objectively but requires interpretation to give it meaning. The process of judicial interpretation necessarily involves a highly subjective element. It is the subjectivity of the law that permits and even encourages judges to apply their own values and prejudices in making decisions. And, on the Supreme Court, where the justices must work in close contact with their colleagues, interpersonal realtionships among "the Brethren" may influence the outcome of a case as much as the ideological orientation of the justices.

The private world of the Supreme Court, like that of the other branches of the government, is characterized by the justices' maneuvering to gain internal power and status. The highly personal and political dimension of Supreme Court decision making has generally been overlooked in the study of constitutional law. The following selection gives a behind-the-scenes view of the role of personalities in the historic Supreme Court decision that held that women have a constitutional right to obtain abortions.

29 Bob Woodward and Scott Armstrong
THE BRETHREN AND
THE ABORTION DECISION

Douglas had long wanted the Court to face the abortion issue head on. The laws in effect in most states, prohibiting or severely restricting the availability of abortions, were infringements of a woman's personal liberty. The broad constitutional guarantee of "liberty," he felt, included the right of a woman to control her body.

Douglas realized, however, that a majority of his colleagues were not likely to give such a sweeping reading to the Constitution on this increasingly volatile issue. He knew also that the two cases now before the

Court—challenging restrictive abortion laws in Georgia and Texas (*Doe v. Bolton* and *Roe v. Wade*)—did not signal any sudden willingness on the part of the Court to grapple with the broad question of abortions. They had been taken only to determine whether to expand a series of recent rulings limiting the intervention of federal courts in state court proceedings. Could women and doctors who felt that state prosecutions for abortions violated their constitutional rights go into federal courts to stop the state? And could they go directly into federal courts even before going through all possible appeals in the state court system? Douglas knew the Chief wanted to say no to both these jurisdiction questions. He knew the Chief hoped to use these two cases to reduce the number of federal court cases brought by activist attorneys. The two abortion cases were not to be argued primarily about abortion rights, but about jurisdiction. Douglas was doubly discouraged, believing that his side was also going to lose on the jurisdiction issue.

These are difficult cases, the Chief said. No one could really tell how they would come out until the final drafting was done. . . .

Brennan and Marshall counted the vote five to two—Douglas, Brennan, Marshall, Stewart, and Blackmun for striking the laws; the Chief and White dissenting.

Douglas, however, thought there were only four votes to strike the laws. Blackmun's vote was far from certain. He could not be counted on to split with the Chief on such an important issue.

For his part, Blackmun was for some kind of limited ruling against portions of the laws, but he had not decided what to do. . . .

. . . The puzzle was Blackmun.

The Chief's assignment sheet circulated the following afternoon. Each case was listed on the left side in order of the oral argument, the name of the justice assigned to write each decision on the right.

It took Douglas several moments to grasp the pattern of the assignments, and then he was flabbergasted. [Flouting Court procedure,] the Chief had assigned four cases in which Douglas was sure the Chief was not a member of the majority. These included the two abortion cases, which the Chief had assigned to Blackmun. He could barely control his rage as he ran down the list. Was there some mistake? He asked a clerk to check his notes from the conference. Douglas kept a docket book in which he recorded his tabulation of the votes. It was as he suspected. . . .

Never, in Douglas's thirty-three years on the court, had any chief justice tried to assign from the minority in such fashion. For two terms now there had been incidents when the Chief had pleaded ignorance, had claimed he hadn't voted, had changed his vote. Until now they had been isolated instances.

On Saturday, December 18, Douglas drafted a scathing memo to Burger, with copies to the other justices. He, not the Chief, should have assigned the opinions in four of the cases. And, Douglas added, he would assign the opinions as he saw fit.

The Chief's response was back in a day. He conceded error in two of the cases, but insisted that the voting in the two abortion cases was too complicated. "There were . . . literally not enough columns to mark up an accurate reflection of the voting," Burger wrote. "I therefore marked down no votes and said this was a case that would have to stand or fall on the writing, when it was done.

"This is still my view of how to handle these two sensitive cases, which, I might add, are quite probable candidates for reargument."

Douglas ascribed to Burger the most blatant political motives. Nixon favored restrictive abortion laws. Faced with the possibility that the Court might strike abortion laws down in a presidential-election year, the Chief wanted to stall the opinion, Douglas concluded.

Blackmun was by far the slowest writer on the Court. The year was nearly half over and he had yet to produce a first circulation in a simple business case that had been argued the first week. . . . It was the kind of case in which Douglas produced drafts within one week of conference. But in the abortion cases, Douglas had a deeper worry. The Chief was trying to manipulate the outcome.

Blackmun might circulate a draft striking portions of the restrictive abortion laws. But as a judicial craftsman, his work was crude, A poor draft would be likely to scare off Stewart, who was already queasy, and leave only four votes. Of if Blackmun himself were to desert the position—a distinct possibility—precious time would be lost. Either defection would leave only a four-man majority. It would be difficult to argue that such a major decision should be handed down on a four-to-three vote. There would be increasing pressure to put the cases over for the sort of case that Nixon had in mind when he chose Powell and Rehnquist.

Blackmun was both pleased and frightened by the assignment. It was a no-win proposition. No matter what he wrote, the opinion would be controversial. Abortion was too emotional, the split in society too great. Either way, he would be hated and vilified.

But from Blackmun's point of view, the Chief had little choice but to select him. Burger could not afford to take on such a controversial case himself, particularly from the minority. Douglas was the Court's mischievous liberal, the rebel, and couldn't be the author. Any abortion opinion Douglas wrote would be widely questioned outside the Court, and his extreme views might split rather than unify the existing majority. Lastly, Blackmun had noticed a deterioration in the quality of Douglas's opinions; they had become increasingly superficial.

Brennan was certainly as firm a vote for striking down the state abortion laws as there was on the Court. But Brennan was the Court's only Catholic.

As such, Blackmun reasoned, he could not be expected to be willing to take the heat from Catholic antiabortion groups. Marshall could not be the author for similar reasons: an opinion by the Court's only black could be unfairly perceived as specifically designed for blacks. That left only Stewart. Blackmun believed that Stewart could certainly relish the assignment, but he clearly had trouble going very far.

Blackmun was convinced that he alone had the medical background and sufficient patience to sift through the voluminous record for the scientific data on which to base a decision. He was deeply disturbed by Douglas's assumption that the Chief had some malicious intent in assigning the abortion cases to him. He was *not* a Minnesota Twin.

True, Blackmun had known the Chief since they were small children and had gone to Sunday school together. They had lived four or five blocks apart in the blue-collar Daytons Bluff section of St. Paul. Neither family had much money during the Depression. The two boys had kept in touch until Blackmun went to a technical high school.

Blackmun's seven years at Harvard, however, put the two men worlds apart. Burger had finished local college and night law school in six years and was already practicing law when Blackmun came back to clerk for a judge on the court of Appeals. Blackmun was best man at Burger's wedding, but the two drifted apart again as they established very different law practices.

Blackmun tried to tell his story every chance he got. His hands in his pockets, jingling change uncomfortably, he would explain how he had practiced in Minneapolis, where large law firms concentrated on serving major American corporations. Burger had practiced in St. Paul, across the river, in the political, wheeler-dealer atmosphere of a state capital.

"A Minneapolis firm," Blackmun would say, "will never practice in St. Paul or vice versa." Left unsaid was the disdain so obvious in the Minneapolis legal community for St. Paul lawyers.

But Blackmun was a hesistant and reserved storyteller, and he was never sure that the others got the message. Douglas, however, should have realized by now that Harry Blackmun was no Warren Burger twin.

Blackmun had long thought Burger an uncontrollable, blustery braggart. Now, once again in close contact with him, he was at once put off and amused by the Chief's exaggerated pomposity, his callous disregard for the feelings of his colleagues, his self-aggrandizing style. "He's been doing that since he was four," he once told Stewart.

Blackmun was just as aware as Douglas was of the Chief's attempts to use his position to manipulate the Court. Douglas was correct to despise that sort of thing. But this time, Blackmun felt, Douglas was wrong. When he arrived at Court, Blackmun had assumed the Chief's job as scrivener for the conference. Burger had finally given up trying to keep track of all the votes and positions taken in conference, and had asked Blackmun to keep notes and stay behind to brief the Clerk of the Court. Even then the Chief sometimes misstated the results. Blackmun would deftly field the Chief's hesitations, filling in when he faltered. When Burger misinformed the Clerk of the Court, Blackmun's cough would cue him.

"Do you recall what happened there, Harry?" the Chief would then say. "My notes seem to be a bit sporadic."

Blackmun would fill in the correct information as if Burger had initiated the request.

Part of the problem was that the Chief spread himself too thin. He accepted too many social, speaking, and ceremonial engagements, and exhibited too little affection for the monastic, scholarly side of the Court's life. As a result, Burger was often unprepared for orals or conference. Too often, he had to wait and listen in order to figure out which issues were crucial to the outcome. His grasp of the cases came from the summaries, usually a page or less, of the certified memos his clerks prepared. The Chief rarely read the briefs or the record before oral argument.

The problem was compounded by Burger's willingness to change his position in conference, or his unwillingness to commit himself before he had figured out which side had a majority. Then, joining the majority, he could control the assignment. Burger had strained his relationship with everyone at the table to the breaking point. It was as offensive to Blackmun as it was to the others. But one had to understand the Chief. For all his faults, here was a self-made man who had come up the ladder rung by rung. Blackmun did not begrudge him his attempts at leadership.

The abortion assignment really amounted to nothing more than a request that Blackmun take first crack at organizing the issues. It was one of those times when the conference had floundered, when the briefs and oral arguments had been inadequate, when the seemingly decisive issue in the case, jurisdiction, had evaporated. The Court had been left holding the bull by the tail.

Blackmun was not so naive as to think that the Chief had given him the abortion cases with the intention of having him find a broad constitutional right to abortion. But he was distressed by Douglas's implicit suggestion that he was unfit for the assignment or was somehow involved in a deception.

Blackmun also knew that he, after all, had a unique appreciation of the problems and strengths of the medical profession. At Mayo, he had watched as Doctors Edward C. Kendall and Philip S. Hench won the Noble prize for research in arthritis. He rejoiced with other doctors after their first successful heart-bypass operation, then suffered with them after they lost their next four patients. He sat up late nights with the surgical staff to review hospital deaths in biweekly meetings, and recalled them in detail. He grew to respect what dedicated physicians could accomplish. These had been terribly exciting years for Blackmun. He called them the best ten years of his life.

If a state licensed a physician to practice medicine, it was entrusting him with the right to make medical decisions. State laws restricting abortions interfered with those medical judgments. Physicians were always somewhat unsure about the possible legal ramifications of their judgments. To completely restrict an operation like abortion, normally no more dangerous than minor surgery, or to permit it only with the approval of a hospital committee or the concurrence of other doctors, was a needless infringement of the discretion of the medical profession.

Blackmun would do anything he could to reduce the anxiety of his colleagues except to spurn the assignment. The case was not so much a legal task as an opportunity for the Court to ratify the best possible medical opinion. He would take the first crack at the abortion case. At the least, he could prepare a memo to clarify the issues.

As was his custom, Douglas rushed through a first draft on the cases five days after conference. He decided not to circulate it, but to sit back and wait for Blackmun. He was still bitter toward Burger, whom he had taken to calling "this Chief," reserving "The Chief" as an accolade fitting only for retired Chief Justice Earl Warren. But Douglas broke his usual rule against lobbying and paid a visit to Blackmun. Though he would have much preferred that Brennan write the draft, he told Blackmun, "Harry, I would have assigned the opinion to you anyway."

Reassured, Blackmun withdrew to his regular hideaway, the justices' second-floor library, where he worked through the winter and spring, intially without even a law clerk to help with research.

Brennan, too, had little choice but to wait for Blackmun's draft. But in the interval, he spotted a case that he felt might help Blackmun develop a constitutional grounding for a right to abortion. Brennan was writing a majority opinion overturning birth-control activist Bill Baird's conviction for distributing birth-control devices without a license (*Eisenstadt v. Baird*). He wanted to use the case to extend to individuals the right to privacy that was given to married couples by the 1965 Connecticut birth-control case.

Brennan was aware that he was unlikely to get agreement on such a sweeping extension. He circulated his opinion with a carefully worded paragraph at the end. "If the right to privacy means anything, it is the right of the individual, married or single, to be free from unwarranted governmental intrusion into matters so fundamentally affecting a person as the decision whether to bear or beget a child."

That case dealt only with contraception—the decision to "beget" a child. He included the reference to the decision to "bear" a child with the abortion case in mind. Brennan hoped the language would help establish a constitutional basis, under the right to privacy, for a woman's right to abortion.

Since the last paragraph was not the basis for the decision, Stewart could join it without renouncing his dissent in the 1956 case. Brennan got Stewart's vote.

But Blackmun was holding back. The Chief was lobbying Blackmun not to join Brennan's draft. Brennan's clerks urged their boss to lobby Blackmun.

Brennan refused. Blackmun reminded him, he said, of former justice Charles E. Whittaker, who had been paralyzed by indecisiveness. Whittaker's indecision had ended in a nervous breakdown and his resignation. Former Justice Felix Frankfurter had misunderstood Whittaker's indecision and had spent hours lobbying him. Instead of influencing him, Frankfurter had drawn Whittaker's resentment. No, Brennan said, he would not lobby Blackmun.

Blackmun finally decided not to join Brennan's opinion, but simply to concur in the result. That worried Brennan. Without adopting some logic similar to that provided in the contraception case, Blackmun would have difficulty establishing a right to abortion on grounds of privacy.

With the official arrival of Powell and Rehnquist, the Chief scheduled a January conference to discuss which cases should be put over for reargument before the new nine-man Court. Burger suggested that cases with a four-to-three vote should be reargued. His list included the abortion cases, . . .

Blackmun spent his time—apart from oral argument, conferences, and a bare minimum of office routine—in the justices' library. Awesome quantities of medical, as well as legal, books were regularly carried in. But all indications pointed toward no circulation of a first draft until much later in the spring. . . .

Blackmun began each day by breakfasting with his clerks in the Court's public cafteria, and clerks from the other chambers had a standing invitation to join them. Blackmun would often spot a clerk from another chamber eating alone and invite him over. He seemed, at first, the most open, unassuming, and gracious of the justices.

Breakfast-table conversation generally began with sports, usually baseball, and then moved on to the morning's headlines. There was an unspoken rule that any discussion of cases was off limits. Where other justices might openly debate cases with the clerks, Blackmun awkwardly sidestepped each attempt. The law in general was similarly out of bounds. Blackmun turned the most philosophical of discussions about law around to his own experience, or to the clerk's family, or the performance of a younger sibling in school.

The clerks in his own chambers saw a different side of Blackmun which betrayed more of the pressure that he felt. The stories were petty. An office window left open all night might set him off on a tirade. It was not the security that worried Blackmun, but the broken social contract—all clerks were supposed to close all windows each night. Number-two pencils, needle-sharp, neatly displayed in the pencil holder, need include only one number three or a cracked point to elict a harsh word. If Blackmun wanted a document photocopied, and somehow the wrong one came back, he might simply fling it aside. An interruption, even for some important question, might be repulsed testily.

The mystery of the Blackmun personality deepened. His outbursts varied in intensity and usually passed quickly. "Impatient moods," his secretary called them. But they made life more difficult; they added an extra tension.

Yet none of his Court family—clerks, secretaries, or his messenger— judged Blackmun harshly. They all knew well enough the extraordinary pressures, real and imagined, that he worked under.

From his first day at the Court, Blackmun had felt unworthy, unqualified, unable to perform up to standard. He felt he could equal the Chief and Marshall, but not the others. He became increasingly withdrawn and professorial. He did not enjoy charting new paths for the law. He was still learning. The issues were too grave, the information too sparse. Each new question was barely answered, even tentatively, when two more questions appeared on the horizon. Blackmun knew that his colleagues were concerned about what they perceived as his indecisiveness. But what others saw as an inability to make decisions, he felt to be a deliberate withholding of final judgment until all the facts were in, all the arguments marshaled, analyzed, documented.

It was a horribly lonely task. Blackmun worked by himself, beginning with a long memo from one of his clerks, reading each of the major briefs, carefully digesting each of the major opinions that circulated, laboriously drafting his own opinions, checking each citation himself, refining his work through a dozen drafts to take into account each justice's observations. He was unwilling, moreover, to debate the basic issues in a case, even in chambers with his own clerks. He preferred that they write him memos.

Wearing a gray or blue cardigan sweater, Blackmun hid away in the recesses of the justices' library, and his office had instructions not to disturb him there. The phone did not ring there, and not even the Chief violated his solitude. Working at a long mahogany table lined on the opposite edge with a double row of books, Blackmun took meticulous notes. He spent most of his time sorting facts and fitting them to the law in a desperate attempt to discover inevitable conclusions. He tried to reduce his risks by mastering every detail, as if the case were some huge math problem. Blackmun felt that if all the steps were taken, there could be only one answer.

These abortion cases were his greatest challenge since he came to the Court. Beyond the normal desire to produce an opinion that would win the respect of his peers in the legal community, Blackmun also wanted an opinion that the medical community would accept, one that would free physicians to exercise their professional judgment.

As general counsel at the Mayo Clinic, Blackmun had advised the staff on the legality of abortions the hospital had performed. Many of them would not have qualified under the Texas and Georgia laws now in question.

Blackmun plowed through both common law and the history of English and American law on the subject. He was surprised to find that abortion had been commonly accepted for thousands of years, and that only in the nineteenth century had it become a crime in the United States. At that time, abortion had been a very risky operation, often fatal. The criminal laws had been enacted largely to protect pregnant women.

The use of antiseptics and the availability of antibiotics now made abortion relatively safe, particularly in the first few months of pregnancy. The mortality rates of women undergoing early abortions were presently lower than the mortality rates for women with normal childbirths. That medical reality was central for Blackmun. It was itself a strong medical justification for permitting early abortions.

A decision to abort was one that Blackmun hoped he would never face in his own family. He presumed that his three daughters felt that early abortions should be allowed. He claimed to be unsure of his wife Dottie's position. But she told one of his clerks, who favored lifting the restrictions, that she was doing everything she could to encourage her husband in that direction. "You and I working on the same thing," she said. "Me at home and you at work."

By mid-May, after five months of work, Blackmun was still laboring over his memorandum. Finally, he let one of his clerks look over a draft. As usual, he made it clear that he did not want any editing. The clerk was astonished. It was crudely written and poorly organized. It did not settle on any analytical framework, nor did it explain on what basis Blackmun had arrived at the apparent conclusion that women had a right to privacy, and thus a right to abortion. Blackmun had avoided extending the right of privacy, or stating that the right to abortion stemmed from that right. He seemed to be saying that a woman could get an abortion in the early period of pregnancy. The reason, however, was lost in a convoluted discussion of the "viability of the fetus," the point at which the fetus could live outside the womb. Blackmun had added the general notion that as the length of the pregnancy increased, the states' interest in regulating and prohibiting abortions also increased. But there was no real guidance from which conclusions could be drawn. Blackmun had simply asserted that the Texas law was vague and thus unconstitutional.

The clerk realized that the opinion could not settle any constitutional question. It did not assert, or even imply, that abortion restrictions in the early months of pregnancy were unconstitutional. The result of this opinion would be that restrictive laws, if properly defined by the states, could be constitutional.

The draft seemed to fly in the face of Blackmun's statements to his clerks. "We want to definitely solve this," he had told them. But he seemed to be avoiding a solution.

In the Georgia case, he had found that the law infringed on a doctor's professional judgment, his right to give advice to his patients. Blackmun proceeded from the doctor's point of view; a woman's right to seek and receive medical advice did not seem an issue.

Blackmun's clerk, who favored an opinion that would establish a woman's constitutional right to abortion, began the laborious task of trying to rehabilitate the draft. But Blackmun resisted any modification of his basic reasoning or his conclusions. He circulated the memo to all chambers with few changes.

Stewart was disturbed by the draft. Aside from its inelegant construction and language, it seemed to create a *new* affirmative constitutional right to abortion that was not rooted in any part of the Constitution. Stewart had been expecting a majority opinion. Blackmun's memo did not even have the tone of an opinion, merely of a tentative discussion.

Stewart decided to write his own concurrence, specifying that family-planning decisions, including early abortions, were among the rights encompassed by the Ninth Amendment, which says that all rights not specifically given to the federal or state governments are left to the people. Rather than identify the rights that women or doctors have, Stewart preferred to say that states could not properly interfere in individuals' decisions to have early abortions. He circulated his memo two weeks after Blackmun's but immediately joined Blackmun's original.

Douglas saw no shortage of problems with the Blackmun draft, but Blackmun had come a long way. At least it was a step in the right direction. Though Douglas was still holding on to his concurrence, he did not circulate it. Instead, he joined Blackmun.

At the time, the Court was considering an antitrust case against a utility company, the Otter Tail Power Company, which operated in Minnesota. Douglas saw an opportunity to flatter Blackmun. "Harry, you're not a Minnesota Twin with the Chief," he told him. "I am the real Minnesota Twin, . . . We were both born in Minnesota and you were not."

Blackmun appreciated the point.

"Furthermore, Harry, I belong to the Otter Tail County regulars. You can't belong, because you weren't born there."

Douglas regaled Blackmun with stories of his father's life as an itinerant preacher in Otter Tail County, and he praised Blackmun's abortion draft. It was one of the finest presentations of an issue he had ever seen, he said. Blackmun was ecstatic. Douglas, the greatest living jurist, had freed him of the stigma of being Burger's double. Soon, Blackmun had five votes—his own and those of Douglas, Brennan, Marshall, and Stewart. It was one more than he needed; it would have been a majority even if Powell and Rehnquist had participated.

For White the term had its ups and downs like any other year at the Court. He had been a fierce competitor all his life. He loved to take control of a case, pick out the weaknesses in the other justices' positions, and then watch them react to his own twists and turns as he pushed his own point of view. When he could not, which was often, he took his frustrations to the third-floor gym to play in the clerks' regular full-court basketball game.

Muscling out men thirty years his junior under the boards, White delighted in playing a more competitive game than they did. He dominated the games by alternating savage and effective drives to the basket with accurate two-hand push shots from twenty feet. White consistently pushed off the clerk trying to cover him, calling every conceivable foul against the hapless clerk, while bitching about every foul called against himself. He regularly took the impermissible third step before shooting. The game was serious business for White. Each man was on his own. Teamwork was valuable in order to win, not for its own sake.

One Friday afternoon White was out of position for a rebound, but he went up throwing a hip. A clerk pulled in the ball and White came crashing down off balance and injured his ankle.

The justice came to his office on crutches the next Monday: He would be off the basketball court for the rest of the season. He asked the clerks to keep the reason for his injury secret. The clerks bought him a Fussball game, a modern version of the ancient game of skittles. It was competition, so White enjoyed it, but it lacked for him the thrill of a contact sport like basketball—or law.

On Friday, May 26, Byron White read a draft dissent to Blackmun's abortion decision that one of his clerks had prepared. He then remolded it to his liking. The structure of Blackmun's opinion was juvenile; striking the Texas law for vagueness was simply stupid. The law might have several defects, but vagueness was not among them. The law could not be more specific in delineating the circumstance when abortion was available—it was only to protect the life of the mother.

Blackmun was disturbed by White's attack, but whether it made sense or not, it showed him that he had more work to do. The more he studied and agonized over his own memo, the less pleased he was. He needed more information, more facts, more insight. What was the history of the proscription in the Hippocratic oath which forbade doctors from performing abortions? What was the medical state of the art of sustaining a fetus outside the womb? When did life really begin? When was a fetus fully viable? What were the positions of the American Medical Association, the American Psychiatric Association, the American Public Health Association?

These and dozens of other questions plagued Blackmun. His opinion needed to be stronger. It needed more votes, which could mean wider public acceptance. A nine-man court was essential to bring down such a controversial opinion. "I think we can get Powell," he told his clerks.

One Saturday toward the end of May, the Chief paid Blackmun a visit, leaving his armed chauffeur-bodyguard in the outer office. Blackmun's clerks waited anxiously for hours to find out what case the Chief was lobbying. The Chief finally left, but Blackmun also departed without a word to his clerks. The next week, the Chief shifted sides to provide the crucial fifth vote for Blackmun's majority in an antitrust case against professional baseball (*Flood v. Kuhn*).

The following Saturday, June 3, Blackmun drafted a memorandum withdrawing his abortion opinion. It was already late in the term, he wrote. Such a sensitive case required more research, more consideration. It would take him some time both to accommodate the suggestions of those in the majority, and to respond to the dissenters. Perhaps it would be best if the cases were reargued in the fall. He asked that all copies of his draft memo be returned.

Douglas was once again enraged. The end of the year always involved a crunch. Of course, there was tremendous pressure to put out major opinions without the time to fully refine them. That was the nature of their work. The pressure affected them all. It was typical that Blackmun could not make up his mind and let his opinion go. Douglas had heard that the Chief had been lobbying Blackmun. This time, Burger had gone too far. The opinion had five firm votes. It ought to come down. It was not like cases with only four votes that might change when Powell's and Rehnquist's votes were added. Douglas also did not want to give the Chief the summer to sway Blackmun.

Burger was taking the position that there were now five votes to put the case over to the next term—Blackmun, White, Powell, Rehnquist, and himself. Douglas couldn't believe it. Burger and White were in the minority; they should have no say in what the majority did. And Powell and Rehnquist had not taken part; obviously they could not vote on whether the case should be put over.

The looming confrontation worried Blackmun. There were no written rules on such questions, and Douglas's apparent willingness to push to a showdown would further inflame the issue. Finally, Blackmun turned to Brennan, who was sympathetic. Obviously the opinion could not come down if its author did not want it to come down. But Brennan also wanted it out as soon as possible.

Blackmun said he understood that Douglas did not trust him, but insisted that he was firm for striking down the abortion laws. The vote would go the same way the next year. They might even pick up Powell. That would make the result more acceptable to the public. He would be able to draft a better opinion over the summer.

Brennan was not so certain of Blackmun's firmness. At the same time, he did not want to alienate him. He agreed to tell Douglas that he, too, was going to vote to put the case over for reargument. He was fairly certain Marshall and Stewart would join. That would leave Douglas protesting alone.

Douglas was not pleased by the news of Brennan's defection. But the battle was not yet over. He dashed off a memo, rushed it to the secretaries for typing and to the printers for a first draft. This time, Douglas threatened to play his ace. If the conference insisted on putting the cases over for reargument, he would dissent from such an order, and he would publish the full text of his dissent. Douglas reiterated the protest he had made in December about the Chief's assigning the case to Blackmun, Burger's response and his subsequent intransigence. The senior member of the majority should have assigned the case, Douglas said, . . .

Douglas knew a fifth Nixon appointment was a real possibility on a Court with a seventy-four-year-old man with a pacemaker; with Marshall, who was chronically ill; and with Brennan, who occasionally threatened to quit. . . .

Borrowing a line from a speech he had given in September in Portland, Douglas then made it clear that, despite what he had said earlier, he did in fact view the Chief and Blackmun as Nixon's Minnesota Twins. "Russia once gave its Chief Justice two votes; but that was too strong even for the Russians. . . ."

"I dissent with the deepest reget that we are allowing the consensus of the Court to be frustrated."

Douglas refined his draft three times, circulated it, and left for Goose Prairie.

The Court erupted in debate over whether Douglas was bluffing or was really willing to publish the document. Though sympathetic to his views, Brennan, Marshall, and Stewart could not believe that Douglas would go through with it. No one in the history of the Court had published such a dissent. The Chief might be a scoundrel, but making public the Court's inner machinations was a form of treason. And the reference to the Russian Chief Justice with two votes was particularly rough. They pleaded with Douglas to reconsider. His dissent would undermine the Court's credibility, the principal source of its power. Its strength derived from the public belief that the Court was trustworthy, a nonpolitical deliberative body. Did he intend to undermine all that?

Douglas insisted. He would publish what he felt like publishing. And he would publish this if the request to put over the abortion decision was not withdrawn.

But, the others argued, what good would it do to drag their internal problems into public view?

It would have a sobering influence on Blackmun, Douglas retorted. It would make it harder for him to change his mind over the summer.

Brennan's impatience with Douglas turned to anger. Douglas had become an intellectually lazy, petulant, prodigal child. He was not providing leadership. Douglas was never around when he was needed. His departure for Goose Prairie was typical. He was not even, for that matter, pulling his share of the load, though he certainly contributed more than his share to the tension. The ultimate source of conflict was the Chief. But Douglas too was at fault.

Finally, Brennan gave up arguing.

Blackmun then took it up, pleading with Douglas to reconsider. He insisted that he was committed to his opinion. He would bring it down the same way the next term; more research would perhaps pick up another vote.

Douglas was unconvinced. He needed time to think it over. His clerks would remain instructed to publish the opinion if the cases were put over for reargument.

But Blackmun had made his point. Douglas finally decided that he couldn't publish. It would endanger next term's vote on the abortion cases.

No longer speaking to his own clerks, whom he blamed for slow mail delivery to Goose Prairie, Douglas called Brennan and told him to have his dissent held. A memor came around to the Justices from Douglas's chamber asking for all the copies back.

The conference agreed to put over the abortion cases, but they would not announce their decision until the final day of the term. . . .

Harry Blackmun returned to Rochester, Minnesota, for the summer of 1972, and immersed himself in research at the huge Mayo Clinic medical library. Rochester and the clinic were home to Blackmun, a safe harbor after a stormy term. He worked in a corner of the assistant librarian's office for two weeks without saying a word to anyone on the Mayo staff about the nature of his inquiry.

In his summer office in a Rochester highrise, Blackmun began to organize the research that would bolster his abortion opinion. He talked by phone nearly every day with one of his clerks who had agreed to stay in Washington for the summer. . . .

The clerk who was working on the opinion began to worry that one of the other clerks, strongly opposed to abortions, might try to change their boss's mind. He took no chances. Each night he carefully locked up the work he had been doing for Blackmun. At the end of the summer, he carefully sealed the latest draft in an envelope, put his initials across the tape, and had it locked in Blackmun's desk. Only Blackmun's personal secretary knew where it was.

Powell also made abortion his summer research project. As a young lawyer in Richmond in the 1930s, Powell had heard tales of girls who would "go away" to Switzerland and New York, where safe abortions were available. If someone were willing to pay for it, it was possible to have an abortion.

Powell understood how doctors viewed abortion. His father-in-law had been a leading obstetrician in Richmond, and his two brothers-in-law were obstetricians. Powell had heard all the horrifying stories of unsanitary butchers and coat-hanger abortions.

Nevertheless, Powell came quickly to the conclusion that the Constitution did not provide meaningful guidance. The right to privacy was tenuous;

at best it was implied. If there was no way to find an answer in the Constitution, Powell felt he would just have to vote his "gut." He had been critical of justices for doing exactly that; but in abortion, there seemed no choice.

When he returned to Washington, he took one of his law clerks to lunch at the Monocle Restaurant on Capitol Hill. The abortion laws, Powell confided, were "atrocious." His would be a strong and unshakable vote to strike them. He needed only a rationale for his vote.

In a recent lower court case, a federal judge had struck down the Connecticut abortion law. This opinion impressed Powell. The judge had said that moral positions on abortion "about which each aide was so sure must remain a personal judgment, one that people may follow in their personal lives and seek to persuade others to follow, but a judgment they may not impose upon others by force of law." That was all the rationale Powell needed.

Brennan and Douglas worried that votes might have shifted since the previous spring. Blackmun remained a question mark, Stewart might defect, and they were not sure what Powell would do.

At conference on October 12, Blackmun made a long, eloquent, and strongly emotional case for striking down the laws. Stewart too seemed ready to join. But the big surprise was Powell. He made it six to three.

Immediately after conference, Douglas called Blackmun to tell him that his presentation had been the finest he had heard at conference in more than thirty years. He hoped the call would sustain Blackmun for the duration.

Before the end of October, Blackmun's new draft in the abortion case was circulated to the various chambers. . . .

The clerks in most chambers were surprised to see the justices, particularly Blackmun, so openly brokering their decision like a group of legislators. There was a certain reasonableness to the draft, some of them thought, but it derived more from medical and social policy than from constitutional law. There was something embarrassing and dishonest about this whole process. It left the Court claiming that the Constitution drew certain lines at trimesters and viability. The Court was going to make a medical policy and force it on the states. As a practical matter, it was not a bad solution. As a constitutional matter, it was absurd. The draft was referred to by some clerks as "Harry's abortion."

By early December, Blackmun's final draft had circulated. Stewart's and Douglas's concurrences were finished, and White's and Rehnquist's dissents were ready. There was still nothing from Burger. . . .

Stewart and Brennan thought he was stalling. The Chief was scheduled to swear in Richard Nixon for his second term as president on January 20. It would undoubtedly be embarrassing for Burger to stand there, swearing in the man who had appointed him, having just supported a sweeping and politically volatile opinion that repudiated that man's views.

At the Friday, January 19, conference, the Chief said that his schedule had been busy, and he still had not gotten to the abortion decision. Stewart figured that, having manipulated a delay until after the inaugural, Burger would acquiesce. The others wanted a Monday, January 22, announcement, three days later, and Burger said that he would have something.

Over the weekend, he wrote a three-paragraph concurrence. Ignoring the sweep of the opinion he was joining, Burger said that one law (Texas) was being struck because it did not permit abortions in instances of rape or incest, and he implied that the other law was being struck because of the "complex" steps that required hospital board certification of an abortion. He did not believe that the opinion would have the "consequences" predicted by dissenters White and Rehnquist, and he was sure that states could still control abortions. "Plainly," he concluded, "the Court today rejects any claim that the Constitution requires abortion on demand."

The day of the scheduled abortion decision the Chief sat in his chambers reading the latest edition of *Time* magazine. "Last week *Time* learned that the Supreme Court has decided to strike down nearly every antiabortion law in the land," an article said. The abortion decision had been leaked.

Burger drafted an "Eyes Only" letter to the other justices. He wanted each justice to question his law clerks. The responsible person must be found and fired. Burger intended to call in the FBI to administer lie-detector tests if necessary.

Dutifully, Rehnquist brought up the matter with his clerks. It was harmless in this case, he said. But in a business case, a leak could affect the stock market and allow someone to make millions of dollars. None of Rehnquist's clerks knew anything about the leak, but they asked him if it were true that the Chief was thinking of lie-detector tests. "It is still up in the air," Rehnquist said. "But yes, the Chief is insisting."

Rehnquist's clerks were concerned. Such a witch hunt would be met with resistance. Certainly, some clerks would refuse to take such a test and would probably have to resign. The Chief is mercurial, Rehnquist explained. "The rest of us will prevail on him."

Brennan summoned his clerks and read them the Chief's letter. It was another example, he said, of the Chief usurping the authority each justice had over his own clerks, "No one will question my law clerks but me," Brennan said. Then in a softer voice, he added, "And I have no questions." The real outrage for Bennan was not the leak but the delay. If the Chief had not been intent on saving himself and Nixon some embarrassment on Inauguration Day, there probably would have been no damaging leak.

Marshall asked what his clerks knew about the incident. When he was assured that they knew nothing, he told them to forget it.

Douglas treated the letter as he had treated a request from the Chief the previous term that all clerks be instructed to wear coats in the hallways. He ignored it.

Powell was out of town, so one of his clerks opened the Chief's letter. The clerk had talked to the *Time* reporter, David Beckwith, trying to give him some guidance so he could write an intelligent story when the decision came down. But the delay in announcing the decision had apparently left *Time* with a scoop, if only for half a day.

The clerk called Powell and told him about the Chief's letter and his own terrible mistake in talking with Beckwith. He volunteered to resign.

That would not be necessary, Powell said. But a personal explanation would have to be given to the Chief.

Powell called Burger and explained that one of his clerks, a brilliant and talented young lawyer, was responsible. The clerk realized his mistake and had learned his lesson. The clerk went to see the Chief.

Burger was sympathetic. Reporters were dishonest and played tricks, he said. It was a lesson everyone had to learn.

Apparently never expecting to learn so much about the little deceptions of both reporters and sources, Burger pressed for all the details. It took nearly forty-five minutes to satisfy his curiosity.

The clerk concluded that Burger understood, that he was being a saint about the matter. Burger wanted a memo detailing exactly what happened. The clerk would not have to resign.

Later, the Chief met with top editors of *Time* in an off-the-record session. He labeled Beckwith's efforts to get inside information at the Court improper, the moral equivalent of wiretapping.

Blackmun suggested to his wife, Dottie, that she come to Court to hear case announcements on Monday, January 22. He did not tell her why. As Blackmun announced the decisions, Powell sent a note of encouragement to Blackmun's wife. Powell suspected that they were about to witness a public outcry, the magnitude of which he and Blackmun had not seen in their short time on the Court.

"I'm very proud of the decision you made," Dottie later told her husband.

After the abortion decision was announced, Blackmun took congratulatory calls through most of the afternoon. But former President Lyndon Johnson died that same day, and the news of his death dominated the next morning's newspapers.

Blackmun was unhappy that the abortion decision did not get more attention. Many women, especially the poor and black, would not learn of their new rights. But the outcry quickly began, led by the Catholic Church. "How many millions of children prior to their birth will never live to see the light of day because of the shocking action of the majority of the United States Supreme Court today?" demanded New York's Terrence Cardinal Cooke.

John Joseph Cardinal Krol, of Philadelphia, the president of the National Conference of Catholic Bishops, said, "It is hard to think of any decision in the two hundred years of our history which has had more disastrous implications for our stability as a civilized society."

Thousands of letters poured into the Court. The guards had to set up a special sorting area in the basement with a huge box for each justice.

The most mail came to Blackmun, the decision's author, and to Brennan, the Court's only Catholic. Some letters compared the justices to the butchers of Dachau, child killers, immoral beasts, and Communists. A special ring of hell would be reserved for the justices. Whole classes from Catholic schools wrote to denounce the justices as murderers. "I really don't want to write this letter but my teacher made me," one child said.

Minnesota Lutherans zeroed in on Blackmun. New Jersey Catholics called for Brennan's excommunication. Southern Baptists and other groups sent over a thousand bitter letters to Hugo Black, who had died sixteen months earlier. Some letters and calls were death threats.

Blackmun went through the mail piece by piece. The sisters of Saint Mary's hospital, the backbone of the Mayo Clinic, wrote outraged letters week after week. He was tormented. The medical community and even his friends at Mayo were divided. Blackmun encountered picketing for the first time in his life when he gave a speech in Iowa. He understood the position of the antiabortion advocates, but he was deeply hurt by the personal attacks. He felt compelled to point out that there had been six other votes for the decision, besides his, that the justices had tried to enunciate a constitutional principle, not a moral one. Law and morality overlapped but were not congruent, he insisted. Moral training should come not from the court but from the church, the family, the schools.

The letters continued to pour in. Every time a clergyman mentioned the decision in his sermon, the letters trickled in for a month from members of the congregation. The attack gradually wore Blackmun down. At breakfast with his clerks, when the discussion turned to the decision, Blackmun picked up his water glass reflectively, turning it slightly on edge and staring into it in silence.

The criticism also drew Blackmun and Brennan closer. Blackmun wrote Brennan a warm thank you note: "I know it is tough for you, and I thank you for the manner in which you made your suggestions."

Brennan tried to cheer up Blackmun. Doing the right thing was not often easy, he said. The one thing in the world Brennan did not want known was his role in molding the opinion.[1]

Blackmun did not cheer up easily. The hysteria on each side of the issue convinced him that any decision would have been unpopular. However, the deepest cut came when the state of Texas filed a petition for rehearing that compared Blackmun's conclusion, which held that a fetus was not a person, to the Court's infamous 1857 decision that said that Dred Scott, a slave, was not a citizen or person under the Constitution. Blackmun thought that

---

[1] When the clerks later put together bound volumes of the opinions Brennan had written that term, they included the abortion opinions, and on page 156 they wrote, "These cases are included with Justice Brennan's opinions for the October term 1972 because the opinions for the Court were substantially revised in response to suggestions made by Justice Brennan."

comparing his opinion with the Court's darkest day of racism was terribly unfair. And, after all, it had been Stewart who had insisted on that part of the opinion.

Months later, Blackmun gave a speech at Emory Law School in Atlanta. He was chatting with students and faculty when a petite young woman with black curly hair ran up the steps to the stage. She squeezed through the group, threw her arms around Blackmun and burst into tears. "I'll never be able to thank you for what you have done. I'll say no more. Thank you."

The woman turned and ran from the room.

Blackmun was shaken. He suspected that the woman was probably someone who had been able to obtain an abortion after the Court's decision. He did not know that "Mary Doe," the woman who had filed one of the original suits in Texas under a pseudonym, had just embraced him.

W ITH THE POSSIBLE EXCEP-
tion of the Supreme Court's desegregation decision, *Brown
v. Board of Education*, 1954), its most
controversial decision was *Roe v. Wade*
(1973), upholding a woman's absolute
right to have an abortion during the first
trimester of a pregnancy. The *Roe* decision came under increasing attack as
Right to Life groups mobilized against it.
In the Reagan and Bush administrations,
leading conservatives on the Court, Chief
Justice Rehnquist and Justice Antonin
Scalia, wanted to overturn *Roe*.

Justice Harry Blackmun wrote the
Roe opinion, which was not only attacked by conservatives, but, ironically,
by some jurists and scholars who supported the decision but found Blackmun's reasoning in the opinion to be
weak because it was based more on medical evidence than on constitutional law.
The following selection describes what it
is like to stand virtually alone on the
Supreme Court in defense of a highly
controversial opinion and decision.

30 Ruth Marcus
ROE'S LONELY DEFENDER ON THE COURT

When Supreme Court Justice Harry A. Blackmun interviews young lawyers
applying for clerkships, there comes a point in the conversation when the
justice brings up a delicate subject, something he fears could interfere with
their working relationship.

"I've been somewhat controversial," the soft-spoken Blackmun advises
the applicant, according to a number of former clerks. "I wrote an opinion
you may have heard of. It's called *Roe v. Wade*."

Any first-year law student—like millions of Americans without a day of
legal training—is aware of *Roe v. Wade*, the 1973 ruling that established a
constitutional right to abortion, and of Blackmun's authorship of the
decision, one of the most praised and most reviled in the high court's
history.

Now, 19 years later, Blackmun is the sole member of the original *Roe*
majority remaining on the high court—and the decision, in the assessment
of the justice himself, teeters on the brink of extinction.

"The court hasn't dared to overrule it directly yet, but the votes are there.
The votes are there," Blackmun said in a speech last October.

That could happen—in practical effect, if not explicitly—by the time the
court recesses in July. On April 22, the court took up an abortion case from

Pennsylvania that calls on the justices to explain what special constitutional protection remains for the right to abortion, if any. Besides Blackmun, only one other justice, John Paul Stevens, named to the court by President Gerald R. Ford, has supported abortion rights.

Blackmun's question to his young applicants reflects what Washington & Lee Law School Dean Randall Bezanson, who clerked for Blackmun the year *Roe* was decided, describes as his "genuinely humble" demeanor. He is a justice who humorously calls himself "Old Number Three," a self-effacing reference to the fact that President Richard M. Nixon tapped him for the high court in 1970 only after his first two choices were rejected by the Senate.

The question also illustrates the remarkable degree to which the 83-year-old Blackmun has become personally identified with the ruling in *Roe*. "A lot of people have personalized this, thinking it's the work of the devil—to wit, me—forgetting there were seven votes for that opinion," Blackmun lamented in 1978.

"I think it's peculiar that he has become so closely associated with *Roe*," says Charles Rothfeld, a Washington lawyer and former Blackmun clerk. "He was not the most liberal member of the court when he was assigned to it, and the idea that he was a crusader for abortion rights is somewhat odd."

Inevitably, however, his authorship of *Roe* made the private, reserved Blackmun the personal embodiment of the divisive national debate over abortion. He has been called, he once said, every name in the book, "Butcher of Dachau, murderer, Pontius Pilate, King Herod, you name it," but has also received "some of the most wonderful letters that one can imagine."

Blackmun has said of the criticism, "of course, it hurt at first. It doesn't hurt so much anymore, because I think one's hide gets a little thick."

Roe "has made an extremely private man a public figure," says one former clerk. "That mantle does not always rest easily on his shoulders."

Blackmun, who declined to be interviewed for this article, is both proud and fiercely protective of *Roe*. He has maintained, in the face of both political and academic criticism, that the case was correctly decided and has become over the years an even more fervent advocate of abortion rights.

The father of three daughters, he has said that even "if it goes down the drain, I'd still like to regard *Roe v. Wade* as a landmark in the emancipation of women."

Although Blackmun's authorship of *Roe* is something of an "accident of history," Rothfeld says, "*Roe* having then become such a lightning rod and he having been so personally vilified, I think it's brought home to him his role as a protector of the right to privacy."

"In a way, *Roe* is his life on the Supreme Court," says University of Virginia law professor Pamela Karlan, a former Blackmun clerk. "He recognizes it's the case that . . . most defines his role."

As he recounted the story in a 1979 speech in Paris, Blackmun was a reluctant author of the decision. When the justices conferred after the case was first argued in December 1971, he later recalled, "none of us was very eager to receive the cases for writing" and "I accepted the assignment without enthusiasm."

Normally, a case is assigned by the chief justice, if he is in the majority, or by the senior justice in the majority if the chief is among the dissenters. When the court talked about the abortion cases, Blackmun said, the vote was "indecisive."

Chief Justice Warren E. Burger, though he was inclined to vote to uphold the laws, assigned the case to Blackmun. Blackmun later surmised that Burger gave him the case because of Blackmun's interest in medicine (he had toyed with the idea of becoming a doctor) and his decade of experience as resident counsel at the Mayo Clinic.

At the time, debate over the philosophy of the junior justice centered on just how conservative he was; with a voting record that closely matched that of Burger, his childhood friend in Minnesota, Blackmun was often derided as the conservative Burger's "Minnesota Twin."

Blackmun drafted a memorandum on the abortion laws—one from Texas, another from Georgia—that were challenged in *Roe* and another pending case, "leaning toward the results that eventually were forthcoming," he said. He also called on the court to put off the matter until after Lewis F. Powell Jr. and William H. Rehnquist were confirmed to fill the two vacancies on the court.

The liberal Justice William O. Douglas vehemently objected, Blackmun recalled. "I think now that he was concerned that the addition of two new justices and the passage of a summer might change the result, including my own attitude."

Blackmun prevailed, and the case was set for reargument during the coming term. The justice set about preparing for it in classic Blackmun fashion: laboriously and agonizingly.

"That summer, I spent two full weeks in the medical library of the Mayo Clinic in Rochester, Minnesota," he remembered. "I traced down, as I hoped to be able to do, the attitudes toward abortion of the American Medical Association (it had changed over the years), of the American Public Health Association, and of the American Bar Association. I wished, furthermore, to study the history of our state abortion statutes, and I wished to ascertain the origin and acceptance of the Hippocratic Oath [which forbids doctors to perform abortion]."

The eventual opinion reflected that tedious work: Blackmun went through a lengthy historical discussion that ranged from "Persian Empire abortifaciants" and Greek and Roman law through the status of abortion in common law and at the time the Constitution was adopted. He opened with a straightforward acknowledgment of the "sensitive and emotional nature of the abortion controversy" and the "deep and seemingly absolute convictions that the subject inspires."

Later, Blackmun was to say that he "did what Hugo Black had told me when I first came here not to do; namely, never display any agony in the decision-making. I think that's usually pretty good advice, but I purposefully did not follow it here."

The opinion, with its announcement of a trimester framework for testing the legality of abortion law, spawned academic criticism from low professors of various ideologies who found the outcome more of legislative compromise than constitutional analysis.

It also triggered an avalanche of mail that continues to this day. The justice, who once estimated that about 75 percent of the mail is critical of the ruling, reads much of it himself, replies to some, and likes to read from both the positive and negative letters at his speeches. "I like to know what people are thinking," he has said.

"Several of us have tried to dissuade him" from reading and answering the mail, said University of Chicago law school professor Norval Morris, who holds an annual "Roe Day" with Blackmun each summer at the Aspen Institute, where the justice discusses the opinion. "He keeps writing. He's stubborn."

Some Blackmun observers credit the letters, briefs in later abortion cases, and other reaction to *Roe* for a shift in Blackmun's thinking about abortion rights, moving from a focus on the physician to the woman herself.

Much of the conclusion in *Roe*, and its establishment of a trimester framework for testing the legitimacy of abortion regulations, was grounded on medical knowledge and the physician's right to exercise medical judgment.

Until the point of viability, approximately the third trimester of pregnancy, Blackmun wrote, "the attending physician in consultation with his patient, is free to determine, without regulation by the state, that in his medical judgment, the patient's pregnancy should be terminated."

In more recent abortion cases, Blackmun has emphasized the woman's right. In a thunderous dissent, read from the bench, in the *Webster v. Reproductive Health Services* ruling three years ago, Blackmun wrote, "For today, the women of this nation still retain the liberty to control their destinies. But the signs are evident and very ominous, and a chill wind blows."

Karlan, the former clerk, attributes the change in Blackmun's emphasis to his on-the-job education from the women whose lives were affected by his ruling. "I think it changed his sense of just how central it was to the way women think about who they are, understanding that it's not just a medical decision but something that's affected women's lives."

Blackmun, who was reported to have been depressed after the retirement two years ago of Justice William J. Brennan Jr., is in good spirits these days, those who know him say. He has been interviewing clerks for the term starting next October but has told people he will make no promises about whether he will remain after that.

Today, with the court solidly dominated by conservatives, Blackmun finds himself alone with his fellow Republican appointee Justice Stevens in what has become, by default, the court's liberal wing. He has griped to friends that "it's too bad that Nino has two votes"—an apparent reference to Justice Clarence Thomas's nearly unanimous agreement with Justice Antonin Scalia, the court's most conservative member.

Although the Harvard Law Review concluded in 1983 that he had "undergone a remarkable transformation" since his appointment to the court, Blackmun disputes that assessment, saying that it is the court that has shifted, not he.

"I get accused of having changed horses in the middle of the stream, but I think I am the same person I was on the Court of Appeals," he said last year. "Republicans think I am a traitor and Democrats don't trust me. So I twist in the wind, owing allegiance to no one, which is precisely where I want to be."

31

Paul M. Barrett
DAVID SOUTER: INDEPENDENT JUSTICE AND REFLECTIVE MODERATE

To acquaintances, Justice David Souter still seems amazed at times to find himself on the Supreme Court.

"He is almost reverent about . . . the Court," says Thomas Rath, a lawyer and close friend. "He sees his role and the Court's as healer of the divisions in the country."

That's a far cry from what conservatives thought they were getting when President Bush in July 1990 chose the obscure New Hampshire jurist to succeed liberal giant William Brennan on the high court. The White House assured the GOP hard right that David Souter would be "a home run."

The Bush administration was "miserably inaccurate," complains Thomas Jipping, vice president of the Free Congress Foundation, which coordinated support for the nomination among conservative groups. He says that Justice Souter has been "horrible in some of the real fundamental areas." Exhibit A was last June's abortion ruling, in which the court, by a 5–4 vote, rebuffed the Bush administration's push to overturn *Roe v. Wade*, the 1973 decision that established a constitutional right to abortion. Justice Souter contributed an assertive opinion for the majority stressing the court's need to maintain precedent and resist outside political pressures.

Justice Souter, 53 years old, is far from a flaming liberal. But as his third term unfolds, the man who was called a "stealth nominee" has surprised legal scholars who had questioned his credentials and seemingly narrow life experience as a reclusive bachelor. He is becoming a major force on the conservative court by means of independent thinking and strong personal alliances with other justices. Should President Clinton appoint one or more liberal justices, some scholars predict that Justice Souter would emerge as the anchor of a moderate center on a divided court.

Judge Who?

"Who is this guy? I never heard of him," was law professor David Strauss's first reaction to word of the Souter nomination 2½ years ago. Now the University of Chicago constitutional law expert calls Justice Souter "unusually thoughtful."

In the 18 cases decided by a 5–4 vote last term and so far this term, Mr. Souter has been in the majority 14 times—more often than any other justice.

Moreover, he has shown he is willing to do battle with the court's most articulate conservative, Justice Antonin Scalia. They are likely to clash again in two cases on religion in public education that will be argued later this month.

"People tried to make him into something he was not," explains Mr. Rath. They mistook a person who is conservative politically for one who would be a conservative activist on the bench.

Along with Justices Sandra Day O'Connor and Anthony Kennedy, two colleagues attracted by his cautiously conservative jurisprudence, Justice Souter is part of a threesome who serve as a brake on more ambitious forays to the right by Chief Justice William Rehnquist and Justices Scalia and Clarence Thomas. All of the justices have been charmed by his courtly, if occasionally eccentric, personality.

Jingle Bells

Justice O'Connor immediately took to Mr. Souter, helping him find a church in Washington and inviting the lifelong bachelor to join her and her husband, John, for holiday meals and strolls along the city's C&O Canal. Justice Kennedy likewise went out of his way to tutor him in the court's peculiar traditions, including the rule that the most junior justice must answer the door if anyone knocks during the weekly secret conference to discuss cases. Justice Souter has returned the favor by privately defending Justice Kennedy against accusations that he flip-flops on controversial issues.

Though sometimes stuffy in his legal prose, Justice Souter isn't pompous in person. Asked why he sings along with the chief justice at Mr. Rehnquist's annual Christmas carol party, he replies: "I have to. Otherwise I get all the tax cases."

On a court riven with resentments, he quickly endeared himself to his colleagues. Liberal Justice Harry Blackmun told a judicial conference in Minneapolis last summer that Justice Souter may be "the only normal person on the Supreme Court." With a smile on his face, Justice Blackmun added, "I won't expand on that."

The cryptic compliment could well refer also to Justice Souter's ability to confront Justice Scalia without rancor. "There is no question that he doesn't take [criticism from Justice Scalia] as personally as Kennedy and O'Connor," says a lawyer who clerked last term for another justice. Frequently during oral argument, Justices Souter and Scalia, who sit next to each other, will duck their heads to share a private joke. And Justice Scalia surprised his benchmate one day by bringing him an oil portrait he had come across of a 19-century justice named Levi Woodbury, the only other person ever to be living in New Hampshire when named to the high court.

Yet despite his inclination to mix it up on the job, Justice Souter hasn't abandoned his ascetic New England ways. Most days, he drives himself to the court in a Volkswagen, lunches on yogurt and an apple, works late into the evening and returns to a tiny rented apartment that friends say remains virtually undecorated. Renowned for his penny-pinching, he was dismayed one day at the $8 price of a judicial luncheon at the high court. "Oh David, you're so silly," Justice O'Connor laughed. "What's so silly about that?" a genuinely confused Justice Souter later asked his staff.

Unabashed in his parochialism, Justice Souter would be happier living in the ramshackle Weare, N.H., farmhouse where he grew up and still spends summers. He avoids the Washington cocktail circuit and, despising travel of any sort, skips the out-of-town speaking gigs that a number of his colleagues enjoy. "He told us he likes to sleep in his own sheets," says a former Souter clerk.

For current events, he regularly reads only the Sunday *New York Times.* "I gave him a color TV, but he never plugged the damned thing in," says former New Hampshire Sen. Warren Rudman. Widely read in history, law and philosophy, the former Rhodes Scholar keeps up with contemporary politics mostly by means of updates from a tight circle of Harvard classmates and longtime New Hampshire friends like Mr. Rudman.

A Friend to Prisoners

Those for whom he makes time in his work-dominated life find him generous, gregarious and entertaining, whether recounting little-known facts about Oliver Wendell Holmes or war stories from New Hampshire politics.

On a recent rare stop at a McDonald's, Justice Souter mused to a companion that he hadn't been in one of the fast-food restaurants for 20 years. The last time, he recalled, had been in the early 1970s, when as New Hampshire attorney general he supervised the early-morning arrest of dozens of protestors at the Seabrook nuclear power plant. Afterward, prosecutor Souter went to a McDonald's and used his own money to buy coffee and breakfast for his detainees.

Justice Souter doesn't give formal interviews. But he has compared his first term on the high court to walking into a tidal wave. Friends say that he staggered back to New Hampshire in the summer of 1991 looking drawn and harried. Last summer, by contrast, he was "much more at ease, more self-confident," says federal Judge Hugh Bownes of Concord.

His self-deprecation characterizes some of Justice Souter's jurisprudential clashes with Justice Scalia, who isn't known for understatement. In a case decided last June, Justice Scalia attacked a Souter majority for resorting "to that last hope of lost interpretative causes, that St. Jude of the hagiology of statutory construction, legislative history." Contending that congressional debates and committee reports are unreliable, Justice Scalia has pushed the court to stick to the "plain meaning" of statutory text.

The Frankfurter Tradition

In a footnote answering the Scalia gibe, Justice Souter maintained that "the shrine" of legislative history "is well peopled (though it has room for one more) and its congregation has included such noted elders as Mr. Justice Frankfurter" (whose 23 years on the court ended in 1962). Justice Souter has launched a forceful counteroffensive against the stringent plain-meaning approach. He contends that when the court ignores other evidence of what legislators had in mind, it may distort the purpose of laws it is asked to interpret.

Legal scholars say Justice Souter brings a fresh approach to such debates. He "struggles with the arguments on both sides of cases," says Prof. Strauss. "You see a kind of humility, which is lacking in some other members of the court." Liberals disagree with many of Justice Souter's views but have been relieved by his performance. "He is certainly conservative on many issues," including criminal law, says Elliot Mincberg, legal director of People for the American Way. "But we could have done a lot worse. He has shown some real intellectual independence from the Scalia wing."

Justice Souter has expressed particular pride to friends in having re-shaped debate on the court over religion and abortion.

Founders' Intentions

Church-state disputes, for example, inevitably provoke questions about constitutional history—which Justice Scalia views as much more relevant than legislative history. Justice Scalia contends that to prevent judges from reading their own values into the Constitution, such vague provisions as the First Amendement's ban on official "establishment of religion" should be enforced only as they were understood by the men who drafted them. Justices Kennedy and O'Connor, while repelled by the more expansive interpretations of the Warren and Burger courts, can't bring themselves to accept the unbending Scalia view, either. Justice Souter argues that while history is vital in making constitutional judgments, it provides few clear-cut answers.

The ferment was on display in last June's 5–4 ruling in *Lee v. Weisman*, which said that official prayers at a public-school graduation violated the First Amendment. In a scathing dissent, Justice Scalia attacked the majority opinion by Justice Kennedy for failing to take a distinct historical point of view. Justice Scalia cited religious passages from early presidential addresses to show that officially sponsored prayer has been accepted since the country's founding.

Justice Souter joined the majority but wrote a separate opinion that confronted Justice Scalia. Justice Souter meticulously recounted the drafting and revision of the First Amendment to reach the conclusion that "history neither contradicts nor warrants reconsideration of the settled principle" that the First Amendment forbids government support for religion in general no less than for one religion over others. As for those early presidents who breached the wall separating church and state, he noted historical evidence that James Madison and others were ashamed of having done so.

Free From Politics

Justice Souter felt so strongly about last term's abortion decision that he used it to make a personal statement about the high court's place in the political system.

Months before the justices even knew which abortion case they might consider, he began studying the question of whether the court should overrule *Roe v. Wade*. Persuaded that the court had overreached its authority on abortion, Justice Souter was nonetheless troubled about the appearance of bowing to conservative pressure to overturn Roe.

After oral arguments last April in the abortion case from Pennsylvania that the court ultimately agreed to decide, there were four votes to overrule: the chief justice and Justices Scalia, Thomas and Byron White. At the other extreme were *Roe*'s stalwart defenders: Justices Blackmun and John Paul Stevens.

On shaky middle ground were Justices O'Connor and Kennedy. Long a critic of *Roe*'s reasoning, Justice O'Connor wanted to give states more leeway to regulate abortion, but worried about going too far. She sought to replace *Roe*'s rigid approach based on the trimesters of pregnancy with a flexible standard that would allow more state regulation but still let judges strike down restrictions they deem excessive.

Justice Kennedy was even less certain of how to proceed. Though on the record as opposing *Roe*, he felt uncomfortable with the conservative argument that the Constitution didn't rank the right to abortion any higher than the right, say, to a driver's license.

Justice Souter also wanted to compromise but had far more confidence in his solution: *Roe*, in some form, must be reaffirmed, he thought. For the court to reverse itself on such a contentious issue would encourage the impression of it as moved by raw politics, not reason. In late April, he and Justice O'Connor separately began work on pieces of what would eventually form a plurality opinion.

Powerful Threesome

The Souter-O'Connor effort provided Justice Kennedy with the alternative to overruling *Roe* for which he had been groping. He joined their opinion and added a section of his own. The core of the cooperative product was Justice Souter's assertion that "to overrule under fire in the absence of the most compelling reason to reexamine a watershed decision would subvert the court's legitimacy beyond any serious question." He called on combatants in the abortion clash "to end their national division by accepting a common mandate rooted in the Constitution."

In heated dissenting opinions, the chief justice and Justice Scalia sought to identify weaknesses in Justice Souter's reasoning. For one thing, they said, this paean to upholding precedent had a peculiar echo when followed by Justice O'Connor's thorough rewriting of *Roe* to narrow the abortion right. Moreover, they noted that the plurality opinion also casually overturned outright two other major decisions on abortion from the 1980s.

Though troubled by these inconsistencies, Justices Blackmun and Stevens nevertheless signed onto Justice Souter's piece of the plurality, forming a fragile 5–4 ruling that reaffirmed a narrowed version of *Roe* and prohibited states from banning abortion altogether.

On Sunday, June 28, the day before the Pennsylvania abortion decision was announced, Justice Souter telephoned his friend Mr. Rath in New Hampshire. "I think my name may be in the paper after tomorrow," the justice said.

HAD HE WRITTEN A POLITI-
cal novel, Horatio Alger
would have chosen as a pro-
tagonist Clarence Thomas, the second
African-American to be nominated and
confirmed to a seat on the Supreme
Court. Thomas not only came from a
poor background, but the color of his skin
subjected him to discrimination at every
turn, an added burden that only the most
talented, self-confident, and determined
individuals can overcome. "Affirmative
action" in law and attitude may have
helped Thomas in his pursuit of higher
education and a career on the bench, but
in his early years poverty and racism
defined his world. While Clarence Thomas's name will be forever linked with
Anita Hill's and her charges of sexual
harassment (see Chapter, 1 Selection 6),
the following two selections depict a
multidimensional Thomas, recounting
his remarkable career and climb to the
top.

32 John Lancaster and Sharon LaFraniere
THE LONG CLIMB
OF CLARENCE THOMAS

The gathering was a friendly one, high school classmates getting together at
a restaurant a few months after their graduation. But Clarence Thomas had
something he wanted to get off his chest.

As his classmates listened uncomfortably, Thomas bitterly unburdened
himself of the slights and humiliations he had suffered as the first black to
graduate from their small Catholic boarding school near Savannah, Ga.

He reminded his dinner companions of the taunts and racial gibes and of
the classmates who at mealtime acted as though he had a contagious
disease, recalls Mark Everson, now a child psychologist in North Carolina.
But perhaps Thomas's most poignant recollection was of a subtler shade of
racism.

"He had a pair of shoes that were much more fashionable than we had,
and we would tease him about those shoes, which were something more
acceptable in a black school," Everson says. "And he commented . . . about
how hard it was to try to fit in with his black friends one way and then at
[school], where we would tease him for the way he dressed."

Everson says Thomas's revelations left him deeply moved. "We were
products of a certain time and generation in Georgia," he says. "I was
saddened that we had been that way."

If there was one constant in the early life of Clarence Thomas, whose confirmation hearings for a seat on the Supreme Court began last Tuesday, it was his knowledge of how his skin color set him apart.

Racism affected Thomas in ways both large and small, dictating his choice of schools, barring him from the James Bond movies he yearned to see and even drawing taunts from fellow black children, who mocked his exceptionally dark complexion. Once it got him ejected from a Shakey's pizzeria. Ultimately it helped drive him off the path to the priesthood.

But if Thomas knew firsthand the pain of racial injustice, he also suffered from its remedy. First as a seminary student and then as a college student on the vanguard of integration, Thomas often expressed feelings of loneliness, self-doubt and isolation—a black man in a white world with the wrong shoes.

The details of Thomas's past have assumed special importance since President Bush named the 43-year-old federal appeals court judge to succeed retiring Supreme Court Justice Thurgood Marshall. In an unusual twist, it is Thomas's life—more than his work—that supporters have emphasized as his primary qualification for the high court.

The legal experience of the former chairman of the Equal Employment Opportunity Commission is limited, and his 18 months on the federal bench have yielded little in the way of a comprehensive judicial philosophy.

But Thomas's backers suggest that in his gutsy climb from the poverty and racism of the segregated South, Thomas acquired a perspective greater than legal scholarship. Bush touched on this theme when he announced Thomas's nomination in July, calling his life "a model for all Americans."

Thomas, who declined to comment for this article, has emphasized his up-from-the-bootstraps background to explain his opposition to racial quotas and other forms of preferential treatment for minorities, which he says create a false impression that blacks cannot make it on their own.

Thomas's conservative views have earned him scorn from civil rights leaders, who call them a betrayal by a man who in college and law school was himself a beneficiary of affirmative action. Abortion-rights activists fear that his expressed view that the Constitution should be interpreted in light of a "higher law" could signal his opposition to legalized abortion.

But few question the power of Thomas's life story, a modern-day morality play defined by grit, self-denial and competitiveness so intense that he once said he treated college vacations as an opportunity to stay on campus and "get ahead" of his mostly white classmates "while they played."

Yet for all Thomas's outspokenness on matters of race and civil rights, his portrait remains incomplete. Even as the Senate considers his nomination, many people are wondering what to expect of this tough, proud, warm, gregarious, complex and sometimes bitter man. The answers may lie in his past.

In the more than two months since Thomas was nominated, his childhood in the rural neighborhood of Pin Point, Ga., outside Savannah, has taken on familiar and even mythic proportions: His birth to a teenage mother on June 23, 1948, his abandonment by his father while still a toddler, his early years in the simple wood-frame house at the edge of a tidal marsh.

But Thomas did not remain in Pin Point for long, and the events that followed the destruction by fire of the family home in 1955 ultimately played a far greater role in shaping his life. For it was the fire that sent him to Savannah and into the home of his grandparents, Myers and Christine Anderson.

The move was born of desperation. For some months after their arrival in Savannah, Thomas's mother, Leola Williams, had tried to keep the family together, living with 6-year-old Clarence and his younger brother in a squalid one-room tenement with an outdoor toilet.

But it was a precarious existence, sustained only by the $14 a week she earned as a maid, she recalls. So in the summer of 1955, deciding that "you needed a man over your boys," Williams sent her sons to live with her parents. (Their older sister had remained in Pin Point with relatives.)

Myers Anderson was a somber, thick-shouldered and deeply religious man who would emerge as the greatest single influence on Thomas's life. Born into poverty, raised by an uncle, Anderson had built a small but successful business delivering wood, coal, ice and heating oil. He owned several modest rental homes and a small farm in nearby Liberty County.

"Everyone is emphasizing that [Thomas] grew up in Pin Point in poverty, but when his grandfather took over, Clarence moved into what would be considered a fairly successful black middle-class family," says Floyd Adams, a childhood friend whose father bought heating oil from Anderson.

Though Anderson had only completed the third grade—Thomas would later recall "his slow poring over the Bible so that he could pass the literacy test to vote"—he placed great stock in education, promptly enrolling Clarence in the all-black Catholic school affiliated with his church, St. Benedict the Moor. Annual tuition was $20. Staffed by Franciscan nuns, many of them Irish, St. Benedict's was an oasis of stability where the students wore blue and white uniforms and stood in unison whenever an adult entered the classroom.

Sister Virgilius Reidy remembers Thomas as a bright, mischievous, ordinary youth, "not a genius," but hard-working and always polite to his elders. He was a patrol boy and won the altar-boy-of-the-year award in 1961, recalls Robert DeShay, a childhood friend.

Thomas's home life provided little respite from the demands of church and school. The muscular, forbidding grandfather whom the boys addressed as "daddy" was a stern taskmaster who Thomas would later claim had never slept past dawn. His attitude toward life was captured by his favorite homily: "Old Man Can't is dead—I helped bury him."

Every afternoon after school, the boys helped out on the Anderson Fuel Co.'s tanker truck, pumping heating oil while their grandfather took care of the paperwork, Adams recalls. Summers were consumed by farm chores in Liberty County.

"Today, I understand what they were doing and why they were so hard on my brother and me," Thomas said in a 1986 speech. "They were preparing us for survival in a racist, hostile environment."

Reminders of that environment were everywhere, even at St. Benedict's, where Thomas suffered from a "caste system" in which dark-skinned blacks ranked at the very bottom, a childhood friend recalls. Thomas himself once told an interviewer that he was known as "ABC," for America's Blackest Child.

But the gravest insults emanated from the institutionalized racism of segregation. "I can still see myself sitting on the tractor, alone, back of the field, plowing in uninterrupted solitude," he recalled in a 1986 speech. "Usually, I would think about a world that was unlike the one we were supposed to live in I would wonder about the tremendous contradictions and discrepanices between the way we live and the way our Constitution and Bill of Rights read. Since I was raised a devout Catholic, I wondered why the church and schools were segregated. Weren't we all equal in the eyes of God?"

With the dawn of the civil rights era, some of Thomas's daydreams were realized. But in many ways these new opportunities only intensified his sense of being an outsider.

As the rector of St. John Vianney Minor Seminary, a preparatory school for aspiring priests in a rural area near Savannah, Father William Coleman was well-known for his enlightened views on race relations. During communion, he used a gold chalice decorated with a black gem, a symbol of his dedication to "improving the lives of blacks," recalls Mark Everson, the child psychologist and Thomas's old friend.

In that spirit, St. John proudly enrolled its first two black students in the fall of 1964. Sixteen-year-old Clarence Thomas was one of them.

Thomas came to St. John from all-black St. Pius X High School, where he had spent the ninth and tenth grades. Preparing to fulfull a mission inspired by his grandfather, Thomas spent three years at St. John and another year at Conception Seminary College in Missouri, where he was supposed to complete his training.

But for all the good intentions of Coleman and others who took an interest in his success, Thomas's first experiences in the white world were not happy ones. Racism, it seemed, knew no boundaries.

Life at St. John was nothing if not isolated. Each grade slept in a single, barracks-like room; classes met six days a week; and before vacations Coleman would admonish the future priests to avoid the dangers of "mixed company," otherwise known as girls.

But Thomas, steeped in his grandfather's discipline, seemed to thrive on these monastic rigors. He repeated the tenth grade, catching up on his Latin, but he was an excellent student who also found time to write for the school paper and manage the student yearbook. A printed comment beneath his senior photo reflected his enduring obsession with grades: "Blew that test, only a 98."

A similar competitive zeal revealed itself on the playing field. "Clarence was the only guy who was a real athlete," says Steven Seyfried, who played on an intramural basketball team with him. "We would meet before the game and say, 'Today's game plan is to get the ball to Clarence.' "

Seyfried, a good friend at the time who remembers Thomas as "a very gentle, lovely guy," says Thomas fit in well at the school. "There was a great deal of closeness and camaraderie among the students," he says.

But Thomas would remember things differently, telling an audience in 1985, "Not a day passed that I was not pricked by prejudice." He once told an interviewer that when the lights were doused in his dorm room, one of his classmates would crack, "Smile, Clarence, so we can see you."

Things were little different at Conception Seminary College, a lonely outpost of redbrick buildings surrounded by cornfields where the 19-year-old Thomas enrolled in 1967. Many of his classmates were from neighborhoods that were "99.9 white," as one puts it, and Thomas—one of only three black students—was something of a curiosity. His roommate, an irrepressible sort who later become a friend, whipped out a knife when he met Thomas in a joking play on racial fears. Tom O'Brien, who later became Thomas's closest friend there, remembers wincing at the welcome.

Thomas seemed shy to some classmates, but O'Brien and other friends remember a funny, more gregarious side to him. One of the other black students "made everyone feel kind of guilty, but Clarence never displayed that kind of baggage," says Father Benedict Neenan, a former classmate of Thomas's and now the seminary's prior. "He did everything we did, he seemed to us really just like the rest of us. He probably consciously worked at that."

But Thomas's hard work did little to assuage the racism of some white classmates. A month or two before the end of the term, he went to O'Brien's dorm room to inform him, teary-eyed, that he wouldn't be returning the next year. "I've run into too many rednecks," O'Brien recalls him saying.

In speeches and interviews, Thomas has recalled that the final straw came when he overheard a white seminarian's response to the news that the Rev. Martin Luther King Jr. had been shot: "Good—I hope the SOB dies." Later, Thomas wrote to O'Brien that he had left Catholicism entirely—a decision he changed several times—partly because of O'Brien's pastor in Kansas City who "can call himself a Christian and a [George] Wallace supporter at the same time."

Thomas's bitterness over his treatment by white seminarians permeated a 1984 interview with the Holy Cross alumni paper, in which he described himself as "the black spot on the white horse" and recalled that "the students temporarily discontinued awards, like Athlete of the Year, that I was likely to win."

Thomas's unhappy memories do not always gibe with those of former teachers and classmates. In fact, Thomas was named "class superjock" by his classmates at Conception, according to the school newspaper. And in the case of St. John, where Thomas captained several intramural teams, none of the former students or teachers interviewed for this article could recall an episode similar to the one Thomas described.

But if Thomas erred on the details, Everson suggests that the bigotry he encountered was real. "Some of the students were openly racist," he says. "Most of us were just insensitive."

The King assassination in 1968 sent a tidal wave of guilt across the colleges and universities of white America, and Holy Cross College in Worcester, Mass., was no exception. Within days of the killing, administrators at the conservative, Jesuit-run school had set up a King scholarship fund and embarked on a crash recruiting drive at black Catholic high schools nationwide.

Their efforts would have a profound effect not just on Holy Cross, but also on Clarence Thomas.

Although Thomas was not directly recruited to Holy Cross—he applied at the urging of one of the Savannah nuns, according to a longtime friend—he did receive one of the first King scholarships and in that sense "certainly" benefited from a form of affirmative action, according to the Rev. John E. Brooks, now the president of Holy Cross.

Brooks say, however, that the school had no formal preferential admissions policy for blacks beyond a general desire to attract more. In any event, the effort paid off: Nearly as many blacks entered Holy Cross in the fall of 1968 as had graduated from the school in its 125-year history.

Arriving at the staid, overwhelmingly white campus, with its handsome Georgian buildings perched on a hill overlooking the gritty New England factory town, Thomas felt more of an outsider than ever. He would later recall the blank look he got from a newspaper vendor when, after purchasing his first copy of The New York Times, he returned and asked for the comics.

Thomas also was impressed by his fellow students' high SAT scores, writing O'Brien not long after his arrival, "There are some souls with college board scores ranging from 650–750." Friends remember he had little confidence in his attractiveness to women and seemed anxious to get married.

Thomas's apprehensiveness about his reception at Holy Cross was not entirely misplaced. In a 1971 campus survey, three years after his arrival, 35.6 percent of the respondents attributed the presence of black students at Holy Cross to "tokenism" while nearly half agreed with the statement, "Negroes tend to have less ambition."

Thomas seemed determined to prove them wrong. By all accounts, he studied furiously, on one occasion petitioning campus administrators to reverse a planned cutback in the library's Saturday night hours. "He was always in the library, down in the basement carrels," says Jaffe Dickerson, a college friend.

Besides his academic duties, Thomas ran on the track team, held a job in the school cafeteria and one morning a week rose at dawn to serve breakfast to poor children in a church basement in Worcester. "He was always a little bit more mature than the rest of us," Dickerson says.

Thomas had a reputation as a grind, but classmates also recall him as warm, straightforward, even jovial. A standout in touch football and pickup baseball games, he went by the nickname of "Cousy," after Bob Cousy, a famous Holy Cross basketball star of the 1950s. Several remember him as a surrogate big brother to younger blacks who had followed him to Holy Cross from Savannah.

Thomas also seemed to share his black classmates' enthusiasm for the radical politics of the day. He wore a goatee, Army fatigues and combat boots, and a poster of Malcolm X adorned his dormitory room, according to a former roommate. In January 1969 he joined a number of other students in founding the Black Student Union, serving as its first treasurer and writing its constitution. Thomas later lost a close election for president of the union, recalls Leonard Cooper, a college friend and fellow activist.

Thomas participated in several civil rights protests in Worcester, including one outside a Thom McAn shoe store accused of denying jobs to blacks, Cooper says. His most celebrated act of defiance occurred during his junior year, following the suspension of four black students for their involvement in blocking access to the campus by corporate recruiters. Complaining that the four had been singled out because of their race, the black students staged a news conference in which they ceremoniously threw down their student ID cards, then left the campus in a caravan of cars.

But Thomas, who does not appear to have played anything other than a supporting role in the walkout, was hardly an extremist. Cooper notes that Malcolm X's autobiography was on the 1968 freshman reading list. And others dismiss the suggestion that Thomas's penchant for Army surplus clothing constituted a political statement.

"He wore combat boots because there was snow all over the place," says Dickerson, who like others recall Thomas less as a firebrand than as an independent, frequently moderate voice who didn't hesitate to take a contrary view.

"Everybody respected 'Cousy'—he always had his own mind, says Dickerson, now an attorney in Los Angeles. "You had a left view, a right view, a center view and then you had 'Cousy's' view."

In the spring of 1969, when the black students took up the question of whether to seek an all-black dorm corridor, Thomas cast the only no vote out of 25 because, he explained later, "If one was at Holy Cross, he should profit from the experience by learning to associate [with] and understand the white majority."

The next fall, when Thomas moved onto the black corridor—which included several whites—he surprised some black classmates by bringing with him his white roommate from the previous year.

The isolation and academic pressures took their toll. Thomas considered dropping out on several occasions. In the fall of 1969, he told the alumni paper, "I had my trunk all packed. I had decided that it was true, what the other blacks had been saying: that Holy Cross was a crusher, that it would break your spirit." Brooks, then the vice president, helped persuade him to stay. But by the spring of 1970, Thomas again told friends he was tired of school and would have left but for his fear of being drafted during the Vietnam War. He was later disqualified because of a back condition.

Still, ever conscious of his grades, he wrote O'Brien that he was keeping up a 3.7 grade point average.

A development in Thomas's personal life may ultimately have been responsible for keeping him in Worcester. Friends at Holy Cross had introduced him to Kathy Ambush, a demure, pretty student at a nearby college and the daughter of a Worcester dental technician. Within days of their meeting, says Eddie Jenkins, "I remember him telling me he was in love."

On June 5, 1971, the day after Thomas's graduation, the two were married at All Saints Episcopal Church in Worcester. Nelson Ambush, Kathy's father, loaned Thomas $15 to buy his senior yearbook.

33

Sharon LaFraniere
LONELY AT THE TOP,
AND ALL ALONG THE JOURNEY

To John Lewis, the January 1987 meeting was just another of the get-acquainted sessions that packed his calendar as a newly elected Democratic congressman from Atlanta.

But to Clarence Thomas, chief of the Equal Employment Opportunity Comission for the Reagan administration, the 45 minutes he spent in Lewis's half-decorated office was more noteworthy. As Thomas rode back to the EEOC office in his chauffeured government car, he told his aide, Charles A. Shanor, that Lewis seemed unusually receptive to his overture.

Thomas had been EEOC commissioner for five years by then, but "he told me Lewis was the first black congressman who would meet with him," Shanor says. "Every other black congressman had rebuffed him. I was really surprised. It made me feel he had been ostracized to a much greater degree than I was aware."

Thomas was right about the animosity he engendered from black members of Congress; they have voted overwhelmingly to oppose his nominations to the Supreme Court, which moved to the Senate Judiciary Committee last week. If he overstated the case—several black congressmen say Thomas never requested a meeting—it only showed how keenly he felt his isolation.

The child who saw his white classmates cross to the other side of the street when he approached grew up to tell the *Legal Times* in 1984: "I don't fit in with whites and I don't fit in with blacks." If anything, Thomas felt more alone as an adult than he did during a childhood of solitude and struggle. His sense of exclusion seemed only to grow with his achievements.

As EEOC commissioner and later, as a federal appeals court judge, Thomas filled his speeches and interviews with scenes of rejection. His notes for a speech last year to Savannah State College students began in a typical vein: "It is one of the few times I have been invited to my hometown to participate in any event."

Essentially a private man, Thomas revealed more about his experiences in his speeches than he did in talks with many of those who make up his wide and loyal circle of friends. Key events of his adult life, like his successful search for the father who abandoned his family when Thomas was a year old, remain a mystery to even his closest associates.

In his everyday dealings, Thomas seems remarkably able either to conceal or put aside his feelings of estrangement. Throughout his adult life, Thomas has impressed professors, colleagues and superiors as warm, engaging and wholly unpretentious, even with his increasingly prestigious titles.

"I expected maybe someone with a chip on his shoulder," says Alex Netchvolodoff, who worked with Thomas in Thomas's first job after law school. "He wasn't what I expected. He was funny, he was gregarious, he loved conversation. He was very interested in other people."

At the same time, however, Thomas continued to note the racial presumptions he faced, now more subtle than those in segregated Savannah, Ga. He told *The Washington Post* in 1980 that white professors and students at Yale Law School assumed black students were "dumb" and "resented our very presence." He told black students at Emory Law School last year that he had saved the letters of rejection from leading Atlanta law firms that refused to hire him after he graduated from Yale.

Years later, when his legal background was in corporate and energy law, he was insulted that the only jobs he was offered by the Reagan administration had to do with civil rights.

Thomas suggested in a 1987 Heritage Foundation speech that he was alternately patronized, ignored and circumvented by administration officals. "It often seemed that to be accepted . . . a black was required to become a caricature of sorts, providing sideshows of anti-black quips and attacks," he said.

But what Thomas seemed to anguish over were his conflicts with black leaders. "That was what upset him emotionally," says his friend Lovida Coleman, who met Thomas in law school.

Coleman, whose father is William T. Coleman Jr., chairman of the NAACP Legal Defense Fund and a close friend of retiring Supreme Court Justice Thurgood Marshall, remembers Thomas sitting on the sofa in her living room one evening near the end of President Ronald Reagan's first term, shifting back and forth in his seat in agitation. "He had hit a kind of crisis," Coleman says. "The criticism was really getting to him. It made him boil inside."

"It's lonely, I mean really lonely," Thomas told the *Washington Times* in 1990. "I hate that people of my race think, 'Here's this black guy bashing everything that's good for us.' "

Thomas has said his life taught him that the solution to the problems of black America lies in values and education. All else—affirmative action, welfare, busing, government set-asides—drains away motivation and creates generations of dependency.

He had his grandfather's values and good teachers, so he succeeded, he said in interviews with *The Washington Post* in 1980 and 1983. His sister lacked those advantages, so she lived on welfare with trash in her yard and beer cans in the driveway. "Those were passions that moved him, his relationship with his family and his own vivid sense of the price of dependency," one friend says.

Such views by a black person were in demand when Thomas made his public debut as a conservative at age 32. The Reagan administration desperately needed senior black appointees to counter its lily-white image, and in President Bush's White House, Thomas's philosophy—combined with his extraordinary life journey—more than made up for his paucity of legal scholarship and judicial experience.

Neither his law professors, employers, colleagues in the Reagan administration nor his colleagues on the U.S. Court of Appeals for the District of Columbia Circuit saw in Thomas a brilliant legal mind destined for the Supreme Court. A typical assessment comes from Richard W. Dusenberg, general counsel for Monsanto Co., where Thomas worked for 2½ years as a corporate attorney: "In a staff of extremely competent and bright lawyers, Clarence Thomas could and did hold his own."

The contours of Thomas's legal philosophy remain largely unclear beyond his view that the Constitution is color-blind and racial preferences are wrong. "He's still sifting and sorting," says a federal appeals judge who serves with him on the D.C. Circuit. "He has not yet had the time or occasion to develop a judicial philosophy."

Twenty years ago, Thomas was skeptical of the few conservatives who banded together in the liberal world of Yale Law School. Only a year before he enrolled in 1971, students and faculty shut down Yale University in a protest over the Black Panthers murder trial and "the norm was a certain amount of questioning of authority," says Reed Hundt, a former classmate. "Clarence was just as questioning as everyone else."

A registered Democrat since age 18, Thomas voted for George McGovern in 1972, like many of his classmates. His internships reflected a liberal bent: He worked two years for the New Haven Legal Assistance Association, then sought summer work with a small, Savannah law firm that specialized in civil rights and criminal cases.

Fletcher Farrington, a partner in the now-disbanded firm, remembers that Thomas worked partly on class-action suits alleging racial discrimination in the workplace—suits he later sought to limit at the EEOC. "I wouldn't say he was brilliant, but he impressed me as being very intelligent," Farrington says. "He was smart enough that he could keep up with the people around here."

On Yale's grading scale of honors, pass, low pass and fail, he received mostly passes, according to school officials. He earned honors in at least two classes, including one entitled "Anatomy of the Corporate State," as well as at least one low pass, school administrators and professors say.

His professors and fellow students remember him as visible and vocal, despite his later assertions that he hid in the back of classrooms so he would be judged only on the basis of his work. "I remember him taking stands and aggressively defending them," says Quinton Johnstone, who taught him in three classes.

But though he seemed to fit in both academically and socially, Thomas later described his experience at both Yale and Holy Cross as "years of rage" in his notes for a 1988 Emory University speech.

Most of Yale's other black students came from what Thomas liked to call "the black elite." Thomas befriended those who grew up in families more like his own, including Harry Singleton, whose father was a janitor, and Frank Washington, the first in his family to attend college.

Around Singleton's kitchen table, the three friends discussed the black students who won clerkships through family connections, while they had to make it "on pure ambition," Singleton says. They also discussed the caste system that relegated children like Thomas, with his dark complexion and uneducated family, to the bottom rung of black society.

Most often, however, they discussed how white students and professors automatically doubted their abilities. "It was in the air," says Wallace D. Loh, an Asian American, now dean of the University of Washington School of Law, who felt the same skepticism. "There were some students, some faculty members, who directly or indirectly made it known: 'Gee, if it wasn't for our largess, our altruism, you guys wouldn't be here.' "

Thomas seemed to discount any benefit from the program. "This thing about how they let me into Yale—that kind of stuff offends me," Thomas told *Washington Post* reporter Juan Williams in 1987 profile for *The Atlantic Monthly*. "All they did was stop stopping us" from being admitted.

In fact, Yale did more. Without affirmative action, many of its minority students would not have been admitted because their academic records were weaker than those of other white applicants, according to Ralph K. Winter, a former professor who served on the admissions committee, and other professors and administrators.

The third-year job interviews with law firms provided Thomas with fresh evidence of how readily whites questioned his achievements. He said in a 1990 speech at Savannah State College that recruiters interrogated him about his grades in college, high school, even grammar school.

He told the *Legal Times* in 1984, "They would always want to talk to me about pro bono work [work done without a fee for charity groups or the poor]. . . . They've got to say something 'black' to me."

So Thomas accepted a job in Jefferson City, Mo., with the state's young Republican attorney general, John C. Danforth. It was a $10,800-a-year position with a crushing workload, but the association with Danforth proved invaluable.

In rural Jefferson City, where Thomas was the only black among about 30 staff attorneys, he began to question the efficacy of government solutions for the social and economic problems of his race. "I just rethought everything," Thomas said in a 1987 interview with *Reason* magazine.

He clipped newspaper stories about the problems and progress of black Americans. He registered as a Republican. And he became a devotee of

Thomas Sowell, a conservative black thinker who contends that the main cause of poverty among blacks is not white oppression but slavery's legacy of illiteracy, indolence and dependence.

Thomas shared his growing conviction in self-help over governmental solutions with students at Lincoln University, a predominantly black college in Jefferson City. He told one group that African studies was not enough of a major to train them for the tough world ahead, according to Dick Weiler, another state government attorney and friend. Asked what he majored in, Thomas told the students: English, because it was his hardest subject.

Thomas's job came to a logical end when Danforth was elected to the Senate, but Danforth was eager to help him find another. He recommended him to officials at Monsanto, a chemical and agricultural firm headquartered in St. Louis.

After 2½ years in the corporate world, Thomas was ready to rejoin Danforth in Washington, with certain conditions. He would work on environmental, energy and regulatory issues—not civil rights.

Thomas quickly turned his tiny cubicle in the senator's office into a kind of outreach center for black conservatives. Another Thomas aid, Christopher Brewster, remembers handing Thomas a copy of *Lincoln Review*, a publication of black conservative writers. Not an hour later, he heard Thomas's booming voice over the divider. He had the editor on the phone, Brewster says, and was telling him, "I'm Clarence Thomas . . . and I like what you've got to say."

"He'd just keep after them until he found them. I was kind of flabbergasted," Brewster says. After one conversation, Thomas flopped in the leather chair next to Brewster's desk. "He said, this was just the most amazing thing for him. He hadn't realized there were other people like him."

The month after Reagan's election as president, Sowell invited Thomas to a San Francisco conference of well-known black conservatives. The young congressional aide who paid his own way took heart from Edwin Meese III, head of Reagan's transition team, who said the White House would hire blacks in their areas of expertise, not limit them to "black" issues.

So Thomas was disappointed a few months later when he received his job offer. On a window seat outside Danforth's office, Thomas and Allen Moore, Danforth's director of legislation, talked over whether Thomas should accept the offer of a position as assistant secretary for civil rights for the Education Department.

"His gut instinct was not to take it. He felt he would be on the minority track, the track saved for symbols," Moore says.

Moore responded, "You are nuts. You are 32 years old, a legislative assistant and you have been handed an opportunity to run an office in a federal agency with a large staff. Forget about being a stereotype. This is visibility, responsibility, a presidential appointment."

While his career leapt forward, Thomas's marriage of 10 years collapsed under the strain of what one friend calls "a mismatch of ambition." Thomas separated from his wife in July 1981, the month he was sworn in as assistant secretary. She kept their 8-year-old son, Jamal, until their divorce three years later when Thomas took over his care.

Thomas barely got his feet wet at the Education Department before he was sworn in nine months later as EEOC commissioner, in charge of 3,100 employees and 48 field offices. He described the job in a 1990 speech to a law firm as "much more than I had been warned about and far more than I had bargained for."

At the Department of Education, Thomas told the National Journal, he was "a curiosity more than anything else." But at the EEOC he was a target. Civil rights leaders and Senate liberals told him "no self-respecting black" would carry out Reagan administration policies, he said in his speech notes.

Even some of Thomas's aides were disturbed by his apparent failure to acknowledge that he benefited from affirmative action or to address the question of what to do for black children without his advantages—the support of a loving, disciplined grandfather and the special care of nuns at a private school.

Anita Hill, a former special assistant to Thomas at the Education Department and the EEOC, was particularly disturbed by Thomas's repeated, public criticism of his sister and her children for living on welfare. "It takes a lot of detachment to publicize a person's experience in that way" and "a certain kind of self-centeredness not to recognize some of the programs that benefited you," says Hill, now an Oklahoma law professor. "I think he doesn't understand people, he doesn't relate to people who don't make it on their own."

If liberals considered him a traitor, conservatives within the administration suspected he was a closet liberal, Thomas said in a 1987 speech.

His old friend Harry Singleton, who succeeded Thomas at the Education Department, says he and Thomas continually discussed the "punishing position" they occupied within an administration that often seemed to go out of its way to offend blacks with policies such as support of a tax exemption for a school that banned interracial dating.

"He would tell me, 'Harry, we've got to hang in there and fight. Who would be in our place if we are not here to try and hold the line?' "

To another longtime friend, Jaffe Dickerson, Thomas suggested the influence he wielded was worth the discomfort. "You should switch parties," Thomas told Dickerson on the phone one day.

"I howled," Dickerson recalls, but Thomas continued: "Think about this. I can pick up the phone and get an appointment with the president any time I need that. Coretta Scott King can't get that. Jesse Jackson can't get that."

On certain issues, Thomas took a more cautious approach than the administration's designated hitters on civil rights, William Bradford Reynolds, head of the Justice Department's civil rights division, and Michael Horowitz, a special counsel at the Office of Management and Budget.

Thaddeus Garrett, who was domestic policy adviser for Vice President Bush, remembers how Thomas resisted pressure from both men to rewrite the Uniform Guidelines on Employee Selection Procedures. Thomas publicly criticized the rules, which serve as a guide to private and public employers on how to adhere to anti-discrimination laws. He vowed to rewrite them. But in his eight years as commissioner, the EEOC only studied them.

"He had such a powerful need not to be patronized or controlled. I've never quite seen the equal of it in any other person," a former Reagan administration official says.

On another key issue, Thomas waffled. He initially supported the imposition of hiring goals and racial preferences as "a last resort . . . against proven discriminators" in 1982, according to a recent book by former solicitor general Charles Fried.

But in February 1986, Thomas told *The Washington Post* he opposed the use of hiring or promotion goals and timetables. About a year later, he said the agency would seek to resume imposing such remedies because the Supreme Court had upheld their use, but he indicated his personal "reservations."

By 1987, Thomas appeared to have stiffened his conservative resolve. "I believe firmly I should have taken a more aggressive stand against opponents of free enterprise and opponents of the values that are central to success in this society," Thomas told the Heritage Foundation.

At home, Thomas assumed the ways of his grandfather, insisting on strict discipline and the best education he could afford for his son. Even on a congressional aide's salary, he paid $1,400 a semester to send Jamal to private school.

Thomas later described the mid-'80s, when he took over primary responsibility for his son and struggled to gain his footing within the administration, as one of the hardest chapters in his life. The next one was much happier.

After a meeting in New York of the Anti-Defamation League, Virginia Lamp, then a lobbyist for the U.S. Chamber of Commerce, offered to share a cab. In 1987, the two were married at a Methodist Church in Lamp's home state of Nebraska. Thomas did not mention to many of the friends he invited to the Washington reception that Lamp, now a legislative officer at the Labor Department, is white.

Two years later, Bush nominated Thomas to the D.C. Circuit, considered the nation's second most important court. Thomas told friends he was delighted to trade in the spotlight for the cloistered world of a federal appeals judge. He has written 19 opinions in the 18 months he has served, most dealing with regulatory disputes and criminal appeals.

"I think he has been very comfortable on this court, and I would hope that that would have diminished his feeling of isolation," says a judge who serves with him on that court. Two judges characterize Thomas as thoughtful and collegial, while noting his comparative lack of experience in many areas of the law. "He's a very young person in terms of a judge," one says.

Some things were already familiar. Thomas told friends about the day he paused to check the traffic before pulling out of the federal courthouse garage in his government car. Another federal judge, mistaking him for a chauffeur, jumped in the back seat. "Take me to the Hyatt Regency!" the judge ordered.

"Lonely at the top," Thomas wrote in his notes for one of his first speeches as a judge. "True."

T HE FOLLOWING PORTRAYAL
of the Supreme Court's most dynamic conservative illustrates
how a forceful personality combined
with a powerful intellect and strong views
produce a leader.

34

Jeffrey Rosen
THE LEADER
OF THE OPPOSITION

Conservatives now have only the courts to carry on their thirty-year battle against entitlement liberalism, and only Antonin Scalia to bear their standard. Scorning other justices, who have refused to take some of the positions for which they were appointed, conservatives hail Scalia as the only justice guided by principle rather than politics. Scalia is the purest archetype of the conservative legal movement that began in the 1960s in reaction to the Warren Court. His increasing inability to command majorities is viewed as proof of his virtue.

From a dramatic standpoint, too, Scalia stands out. Of the three justices who regularly write their own opinions (David Souter and John Paul Stevens are the other two), only Scalia writes with flair. At his most melodramatic, he is more entertaining than the best *Wall Street Journal* editorial writers: "It is instructive to compare this Nietzschean vision of us unelected, life-tenured judges, leading a Volk who will be tested by following, with the somewhat more modest role envisioned by the Founders," he wrote in his abortion dissent last June. Scalia is also a showoff at oral argument, to the obvious irritation of his colleagues. When a lawyer tried to defend the FCC's set-aside program for black broadcasters, arguing that their background had given them a unique perspective, Scalia exclaimed: "Blood, Mr. Wollenberg, blood! Not background and environment. Isn't that right? Blood!" At times, Scalia seems the only justice large enough for the role he has been assigned to play.

When I wrote to Justice Scalia, asking if he would agree to be interviewed for an article about his jurisprudence, he sent back a charming note:

> Since being a judge, I have had a uniform policy of declining interviews for articles about me. That policy undoubtedly has its costs, but is in accord with our judicial tradition of avoidng publicity. (As you know, I am big on tradition.) It is tempting to make an exception for a piece of the rare sort you describe, but a rule is a rule. (I am also big on rules.) I am sorry to disappoint—and wish both of us good luck in your article.

This is an exquisite miniature of a Scalia decision. Speaking for himself, Scalia explains, he might be tempted to grant the interview; but a judge's job is to restrain his personal preferences, and to resist temptation. By refusing to make an exception to a rule he has imposed on himself, Scalia shows that he is governed by law rather than whim. Justice Sandra Day O'Connor, for example, might have balanced the benefits of granting the interview against the costs of refusing it, but Scalia is bound up by history, by tradition. The note is so well executed that it makes me admire him for having turned me down. (He had done this once before, incidentally, when I applied for clerkships with all the justices.)

Scalia's speeches and opinions provide more details of the judicial philosophy that he called, in his 1989 Holmes Lecture at Harvard, "The Rule of Law as a Law of Rules." When interpreting statutes, Scalia claims to be a "textualist," refusing to look beyond the "plain meaning" of the words for evidence of the original intentions of Congress. When interpreting the Constitution, however, Scalia claims to be an "originalist," insisting that each provision should be interpreted in light of the original understanding of its framers and ratifiers. Finally, and most controversially, Scalia says that judges should refuse to enforce rights that do not appear explicitly in the Constitution unless they are rooted in long-standing tradition or very specific historical practice. Above all, Scalia claims to be consistent. "The only check on the arbitrariness of federal judges," he wrote in a 1989 issue of the *Case Western Law Review*, is "the insistence upon consistency."

Radical self-restraint. Scrupulous attention to text and history. Consistency. These are exacting principles, but Scalia properly demands to be judged by them, and he deserves to be taken seriously. In some cases, admirably, Scalia's principles do restrain his passions. Unfortunately, in the cases Scalia feels most deeply about, his passions lead him to betray his principles. In constitutional interpretation, he has ignored or misrepresented evidence of the original understanding of the framers and ratifiers when it conflicts with his own policy views. In statutory interpretation, he has ignored or misrepresented the "plain meaning" of the text in ways that Congress clearly did not intend. For all his self-righteousness, in short, Scalia often chooses among conflicting principles—textualism, originalism, tradition and precedent—in ways that appear no less restrained than justices who do not claim to be guided by systematic principles in the first place.

Affirmative action is a dramatic example of how Scalia's personal preferences seem to get the better of his originalist methodology. Scalia has never disguised his scorn, as the son of an immigrant from Sicily, for the idea that he should atone for the sins of earlier immigrants. In a brutally autobiographical essay in the 1979 *Washington University Law Quarterly*, he confesses his ethnic resentment of WASP judges like "the Wisdoms and the Powells and the Whites," whose ancestors oppressed blacks and who now try to rectify the error through affirmative action programs at the expense of more recent immigrants. "My father came to this country as a teenager," Scalia wrote. "Not only had he never profited from the sweat of any black man's brow, I don't think he had ever seen a black man."

Given Scalia's raw feelings on the subject, one would expect him to tread gingerly in considering the constitutionality of affirmative action. Instead, his opinions are remarkable for their failure to apply the originalist methodology and to examine the contemporary understanding of the Fourteenth Amendment. In a 1989 case, *City of Richmond v. J.A. Croson Co.*, O'Connor struck down a set-aside program for minority contractors, holding that states can discriminate on the basis of race only to "ameliorate the effects of past discrimination." In Scalia's view, O'Connor's position was too moderate: "Only a social emergency rising to the level of imminent danger to life and limb" could justify an exception to "the principle embodied in the Fourteenth Amendment that '[o]ur Constitution is color-blind, and neither knows nor tolerates classes among citizens.' " Scalia offered no historical support for this sweeping proposition except for two irrelevant quotations: one from James Madison on the dangers of faction, and another from Alexander Bickel on the immorality of racism.

Scalia conspicuously ignored an amicus brief for the NAACP, written by Eric Schnapper of Columbia Law School, arguing that the framers of the Fourteenth Amendment not only tolerated, but voted for social welfare programs for the exclusive benefit of blacks. Administered by the Freedman's Bureau, the programs were open to all blacks, not only to recently freed slaves; and the offered assistance—which included land, education, job training and employment set-asides—was not in any way tied to the injury suffered by the recipient. A judge who claimed to be less bound by the specific understanding of the framers and ratifiers might be able to interpret the text of the amendment (no person shall be deprived of "the equal protection of the laws") more generally, but Scalia offers no excuse for ignoring his originalist principles.

Three major opinions Scalia issued last June—on property rights, executive power and school prayer—provide more specific evidence of how his political passions overwhelm his originalist principles. In *Lucas v. South Carolina Coastal Council*, Scalia held that when the state regulates land in a way that strips it of economic value, the landowner must be compensated, unless the prohibited use of the land was a nuisance under state common law. Scalia conceded that the framers would not have applied the Takings Clause ("private property [shall not] be taken for public use, without just compensation") to economic regulations: they understood it to cover only the physical taking of land. But instead, he relied on a subjective test Justice Oliver Wendell Holmes made up in 1922: a regulation is unconstitutional if it "goes too far" in reducing the value of land. This sounds very much like the mushy, judge-created "undue burden" test that Scalia attacked in *Planned*

Parenthood v. Casey, the abortion case. And in a 1990 decision, Scalia took precisely the opposite approach, insisting that police officers who chased a teenager did not "seize" him, because the Founders understood "seizures" to be limited to physical contact.

In *Lujan v. Defenders of Wildlife*, Scalia again violated his originalist principles when he struck down scores of statutes in which Congress had allowed citizens to sue the president for his refusal to enforce environmental laws. In 1983, as a law professor, Scalia had written an article in the *Suffolk Law Review* proposing the theory on which the decision rests: if you are the object of a legal regulation, Scalia wrote, you should always have "standing" to challenge an agency's failure to enforce it; but sometimes even Congress cannot give you "standing" to challenge an agency's failure to regulate someone else. The problem, as Cass Sunstein of the University of Chicago argues in the November issue of the *Michigan Law Review*, is that Scalia's neat theory clashes dramatically with the original understanding and historical practice in England and America. Sunstein shows that the citizen suit was well established in the eighteenth and early nineteenth centuries; to establish "standing" throughout most of American history, you merely had to show that Congress or the common law had given you a right to sue. Scalia's conclusion that Congress can never grant standing to challenge the president's failure to enforce the law is, in short, perverse. But instead of examining the historical evidence, he relied heavily on an incoherent case from the 1970s, written by the liberal activist William O. Douglas, which is clearly inconsistent with the text and original understanding of the Constitution.

And then there is religion. In *Lee v. Weisman*, a 5–4 majority held that it is unconstitutional to recite a nondenominational prayer (actually a paraphrase of Micah 6:8) at a public high school graduation. Scalia confessed his "personal preferences" at the end of his dissenting opinion: "To deprive our society of [this] important unifying mechanism, in order to spare the nonbeliever what seems to me the minimal inconvenience of standing or even sitting in respectful nonparticipation, is as senseless in policy as it is unsupported in law." In attacking the majority, Scalia did not bother to conceal his rage: the Court's "psycho-journey" is nothing short of ludicrous. . . . Interior decorating is a rock hard science compared to psychology practiced by amateurs." (This is a wicked dig at O'Connor's earlier holding that the city of Pittsburgh could not display a crèche without also constructing a "secular" monument, such as a "rotating wishing well.")

Although Scalia dismissed the majority opinions as "conspicuously bereft of any reference to history," Souter's concurrence, in fact, reviewed the evidence of the framers' intentions in meticulous detail, concluding that "history neither contradicts nor warrants reconsideration of the settled principle that the Establishment Clause forbids" nonpreferential as well as preferential support for religion. Scalia simply ignored Souter's arguments about the intent of the framers. Instead, he disingenuously shifted his focus from original intention to subsequent practice or "tradition." He made much of the fact that presidents have traditionally issued Thanksgiving proclamations. But as Souter took pains to point out, Madison later apologized for his Thanksgiving proclamation (which he had issued only to win the War of 1812) on the grounds that he felt all ceremonial uses of religion "a palpable violation of . . . Constitutional principles." And in a footnote in his abortion dissent, Scalia had argued that "tradition" can never trump a right enumerated in the Constitution. Scalia's failure to engage Souter's originalist arguments leaves the impression that he has nothing to say; and *Weisman* will be remembered as the case in which Souter challenged Scalia on his own terms, and won.

Scalia applies his "plain meaning" methodology in statutory interpretation as inconsistently as he applies his "originalist" methodology in constitutional interpretation. There is an apparent tension, first of all, between Scalia's insistence on consulting extrinsic evidence of the framers' intentions and his refusal to consult extrinsic evidence of Congress's intentions. Scalia's response is that "legislative history"—especially committee reports—is often unreliable evidence of the intentions of the average congressman.

But even if Scalia is correct, he has repeatedly interpreted the "plain meaning" of laws in ways that thwart Congress's clearly expressed intentions. Scalia wrote two of the seven opinions that Congress repudiated in the Civil Rights Act of 1991, and most of the other five relied on his "plain meaning" methodology. In some of the cases, the Court misconstrued intentions that Congress had expressed precisely the first time. In a 1991 cases, for example, the Court held that Congress did not intend the Civil Rights Act of 1964 to apply to American companies employing Americans abroad. Although in recent cases the Court had presumed that Congress intended laws to apply overseas unless it explicity said otherwise, Chief Justice William Rehnquist and Scalia resurrected an older rule, applying the opposite presumption. But they also ignored explicit language in the Civil Rights Act, declaring that Congress did not intend it to apply to American employers who hire *aliens* abroad. As Stevens pointed out in dissent, if the statute was not intended to apply outside the United States, the exception for aliens would have been unnecessary.

In 1982 Congress amended the Voting Rights Act to prohibit unintentional, as well as intentional, discrimination. Congress obviously intended the amendment to extend the scope of the act, which had always been understood to cover the election of state judges as well as state legislators. In two 1991 dissents, however, Scalia pounced on language in the amendment about giving voters the chance "to elect representatives of their choice." He argued that elected judges are not representatives "within the ordinary meaning of language"; so judicial elections should no longer be covered by the extended Voting Rights Act. Scalia seemed to relish the prospect of forcing Congress to live with a preverse result that it had not anticipated. The centerpiece of his odd argument: if all elected officials were "representatives," the Voting Rights Act would cover "the fan-elected members of the baseball All-Star Teams."

Finally, Scalia has joined habeas corpus cases in which the misconstructions of Congress's "plain meaning" seem even more willful. Over the past four years, Rehnquist has lobbied Congress to amend the habeas corpus statute in a way that would eviscerate it, requiring federal courts to defer to state courts if their legal judgments are "reasonable," rather than deciding independently if the judgments are correct. Congress has repeatedly rejected Rehnquist's proposals. Last June, however, Thomas, Scalia and Rehnquist not only indicated their willingness to adopt the relaxed standard of review, they denied that Congress had repeatedly rejected it. Instead of overruling the Warren Court cases that Congress had codified, all three pretended the cases meant the opposite of what they said.

In an exhaustive survey for the *Yale Law Journal* of all Supreme Court opinions repudiated by Congress in the last twenty years, William Eskridge of Georgetown Law School discovered that more than half relied on Scalia's methodology of "plain meaning" or general rules of construction. Only 20 percent of the decisions that were overturned relied primarily on legislative history. Scalia claims that being repudiated by Congress does not bother him, since his goal is to encourage Congress to express its meaning more precisely. But his tendency to misconstrue Congress's meaning even when it is precisely expressed suggests that his methodology often fails on its own terms.

Former Scalia clerks insist that Scalia genuinely struggles to be guided by principle rather than politics and is not aware of his own inconsistencies. "He is fundamentally Catholic and Christian," said one clerk, "and wants to believe what he is doing is true and good." In an early review of Scalia's jurisprudence, George Kannar of the University of Buffalo attributed Scalia's "constitutional catechism" to his education at a Jesuit military academy in Queens. Politically and religiously, Scalia was an archconservative in high school. "At the age of 17," William Stern, a high school friend, told *The New York Times*, "he could have been a member of the Curia." In the 1950s Scalia moved on to Georgetown and Harvard Law School, where he was steeped in the Legal Process school of Felix Frankfurter and Henry Hart, with its scrupulous concern for neutrality and restraint. But Kannar argues that Scalia's religious education began his struggle to separate his personal preferences from his actions, to be "strong enough to obey." In this respect, Scalia bears a striking resemblance to another legal purist of the conservative

Kulturkampf, Joseph Ratzinger, whose own Augustinian submission to the will of the law has just produced a new universal Catholic catechism.

In the cases where Scalia's passions are less engaged, there is no doubt that his principles sometimes do lead him to libertarian positions that conflict with his proexecutive politics. "Scalia's judicial asceticism requires him to reach results that are unjust," says Larry Kramer of the University of Michigan. "He reaches a result, he knows it's unjust and now he feels good about himself because he knows the law controls him, because this is a result he knows is crazy." A more sympathetic way of putting the same point is that Scalia sometimes enjoys being forced by his principles to take positions with which he disagrees. This distinguishes him from colleagues like Rehnquist and Byron White, who are so result-oriented that they often remove the legal reasoning from the drafts of their clerks. In a 1991 dissent, for example, Scalia's examination of colonial common law led him to conclude that a suspect could be held without a probable cause ruling for only twenty-four hours (O'Connor thought forty-eight hours was "reasonable"). In a recent speech at Harvard Law School, Scalia pointed to a 1987 dissent in which he held that a search and seizure had occurred as soon as a policeman touched a stereo. "I let people burn flags," Scalia added proudly. In short, even though Scalia often betrays this jurisprudential principles, these cases show that he deserves respect as one of the few justices who has a jurisprudence to betray.

Why do Scalia's passions overcome him in the most controversial cases? Part of the problem is the lack of intellectual debate among the justices of the Rehnquist Court. Traditionally, justices discussed their reasons before voting at conference; but Rehnquist, who is concerned about efficiency above all, changed the rules of the conference so that the justices now go around the table only once, to announce their tentative votes. There is also tremendous pressure to join draft opinions as soon as they circulate. Scalia, to his credit, has publicly proposed that no opinions should be joined until the dissent has circulated. For now, however, there are few opportunities for Scalia's colleagues to save him from his worst instincts.

But the most convincing explanation for Scalia's inconsistencies is that arrogance has blinded him to them. After interviewing scores of law clerks last April, Paul Barrett of *The Wall Street Journal* confirmed what is obvious from Scalia's published opinions and questions at oral argument: that he has intellectual contempt for most of his colleagues. "What's a smart guy like me doing in a place like this?" he periodically asks his own clerks. Because his colleagues seldom check his excesses by engaging his arguments, his treatment of constitutional history has grown increasingly cavalier. Privately dismissing O'Connor and other justices as "politicians," he has convinced himself as he wrote in a 1989 abortion dissent, that their less categorical approach to juding "cannot be taken seriously."

As a result, Scalia has been slow to acknowledge the rise of David Souter, an intellectual equal who is proving to be more scholarly, and less political, than Scalia himself. As Souter does the hard and lonely work of original historical research, many of Scalia's best ideas are increasingly derivative. In *RAV v. St. Paul*, the cross-burning case, for example, Scalia's ingenious extension of the First Amendment (he held that even fighting words and obscenity cannot be regulated selectively) was suggested by an amicus brief on behalf of the libertarian Center for Individual Rights, which relied on decisions by Richard Posner and Frank Easterbrook, two esteemed appellate judges in Chicago.

Souter's displacement of Scalia as the intellectual leader of the new majority is a dramatic reprise of Felix Frankfurter's eclipse at the hands of Hugo Black. The last academic to serve before Scalia, Frankfurter was so convinced of his own intellectual superiority, so busy condescending to his colleagues and dismissing them as "politicians" rather than "judges," that he failed to recognize the profundity of Black's competing judicial philosophy. As Black spent long evenings in the Library of Congress communing with original texts, Frankfurter went to dinner parties. ("Ah yes," Scalia joked to David Savage of the *Los Angeles Times*, who saw him leaving the Court in a dinner jacket. "Esteemed jurist by day; man about town at night.")

Eventually, Frankfurter lost the majorities he had commanded in his earliest years. His most cherished decisions were overturned—he had briefly convinced his colleagues to uphold mandatory flag salutes for Jehovah's Witnesses—and he was reduced to increasingly bitter and personal dissents. Today Frankfurter's stock among scholars is very low: many of his historical claims have been exposed as dishonest; his pro-executive bias appears sycophantic; and his sanctimonious claims about being guided by principle rather than politics seem self-deluded.

The resemblance continues to grow. One of Scalia's most controversial opinions, *Employment Division v. Smith*, said that "neutral laws of general applicability" do not violate the First Amendment, even if they have the "incidental effect" of making it impossible for minorities to practice their religion. The precedent on which Scalia based his theory, amazingly, was Frankfurter's infamous opinion in the flag salute case. (Scalia ignored the fact that the decision had been overturned.) In a 1991 case, Souter criticized Scalia's theory; and scholars have collected extensive evidence—which Scalia also ignored—suggesting that the framers of the First Amendment intended to make exceptions for religious minorities. Eventually Souter could persuade a majority that Scalia's theory has no basis in the First Amendment, just as Black eventually abandoned Frankfurter.

Jurisprudentially, however, the roles have been reversed. Scalia claims to embrace the principles of Black: strict construction, constitutional literalism; objective rules over subjective standards. Souter, in turn, has taken up the mantle of Frankfurter and his disciple, John Harlan: respect for precedent; case by case balancing; Burkean continuity with the past. Souter's Harlanesque approach has its virtues, but at its worst, it leads to a refusal to work the law pure, preserving precedents—like *Roe v. Wade*—that were wrong from the start. In Black's hands, by contrast, strict constructionism led to some of the greatest civil libertarian decisions of the century, as well as to some of the most impressive demonstrations of judicial restraint (such as Black's dissent in *Griswold v. Connecticut*, the contraceptives case).

Black's principles are worthy principles; they deserve a champion who can apply them more consistently than Scalia has done. Many of the conservative criticisms of the Warren and Burger Courts, furthermore, were worthy criticisms. They should not be obscured by the hypocrisy of conservative judges, who have proved no less political—but far more self-righteous—than their liberal opponents. Instead of continuing to use the courts as an instrument of politics, President Clinton could end the cycle. He could appoint scholarly, principled justices—political liberals as well as conservatives—whose politics are geniunely distinct from their jurisprudence. (When interpreted scrupulously, constitutional text, history and structure should lead to liberal as well as conservative results.) As for Scalia, with some recognition of his own fallibility, he could play a genuinely constructive role in the future, rather than being reduced to writing sarcastic editorials. The best gift that Clinton could give to liberals and conservatives would be colleagues capable of challenging Scalia on his own terms.

Perhaps the Clinton justices could also persuade Scalia to re-examine his most conspicuous misreading of text and history, which occurs in his statement of principle itself. "I stand with Aristotle," Scalia says, in the view that law should be understood as a system of rules, rather than an exercise of personal discretion. But as Richard Pildes of the University of Michigan points out, this turns Aristotle on his head. Aristotle rejected the formalistic view of law as a series of fixed principles. Instead of applying straight rules to fluted columns, Aristotle argued in the *Nichomachean Ethics*, judges should be guided by the Lesbian Rule, a flexible strip of metal, used by the builders of Lesbos, that "bends to the shape of the stone and is not fixed." By betraying many of his own principles, Scalia proves a more faithful Aristotelian than he intended.